As I know that many have already written about these matters, I fear that I shall be considered presumptuous in writing about them, too – moreso because, in treating this subject, I depart from the rules set down by others. But since it is my intention to write something of use to those who will understand, I deem it best to stick to the practical truth of things rather than to fancies. Many men have imagined [things] that never really existed at all. Yet, the way men live is so far removed from the way they *ought* to live that anyone who abandons "what is" for "what should be" pursues his downfall rather than his preservation. A man who strives after goodness in all his acts is sure to come to ruin, since there are so many men who are not good.

Niccolo Machiavelli, *The Prince*

We know our problems – we're unsure of our strengths.

Dolores Curran, *Traits of a Healthy Family*

It does little good to ameliorate symptoms without acknowledging the disease that causes them.

Christopher Locke, *Gonzo Marketing: Winning Through Worst Practices*

It's important to have someone living out the goals of any political change even before it's achieved, so that the new political conditions can be compared to a living reality, however small and insignificant, instead of just to some visionary fantasy.

Philip Slater, *The Pursuit of Loneliness*

Our deepest fear is not that we are inadequate. Our deepest fear is that we are powerful beyond measure.

Nelson Mandela

Taking care of your people doesn't mean being nice to them. It means teaching them what they need to know.

Capt. John Pickering, last shipyard commander of the Long Beach Naval Shipyard

Polyamory: Roadmaps for the Clueless and Hopeful

Anthony D. Ravenscroft

Fenris Brothers
an imprint of the Crossquarter Publishing Group

Unless otherwise noted, all persons mentioned in the following text are fictionalized. The various tales herein are based stoutly in reality, but situations, genders, sequentiality, &c., have been modified either to grant them some measure of privacy, or because I thought it made the story better for publication. In a few cases, where the circumstances are unique enough that I felt disguise would only cloud the impact, I have sought explicit permission from the persons involved, and am indebted to those who have granted me the leeway to stay close to the wonderful truth of real life.

Library of Congress Cataloging-in-Publication Data
Ravenscroft, Anthony, 1958-
  Polyamory : roadmaps for the clueless and hopeful : an introduction on pol=
yamory / by Anthony D. Ravenscroft.
      p. cm.
  Includes bibliographical references.
  ISBN 1-890109-53-3 (pbk.)
  1. Non-monogamous relationships. 2. Man-woman relationships. I. Title.
  HQ980.R38 2004
  306.84'23—dc22
                        2004008579

Acknowledgements

Two decades and a mammoth book to boot – obviously, the subject has been a major feature of my life. Thorough thanks to everyone who has had even a major role is impossible, so I will restrict myself to the highlights of the moment.

Wolfgang Gregorii Zeuner is a convenient literary device living in Minneapolis, and can be found on the Web sites for Loving More and PMM, among others.

This project could not have happened without the able assistance of Robert Ford Carpenter, whose underlying belief is that anything is possible with a big enough hammer.

Playing regularly in the background have been dozens of CDs from the mammoth output of Bill Nelson, everything from his orchestral atmospherics to his guitar-driven jazz and rock, depending on my moods. You really need to listen to this guy.

Working writers and independent cafés are made for each other. A few Minneapolis coffee shops have been a blessing, providing me sanctuary for the price of a little coffee. This book began to take shape at The Purple Onion, and returned to begin taking final form a year later; I am also grateful for the Anodyne and the Magpie, and for much-needed late breakfasts at the Hard Times. My Santa Fean thanks as well to Las Chivas for white chocolate mochas that could (and do) rouse the dead, and the Second Street Brewery for their procession of fine ales and bitters.

My children, as ever, remain a prime inspiration. So, Graeme and Inanna, here's another one. (And a wave to the co-father of these remarkable and exhausting young beings, Dan Brady – tag.)

There are very few people in my life whose experiences roughly correspond to my own, even in a distorted parallel-world kind of way. Jules Raberding got this project started by briefly outlining her own book proposal. When her story comes out, there'll be little overlap in our work. Still, knowing that someone else is thinking in this direction has kept me going, as I wanted a book that will sit comfortably beside hers at the bookstore. As always, my warmest thoughts to Jules and her extended family.

Most of all, the existence of this book is due to the love and lessons of two of the best friends a man could ever hope to have, Therese Francis and Nancy Hansen. They have been in my life for more than 15 years, have cared for me and challenged me, have given me both problems and solutions. Thank you for standing by me, and for believing in me even in the darker times. This book simply would not have happened without knowing with absolute certainty that you were there.

Organizations Referred To In The Text

Over the years, I have associated with social organizations that form the backbone of what exists of "the polyamorous community"; though I mention them in greater detail elsewhere, I feel that I would be remiss if I didn't properly credit them *before* you encounter their mention.

While I first encountered the concept of group marriage in the early 1970s on some NBC Television magazine program, and made the first efforts to bring nonmonogamy into my life in 1977, it wasn't until 1981 that I saw three members of **Kerista Commune** on *Phil Donahue* and realized that I wasn't alone. A few years later, I happened to see a classified advertisement for the group in a major magazine (I'm relatively certain it was *Mother Jones*), and subsequently didn't fall off their mailing list for years. Space is too short to do justice to the rise, blossoming, and collapse of Kerista, though it has been covered in articles elsewhere (specifically those of Mitchell Slomiak and Eve Furchgott in *Communities* Journal, an excellent magazine published by the Fellowship for Intentional Community). Between the early 1960s and the early 1990s, Kerista's publishing arm, **PASS**, put out an amazing number of books, pamphlets, and tabloids, generally distributed for free. I have never had a chance to meet any of these people, but their efforts formed an important facet in my understanding of nonmonogamy and community.

In the mid-1980s, another classified advertisement put me in touch with Polyfidelitous Educational Products, more widely known as **PEP**, a project run by a three-person household in Eugene, Oregon. Though a group effort, the name most generally associated with PEP is Ryam Nearing. For the next few years, I was a regular contributor to the quarterly PEP newsletter, *Loving More*, which was reborn in 1995 as a proper magazine that persists to this day. Their Internet presence is *www.lovemore.com*, and I recommend it highly.

I found a new group in 2001, which exists almost entirely in cyberspace, **Poly Matchmaker**, at *www.polymatchmaker.com* – don't be fooled by the name: this is not a mere "personals" site.

Besides these, I have visited dozens of related social and personal sites, and have found something good in all of them. I would finally like to thank one particular real-world group, the Twin Cities Polyamory Discussion Group (**TCPDG**), for inspiration.

Note from the trenches

Hello, everyone. I thought I'd share an update.

I had a good weekend, went off camping with (ultimately) nine people:

- my son & daughter (whom I don't see half enough)
- my ex-wife & her boyfriend (call him Bob)
- their former roommate
- my ex-lover (& Bob's)
- her two male SOs
- Mike, a friend of one, who is quickly becoming the SO of a woman I've dated for years.

I simply can't imagine this sort of agglomeration as having any possible analogy within monogamous society – it was so cool!! Us ex-spouses were actually quite pleasant to each other, and I told Mike that if he dared to back down from a primary relationship with the woman we've been dating, I'd never let him hear the end of it (in other words, we got along great).

Got back Sunday. Showered. Went to a birthday party for Winnie, the third partner of our aforementioned ex-marriage. Hung out with, among others:

- Winnie
- her recently ex-husband
- his previous ex-wife (who I'm dating)
- my recurring lover/friend (we've been "involved" for 16 yrs)
- the birthday girl's sister, her daughter & SO
- and a secondary of the ex-girlfriend I'd just been camping with.

And my primary is coming to town tomorrow for a few weeks.

Life is good.

Preface

> Anybody can write a short story – a bad one, I mean – who has industry and paper and time enough; but not every one may hope to write even a bad novel. It is the length that kills.
>
> Robert Louis Stevenson

I'm going to begin with a confession:

I'm clueless.

I'm okay with that, because I know you're clueless, too.

Having been sexually active for more than a quarter-century, I really have no tried-and-true advice for creating or preserving a relationship, whatever its form or structure. And though I've been openly nonmonogamous for two decades, I can't tell you why some things work and some don't.

This shouldn't come as much of a surprise, if you've thought about it. Most people who stake their allegiance firmly in monogamy – the cultural standard, thousands of years in the making, support of Church and State, blah blah blah – are no better off, but they've got the weight of all that history behind them and, however inaccurate the information provided might be, only a fool would be unaware of the force of long-established tradition.

By analogy, let's compare little polyamorous me with some hapless representative of the majority, and momentarily pretend a lifestyle can be seen as a trip into the deep forest. I don't have a map for the territory I'm wandering around in, and the sun has set besides, and I'm mostly cold, damp, and confused. In comparison, if you're monogamous, you've not only got a map of your own respective territory, but a flashlight as well… except that the map is largely speculative, mostly showing what ought or could or will eventually be there, sort of like a tour guide for a theme park that hasn't been built yet. I suppose it's nice to know that the swampy patch you're standing in will someday be a hospital or a deli, but if you're bleeding or hungry, that pretty map might appear a little inadequate. In any case, lifestyle differences aside, we're all out here without tents, wondering to some degree about what the hell is happening.

*　　*　　*　　*　　*

This book is essentially being written by, about, and for middle-class Caucasians raised in the United States in the latter half of the twentieth century AD. In many of the topics covered herein, I truly do not know my own biases well enough to correct for all of them, and so cannot in any way assure you that they are entirely applicable to your situation. Then again, even if you fit the above criteria exactly, I wouldn't give you better than even odds that you'll identify with more than half of what I present.

Cool. If what I have to say doesn't quite work out for you, articulate your disagreement. I would like to see more intelligent, thoughtful books on this and related subjects added to shelves of bookstores and libraries.

Leaving aside this disclaimer of omniscience, all I offer is my own confused attempts at honesty.

*　　*　　*　　*　　*

As you may have heard, "If you meet the Buddha on the road, kill him."

Likewise, one of the most profound statements I've ever heard is, "I believe, O Lord – help me in mine unbelief!"

Take these two together. Only someone who is sincerely attempting to understand a situation is secure enough to admit that s/he doesn't know every-thing. Beware the True Believer who is convinced of his or her own infallibility – such fanaticism is, at best, incorrect.

In short, whatever sort of relationship structure fits your personal worldview, you're clueless. Welcome to the human condition.

On the other hand, some of us have been spending half a lifetime or more by running about, and finding every misplaced bear-trap in the time-honored way: we poke a toe around in the brush until we hear a jolly metallic snap! and then triumphantly shout "I found it!" just before passing out from the pain. Since us polyamorous-type people started out with no map whatsoever, we've had to make our own, simply to avoid getting stuck in drearily experiencing the same mistakes over and over again.

It's messy and it's painful and we make lots of fascinating mistakes, but we've learned to pay attention to what works, discard what doesn't, and live a rewarding life despite (and, some would argue, perhaps because of) the discomforts of a non-stop learning experience. Follow along and profit from our mistakes, or maybe learn the secrets of maximizing the retention of your toes through a long and (in final balance) happy and exciting life.

*　　*　　*　　*　　*

When exploring dangerous territory, it's considered a common courtesy to main-tain a log, whether a handwritten diary or voice recording. This probably won't help you do much more than organize your thoughts and memories, but the next person to come on shift will benefit. Or, since exploration is generally a dangerous profession, someone once summarized this courtesy as "Always tell the next guy what killed you."

This book is nothing more than a summary of my duty log (though the events chronicled haven't quite killed me yet). I'm at the beginning of my third decade of openly maintaining multiple long-term intimate relationships that are sexually and emotionally nonexclusive. I have over 100,000 words of notes, based on more than twice that bulk of extracted source material. Most of it has been left out and, necessarily, much of it has been glossed over. As I put it to my partners, "I don't need to describe every deadfall to you, when the important part is to tell you that deadfalls exist and how to watch for them."

If you should come to consider yourself as part of the "polyamorous commu-nity," then the most valuable thing you can do for your comrades is to keep your own log of the highs and lows. If you aren't compulsive enough to write things down, then work on your storytelling'– become a living work of history. Let us all know about the good times and bad, equally, as well as how you got there, what you learned, how you moved along, and how you applied your learning in subsequent situations.

*   *   *   *   *

Throughout the book, I have regularly repeated myself, without so much as calling attention to the apparent redundancy. Please don't hold my editors responsible for this! This is not at all an accident. In my years of speaking with people about their relationships, I find that some seemingly small and fundamental points about interpersonal dynamics and sense of self are widely overlooked in our culture, and I feel as if I'm repeating them constantly, not only as I move from audience to audience, but even to the same people on ongoing counseling situations. Given the choice between nagging reuse and allowing an information gap to remain, I will always prefer the former.

Therefore, it was pointed out to me that my use of phrases like "I feel the need to repeat..." were themselves getting rather repetitious in the original draft. Upon consideration, I further agreed that there is no particular need to read what follows (or subsequently refer to it) in a linear manner. Because of this, the reader who slogs through beginning-to-end would tire of seeing the warnings of repetition, where the random-access reader wouldn't know (or particularly care) that any given phrase was a reiteration.

While calling attention to these repetitive fillips is perhaps good form, I hope you'll accept my assurance that the present structure is more pleasant and no less readable.

*   *   *   *   *

Since I'm taking a moment for self-disclosure – a necessity for polyamory, really, but occasionally irritating to the uninitiated – let me explain the tone of the book.

Once in a while, someone gives me a hard time for using "I" and "me" almost constantly. I won't apologize for this. I don't pretend to speak for all others who share a lifestyle with me, or even for my social circle or my intimates. I'm highly opinionated, and it should be made clear at every turn that your experience may vary from mine. Still, I've been through many twists and turns in life, and there's really no good reason that good-hearted, intelligent people should repeat my more obvious gaffes.

The book you hold in your hands is written in an intensely personal style, from observations of people with whom I share a way of life that has apparently always been a part of me, and that I will never change. The book is written as a grossly extended letter to a friend, as I consider all good-hearted, intelligent people who take the emotional risks required by polyamory to be my friends. I truly hope that every such person will find happiness, and my experience gives me many, many reasons to be concerned.

*   *   *   *   *

When I was studying sociology, we had a joke: "There are two types of people in the world: those who divide the world into two types of people, and those who don't."

In the following text, I have essentially divided the world into two groups, monogamous and polyamorous. I readily admit this simple-seeming dichotomy is actually (like most) quite full of holes, and prone to movement, and doesn't fully encompass the amazing range of corners and dead-ends into which the human race is able to walk. However, if the discussion is going to proceed at all, and without turning this little book into some musty philosophical treatise the size of the Manhattan telephone directory, compromises have to be made. So, if I appear to lapse into moments of "poly versus mono" diatribe, please bear with me until the smoke clears.

For clarity, though, let me say this first: I have nothing against monogamy, and much of my writing and counseling consists of encouraging couples to work past obstacles created by simplistic assumptions they have absorbed from the culture around them and imported into their interactions with others. These same assumptions have, of course, likewise been dragged along as people move into more complex forms of intimacy.

Conversely, therefore, I wish to emphasize that calling yourself "poly" is in no wise a guarantee that you are sincere or (once achieving sincerity) that you will act with sincerity forever, consistently, or even regularly. The vast majority of self-described polyamorous people are toting huge amounts of unconscious baggage. The "true believer" exists everywhere, and is no more likely to be an absolute and irrefutable authority whether polyamorous or monogamous.

*　*　*　*　*

And, thanks to my nit-picking friends, I wish to make another apology *cum* disclaimer. In order to actually begin putting this darned thing together, I restricted myself as much as possible to speaking about heterosexuals. Being more widely inclusive would have added greatly to the potential complexities of the discussion, which I would've then felt obligated to analyze fully, resulting in assorted apoplectic attacks at the offices of my publisher, who thought they would be getting a nice 70,000-word book, a limit I've significantly exceeded. More importantly, I in no way consider myself a representative of gay men, much less of lesbians. Ideally, others better qualified than me might use this book as inspiration, and properly examine the role of responsible nonmonogamy in their own milieu. In the meantime, I do hope that much of what I have to say applies with sufficient accuracy to the human condition in general.

*　*　*　*　*

Whatever your experience may be, or might someday encompass, I bid you welcome. Perhaps you are happily monogamous and will be for the rest of your life, in which case I have every best wish for your continuing happiness and satisfaction, no less than I wish upon experienced polyamorists and those who (like me) remain plainly baffled but fascinated by the possibilities.

Reader that you are, I hope you enjoy the following tales and ruminations, and that, if you have any troublesome questions about your experience with life and relationships, you might stumble across even a single small insight that will make your life and the lives around you more rewarding.

There's one demographic I don't talk to much in the following. If you already have what it takes to live polyamorously, without effort, then you're not reading this book. See, if that's you, you're having fun, your days slide by in radiant bliss, and there's no way in Hell you'd be looking to find out what you're supposed to be doing – you're already doing it, and far too busy anyway to read such a stupid, obvious book. In fact, I don't know why I'm talking to you, but then, I have arguments with myself, which at least gets me a seat on the bus in the worst parts of town, the sort of respect all dangerous lunatics aspire to.

The rest of you have questions, concerns, and simple abject curiosity that you're here to assuage. The best way to do that is to tell you stories, and then to examine them. Some are quite funny, some pathetic, and one or two will be surprisingly familiar to you.

Let's get started.

What You Can Get From This Book

As with so many things in this world, there are two levels of advice, which I'll group loosely as *strategy* and *tactics*. Strategy looks at the whole picture, the entire situation, that situation's place in the lineage of what has come as well as how it will be viewed from the future. The tactical approach lacks that historicity, and is concerned mainly with what needs to be done, right here, right now, with the resources that are actually at hand.

Both are exceedingly powerful – when paired. By themselves, they can be pedantic at best, dangerous at worst. Tactics without strategy gives you only what is best in a single moment disconnected from time; as any responsible adult can testify, true gains are measured in the long term, requiring sacrifice, compromise, and other hindrances to immediate gratification of desire. Meanwhile, strategy without tactics skews your thinking toward the merely historical – you could fritter away your energy and concentration in endlessly analyzing what's already happened.

Strategic thinking is of the past. Tactical thinking is of the present. Connecting these two points gives you the minimum required to create a line – in this case, a line that extends also into the future.

Sociology and history give us the past, which is why some people refer to them as retrospective sciences. Some disciplines such as social anthropology and social psychology are very good at studying the present, though they easily become an aimless (if meticulous) gathering of descriptors for the behaviors of the moment, without being overly concerned about the meanings of these behaviors. With the intent of reaching toward the future, we are going to take a whirlwind tour through some of these things.

The practices, the social organization, the psychological and social ramifications that are comprised by what we call "polyamory" are hardly unique to polyamorous thought and action. You could say that polyamory is really nothing more than a symbol system, a way of letting like-minded people communicate without constantly re-creating the language that is needed to enable the communicators to be both concise and clear. There's little else that is truly innovative about polyamory. Nevertheless, these small-seeming innovations are powerful.

Back in the early 1980s, before the term *polyamory* had become common outside of a few dozen people on the planet, some of us used *responsible nonmonogamy*. You could probably make a case that this is a rather negative definition, and you would be correct. However, it is also complete and accurate, with little room for misunderstanding. Until the 1980s, common wisdom, even among counseling and therapeutic professionals, was that nonmonogamy was immoral, or irresponsible, or at least (as the Freudians would say) immature. The term also led to an interesting topic, where we would discuss the many examples most of us have witnessed or experienced of *irresponsible monogamy*, the counter-case.

When we started using such terms, it was with the intent of creating continuity over time. With a unified vocabulary, even a small one with a few terms for commonly discussed concepts, we were able to immediately have useful discussions of past experiences, present situations, and thus to rehearse the hopes and plans we held for the future.

If there's a theme for this book, it's this: "What would a real handbook for newly polyamorous people look like? Could we produce a sort of *Nonmonogamy for Dummies*? Can we provide structures to answer 90% of the questions and problems that are going to arise when a household of roommates suddenly turns sexual?"

*   *   *   *   *

In scientific method – something employed to solve problems by every thinking being, not merely scientists – there are four basic stages:

- observation
- hypothesis
- prediction
- verification

As we apply these to a given problem, some stages recur to give us the ability to peel apart further questions that are revealed by analysis. For instance, analyzing a given problem might follow the stages of observation, hypothesis, prediction, further observation, amended hypothesis, observation, hypothesis. Data overlooked at the first pass may become necessary; data collected may be discarded as irrelevant to the main question.

This book is an attempt to address vast gaps that have existed in the literature (popular and scholarly alike) for quite some time, rendering it virtually useless for productive discussion. I want to make a start at dissecting what it is that polyamorous people do, so that anyone who encounters polyamory, even if peripherally or momentarily, will be in a position to apply scientific method to adapt the necessarily limited information from its source. Perhaps I can't offer a complete toolbox, but I have a goal to offer at least a new tool or technique to every reader.

This book began largely from my irritation at having so few good books to recommend on nonmonogamy. Leaving aside the question of quality, there are (for instance) more books about the history of Canadian rock-and-roll bands than about nonmonogamy, even if you expand the latter category to include studies of swinging and extramarital affairs.

Then there is the question of quality, and another of utility. Nonmonogamy has been addressed as a set of observable behaviors, and also as a collection of utopian dreams and attitudes that extend therefrom. Virtually no attempt has been made to connect these two data sets. The result has been a disjoint mishmash of statistics and secondhand conjecture. When you go searching for books and articles about relationships in general (of which there are hundreds in print at any given moment, joining the many thousands that have gone before, in printed form and on the Internet), you may notice that most of them can quickly be dropped into groups: observation that is highly biased or largely uninformed; hypothesis that is based on a questionable interpretation of what is past and what is possible; prediction predicated on the occurrence of a certifiable miracle in the state of the world or human nature, with little or no attempt at verification, except to begin the cycle anew.

Life is packed full of uncertainty. Yet, to move forward, we must make decisions upon which to act, and intelligent decisions require some web (however tenuous) of facts. We seek to expand our knowledge so that we can get on with our lives without leaping from one blind decision to another'– hope can only take us so far. The constant struggle between uncertainty and the inexorable movement of the Universe seemingly requires us to build our castle in a marsh.

I am hugely disappointed by books about interpersonal relationships, and most bitterly so concerning anything outside of the paradigm of life-long heterosexual monogamy. The best collections of data are almost never translated into some form interpretable outside of academia, let alone useful to the very people the data describes. Advice books are based more heavily in the philosophical or religious biases of the author than on anyone's needs.

So, this book. Again, as I cannot possibly say too often: everything in my writing, especially in this book, is highly biased. I would never claim otherwise. This is not a work of "objective journalism" by any stretch. Though I have done my best to stay true to the ideals of both scientific methodology and journalistic integrity, I refuse to claim the protection of either. In fact, those two camps echo the two sorts of book I most wanted to avoid imitating: I didn't want to assemble another stuffy collection of conjecture-puffed facts, but I also wanted to steer it far away from becoming (as a friend called another book on nonmonogamy) a bunch of feel-good, aren't-we-wonderful propaganda.

This book is based upon experience, upon observation, upon discussion, harking back not to the dawn of time but barely further than a mere quarter-century. In addition, I've read a large proportion of the extant books, and done my utmost to pare away the garbage. (At the end, you'll find a somewhat wacky bibliography, which includes many of the books that have influenced my relationships and my writing, with notes about their strengths and weaknesses as appropriate.)

This book will not apply to everyone seeking advice about polyamory, just as it cannot possibly apply to every situation. For those who find some good, I'd deem it highly improbable that they will agree with everything I present. If you find my every word golden, then read it all again, from the beginning, and poke holes in it! You've obviously overlooked all of the ragged details. Enlighten yourself.

If you should read this book and find only one tiny nugget of something akin to wisdom that improves your life and your interaction with those around you, but roundly ridicule all the rest of my verbiage, then I will be satisfied with that small success. And that's the way it oughta be.

I hope you at least find the following entertaining, perhaps even thought-provoking.

Table of Contents

Part I
Background & history

In Part II, I will provide tales and advice that ought to greatly assist in many circumstances, with an emphasis on successful nonmonogamy, especially polyamory.

Before we go charging into that, though, you likely need to be brought up to speed on the concepts that underlie polyamory as a practice, in order to understand how it manages the apparently paradoxical position of being both very radical and somewhat obvious and well-established. Whatever experience or reading you have, much of this will come as a surprise to you.

01. What are we talking about, anyway?

The term **polyamory** is a relatively recent neologism, generally credited to Morning Glory Zell of the Church of All Worlds, from an article published in 1990. The term is a hybrid from the Greek *poly* and Latin *amory*, and so translates to "many loves."

While providing a category of sorts, "polyamory" is a catch-all that covers quite a range of lifestyle choices, outlooks, and interactional patterns. The term says little about any given person's sincerity or experience, let alone what they have in mind for the future. And, of course, an individual's pattern can change with time, circumstance, and opportunity. In short, it's possible to gather a roomful of "poly" people and quickly discover that their ways of life have nothing in common, except that they do not claim to be monogamous, detest being called promiscuous (even in the cases when it's true), and see themselves as something quite apart from swingers. Come back in a year, and you'll find that most of them will be in slightly different situations.

How to spot a polyamorous person
Well, good luck.

Polyamory is not a lifestyle. We cover just about every imaginable combination of economic level, social class, education, upbringing, religion, age, race, political affiliation, gender preference, technological comfort, physical type, living situation, and preferred urban milieu. All in all, we look pretty much like any monogamous or promiscuous person (depending on when you look). If we want to keep our private lives private, then it's a simple matter to hide. You will not be able to spot us at a glance when walking down the street, or among your coworkers, or even among your friends and relatives.

1

However, I can make some assumptions, from years of observation. See, we look like anyone else, really, and we mostly act "normal" too. But we think differently. We have to, as you will see. Whether the thinking pattern led to nonmonogamy, or the reverse, is probably the least consequential of data.

Let me pull up some observable demographics. If a given person identifies with the term "polyamorous," chances are that she or he is a citizen of the United States, raised in a middle-class household by a nominally Christian family with moderate-to-poor communication skills, where folks were loving and supportive but not great at showing how they felt. (Not so long ago, I would've stated that 95% of people who know the word "polyamory" and apply it to themselves would be purebred European stock, but that has changed in recent years, and I'd say it's now relatively safe to guess 75%.) He or she is most likely of high intelligence, has spent two or three years in college, is conversant in technology and the Internet, and has distinct entrepreneurial and artistic leanings. This person is probably a self-described bisexual, though recent sexual experience with lovers of both genders may be lacking. They love the members of the family into which they were born, but are probably not "out" to them, and have found that a few visits per year seems to leave everyone an adequate comfort zone; given an opportunity, they prefer to live in a different city from their parents. As far as jobs, they aren't usually very career-oriented, though they sometimes seem to stumble into long-term job situations by sheer force of their overall curiosity and competence. In fact, their job status and income level might seem to be inversely proportional to their education.

A distinct subgroup does exist: these are members of the Society for Creative Anachronism, avid readers (far more than the 2 to 6 books per year variously estimated as average for people in the United States), especially of the science fiction and fantasy genres, and professing the Wiccan religion or a sort of "Earth-centered" optimistic agnosticism. The reason such a cluster exists is simple enough: someone who is willing to "go public" about being slightly outside of the mainstream (as with dressing up in medieval garb to attend SCA events, for instance) is more likely than the general population to consider other non-mainstream lifestyle choices as potential options. This "expansive" tendency doesn't necessarily go both ways – there are plenty of people who live in what could be called a polyamorous fashion, but are extremely unadventurous; to put it another way, being open-minded and curious tends to lead toward nonmonogamy, but the reverse doesn't seem to hold at all well.

Overall, though, if I was going to describe a single trait inherent to a polyamorous person, especially someone who would tend to have successful and fruitful interpersonal relationships on all levels, that would be a kind of unremitting general curiosity. Unless his or her life is typically a continuous series of self-created disasters, a polyamorous person has a distinct fascination with the way things work, and enjoys tinkering. Without the flexibility indicated by some inherent problem-solving ability (and in fact a tendency to seek out problems that need solving), the "polyamory" that takes place will either have to be kept at a very emotionally shallow level or it will quickly seem to become nothing but an endless round of chaos, conflict, and melodrama.

There are no experts on polyamory – just a few of us who venture to put forward our ideas. Outside of some very basic and generally agreed-upon standards of conduct, there is no "orthodox" approach to polyamory. There is only rarely a single right way to do things. Unless you are prepared for this, you'll find the experience very disorienting.

This isn't a bad thing; far from it. Rather than trending toward a narrow set of standards, this makes polyamory inherently inclusive, allowing for (see previous) an amazing range of people.

A little terminology

If you hang around with so much as one polyamorous person for more than a few minutes, you'll soon find yourself buried with jargon. This sort of label-glut is common in any non-mainstream area of human endeavor, whether you're talking to a philosophy student or an Internet addict. In polyamory, as in any other slice of life, these terms may be a little overwhelming at first, especially around someone who has recently learned them. However, for the most part, this vocabulary does serve the purpose of providing a useful shorthand, and (hopefully) easing communication.

What follows is admittedly very biased, but for the most part accurate. As they say on the Internet, "your mileage may vary," but I stand by the general accuracy of my statements, and they will at least give you a solid basis from which to join in the discussion.

I'm going to attempt to list some of the more common terms, putting the ones you're most likely to encounter nearer the top.

POLYAMORY: "multiple loves." I prefer to define the term very literally, especially the "love" part. Therefore, these relationships may or mayn't have a sexual component, but I emphasize the openness, honesty, and communication necessary to make each and every relationship one of love, with on-going commitment. While not anathematic toward dating and "friend sex" (or, necessarily, swinging), those forms, even if undertaken with the hope that something long-term might develop, aren't really central to polyamory. The term is commonly shortened to "poly" (and, yes, I'm tired of parrot jokes). You'll occasionally encounter "polyamorist," which is descriptive, but so lumpen that people (myself included) will instead refer to another person as "a poly".

The term *polyamory* is in important ways unrelated to *polyandry* and *polygyny* (and distinct from the much newer *polyfidelity*). While polyamory seems like a combination of the two older concepts, it also implies a lowered tendency to judge other peoples' choices as "immoral" merely because they're different.

DYAD: a unit made up of two people. With rare exception, all complex relationships such as the polyamorous can be examined as a mesh of dyads. Even in absolute monogamy, there's still a dyadic component in how you interact with, say, your best friend, your most usual buddy, and so forth. You will occasionally hear a three-person core group referred to as a *triad*, and (rarely) four as a *tetrad*.

PRIMARY, SECONDARY, TERTIARY: these words have nothing to do with how important a given person is to you, but rather indicate how thoroughly your lives as individuals are intertwined. In part, these terms are a legacy of decades-old sociology, where it was assumed that each person had exactly one primary relationship (spouse or equivalent) and all others were secondary. In modern usage, the terms can be a little vague and slippery, shifting with circumstance, but their utility is nevertheless important for quickly mapping out the territory.

Many people who consider themselves polyamorous don't like this "hierarchal" paradigm. Generally, those very people don't yet have a whole lot of experience with maintaining simultaneous multiple deeply intimate relationships over a period of months, much less years. Life does force us to set priorities (even if they have to change every few days), and ignoring this necessity is both dishonest and willfully ignorant, neither trait particularly predisposing someone for the rigors of this lifestyle.

If I am living with a lover, we likely have all sorts of things we share that won't occur in our interactions with other people: a lease, children, shared bank accounts, housecleaning concerns, pet care. Each of these facets brings with it responsibilities and rewards, which we share in a manner others do not experience with us. People likely think of us as "a couple"; if they see me with a secondary partner, their impression is probably something like "close friends."

A primary relationship has generally survived past its initial bout of NRE (see below), and the partners are capable of having involved productive arguments that don't readily endanger the continuation of the dyad. Some people who don't presently have a primary relationship in this sense might refer to one lover as their primary partner, by which they actually mean "most primary." As we'll get into later, it's almost always a cop-out to say something like "All my relationships are primary," or "Everyone is important."

SO: significant other. A good word, though without much depth, as it seems to mark a transient, of-the-moment feeling for another person, though I find it's usually used interchangeably with *partner* to mark out one of the handful of people who is, well, most significant.

MONOAMOROUS: another way of saying "couple-oriented." This includes monogamy, of course, but also leaves room for a dyad who are open to polyamory, or accept it as a long-term likelihood, though not presently seeking more complexity. Compare this to the next entry.

MONOGAMIST: this interesting neologism is still evolving, so I would like to take a moment for it. In our society, when someone is identified as "monogamous," the term is as vague and muddled as is "polyamorous". Long-term intentions might be at distinct odds with actual behavior.

When Patty was going through an emotionally difficult time after the sudden death of her fiancé, she could not tolerate the idea of sleeping alone, yet was afraid of forming another emotional bond. Being socially gregarious, she regularly encountered eligible males. By her own estimate, she had sex with almost 200 men in one year, only three of them more than one-night stands. Yet, all through this period, she saw herself as monogamous, knowing that she would eventually work through her trauma and gladly settle down with one man. (In fact, she subsequently married my roommate, and they were very happy together.) I would call her mindset at the time monogamist, not monogamous.

Patty is hardly alone, or even particularly unusual in our "monogamous" society, except for a high degree of awareness of her own motivations. When I go to a club to see one of my musician friends perform, I can't help but observe the phenomenon of the "last-call romance," when people who are lonely or bored or just plain horny begin casting around for someone who might be willing to go out for a bite to eat afterward, have sex, or maybe even spend the night. Not unusually, the person they leave with would not have even slowed their roving eye a few hours earlier. That this is a long-accepted facet of a cultural philosophy that claims predominance of life-long one-on-one relationships is absurd, but common, and leads to the next term.

NONINTIMATE SEX: one of my neologisms coined about 1990 to replace the widespread pejorative tone of "casual sex." This latter term seems to have utility only for damning sex outside of the marital (or quasi-marital) bond. Garry Trudeau once defined casual sex as "jeans allowed" – and this is one of the most thoughtful and accurate definitions! Personally, I see nothing inherently wrong with sexual encounters that aren't intended to be part of a committed primary relationship; any valid moral judgment would depend from the situation and the people involved, not merely from the acts.

You likely will find it oxymoronic at first that sex could be anything but intimate. However, intimacy is far more than mere physical proximity, despite any interlocking body parts. You can probably think of some moments of incredibly intimate connection that didn't involve even physical contact. The converse also holds since, though sex offers a channel for incredibly rich interpersonal communication, sex is not of itself communication.

In the foregoing example, Patty was purposefully engaged in nonintimate sex, setting a comfortable distance from deep attachment to other human beings while satisfying her desires for sex and companionship.

SWINGING: once also known as "wife swapping." Usually, couples get together in groups for the explicit purpose of having sex with people they're not married to, whether pairing off to separate bedrooms or having some sort of orgy. While sex between women is tacitly encouraged, these groups are heavily monogamous and heterosexual, to the degree that some groups will boot members who attempt to contact other members outside of sanctioned events, since this could threaten the day-to-day solidarity of the affiliated marriages. Though many poly people can still get quite testy when the two lifestyles are compared, there is nowadays much overlap between polyamory and swinging, with some swing clubs resembling intimate networks (see below) or even group marriages, and swingers trending toward polyamory as they give increasing priority to a few lovers.

NRE: one of the very handiest terms you'll run into, this refers to the phenomenon of "new relationship energy," where the fascination with a relationship tries to overwhelm your common sense. As long as you avoid making any ill-considered commitments, or risking your job, housing, other relationships, etc., you'll probably be okay. When NRE wears off, it's not unusual to ask, "What the hell was I thinking?" A little conscious caution can avoid most related problems. This is sometimes known as the "honeymoon period" where new lovers in a dyad temporarily focus a little more on each other than on their preexisting relationships. Something akin to NRE can also recur when people find themselves falling in love all over again – I can easily think of five distinct times that I fell deeply in love with my wife during our 12 years together, and there were probably three times that number that would count as NRE.

LTR: long-term relationship. On the surface, this looks like a very specific term, but it's not. If Marge and Bob have vastly different work shifts and social lives and thus manage to get only a few evenings together in a typical month, and have been doing this for years, while Marge and Fred have lived together for a year and spend most of their free time with each other, then the former is an established LTR while being secondary to the latter.

LDR: another complicating factor, the long-distance relationship. In this sense, "distance" means more than mileage, as when one or both members of a married couple have a job that takes them all over the country on a regular basis, or otherwise have commitments that keep them apart. Some people feel negative effects from the distance more than they do the time apart, while others are more affected by the separation itself. In fact, being a mere fifty miles apart but unable to align your schedules more than a few times a month might make you more nervous than would any regularly bridgeable thousand-mile gap.

VEE: not an acronym, but referring to a core relationship where one person has two lovers who themselves aren't lovers, which makes a V-shape when you map it out. Though the neologisms begin to quickly pile up, this sort of "open ended" structure appears as well in larger groups and networks.

FMFMFM etc.: originated in swinging, where most males are willing to have a "king triad," female-male-female or FMF, and occasionally a "queen triad" or MFM. In poly, the acronym is too linear to be of much detailed help but is handy for indicating that, say, the core group was created from two couples, or MFMF.

SWEETIE: a very popular buzzword used by those not quite willing to commit to a more specific euphemism: lover, sexual partner, former one-night stand, potential bedmate, close friend, flirtation, etc. In most cases, it tells you nothing more than "We've had sex." (I find it detestably coy, and attempt to not snarl when it appears. Such terms "cutesify" without informing.) Used primarily by the sort of person who refers to a male partner as "hubby" without an apparent clue that "wifey" was a fightin' word a mere couple of decades ago to anyone with the least feminist sensibility.

SISTER-WIFE: usually indicates that someone has been reading a little too much about Native Americans or Mormonism. If someone says they're looking for a sister-wife, they probably mean that they want a closed FMF triad, and likely are new to the concepts of polyamory.

HBB: standard acronym for "hot bi babe," the apparent goal sought after by every straight male, lesbian, and married couple that one day decides to "become poly." Well, that's how the myth goes, anyway. To say that someone "is only here for HBBs" is almost always sarcastic and, unfortunately, far too often true.

PARTNER: watch out for this term! If you think you know what a person is saying, you may find yourself rapidly lost. The modifier could be "business," "life," or "sexual." We'll get to it in a little more detail, but "That's my partner" could as easily signify a casual date, a spouse, a sexual fling, or a long-term intimate relationship (potential or actual). If you want to pin the speaker down quickly, ask what line of business they're in and let them clear it up for you.

SEXUALLY OPEN MARRIAGE: a primary couple, neither of whom presently maintains another relationship that is of as high a priority. A specific case of consentual adultery.

CLOSED GROUP MARRIAGE: a definable unit of three or more adults, who may or may not be sexually involved with all other members, but none of whom has a sexual relationship or love attachment outside of the group, or intends to.

POLYFIDELITY: a special case of closed group marriage, fully egalitarian (equal in as many senses as humanly possible), in which each individual member maintains a primary bond to each other member.

INTIMATE NETWORK: a sort of community, where singles, couples, group marriages, and households are interconnected by varying degrees of on-going intimate relationships, sexual and otherwise. These "nodes" can be of any nonmonogamous form, and can have members who do not have sexual ties but are regularly involved with the social dynamic. An intimate network forms a quasi-familial structure, with most of the mob getting together for parties, outings, gardening, and so on. Usually shortened to just *network* in common use. You may find this also referred to as a *tribe*.

LOVE-TYPE THING: this term is a clean swipe from a friend, for which I'm grateful. They use it to indicate a situation where people are falling in love, but are not quite there yet, or are incompatible in some small but significant way but very attached otherwise. I think it's delightful, and a fitting label for one of those awkward in-between stages of a relationship.

COMPERSION: a feeling of simple joy for the happiness of your partner, compersion is pretty much the inverse of jealousy. (This term survives from Kerista Commune.) It's difficult to describe, but you know it when you encounter it within yourself.

OTHERLOVE: while I don't have anything against this term, and see where it could be very handy in the future, it presently isn't defined well enough to achieve any standardization of usage. Depending on who is speaking, it can refer to a non-primary sexual relationship, an LDR, a lover of a lover, a date, an old friend, a flirtation. The shorter this list gets, the more useful the term will become.

CO-MARITAL: a term that has largely fallen by the wayside, but still possesses great merit as far as historical antecedents to polyamory. This was meant to be a non-pejorative description of responsible, emotionally healthy intimacy outside the married couple, without the negative connotation of *extramarital*. Interestingly enough, the term has been ascribed to the Reverend William Genné, co-author of *Foundations for Christian Family Policy*, published by the National Council of Churches of Christ, to which he belonged.

Why jargon is important

Let me start from the core term. People get into occasional snarls over throwing "polyamory" into a conversation as if we all mean the same thing across a huge variety of circumstances. For instance, some people represent an established couple looking to add another woman, and make clear that none of the resultant three will be involved with anyone outside of the triad. Then again, there are a few who, due to various factors, have multiple intimate encounters, some of them intended to be on-going, but do not presently have and/or are not looking for a primary partner. Arguments crop up here because we start from a faulty premise: "It's all polyamory, therefore it's all the same thing."

Another important concept is *intent*. The terms can get slippery and lead to all kinds of disagreements if past, present, and future aren't the same, which they usually aren't. Think over the following three brief examples, and see where you could make a case for multiple answers.

Say that I've never had a non-monogamous primary relationship, but I want to. Am I polyamorous? You can find staunch, well-thought defenders of either extreme and every shade between.

Let's look at the counter-case: I'm widely experienced in nonmonogamy, but I do not presently have a primary, and I am steadily dating four women, hoping that I will eventually end up monogamous with one of them. Am I therefore monogamous?

Third case: though I've experienced the whole range, I'm not obsessed with any of the alternatives, and will adapt to the circumstances and the people in my life. Am I mono, or poly? open, or closed?

In that last, let's say I settle down with a lover, and we decide that, what with a young child and jobs and evening classes and social groups, we have just enough time and energy to maintain exactly one intimate relationship. But, a few years down the road, the baby is off to school, the classes are done, the job schedules have become more flexible, we've dropped a couple of social groups... and maybe we have the time and stability to start dating others. Have we always been poly, and in denial? Are we really mono, and looking for a little adventure? Have we in some way "changed our minds"?

Terminology is important in another way. I have a friend who adamantly denies that he is gay. "I'm *homosexual*," he insists. "I have a partner, we love each other very much, we don't want anybody else, and we'll probably be together for life. I don't go to the bars, I don't march in parades, I don't put rainbow stickers on everything. I'm a boring old fag, and I'm happy that way." He is very proud of the advances of the queer community, but doesn't feel they represent him, or he them.

Similarly, there are many people whose behavior and outlook appears clearly consonant with polyamory, but have no desire to be "out" or activist. I'm aware of at least one group marriage that has been quietly whirring along since Prohibition, and they have no interest in being part of anyone's movement. Though the comparison is often made, polygynous Mormons are horrified by the openness and flexibility of polyamory.

An increasing number of people say "polyamory" when they are referring to whatever form of extra- or nonmarital sex they have fastened upon as the One Right True Way. To clear this up, read and memorize the following well-established set of nested terms, and make every attempt to apply them correctly and to assure that others do as well. You can't have clear thinking with chronically sloppy language.

- Nonmonogamy is intimacy that cannot fit neatly within exclusive couplehood.
- Responsible nonmonogamy is a subset of nonmonogamy.
- Polyamory is a subset of responsible nonmonogamy.
- Group marriage is a subset of polyamory.
- Closed group marriage is a subset of group marriage.
- Polyfidelity is a subset of closed group marriage.

Therefore, factors that apply to polyamory almost always apply to polyfidelity as well. However, the reverse is most often incorrect. Statements such as, "I have a closed triad, therefore all polyamorous people should be doing the same thing" are absurd.

Words to set aside or leave behind

There are a few words you might be tempted to toss into a conversation, which will instantly mark you as a dabbler.

FAITHFUL: as in, "I don't think I could stand it if I knew my husband wasn't faithful." Polls regularly find that roughly half of marriages that last 15 years or longer have weathered at least one extramarital sexual affair that the nonparticipating spouse knows about. What makes absurd such waving of "faithful" as some sort of moral plateau, though, is that sex outside the monogamous Sacred Bond is usually more a *symptom* of deep-rooted problems than it is a *cause*. More than a few spouses secretly wish they could trade a few bits of that exclusivity for their partner's obsession with social clubs or hobbies. I am exceedingly faithful to all of my friends, whether or not we are (or might become) sexually involved.

LOYAL, TRUE, etc.: see above.

FIDELITY: while related to the previous, we'll be looking at this concept a bit more thoroughly. As with words such as *discipline*, fidelity is something that you have within yourself. Its use, though, usually indicates that the speaker has deep but crumbling reservations about "this whole polyamory thing."

FOOLING AROUND: what many monogamous people think polyamorous people do (other than sleeping and eating). My mother once accused me of this, so I protested that, no, I was entirely serious.

That's enough of verbiage for the moment. Let's move on to more advanced concepts of the "is and isn't" type.

02. Reinventing the wheel: why polyamory won't change the world.

You could say that polyamory is something new, a daring and radical social experiment in which the guinea pigs are running the laboratory.

That is, you could say it, but it'd be silly. In the realm of human goofiness, happy and otherwise, there's really not much new under the sun that doesn't require batteries.

On the other hand, I am not about to make a case for polyamory being something that has been around for centuries and eons, lo these many millennia and all that. Needing to prove a "logical" pedigree, as a route to validation, is no less pointless than needing to prove one does not exist.

Like so many irritating details of the Universe (which, come to think of it, is made up almost wholly of irritating details), the truth is much more complicated than could adequately be covered by a binary yes-or-no, good-or-bad, old-or-new summary. So, walk with me back to the basics, and look more closely at the root assumptions we carry.

The society we live in, and in fact most of the modern-day world, is monogamous. That is to say, the inhabitants, the organized religions, legal codes (housing, taxation, inheritance, etc.), mercantilism, media, the arts, language, and likely anything else you can think of support and reinforce the notion that we are all monogamous, or at least ought to be.

In that context, allow me to take a hand at something you've likely never before experienced: let's define monogamy. Seems simple enough, right? However, there are some serious differences between denotation and connotation, theory and practice, intent and act. To my way of thinking, showing you what a mess "monogamy" is will be my way of enlisting you in the struggle to keep "polyamory" from sliding the same way and thus contributing to the mess caused by vague, imprecise use of language. This is going to take a while, though, so you might want to put on some music and grab yourself a soda before we continue.

At root, the word monogamy can be parsed as meaning "one spouse". This says nothing about love or sex (for starters), just bluntly that you can only be married to one person. And I don't mean "one at a time" – one person, period, that's it, thank you for playing, enjoy the rest of your life as a unit.

A brief history of monogamy

Let's take a step closer to extant reality. As you may have noted, the world has undergone some big changes in the past few decades, and this includes the laws and attitudes toward marriage and the lack thereof. (If you have the least doubt about that statement, you may wish to read Lenore J. Weitzman's *The Marriage Contract* for an excellent overview of the often bizarre and byzantine laws attached to marriage well into the latter half of the 20th century.) Even into the 1970s, to get divorced was only slightly less shameful than pregnancy out of wedlock.

An excess of romance (see *The Hoax of Romance* for the history of this originally laudable philosophy that has now clouded our reason for a few centuries) in our culture leaves us with the impression that the concepts of monogamy, love, sex, and marriage, and everything attached to them, forms some sort of indivisible unit, and always has. Though this complex has indeed existed for centuries, it has always existed more largely in theory and concept than in practice. At best, the pieces have fit together poorly, and required a certain suspension of your disbelief – and bald lying, or even schizophrenic detachment – in order to keep the whole thing going.

While Christianity began to coalesce in the fifth century, the Church needed to unify itself by standardizing its practices and dogma. It commonly did so by bloodily crushing any "heresies", meaning groups that disagreed with policy, or perhaps were merely suspected of the potential for someday getting around to thinking about deviating from core dogma in the least little way. In any case, whether by war, intrigue, execution, or threat, the scions of Christianity became part of the power structure, allied to leaders and warlords, and eventually to the majority. Therefore, I wish to differentiate, for the rest of this discussion, the philosophical beliefs of Christianity from the quasi-political Church.

As elsewhere, the various barbarians of Europe had begun to diverge into two groups: those who did the constant physical work required to keep the community fed and clothed, and those who provided protection from ever-present threat. In time, these evolved (respectively) into the mass that worked the land, and the tiny minority (including the Church) that claimed stewardship of that land; or, to put it another way, peasants and nobility, with a vast unpopulated gulf between.

For most of the people in Europe, sex was a rather simple part of life. You found someone who you could at least tolerate well enough to procreate with and raise plenty of strong, healthy children who would take care of you during illness or encroaching age. Mutual love might be the sole motivator for a particular coupling, but love could just as easily be wholly absent. The focus was on partnership and stability, both of which contributed to the survival of the community and its members. If there was any sort of social recognition of an intent to form a union between a particular man and a particular woman, it was likely to be a party of some sort, with requests to the local gods and spirits to bestow fecundity, much the same sort of thing as was done for the crops and livestock. The Church had little formalized interest in the peasantry, because they weren't much more than draft animals with passable communication skills.

Maintenance of lineage meant little to the serfs. Any sensible man whose children were prone to be born sickly and to die young would easily turn a blind eye if his partner took an occasional fancy to some strapping male whose known offspring were all solid and sturdy. There was, after all, little enough property to inherit, other than maybe a domicile, a few tools, and some bric-a-brac, meaning no particular need to determine who the "real father" might be. The peasants owned little, and certainly no land. Their only legacy was in their children, who ought to be long-lived and healthy enough to care for age-afflicted parents.

The royalty, though, worried about inheritance, and therefore patrimony (and thus, of course, matrimony). Even if the royalty in question sometimes did not believe in it themselves, they knew that a preponderance of the human beings beneath them were much more loyal to a ruler who could demonstrate a genetic right to rule. Thus, lineage was one of the most important factors, regularly outweighing more practical abilities like leadership, courage, economic savvy, battlefield strategy, and diplomacy. The ruling class, especially those at the top, and most especially the topmost male, held a position that was largely as stand-in for, divinely ordained representative of, or incarnation of the gods of the land. They were seen as not only granting but inducing a prosperous harvest. By so-called *droit de seigneur*, a local ruler could go about the countryside, having intercourse at his whim with any woman or girl who took his fancy. If you find this practice barbaric, you fail to consider that this was nominally (at least) considered a blessing, that the mortal incarnation of God Himself would deign to come down and spread his strength and wisdom throughout the bloodlines of the common folk, thereby ennobling them as well. The Church representatives could not be happy about this, but the greatest fallout from the practice was that bastard children – demigods, essentially – might appear from the heaths during a question of royal succession and present an inconveniently valid claim to the throne, with the claimant having only tenuous loyalties to the Church. We'll leave aside the irony that, with a relatively small ruling class, added to the pressures to produce sanctioned offspring (preferably male) as soon as possible to assure a line of succession both legitimate and approved by those who wanted to maintain their jobs, the impregnating ruler was probably genetically inferior to the people he was "improving."

Then, the world began to change more rapidly. (Authorities disagree widely, setting the following phase as occurring anywhere between the ninth and fifteenth centuries. Since this book isn't meant to be a history text, I refuse to go any closer, and leave that for the students and the extremely bored among my readers. I freely admit that I am only skimming over a few highlights relevant to our topic.)

The situation started to get complicated as knowledge expanded. The ruling class started desiring items that could not be grown or created in the areas over which they had dominion. This required trade with other regions. However, this same class was essentially prevented by their inherent godlike status from performing labor other than combat, and could not seek monetary gain except through the passive income of the rents on their lands, augmented by their various conquering hordes pillaging some other region's wealth. Even if the rulers had the money, though, they couldn't go chasing off on supply runs.

And so, a new class was born, the merchants, the first middle class. This never sat particularly well with the nobility, especially the lower strata who might themselves earn little or nothing from whatever holdings they controlled. The merchants were still people who had to work daily for a living, but they were also sidling toward the realm of royalty by accumulating their share of a relatively new form of power: money. Some of the merchants were soon able to acquire for themselves a higher standard of living than available to the lower nobility, albeit at the moral expense of having to run a business, something still seen as far beneath the station of our tattered present-day nobility.

The merchant class took on not only fine garments and comfortable beds, but also many of the social rituals previously reserved to the domain of royalty – such as the Church. Conversely, the Church was not slow to comprehend that there was rising power in this class, whether just when counting warm bodies, or in the combined social and monetary assets this expanding stratum represented. And, since these former peasants now had actual tangible assets, leading matters of inheritance and succession to the fore, lineage and "legitimacy" and birth-order began to take on importance for those not of noble birth.

Though the benefits of inheritable property and capitalism straggled downward through the classes, dreams of a better life, and even upward social mobility, made the trip much more quickly and thoroughly. You couldn't simply become of royal blood, and you likely could never become a merchant or a member of a craft guild (positions that were usually passed along generationally as fathers favored their sons, well into the 20th century). You could, though, aspire to *seeming* more like the upper classes, and marriage was something relatively easy to emulate. In fact, it gave you the possibility of marrying your daughter off to someone of slightly more elevated station, and thus raising your family's standing. Supported by such aspirations, marriage became a matter controlled first by the government (since this simplified somewhat the matter of the census, which in turn streamlined taxation of the lower classes), and eventually by the Church.

A friend of mine, Dean, a costume maker, told me an interesting story. One of his clients asked him why fancy gowns throughout the ages, with all the pounds of cloth they entail and the many resulting folds and layers, didn't have pockets. Dean had actually studied this. As it turns out, most of the fine-crafted gowns have indeed been pocketless. "But when you trace the evolution of a particular style back to its innovator," Dean said, "you'll always find that the original gown may have had more pockets than a shoplifter's trenchcoat, and if you stuffed each one with rocks, it wouldn't hurt the lines a bit. They were masterpieces of both craft and art. The wannabees copied what they saw, which was these lines, and the sumptuous cloth, and completely overlooked the invisible pockets. To ask would've been to admit you were only pretending to the class, so this never came up."

And that's largely what the wannabees have done with everything else as well, from clothing and furniture to religion and marriage. They appropriated what they saw, without stopping to ask themselves whether there might be any overlookable subtleties or artfully camouflaged nuances.

In the arts, this is hardly a bad thing, since "pure" forms quickly become either stale or decadent. The amateurish icons throughout the Russian Orthodox Church are in many cases third- or fifth-hand renderings, copies of copies of copies, by painters with rather poor memories and little skill. Yet, it is that incredible sincerity that shines through in these portraits, the faith and devotion and absolute belief of the artist, that gives these icons a richness and depth that could not possibly be matched by the finest portrait painters of any age.

There is much more danger in attempting to elevate a form of artistic expression above its roots. It is difficult (though not impossible) for a rich suburban boy to learn to play a convincing Delta blues. I've heard many stories of early-1960s kids who tried so hard to make their folk and blues tunes "authentic" that they faithfully reproduced every tiny detail from the old 78s, including poorly tuned guitars and obvious performance blunders. A comfortably middle-class painter who attempts to become a "folk" or "primitive" artist will in all likelihood never come across as anything other than amateurish and uninspired (though they could aspire to being called "derivative" or "imitative"). Art is an expression of worldview, and worldview cannot be purchased at the hardware store.

Depending on your place in the world, you can view such pretension as contemptible, pathetic, ludicrous, inspired, or inconsequential, and you'd find plenty of justification. But in marriage, this sort of thing has been disastrous. To the upper classes, monogamy was a matter of outward show, of state ritual. This meant that offspring shouldn't be scattered liberally around the countryside, and that children should resemble their ostensible fathers. Other than that, all bets were pretty much off.

But what the lower classes saw was an indivisible, life-long pair-bond, one related to prestige and wealth, and not only sanctioned by but endorsed by the ever-powerful Church. Furthermore, life-long marriage, as a concept, had a self-limiting factor: an average human lifespan of perhaps 35 years. Even if you married at age 15, odds were that your spouse, or you, would be dead within a couple of decades, whether from disease, childbearing, famine, overwork, war, or accident; before the era of sulfa-based medications, death from the infection of even a minor wound was not terribly rare. So, if you were fortunate, you could make multiple trips to the altar before your own mortality interceded.

The wide-ranging adoption of marriage was, generally, not a cause of problems. That is, wasn't until about 250 years ago, when something happened that is usually referred to as the Industrial Revolution. Up until that point, life was pretty much based around the community, with sprawling families intertwined by countless generations of marriage, shared tribulations, and so forth. Travel of any distance was experienced by a very few.

The advent of factory-based manufacturing, and the parallel decline of labor-based agriculture, was perhaps the first major blow against community. When crops failed (as they inevitably do), people began to make the choice of moving to the city, where factory work did not depend on vagaries of the weather and assorted blights. In many cases the choice was not so difficult: you could work in the fields twelve or more hours a day, seven days a week, or even longer, often risking your health or even life, only to end up watching your children starve, or you could work twelve or more hours a day, seven days a week, or even longer, often risking your health or even life, and virtually guarantee that your children would be fed, clothed, and housed for as long as you retained your life and most of your limbs and faculties.

Problem is, big sprawling multigenerational families do not transport well. Someone without an immediate purpose in the new situation only added to the risk for everyone. As Susan Faludi phrased it, we became "a society of utility." Bit by bit, *family* referred to fewer and fewer people, pared down in an evolutionary fashion to become leaner and more flexible, until today mention of "a family" equates with "a married male and female, with 2.6 children." As much as the reality of this concept has eroded in the past 50 years, it actually grew in strength over much of the same period, and manages to hold sway over our thinking even now.

For all of the malign effects of the Industrial Revolution, some improvements are inarguable. One of the greatest is that the average human lifespan around the globe has increased. Infant mortality is a fraction of that a few centuries ago. Not only is a cut no longer a potential death sentence, but major damage can be repaired, and spare parts might even be introduced. Childbirth kills very few women. All in all, every person born alive has better than a fifty-fifty chance of living to see the high side of 70; for children born right now in western Europe, the number is estimated to be 105 years.

Which, as you may have pondered, puts an entirely different spin on the "marriage for life" concept. In the Somewhat Dimmer Ages, the odds were fifty-fifty that you or your spouse would be dead by age 35. If you married at 15, that meant about 20 years of wedded potential bliss.

Fast-forward to the latter part of the Twentieth Century. Assume a certain degree of genteel decorum, so your marriage would be delayed to age 25. If you and your beloved are only slightly fortunate, you'll both be alive to celebrate your 50th anniversary.

Nothing wrong with that, except that we live in an era where the concept of delayed gratification has crumbled to practically nothing. There is a great irony in this perverse facet of humans. As we gain, we also become greedy. We are happily frugal until we touch wealth, and then we become selfish and grasping. We alternate hard work with living each day to the fullest, until our jobs ease and our lifespans stretch, and then we become lazy and short-sighted. We become bored or frustrated with anything that demands effort or focused attention.

The half-century marriage is hardly doomed to extinction, but its occurrence is unlikely to grow.

Look at yourself. Be honest. You are likely still recognizably the person you were five years ago, or even ten or more. But can you say that you are the same person, with the same interests, skills, friends, job, home, lover? Assuming that you and your closest intimate have known each other for five years, can you truly say that neither of you has changed significantly, or your relationship? Project this forward, and imagine how far apart people can grow in 10 or 20 or more years.

Unless we suddenly shift our culture away from a jump-cut MTV-ized focus upon immediate gratification, the old paradigm for life-long intimately-monogamous relating cannot survive.

The currently dominant concept probably reached its peak in the 1950s. Since then, the encroachment of life-long monogamous marriage has been steadily eroded, in the general culture, by the Church, and by governmental bureaucracy. As far as societal benefits, few landlords would nowadays eject a cohabiting couple out of hand, an accepted practice not so long ago. Being unmarried doesn't make an employee less desirable. Even the differences in federal tax regulations do not significantly penalize unmarried couples. All in all, marriage-based advantages are minimal.

Until after the middle of the 20th century, many areas of the United States maintained official recognition of common-law marriage. (The term might actually be more accurately "statutory" marriage, or perhaps "de facto.") Briefly, if a man and woman fulfilled certain criteria, such as cohabiting for a specified period, possessing intertwined economics, producing children, or even just claiming to be married, they were then considered to be in fact married – occasionally without actually wanting to be. Marriage had thus gone almost as far as possible, from a privilege of the very few at the pinnacle of society, to a right of a few, then a responsibility of most, until it was finally a bureaucratically imposed requirement.

Though rarely acknowledged, signs are all around us that the established model does not work and is in fact being tacitly scaled back. Common-law marriage has largely been nullified, even for the willing, the regulations having been stricken from the books, although its utility has been recognized somewhat by community-property statutes. The "no-fault" divorce phenomenon swept the United States from state to state, followed by revocation of many laws against adultery. Even as one political administration after another calls for strengthening the family, they participate in cutting ever further into the strength and stability of the pared-to-the-bone couple-and-children form that for so many of us still defines "family."

In brief, then. Monogamy has been with us a long time, at least in the sense of modern human civilization, a caveat that should put any thoughtful observer on notice. In the human unconscious, throughout the recorded history of the world, the pairing of one man and one woman has inherent power, representing the major obvious dichotomy, the genders, and thus various Divine Principles. But this does not in any way mean that lifelong sexual exclusivity is automatically right, or natural, or even commonly practiced. We must differentiate between the pair-bond or dyad and what we generally refer to as monogamy: the former is perhaps natural, the latter is imposed for various rationalistic reasons. I find it amusingly strange that the very people who would state that human beings are far beyond their animal forebears are the same who so readily claim that monogamous pairing is "natural" on the grounds that that's what many animals do.

A few related comments on nonmonogamy

I want to take a moment to potshot at a simplistic countervailing notion. While in many cultures sexual nonexclusivity may have been sanctioned, or even normative, this does those of us who come from the dominant Western culture little good.

We have for so many generations lived with the worldview that lifelong sexually exclusive monogamy is the norm that we start from a base of being blinded to other possibilities. It could be said that, genetics aside, this form of monogamy *is indeed* natural, so ingrained is it. Our thinking patterns, our speech, our arts, and so forth, constantly reinforce this belief, and it is only the minority who are able to stand back and recognize the flaws in the assumptions upon which this worldview is based. Of this minority, few can take the step to envision viable alternatives to the prevailing sentiment; and fewer still can begin to apply such alternatives to their own lives, in the face of constant social pressure.

Briefly, nonmonogamy may be no less natural than rigidly defined monogamy – and perhaps even more natural – but most people are blind to it and will go to their graves that way. As Robert Anton Wilson once said, "Common sense is what tells you that the Earth is flat." To propose an alternative, however viable, to an inherent belief of such power is only slightly less ridiculous than attempting to repeal Newton's law of gravity.

Because it is very much a product of our culture, nonmonogamy is prone to the same sorts of problems that infest monogamy. In fact, since nonmonogamy has never actually existed in a "pure" form in our culture, especially if we take that culture to be that of the United States of America, which is less than 250 years old, I would make the case that the dangers are even greater.

As an illustration, let's look at the group marriage phenomenon. While the term "group marriage" may or may not have been previously coined, it did not enter mainstream usage until the late 1960s.

To lead up to this, I would like to digress a step further. Again, "commune" was certainly a word in the English language before the 1960s, and the concept it indicates has recurred throughout the history of the United States, most famously with the founding of Oneida in 1848. The phenomenon of utopian communes, while inarguably pointing out some of the wonderful ways in which human beings are actually able to cooperate, also points up a litany of disasters.

One of the most scathing descriptions of the "modern" communalist movement of the late 1960s is an article by Vivian Estellachild, "Hippie Communes" (first published in *Women: A Journal of Liberation*, 2:2, Winter 1971, and reprinted in *Intimate Lifestyles: Marriage and its Alternatives*, ed. Joann S. and Jack R. Delora (Goodyear Publishing Company, 1972)). While hysteria and sneering were predictable reactions from conservative mainstream society, this screeching largely drowned out thoughtful and unblinking analysis by people such as Estellachild who had actually lived in communes, hoping to be a part of a movement that would bring a better world into being.

Estellachild's experiences in two communes are chilling. Her contention is largely that, attempting to escape from the structures and limiting roles of mainstream society, the members actually ended up distilling them into their frightful essence. They worked from a faulty assumption: by walking away, they would also leave behind the complex set of assumptions with which they had been indoctrinated from birth. Not only was this entirely incorrect, but this belief formed the basis for rationalizing denial that they were indeed acting as stupidly as anyone in "straight" society.

In the first commune Estellachild describes, the adult males involved (I call them "adult" only by way of age, and am reluctant to even think of them as "men") found themselves with an opportunity to create a fantasyland that, at its best, was an adolescent playground, though at its more-common worst took on degrees of bizarre infantilism. The females were expected to be constantly available for sex, and to otherwise be undemanding, to handle all care of children, to prepare all food and do all cleaning around the grounds and living areas. The males, meanwhile, mostly drank and got high, complained about the condition of the living space, and preened their "revolutionary" intellects. Of Estellachild's two experiences, the second was admittedly much less awful, yet the gender roles were still firmly in place, and more obvious than in the world they all had supposedly abandoned.

Lest anyone think that articles such as "Hippie Communes" is nothing more than sour grapes, I've encountered a few people in the past decade who spent large parts of their childhood in such communes, and they have done nothing but confirm how silly or even bizarre the behaviors of the "adults" appear in retrospect.

By validating each other's utopian intentions, such communalists as Estellachild described unwittingly conspired to avoid taking on the very responsibility that had previously been denied them. No individual wanted to lead, none wanted to have anyone else lead, yet they continued to act as though someone was leading. If your car is rolling down the freeway, and the steering system is so perfectly balanced that it actually follows the curves and remains in the lane as you desire, that is nevertheless a poor indicator that you can sit back and nap. And just because a train is set on fixed tracks will not protect it from the hazards of cow herds, stalled trucks at grade crossings, washed-out bridges, rock falls, etc. Progress can be monitored by all, many, few, or one, but the responsibility must be taken by someone.

In a similar fashion, group marriage as a concept contains the seed of its own decline in its very appellation: marriage. The bald truth is that much "polyamory" is just plain marriage with more people, taking along the very flaws of monogamy and turning up the heat under that pressure-cooker without making any attempt to examine (much less repair!) the problems.

Some 17 years ago, I made the wisecrack: "Polyfidelity is marriage, just with more people... and the same sorry collection of empty mythology, illogical root assumptions, and hyperromantic confabulations." I stand by that. Most triads are created from pasting one more person into a preexisting dyad, just as most quads are formed by pasting two preexisting couples together. Many people who lack the skills to be either monogamous or promiscuous decide to become nonmonogamous, apparently working from the assumption that it's easier to maintain multiple superficial "relationships" than even one stifling, confining, demanding, deep relationship, and the cheap patina of "permanence" attached by claiming to polyamory (or group marriage or whatever) affords a string of glorified one-night stands the next best thing to the sanctified blessing of the Church.

In short, if thoughtless, irresponsible monogamy is a collapsing institution, then thoughtless, irresponsible nonmonogamy is not far behind it on a steep downhill slope. Good riddance to it all, I say.

Where from here? Can we make it better?

Forward, and yes. Though we're likely stuck with the law of gravity, people do have some power to make local changes in relational and familial structures.

Let's look at the two basic models we are left with. I've swiped them, actually, from yin and yang, but in the Western world you'd recognize them more readily as masculine and feminine. A better way to define them would be authoritarian, and cooperative.

We are presently living in the last gasps of the authoritarian predominance in our culture. This can easily be dated back as far as the rise of Confucian influence upon Oriental countries, but the story there has been repeated all over the world. Confucianism as a philosophy of social order and governance really has surprisingly little to do with the writings of Confucius, so if you have read the works ascribed to him, forget it for the moment. In Japan, state Confucianism meant that you were expected to automatically accept someone as an authority figure because they were of higher status than you, had a better job, represented the government, came from a family from a more prestigious region, or were older. Such things are associated with wisdom, and the societal belief was based largely upon the fallacy that, if someone possessed a hallmark of wisdom, then they were wise, and their every word was an expression of their wisdom, however much it might resemble corruption, power madness, or senility.

I'm confident about the "last gasps" diagnosis for authoritarianism, but don't hold your breath: it could easily hold on for another 50 years.

People who want to substitute a matriarchal hegemony for the patriarchal version are wrong-headed. Throughout history, especially in Europe, the few examples we have of female-run societies really didn't do any better overall than did those dominated by males. While there are many moments in the relatively recent past where an obvious thought would be along the lines of "Anything has got to be better than this!" the fact of the matter is that a swing to matriarchy would lead to very little along positive lines, a pittance that would be quickly submerged by the predictable chaos from such a massively symbolic paradigmatic shift.

Though our culture puts great effort into it, we cannot usher in some sort of "new age" by merely changing the terminology, any more than we could improve a worn-out, malfunctioning machine by dusting it off and putting new labels on it. If we've been raised under a dubious set of beliefs rife with assumptions that wouldn't stand up to the cruel logic of a three-year-old – which is pretty much the case – then any movement in the direction of real and constructive change would be immediately undermined by our continuing attempts to restore some Golden

Age or "good old days" that never existed by applying methodologies that never worked in the first place.

This is why changing our culture over from an authoritarian to a cooperative model will be so hard, akin to the traumas rippling through our world as it shifts over from the Industrial Age to the Information Age – and just wait until folks begin to realize that even the much-vaunted Age of Information is already in the process of rolling up to the next era, something like a Paradigm Age that feeds on information as raw material.

I have every confidence that human beings, left to themselves, are cooperative by nature. It is literally part of our genetic makeup, representing many thousands of years of banding together for survival and sharing what surpluses occasionally arose. This is overlaid with a few centuries of egoistic striving, of belief in a culture of perpetual deficit, where all that is required is to get *more* or *better* and then all will be well and we will become saints. As a culture, this can be overcome, with time; as individuals, we're pretty much screwed up and have a single option to fight this for the rest of our isolated lives.

When my daughter went to daycare, all of a year old, one of the founders told us wide-eyed about what our kid had been up to. During periods of unstructured play, she would toddle over to the huge collection of toys and rummage about until she found one that appealed her, play with it momentarily and, apparently finding it suitable, bring it over to another child who seemed to be unoccupied, giving it to them. Then she'd head back to the collection and repeat the act. I like to think that we gave her the understanding that creative giving is rewarding, and much more entertaining than hoarding. We were told that children normally want what another has (and, getting it, quickly covet something else), or will spend their time defending piles of playthings from unwanted use.

What saddens me is that the daycare people, after years of dealing with small children from many circumstances and walks of life, had never seen this behavior before.

By definition, cooperation cannot be imposed or enforced. If people aren't doing it willingly, then they have already proven themselves constitutionally incapable of cooperating. This is, in fact, the classic limitation of socialism.

Stale roles

Chances are, should you decide that you are going follow a polyamorous path, that you will not possess most of the talents that will keep you out of trouble, and it's even less likely that you have the emotional and intellectual tools that will allow you to repair a situation, or at least back out gradually.

We are not born with these abilities. They are supposed to be learned from our deep and ongoing relationships with members of our family and with the community at large. Problem is, as time has rolled along, Western culture has been more and more about flexibility and interchangeability, contact with a sprawling multigenerational family has been reduced to an occasional holiday, and our relationships are defined by superficiality. We never have a chance to learn those old-fashioned "deep processing" abilities – in fact, any sort of clear observation and probing honesty is actively discouraged in a thousand tiny ways.

Essentially, we grow up poisoned to a greater or lesser degree. Given a healthy environment, we can avoid inflicting these toxins upon others as we undergo the painful process of clearing out our souls. I cannot hope, with a mere book, to replace either a talented psychotherapist or a loving community, but we can make a small start here, continue throughout, and hopefully steer you toward a healthier path.

In order to be polyamorous, the collapsing roles have to be depleted of their power over you. Males have to give up many notions: that they are always in command, that they must be the sole or primary wage-earner, that everyone ought to defer to them, that their needs and feelings come first. Women, meanwhile, have to stop seeing themselves as primarily or solely responsible for housekeeping chores, and as bottomless wells of emotional support.

Polyamory requires your fullest possible communication and cooperation. These require honesty, and by that I mean an ability to be honest with yourself, and to communicate honestly without being defensive or attacking. It means that each individual person will have to take on generalized roles as the situation requires, and constantly learn new talents and techniques, possibly to use any given skill only once or for a brief period. It means that each person will need to be conscious of the lessons from the past, the possibilities of the present, and the goals of the future, living fully in each moment yet also constantly steering toward even brighter possibilities. It will mean seeking for a seemingly paradoxical balance between a sense of satiation and completion and happiness with what exists now, and yet learning to hope for more and better in a healthy and sane way without seeing those as promising ultimate completion. It means setting aside striving for goals and learning to savor the process of growing and learning, or of expressing oneself.

These traits and skills are still largely foreign to our culture. We are not raised to consider their necessity, much less their possibility. Because of this, the great majority of people now alive will never be fundamentally able to be openly and responsibly nonmonogamous, let alone polyamorous. Unless very large changes in thinking, outlook, and problem-solving are introduced, I do not think this will improve much in the coming decades, or likely even in the 21st century. In fact, as I write this book, the level of chaos and uncertainty that is being inculcated in so many people around the world, and possibly most drastically in the United States, can only reduce the likelihood that polyamory and its relatives will spread either in breadth or depth in so-called Western society. People will tend to retreat to any illusion of safety and stability, which are (and perhaps will always remain, even in the most fortuitous of circumstances) anathema to polyamory.

Nevertheless, ensocialized nonmonogamy has been around for a long time. Millions of people practice some degree of responsible nonmonogamy, for some amount of time, even if they do not have so much as a name for it. The conjoined rise of the Internet and the personal computer has brought together like-minded people across the United States and around the world, allowing them to compare their thoughts and experiences, learning vicariously from each other's mistakes. In short, nonmonogamy is growing toward the point where it will form a definable community. Until that day, should it ever arise, a few resources (such as this very book) occasionally pop up to help ensure an open dialogue.

03. So, you want to be polyamorous!

No, you don't.

Really, I have to be very blunt about this. If you are indeed actively polyamorous, then what you *want* is a moot point unless you're planning to change; you might as well decide that you're becoming bored with your race or ethnicity and would like a change of pace. As for the rest of you, think some deep thoughts about what you're saying you intend to do to yourself and your loved ones. It's entirely enough of a pain in the ass to simply get through daily life as an individual without adding in the burdens of even one little *monogamous* relationship.

Assuming you likely aren't going to take the foregoing warning to heart, then at least stop and ponder for a minute. Okay, alright, you're not *that* dumb; fine. Go ahead and feel superior for a moment, give yourself a pat on the back and all that. But then, when you're done with the self-congratulation, come back and join me.

For, never forget, human beings are fantasy-driven creatures. It's been said that *Homo sapiens* is the only animal that dreams. I am not speaking here of mere memories or imaginary experiences of such simple pleasures as chasing rabbits or basking in the sun. Leaving aside the random memory interconnections that occur during sleep, which may affect any creature with a few brain cells to rub together that aren't dedicated to motor control, autonomic functions, and other mechanical pursuits like reproducing and getting food and otherwise avoiding death, humans have the capability to imagine the future, and we get ourselves into as much trouble with this facility as we do by ignoring it.

By deciding to become polyamorous, you're taking a step as questionable as deciding to have a religious conversion, or deciding to change your sexual desires. In reality, these are things that simply happen, when circumstances force a change on you and you suddenly feel as if you've been doing things all wrong up to that point. You really can't intellectually decide to make this sort of a catastrophic change any more than you could decide to begin (or end) an allergy.

For the sake of argument, let's say that you have decided that you've chosen to become polyamorous. Look at yourself as an individual. If you are very, very lucky, you have managed to find one person – one single, solitary individual, in all the course of your wanderings around in your life-so-far – with whom you feel that rare mixture of deep friendship and abiding lust. You have perhaps occasionally stopped to reflect upon what a lucky person you are, to have found that one person in the entire world.

Now you've got to go find another one.

And the two of them have to be able to get along.

In fact, each of them has to, minimally, be able to put up with the fact that your heart is not their sole possession.

And, right there, we run into a problem. Or, rather, a myth.

Look at your myths

We are raised to believe (on the surface, at least) that us humans only have so much love to give, and that it comes in a standard round unit: one. After all, we associate love with the heart, and, well, you've either got a whole heart, or you're dead, period. You can't, common wisdom goes, just run around dividing that one heart up freely; to claim to do so means that you're either a fool, or you're dividing up something that is dead.

The same people that believe that sort of thing, though, have no trouble dividing their hearts in actuality, and in fact hold this ability in high regard. All you have to do is say, "So, you're married, eh? Must have stopped loving your mother, then." Or, if you're feeling especially stung after receiving the "only one love" lecture, and the utterer is a parent, try this: "Cute kids. Which one is the one you love? Too bad you had to stop caring deeply about that person you married."

You're going to have to think long and hard about this, and you're going to have to continue thinking about it for many, many years, possibly for the rest of your life. You are fully programmed. However much of a nonconformist or iconoclast you see yourself to be, you have been flooded with all sorts of little messages all your life that are telling you to seek out your One True Love and then everything will be perfect, forever and ever, till death do you et cetera. I can't begin to count the number of "poly" people I've seen over the years who make the big change, spend years dating around, then settle down to a closed monogamous relationship in apparent satisfaction. You might be one of those people, and, if so, more power to you, and I sincerely hope for your prolonged happiness.

There's nothing wrong with monogamy that paying attention and exercising your brain and risking your heart a little couldn't fix. Our enculturated training is to do exactly the opposite. So get it out of your head, right now, that becoming polyamorous is any more the Magic Pill than is Finding The Right One.

One of the myths we're stuck with is that there is some "single right way" to do things. This is nonsense for society in general, and it's almost as silly for any given individual. Perhaps your life is a little less colorful than mine has been, so let me enumerate for a moment. I have known many people who, after years of being one flavor, have suddenly become another; they appeared happy before the change, and they appear happy afterward, so who's to argue? I know five guys who decided to become women, and a woman who's going the other direction. I know scores of people who've changed their sexuality from straight to gay, and vice versa. Some poly folks gravitate toward wedded bliss, and some happy couples decide that their love is strong enough to not only survive but flourish with additional intimate commitments. A few couples even divorce but continue to live together because they figured out that they make excellent friends and roommates. To borrow from John Lennon, life is what happens while you're making other plans.

Another one of the ingrained implicit societal myths is that you either commit wholly, in thought and deed for the rest of your life, to a lifestyle, or you're just fooling around. Ridiculous. Oh, the intent is extremely important, if only to keep yourself sincere and avoid becoming a shallow dabbler, but people change, and if they're aware of what's going on around them, they might stumble across one person who is so unique that long-held beliefs or preferences disappear as if they've never been. For instance, I know two gay people, male and female, who were close friends for years. One fine day, to their surprise, they figured out that they were completely and totally in love with each other. Last I checked, they were happily married and raising their children. While this probably relieved their respective parents, I have never felt that they are any less "gay" in politics or outlook, and they don't feel that they've somehow changed their minds or even "become bisexual" just because they have found a sole individual who is the exception to the rule.

This sort of apotheosis can be a little disturbing for a straight male who suddenly finds himself lusting after another guy (even more confusing if the object of this lust is also straight). By the model handed to us by our societal upbringing, he's going to kick himself around wondering whether he's "really gay" and has been repressing these drives all these years, and likely end up in some sort of therapy in order to root out either the tingly feelings or the fears thereof.

sidebar: Why you probably need sex education

Leaving aside porn films and adolescent experimentation, most males will go to their graves never having seen another guy's erection, much less ejaculation. Call it something like "the lure of the forbidden" if you must, but all that does is raise a question: why on God's green Earth should something so universal be forbidden? One sex education specialist has said that a lot of pubescent anxiety could be assuaged if boys were free to find out that their genitals weren't somehow "weird"–she said that more than half of the questions to a sexual counseling line for teenagers were concerns from young males that their penis was too small, crooked, or otherwise worrisome.

Girls develop similar fears about breast size or body shape, but locker room experience usually minimizes the doubts. Female fears tend to be about more subtle things, like menstrual irregularities, lust, and orgasm (rate, frequency, achievement). I've met a surprising number of women in their 30s who were still clinging to doubts about their own sexual responses because they didn't feel they were orgasming like women in porn films (or an excessively vociferous roommate) or had been negatively compared by a boyfriend to his experiences with others. (If you're female, I'd give good odds that at least one lover has told you that getting you to orgasm is "difficult." Uh-huh, thought so. Chalk it up to their cluelessness, and don't take it personally.)

This is, again, nonsense. An emotionally healthy person (male or female) does not view all physiologically suitable candidates as potential bedmates. You are unlikely to get intimate with someone merely because they're available and your body parts are mechanically compatible. Hundreds (at least) of tiny little factors, not the least of which are mood and circumstances, conspire to get your attention, and you find yourself realizing that this is an exceptional individual and you wouldn't mind falling a little closer to them, emotionally and/or physically.

So, it's an easy bet that, somewhere, there's a member of the "wrong" gender or preference who could really spin your dials, at least as far as sincere flirtation.

An informal study in Minnesota about 1990 found that roughly 40% of women self-described as "lesbian" or "dyke" had voluntarily had sex with a male in the previous two years, generally with someone self-identified as "gay." They didn't feel that they had changed their minds, or sold out, or slipped from grace, or otherwise made a mistake. It was simply a matter of the right person, under the right circumstances.

Similarly, people who are committed to monogamy occasionally realize that they're falling into something dangerously resembling love with someone other than their intended one-and-only. For most folks to whom this happens, they play out the societal script, and reach for one of the limited number of choices they're granted:

- dump the first one in order to pursue True Love with the second
- break off all contact with the second one and spend the rest of your life kicking yourself for even having those feelings

- end both relationships, the first from guilt and the second from anger at being tempted
- keep up appearances with the first and have an affair with the second

This reminds me of how someone described the electoral process in the Soviet Union: you're free to vote for whoever you want, as long as they're a Communist. (Not that we can throw stones. Mostly, in the United States, you can vote for the candidate of your choice, as long as they're Democrat or Republican, otherwise you're just "wasting your vote" or "protesting.")

When someone gives you a limited menu of choices, they are not granting you freedom to decide. At that point, your only actual choice is whether you want to accept the menu that you've been handed. Your actual first choice is whether to play the game as it's presented to you, or walk away from it altogether. If you find yourself heading toward polyamory, you're stuck with the latter, and you might as well get used to the notion.

In polyamory, you will find yourself suddenly adrift in rather large gray areas that, up to that point, you would've sworn were at most either black or white. There's a lot of all-or-nothing thinking that works poorly in monogamy, and will only fare worse in situations of increased complexity. For instance, take a look at the notion that "love" is something that is either full-on 100% – or doesn't exist at all. Even in monogamy, this isn't so; it's possible to have only one deep relationship, yet not be "completely in love" with them. A relationship is like a multi-chambered container, in that there's only so much of anything that each can hold. One relationship might have a large amount of space for friendship, a small amount for sex, and none whatsoever for intellectual stimulation. Another might have vast room for physical expression of passion, a tiny bit for what most people would call romantic love, and larger-than-average capacity for creativity. In some cases, the "capacity" of the dyad relationship is limited by what one or the other of the partners can handle; elsewhere, the individuals might each be able to handle far more than they are allowed by some quirk of the relationship itself.

Here's another pervasive myth that bears regular examination. We're raised to believe that we're going to find one (hapless) partner who is going to be the sole primary connection for us – and I'm not talking mere sex, here, but the whole ball of wax – for the rest of our mutual life. Well, *nonsense!* I mean, just look around you; do you really believe that any two people could possibly *want* to spend up to a century doing *everything* together? (It might happen, but this is hardly a realistic goal, much less a central necessity.)

And even if that were possible for everyone to achieve, it cannot be healthy. Two dynamic, creative, curious beings cannot grow in the exact same direction, at the exact same pace, at every moment over a span of ten or twenty or fifty years.

A few years into our relationship, I told my first lover, Cindy, how I felt: I cannot see myself going through life with one close friend, one lover, one sexual partner, one person to whom I complain about my day and share the scattered victories thereof. I cannot see being forever the sole general-purpose nursemaid to one person, nor can I see where they would want to do that for me. There is absolutely no sense in thinking that there is a single "best" person to be my business partner, roommate, muse, and so on. And why should I have such expectations? Wouldn't that take away from the incredible reality that is right in front of me? What if I find someone who is perfect in everything… except that she has a phobia about germs, and is afraid to be around anyone who is ill? Should I dump her because she's not perfect? Or perhaps all her marks are tops... except she doesn't really like sex much. As important as lovemaking is to me, why should I boot her out of my life?

With Cindy, I had someone who, I knew, was as rich and complicated a soul as was I. We had more points in common than any other two human beings I knew... yet I was also very aware of how many more such points we had that aligned poorly, or not at all. I was a musician, and an amateur historian of guitars; she liked music, but had stopped playing piano years before, and rarely even sang. She became jealous if I went to a guitar store without her, yet when I did bring her, she would be bored and impatient within minutes, thus undercutting my enjoyment of the outing. I could get going on an excited monologue about tonewoods or pickups that puts most sane human beings into a coma in a matter of minutes. Meanwhile, she was an incredible artist and costumer, and would spend many happy hours obsessively hovering in front of her sewing machine or easel. We learned a lot from each other.

An organism becomes stronger through challenge. Intellect develops from applying a combination of knowledge and reasoning that may previously have not been attempted. Creativity springs from pasting things together in new and interesting ways.

An organism that is not challenged becomes dull, as in both definitions of "boring" and "stupid." Lacking stimulation, an organism withdraws, stops being curious, lives increasingly in a fantasy world, and even that begins to roll backward toward the happily fuzzy drug-like state that is probably how we felt in the womb. Though we've all had times in life when we've encountered some degree of longing for that sort of unmindful comfort, we are indeed fantasy-driven creatures, and the dreams of an intelligent, curious mind are entirely incompatible with such a sub-animal state. Yet, we live in a culture that tries to turn our dreams toward fantasies of *ease* and *comfort*.

A relationship is an organism. In order to grow, or even survive, it needs stimulation, it needs novelty, it needs exercise, it needs challenge. Life is like going upward on the down-moving escalator: if you don't keep climbing, you'll eventually end up back at the bottom. Observe how people exercise and diet to whip themselves into shape when they're courting. When they settle down to regular involvement with one lover, they let themselves go a little, preferring to linger over dinner rather than work out at the gym (which is why "working out" is not a positive sign when you peruse the "personals" section of the classified ads – it tells you that what you encounter will likely be an easily-shed illusion).

(There's a newer version of the phenomenon I find very strange, and it is mutating. Women are telling me that an increasing number of otherwise healthy young men are bragging about having a prescription for Viagra. One paraphrased this as, "Hey, baby, you turn me on as much as any other woman!" My, how flattering. As most of these guys are still struggling to make their car payments, and the pills cost their HMO about $46 a dose, you might want to ask yourself where their sex drive, and resultantly their self-esteem, is going to go should they find themselves temporarily out of work, or even with a downgraded health plan that disallows such fripperies. Therapeutic justifications aside, addiction is addiction.)

A dyke friend told me about a phenomenon she called LBD, or "lesbian bed death." I was shocked, then terribly amused, as this gave me a label for something I'd observed for years in straight couples. She described how a relationship begins at the dating-around phase with lots of hot sex and a pervasive sexual tension that energizes life in general, which declines noticeably when the interaction becomes monogamous, then disappears altogether when the relationship is firmly established. After all, no need to keep the hook baited once you've landed your marlin! In other words, for many people, sex is a way of attracting a mate, nothing but a gambit of courtship. I've noticed this phenomenon played out by males and females, straight and gay alike, and even among a bothersome proportion of polyamorous people.

There's an analogy I cannot get out of my head, so I'll foist it on you. If I take up golf, what do I do about my wife? Do I drag her to all the events, so that she can stroll along with me? Don't think it'd be much better if she plays golf herself. Let's assume she's not doing it out of a sense of enforced togetherness, now. Knowing my personality, I'd be a happy duffer, pleased to keep my score under 20 strokes per hole. (For you non-players: with rare exception, every tee-to-hole trip in the known universe is rated between 3 and 5 strokes per.) What if my wife enjoys the game? or, god forbid, is competitive about it, so that I'm always bashing away merrily at the deep weeds while she's setting up her final easy putt?

Where is the "togetherness" in this?

If you took the problem to a marital therapist, couched in slightly different terms to avoid embarrassment – after all, sexual problems are one thing, but no golfer will readily admit to befuddlement about the game! – the advice is predictable. If my wife is becoming frustrated with our differences, then there are only a few choices. I can practice. I can ask her to slow down a little. We can stop being a pair.

Let's say that we manage to work out our differences, I spend more time practicing, and she doesn't go out of her way to stomp my scores into the ground. She's concentrating on her game, very self-conscious of what she does, so that she doesn't make me feel inferior. Meanwhile, I'm remembering everything my golf coach told me at this week's session, as well as all the tricks and methods that seem to be working for me. With all this effort, our scores are actually well-matched, and slowly dropping as we work together.

But, are we really working together? We're each so busy concentrating in our little separate worlds that we've all but stopped talking on the course; the easy camaraderie we had when we first began playing together is almost gone, and our communication is down to nods and grunts, with occasional five-word sentences scattered throughout.

If that's your idea of a good relationship, then stop reading right now, and put the book back on the shelf, because you are not only unsuited at the moment to actually be polyamorous, but you are so far down the ladder that you won't even be able to enjoy the stories (much less benefit from them).

So, my wife and I have fallen into that non-relationship rut. It occurs to us one day that maybe we ought to expand a bit. I have a friend who is a part-time golf coach, but when not on the job or in a tournament greatly prefers the casual sociability approach to golf. Meanwhile, my wife has a friend she met at the clubhouse while waiting for me to finish a session with my golf coach, who, while not a serious player, has had some sporadic successes playing in local competitions. My wife and I both see where we each have a new companion who can add something to our respective enjoyment of the game. But, without working at it, a funny thing happens. Her friend, though capable of nailing an occasional hole-in-one, isn't obsessed, and enjoys conversation while strolling the fairway, and I begin to notice how my wife has loosened up, and seems to be enjoying our outings almost as much as in our early days. Meanwhile, my own buddy is laid-back, but has been giving me some good pointers along the way, and my game is improving, slow and steady, without a fraction the effort I had previously been putting into it.

Does that mean that my wife and I are no longer "really playing golf together"? Does that mean that our twosome has broken up, or that we are about to take such drastic measures?

I'll answer that for you: no.

But when we apply this back to marriage, that's exactly what is generally assumed. Imperfection is okay, right up until the point that it can no longer be ignored, then it's suddenly an elephant in the livingroom. We respond as if this behemoth has suddenly appeared out of thin air when, if we were forced to be entirely honest, we'd at least admit that it's been there for quite some time, growing imperceptibly but steadily until it blocks our view and movement and intrudes upon our consciousness at every moment. The individuals in the couple blame each other for bringing it in, even though they've both been feeding it and encouraging its health and growth, and that neither has had the fortitude to protest its existence or even its residence.

Generally, the institution of monogamy then leaves you a choice: accept the elephant, or end the relationship that spawned it. Most monogamous people, perhaps after some half-hearted or inept feints at the former, end their dyad and part ways. They take along with them the very preconceptions, assumptions, and dubious skills that not only brought the elephant into being, but that generally *require* these problems to exist. We are then free to use this to criticize subsequent relationships, which didn't even spawn the damned thing in the first place. This stuff we cling to, poisoning one relationship after another until we're lucky enough to find a rare immune (or insensitive) individual, is usually called *baggage*. I think we call it "baggage" precisely because it's something we carry around with us from place to place as we search for a true home, and would never consider leaving behind or throwing away because it's become so common a feature of our travels. Maybe we can't entirely get rid of our baggage, but we can certainly learn to become seasoned travelers, and discard what is more trouble to carry than it's worth. If you're going to be nonmonogamous, you have to learn how to travel light, so that you can enjoy the scenery.

The first myth to go

Much of our emotional baggage is rooted in myths, "stories" that are of themselves rickety and poorly constructed, but we've had them with us for our whole lives, and trotting them out is reassuring, even if their display causes upset when they clash with the mythic tales of the people around us. It's time to start putting them back on the shelf, where they belong, rather than perpetually toting the ever-growing stack of tomes with you.

There is a single most pernicious myth that you will have to root out, get rid of, stamp down, and be entirely done with – and I mean you ought to do it no matter what lifestyle choices you make, but determined crushing is *necessary* if you're going to go anywhere near polyamory. Final elimination of this myth is ultimately impossible, because it comes at you in a hundred different ways, and you will find yourself drawn back to it constantly, by your environment and your nature. All you can do is watch for it, and deal with it efficiently when it appears.

This is a never-ending task, and must be met with unflinching honesty and vigilance. If you have ever tried to eradicate quack grass or creeping charlie from your lawn, you may have discovered that even stripping the whole thing down to bare soil and installing carefully grown sod raised elsewhere, or applying enough poisons to render the area as attractive as any other toxic waste site, is possibly only a temporary measure. The weed will tend to return, on the wind or sneaking in under the fence, and resume killing its way through your turf and garden. It becomes a mortal's experience of Sisyphus damned to forever roll his boulder up the mountain, only to have it slip away, perhaps rolling over and crushing him, then the poor bastard to go down the mountain when his bones have knit, and begin the trip yet again. So, too, with our myth – except that it is deep inside of you, part of your very being, built into you from babyhood.

While it's too late for you to be entirely free of it, you can definitely make the life of yourself and of the people around you much easier by paying attention, and perhaps, in future generations, the myth will fade until gone.

As Lenore Weitzman says, marriage is structured to unite two people, a man and a woman, into one being, the couple – and that being will be represented by the husband. Though marriage has undergone drastic changes since the 1970s, this attitude still survives. Take changes of name. A married woman will refer to herself as Mrs. Harvey Smith; no man would happily or automatically call himself Mr. Sheila Smith. If the couple is a little more liberal, he will be Harvey Smith married to Sheila Jones-Smith; of course, if he adopts the hyphenated version, his surname will likely be first for both of them.

That is not the myth that I'm getting at. The myth underlies these attitudes, supports them and is supported by them. It's simple to state:

The man is in charge, the woman is his helpmeet.

Like "monogamy," we all can quickly determine to our satisfaction that this is a load of crap, yet we ignore how much we act as if it is (or ever has been) true in the least.

Males are not in charge by mere dint of being male. The fact that so much of the world is run by males gives absolutely no cachet to the rest of the gender. In the same way, most of the power structure in the United States, and the vast bulk of wealth, is owned or controlled by caucasians, but only a moron would claim that this trickles particularly far down to other white folks.

Do you think you're really free of the crypto-Confucian myths that are so obviously goofy? Consider one common artifact. Let's say that, whatever your current relational circumstances, you are looking to add another female partner to your life. In that case, I can predict, with a very high degree of accuracy, you'll expect not only youth, but someone who is able to live up to your image of perfection.

And why would you be interested in younger women? That's easy, though not obvious: because you know on some deep-down level that you would be in charge. You would have automatic authority over her, based upon a daunting combination of age, experience, and established couplehood, along with such attendant details as home ownership, children, careers, and community standing. You'd likely help this along by expecting that she move in with you, that she not have shared rights over things like *your* house or bank accounts, yet that she take over "her share" of caring for your children, cleaning up the quarters, and so on. A mere few years of difference in age can make a vast difference when coupled with factors such as these.

Plus, as more than one social anthropologist has pointed out, the level of naïveté is notably higher for younger people. (While the cynical side of me enjoys this explanation, I'd like to offer a variant. I tend to be involved with women a decade younger than me, or a little older than me; the former are less likely to have been burned by relationships often enough and badly enough to have fallen into a "safe" rut, while the latter have enough scars that their sense of humor at the absurdity of the whole thing is beginning to return.)

This combines with the more obvious motivations (midlife crisis, fear of senescence, fascination with form over substance, playing out of incest fantasies, etc.) to bias most "married couple looking for bi woman" people into ending up with a manipulative, controlling, flighty – but really cute! – girl a decade or two younger than either of them. Be objective for a moment, and answer this: will this triad likely be a success, or a failure? Unless the couple manages both to hold to their expectations and to ruthlessly treat the youngster as an equal in both rights and responsibilities, it'll end up following the latter.

I'll get into some of the interesting ramifications of this a bit later on. For now, lets just leave it at this point: in almost all cases, relationships in Western culture place a man with a woman some years his junior, and many of the exceptions to this find a woman acting in various mothering ways toward a younger man. Another way to state this myth is that **women have responsibilities, men have rights**. Consider birth control in this light, or child care, or housecleaning. That's some of the baggage we carry, and leaving it out of polyamory as much as possible takes effort. That leads us to the next point of interest, which I address primarily to males, especially non-gay.

Give up control

Back when I was working on my degree, I read an article that's stayed with me over the years.

In Hawaii, one of the traditional competitions is of cliff divers. The art is self-explanatory: they dive off of cliffs, sheer drops to ocean inlets. At first blush, this looks pretty much like Olympic-style high diving, though with much better scenery. But think about it for a moment.

As the piece pointed out, a cliff diver stands at the edge, sometimes for very long minutes, apparently lost in thought. He is thinking about the many factors that will never concern someone in an Olympic event: in very few concrete pools will you ever have to concern yourself with complex intersecting series of waves, for instance, much less potential effects of crosswinds. If you don't time things right, you could make a perfect dive, only to be slammed laterally into jagged rocks. The water might suddenly be high, in which case you won't cut the surface neatly but will meet it before you're ready to part the water cleanly, which could result in various extremities being sprained or broken.

When you dive, you control only one thing: your timing. Everything else comes from inside. You are controlling nothing in the world around you. However, you have the choice, the ability to interact with all the variables, including all your preparation leading up to the moment your feet leave the rock. You are adding your own variables to the many variables, and you are then influencing the outcome.

Our little human-made sphere doesn't do much of a job of differentiating *control* from *influence*. In fact, you likely think that the two concepts are interchangeable. Start working out the stark differences for yourself, and you will be much happier, especially if I haven't thus far dissuaded you from nonmonogamy.

These differences are especially true when dealing with other human beings in close quarters. I have many friends in various types of therapy, and they delight in reminding me that "nobody can *make* you anything." It's beyond the power of mere mortals to *make* me angry, or to *make* me happy. At the very least, it's me who is choosing to stay in such situations, and therefore it's me who is choosing to subject myself to those outcomes. The reality is that others can indeed use a privileged position in order to influence me, sometimes in ways that are so subtle or so programmed into me by prior experience that I do not even consciously note the acts of influence.

You cannot control situations, or other people, or really even yourself – I studied enough yoga that I can do interesting things with my heartbeat, and chances are that you're nowhere near so focused, and if you can't regulate something so simple as your own respiration, what makes you think you can control emotions or other messy details?

However, once you learn to pay attention, and to phrase your desires, you *can* learn how to influence the situation. To put it another way, you need to give up on all-or-nothing thinking, and change over to shaping the currents of the situation. Since that's an underlying theme of this book, I'll leave the explicit discussion for the moment.

Dump mythic romance

Monogamy is heavily predicated upon *assumption*, upon *expectation*, upon *as-if-true*. Mostly, we think of this as *romance*.

Basically, "romance" as a concept was meant to be a way of pining after someone you would never have – courtly love, as it were. If you were actually free to be sexual with them, even for a moment, that was the end of romance. The two cannot coexist because romance *per se* is entirely of the "higher" sentiments, and to bring it down to the carnal destroys it.

What I do not like about monogamy as a myth is not even the inherent restriction, but the sheer active lying that lards it as a cultural artifact. You *have* to lie to yourself, to your (so-called) loved ones, to your family, friends, co-workers, strangers in the street... and they are *required* to lie back to you (though, of course, you can rip each other down to others). Because by doing anything to actually *help* them figure stuff out and maybe even make it work, you'd have to acknowledge, own, and examine the problem and likely many of its underlying and root assumptions. So, we only *console* each other rather than get close enough to the truth to actually make a positive difference.

If people were to marry someone as a life-partner, and to have their primary sexual outlet elsewhere... well, that was covered about 90 years ago, in *The Companionate Marriage*, by Ben Lindsay. (A classic.) I wouldn't have any problem with people running their lives in this manner – but they deny it. Even if that's what they're doing, they'll tell you it's an aberration, an exception, a momentary necessity. But nothing wrong with monogamy, nope. We're not *allowed* to examine the underlying assumptions, and that's an inherent part of the monogamy myth.

Romance is a wonderful thing. It adds much to life, and is a powerful interaction for bringing two people together. Romance, though, is a poor substitute for rationality; if rationality is damaged, ignored, or underutilized, romance becomes little more than a drug, a painkiller that keeps you from seeking help to repair the underlying problems. That is precisely one of the major problems with the practice of monogamy, which would be much better for everyone involved if the necessity of such attributes as strength of purpose, honesty, and empathy were each emphasized at least half as much as is romance.

More myths to leave behind

1. **Relationship failure.** There is a wide-held belief that "failure" is exactly equal to "they broke up." This is pernicious nonsense at its worst, and should not only be avoided in polyamory but should be discarded by monogamous people as well. It is a leap of malign faith, and obscures constructive thought about interpersonal relationships. As one marriage counselor put it to me many years ago, "Most relationships that break up failed years before the actual separation, and some of the worst failed marriages I've seen are still grimly clinging together and poisoning the lives of everyone involved." I've observed divorces that were constructive, and allowed a troubled couple to salvage their friendship.

Starting right now, you need to make a concerted effort at rooting out such assumptions, and to examining situations for what they really are, not for which societally-provided box they happen to fit into most conveniently. Think about some relationships you know of that have become less intimate, and instead of thinking something like, "After ten good years, their marriage failed," try, "Despite the sheer unlikelihood of happiness in this crazy world, they had ten years of success." Makes an interesting difference in your outlook, doesn't it?

Often, a relationship simply fades away when the NRE can no longer mask inherent difficulties between the two people in the dyad, or in the lives of one or both of them. There is usually very little basis for blame, as it's simply a matter of the relationship not quite "catching fire." However, we come from a society where, in order for there to be a winner, there has to be a designated loser. (Try to explain to me why there *has* to be a winner!)

I have a friend who spent years working herself out of a seriously troubled marriage. When the divorce was granted, she rapidly tired of her friends calling up to offer their condolences, and told me, "I'd put in all that effort, I was elated at finally being free, and they sounded like I was dying! I decided to have a party, to celebrate my freedom and the new beginning for my life. Some of my friends got quite angry, telling me that I was being morbid… yet they were the very same people who wanted me to cry on their shoulder!"

If you're unlucky enough to be in the majority, then you likely are not even on speaking terms with most of your previous sexual partners. I find this quite dismaying and more than a little baffling, since I not only keep in touch with most of my ex-lovers – on my present telephone list of 47 most-called numbers, 16 represent former sexual partners – but half of my closest friends have been my sexual intimates at one time or another. Most of my "failed" intimate relationships are still friendships.

2. **Couple-front thinking.** Though you will never get rid of this entirely, you will need to restrict it, and to do that you will need to be conscious of it. I have met many married couples who wanted to add a female and thus become an egalitarian triad, only to find that they cannot do a very good job of shaking off thinking patterns that continue to keep "her" separate from "us" – meaning the original couple.

The couple front is exactly what the book *Open Marriage* presents as pernicious. This message is widely overlooked, as most people to this day mistakenly believe the book advocates the "radical" concept of nonmonogamy – which I suppose only goes to show how few people have actually read it. Actually, the O'Neills were adamant in later articles that the book was **not** about sexual nonmonogamy. The attitude this text presents is very useful, but they back down from examining secondary relating that goes beyond the "close friends" stage. However, its premises *were* very radical for the time, and are still unusual: a dyad should not limit itself to constant togetherness, to only existing as a couple.

The couple front is a poor substitute for a partnership between equals. It does not work very well in monogamy; extending the "couple" part to include more people doesn't make it any less stupid. When you present as a couple, people draw you out about your partner, soliciting good and bad alike. But when you have multiple partners, your friend is much less likely to know how to broach the subject.

It isn't only your close friends who will be stymied by this. After all, monogamistic experience limits their thinking processes. If you, though, are in a situation that inherently calls into question the gaps in this sort of thinking – and I think we can agree that nonmonogamy does exactly that – you will of necessity need a more advanced skill-set.

There is much room for irony here. I regularly observe polyamorous dyads that are trapped in the "couple front" or "closed marriage" stage. They appear obsessed with going everywhere together, of having the same friends, of joining social clubs together, of presenting to the world as a monogamous couple, with an apparent fear of individual hobbies and interests, only wanting to have sexual partners that they can both be involved with, etc. Having worked themselves into such a comfortable little corner, they are ill equipped to add another person who does not have the same "mileage" as part of the in-group.

3. **Courtship ends.** What with locating a suitable partner, examining each other against preconceptions and poorly understood motivations, then establishing a complex relationship that is supposed to last a lifetime, courtship is sadly reserved for only the opening phases. In reality, in a healthy relationship between two adults, it should not end – and, truly, cannot end without eventual consequences that are at least fatal to the love, if not the living situation.

In a nonmonogamous situation, a permanent collapse of interest in pursuing courtship is the equivalent of a lit fuse sparking its way toward a stack of gunpowder: it's not so much a question of *what* is going to happen as *when*. The closer and more complex a given relationship, the faster the fuse. Though marriage is now far easier to get out of than we would ever have imagined in 1970, other bonds are even easier to slip.

What we *think* of as courtship does reach a point at which it ends. For most people, the sole purpose of dating is to find someone to marry. Once you've locked down a relationship with such a person, you can cancel the fitness club membership, get the cable television service hooked up again, and go back to being your normally slovenly self. This makes a skewed sort of sense, as there's really only so long you can continue presenting such an immaculately polished version of yourself – such a high level of image maintenance makes demands on resources (time, money, effort) that could be applied instead to the relationship.

In nonmonogamy, that can't happen. Your courtship might take an occasional hiatus, but it never actually stops. Each dyad will have to undergo regular cycles of courtship, because an intelligent, sane, emotionally healthy individual is (by definition) a work in progress, and so is the dyad, which means that you are dealing with three live beings before you even venture outside of couplehood. When you feed more fuel to an engine, it tends to turn faster, and (done correctly) that is exactly the effect that responsible nonmonogamy has on the people involved. Radical growth may not be a daily occurrence, but all the bits of forward movement can easily be overlooked until one day you note that things have definitely moved along since the last time you paid attention.

To put it succinctly: the partner you loved with all your heart a year ago is not the same person she has become. Think of how a flower goes from a bud to a full bloom; it can take days and more, but it's happening every second, gradually. If you've neglected to notice this evolution in your partner, you can be forgiven… but now you are faced with what **is**, not what **was**, and you can likely never go back to those "simpler times."

4. **Security is the goal.** I don't mean to sound pessimistic when I say that no relationship can guarantee security. It's true enough, but this applies to practically everything in life. Even the best business contracts sometimes fall apart due to unforeseen circumstances, and the finest legal firms in history of the world cannot prevent that.

To expect that a contract so simple as the marriage vows (or unmarried parallels) will survive all confusing shifts, honest mistakes, and active sabotage, and last (possibly for a century) until one partner dies, and do so in a manner that is clearly loving… well, it's an ideal, and as unlikely as sainthood, especially when either is sought after.

If you try to change or ignore this, you are cutting into the relationship's ability to withstand those very quirks of Fate. Security comes first from inside of you. Then, if you are very lucky, you will be in a position to find other people who also possess that sort of security, and build some sort of family or community as a team. You **cannot** do it the other way around, taking people who are unsecure or insecure and putting them into a metaphorical box; community is hardly so simple and, though "family" has largely become a pestilent institution and can refer to a sullen mob under one roof, we can do better than that.

If security is your primary goal, stick to monogamy. It doesn't work very well, but at least you'll have social support. Polyamory has few guarantees, and we're perhaps a century away from widespread acceptance.

Myths to avoid ever starting

1. **All I need is a hot bi babe (or two).** While having a few adoring naked young cuties running around the house might be a fine distraction from your problems and the other lumpy little realities of daily life, stacking up relationships

doesn't solve a damned thing. Unfortunately, we are embedded in a culture that presents this ideal at every turn. You cannot find completion through other human beings. One joy of polyamory is that, if you are already complete in and of yourself, then each relationship you have makes you even better – the trick comes in using the resultant synergy not to obscure weaknesses, but to add so much strength that the flaws become inconsequential. While I might agree that more relationships certainly ought to make you *happier*, I would be very worried if you were seeking more relationships in order to make you *happy*. Merely creating a harem won't do this, even if you can manage to keep it together for any amount of time, and chances are that expending any effort in making this little fantasy happen will cost more than you can pay. You must start from a good place and seek to make it better, not to expect that a crowd is going to solve your problems for you – all you'd be doing is climbing higher so that your eventual fall can be all the harder.

2. **This is good, so we have to take the next step.** There are people who are practically destined to be incredible partners and horrible roommates, and vice versa. There are people who can be in love, and people who can be in business, and forcing either (much less both) is extremely inadvisable. In most cases, successful roommates should not become sexually involved; to a somewhat lesser extent, lovers should not automatically think that they *need* to live together or get married or pool their income. And if you insist on going ahead with this sort of nonsensical "logical" progression, then spare yourselves a lot of pain and make sure that you have options to back out of it before you hate each other. Be very wary of pushing a fantastic relationship until it explodes.

3. **Polyamory is easier than monogamy.** Monogamous people who are going through a hellish period may want to believe it'd be easier to fill their life with relationships kept at a shallower (and thus emotionally safer) level by sheer lack of time. Polyamorous people may as idly consider returning to strict monogamy, because dealing with one person on a long-term intimate basis lacks virtually all of the emotional and temporal complexities of nonmonogamy. Neither of these trains of thought is particularly valid, and both ways (in order to have anything resembling both depth and permanence in the associated relationships) require determination, capacity for deep love, and above-average problem-solving skills.

04. The usual questions

There are indeed questions that keep popping up, which I will address throughout the rest of this book. From presentations and discussions, I can point up some of the more common, as well as a few of the odder ones, which deserve at least a passing mention. As I've learned over the years, there are no stupid questions, only stupid answers (which I will endeavor to avoid). Well, actually, the aphorism is, "The only dumb question is the one you don't ask." Most of the following queries were sincere, if occasionally a bit confrontational.

Why do you hate monogamy?

On the face of it, that's as silly as would be my asking you why you hate anything that you're not – isn't it true that Norwegians hate Italians? Life is far too short for me to properly hate everything that doesn't include me, or even a representative sampling thereof. I think that monogamy, as the almost exclusive paradigm of modern Western culture, therefore includes its share of dissenters and malcontents. I see myself as helping to separate the sheep from the goats, and providing a place for the troublemakers to go that is distinct and separate from those who are satisfied with the status quo. Perhaps I'm taking advantage of ferment, but I'm not causing it.

Can't you go to prison for that?

In certain localities, laws indeed exist that could potentially lead to that end. But these are the sorts of laws that are left in place mostly to make it easier for law enforcement and government to crack down on people to whom they've already adopted a dislike; generally, if you've attracted that sort of enmity, the exact nature of the charges is irrelevant. I've seen people fined or jailed for growing expensive ornamental grasses, for allowing the wrong sorts of weeds to grow among their other weeds, for not painting their porch, for painting their porch an unpopular color, for cleaning up their neighbor's trash, for not cleaning up their neighbor's trash, and so on. No doubt, I could be arrested, depending on where I was at the moment, for adultery, cohabitation, lewd behavior, contributing to the delinquency of a minor, or gods know what all, perhaps even tried for my sins, and even found guilty, without the smallest shred of evidence. But the choice I must make comes down to either living in fear that I've stepped over some invisible line, or shrugging my shoulders and getting on with enjoying life.

How do you deal with jealousy?

Immediately, ruthlessly, and lovingly. I own my occasional jealous feelings, and I look closely at them, but they don't impress me very much. When my partners or their partners get jealous, I might let a little time go by until it doesn't sting quite so badly, but then we talk about it, and see if we can't find out what actually caused the fear or resentment, which gives us something that can actually be fixed.

Do you all sleep together?

Personally, no, though there is nothing like a rule that prevents people from sleeping together. Even a full-size bed gets a bit crowded with three people, and the unlucky one in the middle might quickly find that it's rather like trying to get a good night's sleep in a convection oven. I prefer two criteria: that I have the edge of the bed, and that I won't get shoved off of it.

Do you all have sex together?

Rarely, yes, polyamorous people might indulge in "moresomes." In general, though, it's difficult to coordinate something like group sex without killing off every chance for spontaneity, which can make the whole thing start to feel like an early rehearsal for some rather pointless theatrical production. For the most part, one-on-one sex is superior, both because it's far simpler to focus yourself entirely upon pleasing one person to the best of your ability, and very flattering to be the sole object of another person's attention to the exclusion of the rest of the world.

Do you all live together?

Though there's a strong communitarian undertone in nonmonogamy, and we occasionally make vague noises about mansions and villages, very few of us actually have more than three interrelated adults living under one roof, and most don't get beyond a dyad for any length of time. Multilateral intimate relationships are plenty complicated without piling on the absolute necessity of coordinating housekeeping styles, finances, and other such factors.

How do you work out your schedules?

By insisting that each person have some idea of what they want to do, then presenting it to the others in a timely and reasonable manner. Personal styles must be worked out; for instance, if one partner wants absolute flexibility over his or her planning, including the ability to change plans at a moment's notice, the others might make clear that, reciprocally, that person won't automatically be included in group plans. If Marvin walks in late on a regular basis, but his housemates enjoy having a household dinner at 7:00 every Sunday evening, old Marv can't expect that there'll be a place set at the table for him. Should Maureen's group decide to go to the cabin for a weekend, and Maureen not return any of their calls for a couple of days, she might walk in late Friday to find that she has more time to call her own.

Where do you meet potential partners?

Everywhere. Okay, I'm a little odd in that, but you don't need to wear your polyness on your sleeve. Sometimes I will be seated alone at a restaurant that I've attended over time with various affectional partners, and be engaged in conversation by someone who's very curious about my intimate life. Occasionally, in order to avoid giving the false impression that I'm monogamous and single, I mention something about polyamory, and I'm surprised at the number of times I thereby make a new friend who has encountered the term, been interested in the concept, yet never met someone who is actually experienced.

How do you arrange finances?

Everyone contributes financially, which for all practical purposes looks like paying rent. In one of my householding experiences, we figured out that our overhead was tiny with four of us contributing. So, we set ourselves to paying a monthly amount that was only a little less than typical rents. The excess cash accrued painlessly, and allowed us to keep the house warm through an unusually cold winter, as well as having the kitchen well-provisioned. We set up a checking account just for the household cash, and convinced the bank to let any of us sign. Generally, it's best if one person takes over the "landlord" role and sees to balancing accounts, paying bills, and setting a tentative budget.

What would your parents think?

They roll their eyes a lot. The smarter ones don't ask, and we reciprocate by not going too far out of our way to throw it at them. The established adults among us show up for family visits with a sleeping bag for each, and either keep the bedroom door closed and braced, or spread out on the floor or sofas – I mean, even if we have heavy sexual involvement, we'd stay home if that's what we wanted to do, so giving it a rest for a few days isn't a major inconvenience. My mother gives me a hard time because she can't figure out who gets Christmas cards, and that's the most that it's ever made a difference.

What effect is this having on your children?

At the very least, our children are no more screwed up than those of the overall Western culture. Most times, screwed-up kids are the products of screwed-up relationships between screwed-up adults. Polyamory is just as vulnerable to this as monogamous marriage, but we don't have so much problem with keeping toxic relationships together "for the sake of the children." Some of us are quite prepared for our kids to react against us and flee to monogamy, but since they'd take with them better skills for communication and problem-solving, and thus they'll be likely to find a positive relationship, I'm not worried about this possibility. In general, kids thrive when they have a variety of positive adult role models to choose from, especially if these adults are approachable and supportive.

Aren't you afraid of AIDS?

If I were celibate and living in the high Himalayas a thousand miles from the nearest human being, I would still be "afraid of AIDS," as should *any* rational person. Compared to the ostensibly monogamous society around us, though, we're probably in less danger of contracting venereal diseases in the first place, and the higher level of communication required to simply get from day to day means that we are more likely to discuss any worrisome symptoms immediately, and get any necessary treatment.

05. About swingers

Wife-swapping, swinging, recreational sex–call it what you will, chances are that, even if swinging doesn't freak you personally out, it'll set off someone that you know. This is especially true if the offended parties are self-proclaimed polyamorous, and that's what gives it a faint taste of irony. Like so many other interesting concepts, swinging is far more complex than a commonly used, widely misunderstood categorization would allow you to believe.

In case you've forgotten, recall that one of the underlying themes of this book is that polyamory is a sub-sub-subset of a small area of interpersonal interaction. However, because polyamory contains certain definable philosophical bases, I can therefore write about it in both a general and a specific sense. By comparison, promiscuity is easy to tut-tut over and excellent fodder for gossip about a single case (instance or practitioner), but could only result in a book that is uninformative, unhelpful, and/or kinda boring, due to necessarily vague inclusiveness.

Swinging is generally a couple-oriented form of entertainment, where two or more dyads get together, and amuse themselves by having sex. Other than that, as far as describing what they do, all bets are off. They might interact as couples, off in separate rooms with the doors closed, or the groups could indulge in big sweaty piles, though this is far rarer than popular belief. I was once invited by a very nice couple to join in their sporadic celebration, where they would gather up to a dozen suitable males to have sex with the woman until everyone was happily exhausted; not my scene, really, but I was terribly flattered and thanked them profusely for the offer. Some groups have large erotic parties, with hot tubs and massage tables and professional dancers of either gender or both, even taking over an out-of-the-way hotel for days-long parties and socializing.

Why people confuse poly and swinging

The main culture in which we find ourselves living is notoriously squeamish about sex, alternately repulsed and titillated by their own drives and happily projecting their odd, ill-formed fantasies onto others. So, when anything appears that can be lumped into the "nonmonogamy" slot, people instantly lump away.

One of the more common events, in a city of any respectable size, is the swing dance. Popular fantasies aside, they are pretty much exactly what you'd expect from any other social club, and would probably bore outsiders. Maybe you want to check this out for yourself. A lot of the swingers I know go to the dances in order to… dance. Like many other social groups, they like to get together with others of like sensibility, so that they can let down their guard and not worry that the wrong comment will slip out and alienate them. This is exactly the same reason that nonmonogamous people who are not "shopping" for a new relationship will nevertheless gladly go out of their way to hang around with others. You might despise the majority of people in your profession, but if you've been to a gathering of your peers, you'll likely agree that the sense of kinship is uniquely reassuring and invigorating.

In much of the culture of the United States, adultery is adultery, period. Both polyamory and swinging have an additional black mark against them: we might be cautious, but we are lousy at being furtive. We meet together in bunches, we meet via the Internet and occasionally a magazine or newspaper. We really suck at being *ashamed* about what we do and feel. Obviously, we're not as moral as the moralists who are fascinated by prostitutes, who cheat on or abandon their spouses… right? Apparently, hard-core lying perverts who slink around the back alleys of the world are pardoned because they feel really, really bad about what they do, even though their remorse doesn't extend deep enough that they voluntarily change their ways. Meanwhile, polyfolk and swingers can be quite proud and defensive of what they do, especially when some inflamed moralist attempts to corner them.

Why they are indeed related

What's the difference between poly people and swing people? Less and less. In fact, I'm seeing a steady increase in "poly" people who are looking primarily or solely to get laid, and more and more swingers who are looking for continuity in their intimate relationships.

If swingers are club-based, then you can check out someone's reputation before you get intimate; meanwhile, poly folks have pretty much no way of keeping tabs on someone (bad or good). There are some swingers who, once they trust you, will introduce you to their companions, and let you gossip freely – only a minority aren't rather choosy about who they get involved with, and they extend the courtesy as well.

The term "polyamorous community" isn't yet active. There are social groups and intimate networks, yes, but even among the minority of these that actually have good interrelationship communication, there is a lack of experience with cross-checking (and thus validating) experience. That is, someone who shows up to social events and claims to be polyamorous is free to act in a rather reprehensible manner without criticism, because there are no widespread rules of conduct that define the practice of polyamory.

This is due to a few factors, primarily: lack of individual skills; a gap in perceived empowerment to criticize; no established general policing mechanisms. Polyamorous people are wary of having others' values inflicted upon themselves, and so tend to stay very far away from making such pronouncements, to the point that they will actively ignore predatory behavior that is affecting their own "community." As social outsiders, they are keenly aware that they may not receive sympathetic support from the legal system, even in our litigious world. Though many think of themselves as activist to some degree, the fact is that they are largely disempowered, with their own collusion.

In order to achieve something resembling nascent community, polyamorous people will need to:

- trust themselves enough to consciously acknowledge doubts about others' behavior
- feel that they have not just the right but the *responsibility* to air these doubts
- know that they will not be censured or excluded from their social circle for presenting (or even harboring) these questions
- support each other when such uncomfortable questions arise
- form a social front in agreeing (tacitly perhaps) on control of antisocial behavior, including the possibility of censure or exclusion from the circle
- monitor interaction of offenders in the wider community, such as contacting representatives of other polyamorous groups and organizations to make them aware of problems that have not yet spread, but readily could.

In short, if polyamorists are going to become a community, they will need to establish rules of conduct, and expect that anyone who desires to belong will act within these rules. For these things, polyfolk still have much they can learn from swingers.

Why they are distinctly separate

Until recently, swinging was entirely an artifact of a monogamous heterosexual culture, an attempt to extend some degree of intimacy beyond the couple front. This is changing, but the swing community is at this time still largely couple-oriented and heterosexual.

These two orientations are inherently anathema to polyamory. If an individual or a couple are functionally monogamous and open to polyamory but not presently able or willing to have other lovers, they will nevertheless consider themselves no less polyamorous, and thus uncomfortable with couple-front thinking.

The same can be said for those individuals who are not at a given moment sexually involved with both genders yet would readily describe themselves as bisexual rather than merely "bi-curious." Those polyfolk who are rather basically heterosexual are less likely than most of the members of our culture to shun or ostracize others who aren't so straight in thought and deed.

The near future

At some point, polyamory and swinging will form a sort of continuum. As they continue to become more comfortable with their respective societal niches, each will gain strength. This differentiation, as the dust settles a little, will be healthier for everyone. The differences between the two camps will be clearer, but there will be a small minority that remains comfortably within both camps, as well as a number who transition from one lifestyle to the other, perhaps repeatedly, as their lives and circumstances change. And as the fear and self-doubt decline with the maturation of polyfidelity as a lifestyle choice, any mislabeling as "swinging" will result in increasingly limited backlash against the swing community, allowing calmer explanation in place of reactive denial. Rather than pitting two deviant cultures against each other, they will be able to join forces and share their respective strengths.

In the meantime, if you wish to declare yourself polyamorous, get used to the fact that the confusion is going to remain as a pejorative. Sure, clear up the misunderstanding as much as you can, but don't put too much effort into setting yourself up as a "good," responsible, community-oriented polyamorist by contrasting yourself to the "bad" swingers – they may not be your siblings, but they're definitely your cousins.

06. Avoid the common mistakes

The pitfalls that await you when you venture forth into nonmonogamy are impossible to list completely. The saying goes that "the problem with idiot-proofing technology is that idiots are so ingenious." Well, polyfolk apparently comprise some of the most ingenious idiots you could ever hope to find, and I include myself and many of my loved ones in that category.

I have quite a range of experience in nonmonogamy, yet I am far from perfect, and regularly impress myself with the really ridiculous corners I manage to walk myself into. As I intend to keep learning throughout my remaining years on this planet, I therefore have to keep searching out the boundaries, and trying to extend them, which invariably means I'm going to make mistakes, some of which will be more spectacular than most.

Think of it as storytelling. If you're supposed to go up in front of the class and tell a funny story about yourself, wouldn't you at least like it to be different, to stand out from the rest? Given a chance, wouldn't you want it to be not only funny, but provoke some honest empathy for your foibles, and leave your audience so taken with it that they retell it to all their friends? You'd probably want to make sure that the audience sees your flaws, so that they can form some emotional attachment for your fallible humanity... but you don't want to come across as a total moron!

There's one complex (but hackneyed) plotline I'd like to steer you away from. If you emulate it, most observers would just roll their eyes and groan–even if it doesn't resemble their own story, they've heard it a hundred times.

Assumptions: short-circuiting yourself

There is a chain of assumptions that is guaranteed, tried-and-true, to destroy your foray into polyamory. An individual might wander in at any of these points, but it's impressive how often someone will go completely through the list, start to finish.

1. I have discovered the word. Since all *you* people did it, polyamory must be easy.
2. I am a radical. Polyamory is radical. Therefore, I should be polyamorous.
3. Polyamory is easier than monogamy, because you don't have to focus so intently on one person.
4. Polyamory sounds interesting; therefore, I am polyamorous.
5. My previous monogamy-clouded relational experiences mean nothing, because I have become polyamorous.
6. Since we are all equals here, I know as much about polyamory as you do, and thus I know what is ultimately the right way to do things.
7. In order to be polyamorous, I need to have superior communication skills. I have decided that I'm polyamorous. Therefore, I have superior communication skills.
8. I have found someone with whom I want to have sex. Therefore, s/he is my life-partner.
9. We've got our triad. We are intelligent, and have good intentions, therefore we won't need to talk to you any more.
10. We're having problems, but we are deeply in love, so the situation will sort itself out.
11. The relationship bombed. We had everything we needed, and it didn't work. Polyamory is a load of crap.

Miss that episode

Does that progression sound silly? Don't laugh – I've seen it waft by more than a hundred times. And I don't mean to derogate those who've fallen prey to this sort of thinking, since I've pulled up short of falling into a couple of those reflexive assumptions myself. If you can't find at least one point on the above list that's sneaked up on you, I'd feel justified in calling you a liar or a fool. Even if you avoid getting swept up in it, you'll know someone who isn't so lucky at dodging the bullet, and it would be nice if you helped them out of their corner.

I'm going to follow sage advice from a very experienced author: "Trust your audience." I was originally going to deconstruct each of those points, in order to show the larger flaws in that sort of thinking. Many of these are addressed as separate topics in this book, and I won't chase them around in circles here. Instead, a few more-general comments.

At its core, polyamory requires a balancing act: calm trust in your own feelings and instincts, but a willingness to look at your actions and understandings critically, with a high degree of objectivity – trust, but not blind faith.

The society in which you were raised and educated, in which you have received most or all of your interpersonal experience to date, has loaded you up with a vastly complex set of rules, and patterns of thinking to support those rules. Many of these things don't work very well at the best of times, but there is enough internal consistency that, overall, they at least function.

You, though, are apparently interested in stepping outside those bounds. The social mechanism doesn't work very well, but you will no longer have the luxury of choosing what portions you will keep close to your heart and what portions you will actively ignore. Polyamory is a stripped-down machine, with no excess parts, and where everything that exists is necessary to overall function. On top of this, you cannot expect that, if the going gets a little bumpy, you can just bolt on a few parts from the old machine. Go back and read that list again, and give a little thought to this analogy.

07. Overview: what polyamory actually requires

If you want to take a closed monogamous relationship and magically transform it by force of will into something polyamorous, you're probably in trouble. Oh, and more bad news? If you just try to open it up, that's a little rocky, but can be done, and you'll likely regret it. If you're trying to turn it into a closed foursome, you might just make it, but the odds aren't with you. And if you're going for a closed triad, oh, are you in for a world of frustration… and that's only if you never get it off the ground! But, more on that later.

Here's an analogy (with due thanks to Robert Ford Carpenter):

Let's say I've finally found an incredible site to build my dream house. I've pulled together the financing, and I'm all set to put in years of labor in order to have the house I want to spend the rest of my life in.

Mind you, I still need a place to live in the meantime. The financing I've arranged is only going to cover construction of the mansion, not my rent. I've got a little in savings from my contracting jobs. I figure I can throw together a nice little cabin for myself, a lot like my hunting cabin in the woods. Not the sort of place I want to have a full-dress dinner or costume ball, but plenty good for a couple of years. I'll be able to spend all my spare time working across the way on that mansion.

Since that little cabin is only meant for my convenience, a place to change my clothes and cook the occasional meal, and it only needs to be barely habitable for just a few years, I can cut all sorts of corners to save my time and effort. A kerosene heater keeps me plenty warm when I'm there, and a small generator runs the icebox. Other than that, it's not much more than a roof against the rain and four windproof walls. All in all, it's good enough.

The problem I see with most folks who decide they're going to "get into polyamory" or "become poly" is that they've got my cabin. Sure, it's got some insulation and electrical outlets and pretty paint, but it's still just a little shack.

And what they're proposing to do to that shack is… oh, I don't know, take your choice: foolish, goofy, stupid, ill-advised, rash. Badly planned, in any case.

I need to paint this out with an example, a very typical monogamous married couple. Let's put a name on this couple, and call them Bob and Emily Schell.

They're going to take that rickety little makeshift cabin, and they're going to expand it.

Now, they don't want to go attracting undue attention from the neighbors or the authorities, so they're going to put on an addition, but it's got to look pretty much the same as the original house.

And, if you press the Schells a little bit, they'll admit that they're afraid of change. They're doing so well in their little shack that they don't want to risk anything radical that might disrupt things. [Notice how they say they "don't want to make any changes," in order to defend making radical changes.]

Their new addition is going to have the same cheap foundation, the same makeshift walls. The roof is going to be an extension of same single plane, sloped to let the rain and snow run off, and if the new addition happens to be under the low end of the original roof and the ceiling will slope down to the four-foot mark, well, that's the price that has to be paid for continuity. It's familiarity that counts first to the Schells. If the neighbors notice at all that the shack seems a little bigger, they'll put it off as a trick of their imagination.

Sure, they've made some odd compromises, but it's *sort of* what they had in mind, and thus good enough.

Good enough for what?

There is no room for "good enough" in polyamory. If it ain't "good", then it can't be much better than "not so good." You need to make things the best you can, every step of the way, and to remember where you have cut corners and will eventually need to do some upgrading, or I can guarantee that it'll come back to surprise you in quite interesting and unpleasant ways.

Back to our housing development. Let's leave the Schells alone and look at what you personally would do. As anyone who's been anywhere near contracting can tell you, the most unforgiving parts of a structure are the basics. Anything else, you can fix and patch, or tear out and redo, and the house stays essentially the same, but improves. You select the best **location**, because that's going to be with you for the duration, period. You put in the best **foundation**, because everything subsequent depends on that. You build a solid **frame**, if only because replacing it without tearing down the entire house will be impossible. Then you put a **roof** on it that is going to be adequate to protect all the work that comes after.

Once you reach that point, it's all pretty much down to replaceable stuff. You'll have a lot of flexibility to rearrange interior walls, change the plumbing, upgrade the electrical, even tear the floors down to the joists for reconstruction. You can get away with putting in cheap interior walls so that you can move in and actually begin living in your house, and then deal with the mess as you while away many happy hours going from room to room putting in proper wallboard and woodwork. Repainting every once in a while until you come up with a color scheme that is perfect for your personality and the room's use can be a headache, but it's really minor in the scheme of things.

But: location, foundation, frame, roof. Skimp on any of those, and you'll pay dearly for it eventually.

These not only have to be *good*, they ought to be the *best* you can manage. There won't be much opportunity for a second chance to do them right, short of starting over again. Once the frame and roof are set on the foundation, it'll all settle into place and take on its final form. If you take the house off the top of the foundation and build a new house, the weights will be distributed differently, which will likely mean stresses that the foundation can no longer adapt to. Even the roof, the last of the absolute necessities, has to be solid, as near to perfect as you can get it. If it only looks good, but allows rain to leak in, you could find yourself with damage all through the frame and even down to the foundation before you know anything is amiss. And should that roof blow off in a storm, you ought to pray that you're able to get it replaced before the exposed rooms are further damaged by the elements; during the repair time, you won't be able to use any of those rooms for anything, likely not even storage, and the whole place may be ruled uninhabitable until the repairs are completed.

"I've decided to be polyamorous."

There are a few things you must consider before leaping into the deep end of the poly pool. Once you start lining up that leap, the rules change slightly – you're more committed, not as much as when your feet leave the cliff, but more than when multiple sexual partners was just an amusing thought. Let's consider a few things from this "almost ready to be ready" vantage.

Most people who "get into polyamory" are pretending. While this behavior is cute when a three-year-old has an imaginary friend, it's not the sort of relationship that most adults can rely on. After you reach some poorly-defined age, other folks start calling this sort of thinking delusional. People like to think that they're forever and always practical and logical, but their brains seem to go on "pause" when intimate relationships are involved.

Romance is a good thing. It's an endorphin that lets us get through the bad times. Romance gives us the strength to struggle, a reward at the end of a troubled period. It's a drug, and a very useful one at that.

But romance is a drug nevertheless. Once, when I tore up a bunch of shoulder muscle, the doctor gave me a painkiller, with a stern warning: "When you take this, the pain will go away. This should allow the muscle to heal by decreasing involuntary spasms and voluntary tensing of that shoulder when it twinges. However, you *will* take time to rest and let it heal. If you go back to work, you'll start swinging a hammer again, and you'll feel like Superman because all the little aches and pains that warn you about damaging yourself will be turned down to zero. If you come back in here with even more damage, I will cancel the prescription, and you'll have to get by on aspirin. I know what a stubborn jackass you can be, and if I could put you on something to keep you flat on your back for a week or two, I would, because that's exactly what you need right now. Go home, and don't lift anything heavier than a paperback novel." I decided to follow her advice.

Like many drugs, romance makes you stupid. Enjoy it, by all means! Fall in love, have fun, wallow in the thrills of connecting with another human being... but never forget that you're not a completely rational being. People in the grips of NRE are not entirely sane, and the smart ones are the happy ones, because they don't lose track of this truism for very long.

If the world was entirely made up of truly monogamous people, the dangers of NRE would be at a minimum. You would go out, find someone who sets off a massive NRE attack in you, get married, and live happily ever after. You would never be tempted outside of couplehood, either by some enticing other or from your own questionable needs to roam.

The world, though, isn't monogamous. Even the monogamous aren't completely monogamous! Stop and think for a few minutes, and consider all the people you've known who had a nice steady relationship, apparently happy and productive even according to their closest friends. Then, one day, news comes out about the affair that one of them has been having, followed closely by word of their impending breakup. Not only is "good enough" not good enough once the objective (forming a presentable couple) has been attained, but we keep looking for something better, for True Love and a permanent state of rapture and jobs that are both easy and rewarding.

This is nonsense, but all it takes (apparently) is one tale of the triumph of True Love to justify a hundred, a thousand poorly considered, ill-advised leaps into blatantly foredoomed relationships. "Everybody wants to see Heaven, but nobody wants to die." Everyone wants True Love, as long as it's bestowed by kind gods or smiling Fate, or maybe wand-wielding Fairy Godmothers. *Working* for it, diligently and with personal risk, is the last thing we want to think about. Next time you see an advertisement on television about some get-rich or investment program, read the fine print: "Results are not typical. Returns depend on many factors, including skill and economic conditions." That's excellent advice for relationships, too.

Monogamous practice, though full of holes and going more than a bit mushy in critical places, has the widespread support of society. Therapists know how to deal with it. Courts know how to divide up rights and responsibilities when a relationship falls apart. Churches and schools and social groups make up for some of the more awkward or missing parts of the rickety theory underlying monogamy and marriage.

We don't have that in nonmonogamy. It's unlikely that any nonmonogamous relational form will ever have a tiny fraction of that sort of synergy with social belief and structure. I don't believe that this "outsider" status is a *bad* thing – but that's only true for *you* if you should happen to thrive on being outside of absolute, rigid social controls. If you are never able to make it to that point, but are otherwise sincere, then welcome, and let's see what we can work out. But, if you like the idea of spending the rest of your life riding some *really cool* emotional rollercoasters, then you're in the right place.

Goin' poly: an MF-to-FMF checklist

A closed multiple relationship is marriage, just with more people. We are all aware of the limits of monogamy; a little consideration will show that simply adding more people to a problematic structure won't work any better for intimacy than it does for government or business. Going out of your way to set up a closed group is a little more likely to succeed than winning the Powerball. If you're planning to include someone you haven't even met, then the likelihood of measurable happiness plummets still further.

As far as having a closed triad that is not only functional but very loving, I am certain that it *can* be done: I've been there. It worked for a couple of years. However, we were exceptionally fortunate in that we didn't set out to find anything but a roommate. A young woman living in the far suburbs needed a place to live that was closer to work. She hit it off immediately with my fiancée, becoming close friends even before she moved in. A few months later, though both pretty much inexperienced, their friendship progressed to sex. Our little household went well, and we all had other lovers too, with the three of us living in a loose "vee". A year later, our new partner broke up with her latest boyfriend, and was complaining to me of how she didn't have time for a typical one-on-one primary, with her schedule. I laughingly said, "Well, we're already living together, and we've gotten pretty good at giving each other space." We stopped, looked at each other. I called my fiancée in, and the three of us discussed it; she not only endorsed the idea, but told us it was about time we thought of it! Soon, our schedules were so tight that we didn't have time for other relationships, and we spent the year as a closed triad. All accidental, but approached rationally and openly, with our needs, desires, and limitations stated up-front.

One of the most common phenomena in polyamory is when a couple starts looking around for another female to add to their happy home. Motivations vary widely and can be quite complex. Not uncommonly, the romance in the dyad has begun to fade back toward day-to-day normalcy, the woman would like to keep her partner from straying in search of renewed excitement, and may herself be curious about being sexually intimate with another woman. She might be willing to consider another male partner, but assumes (likely correctly) that she is better able to deal with nonexclusivity than are most males. Finding another "bi-curious" female appears the perfect solution.

If you're with me so far, you'll note a few problems with this presumption. Foremost, many polyamorous people are isolated, even if they are both poly-experienced and living openly; for those who are newer to the concept, the chances that they even know another half-dozen people who *recognize* the term "polyamory" are (literally) slim to none. Therefore, the couple isn't likely to be associating with many polyamorous people, so it's doubtful they know of any apt candidates for the position, or even how to go about finding one. They've got to find someone who is sane and stable, yet has few enough attachments that she is free to leap right into the situation. (As a friend of mine said, "When I meet a guy who is single, I have to wonder a little at first what's *wrong* with him that he's available!") On top of this, they've got to not only sort out the dynamics of the triad, but of two new dyads as well, with little or no experience in the high level of intimate communication skills that will be absolutely necessary. And they've got to do this using only classified advertising or the Internet equivalent. In addition, it is the rare male who can keep up with the sexual desires of one healthy female, let alone two. You could say that I'm not optimistic.

Still, I can't help but feeling that there are ways to improve the chances for a "searching" approach. With that in mind, I want to examine the process that most people would follow to set up a potentially successful closed FMF triad. What is the actual likelihood of finding that one special female who's going to make you a life-long threesome? Pay close attention to the following, and you can at least even your odds a little.

A. PREPARATION

0. If lists and structure make you squeamish, then take two aspirin and lie down in a quiet room: you're just having a fantasy. If you proceed, you may find yourself deciding that love solves everything, or similar recipes for disaster. Love gives you a basis for problem-solving–it does not exempt you from it. If you can't approach this logically, you're looking for a rude awakening when the love suddenly evaporates. Which it will, however briefly.

1. You have to be in an established relationship, living together for at least a couple of years. Your own NRE has to have settled down a little, but you must still be close enough that your dyad can survive the turbulence of each of you forming a new, mutually competing dyad.

2. You have to be financially stable, not searching for another necessary paycheck or housekeeper or babysitter to add to the household. You're looking for another equal partner, not a plaything or maid – right?

3. Your sex life has to be very satisfying for both of you. Adding another lover will place huge demands on your communication skills, so you'd better be experienced at working through difficult situations, because you'll be doing much more of it than you ever will with a healthy one-on-one relationship. In short, another sexual partner will not be a magical cure for preexisting dissatisfaction in bed.

4. Neither of you has had a secret sexual affair while in this relationship. If one of you tends to roam, then having another sexual partner is unlikely to change this for long.

5. You can't be having any on-going problems communicating openly, clearly, and promptly, and solving difficulties in an intelligent, mutual, and efficient manner.

6. You're not living in a community where you're already worried about "what people might say." Assuming you find someone, are you going to have to hide the relationship from your friends? What's going to happen to your social life?

7. You both have some experience with maintaining simultaneous relationships, even if it was just dating.

8. You both have to agree on your sexual expectations for the beginning. Who will a new partner have sex with? Just him? Just her? Primarily one or the other? Both? At the same time? And what happens if one of you doesn't feel that "click" after one or two experiences?

9. Will she be her own person, or will all of her time be divided between the two of you, her job, and the household?

10. Will she be an equal partner, with rights and responsibilities... or is she going to be a plaything and servant?

B. RESEARCH

11. "Make a list" at least insofar as having some way of letting women know you're looking for another partner, probably some sort of "personals" placement in the classified ads. Even if you never actually place the ad, the two of you need to agree completely in your initial expectations.

12. Find women who are emotionally available... but not presently in some sort of intimate attachment.

13. Narrow the list to women who have had at least one long-term committed relationship that was mostly healthy.

14. Trim further to those who are financially stable... but willing to give up a job (if she's far away) or a house (if she's nearby) to move in with you.

15. Ruthlessly prune those who want to be a Lolita, an immature bratty playtoy who will in short order make your life and home a living hell.

16. Assuming anyone makes it this far, contact the respondents.

17. Get together with them.

18. Avoid saying to yourself, "She's the only passable response we've gotten in six months, so we'd better settle." Wrong, wrong, wrong—are you shopping for a used car or searching for a life-long partner?

19. An often-overlooked crux is what a friend calls the "sniff test": "If they don't smell right, it ain't gonna happen." I disagree, but only slightly. If there's no "magic" at the beginning, adults can still make things work out and base an intimate relationship on raw friendship. However, the sniff test can help you determine if you're in danger of going completely overboard: if your first reaction is overwhelming lust, then I can guarantee the blood is not going to your brain.

C. EXECUTION

20. Being left with no more than a handful of candidates, get together again, a few more times. Drop the damned masks–if you expend too much effort on being "pleasant" you are working hard at misleading yourselves. Lay out your expectations, your social structure, your plans, and do it in inarguably bald terms. Talk money. Talk sex. Talk children. Talk pets. Talk friends. Talk ex-lovers. Talk drinking. Emotional and intellectual disclosure greatly helps block the dangers of NRE.

21. Unless one of you is terminally ill, there's no rush. Do not start planning a move-in date! Do not have sex yet, or the relationship's development will likely come to a screeching halt at that point, with all the undiscovered problems frozen in place. Keep getting together, especially two at a time. Take a few evenings to sit around and watch movies on the VCR. Go to a few parties together, so that you can all see how you behave socially. Packing the three of you off to a weekend poly conference is highly advised. Sound like too much work? If you met an attractive stranger, and went out for dinner a few times, would you leap into marrying them at that point? What do you think you're doing now? It's called courtship.

22. In fact, as so few do, this dating-and-courting stuff should be an on-going process. You'll get better at it with more experience, you'll be less likely to leap in and commit to a poor match, and you won't be limiting your candidates to just those women who choose to make their presence known within some narrow little window of time. Your resulting confidence will attract better candidates.

23. For any candidate who's made it this far, have sex on three or four widely separated occasions, with plenty of time to process feelings and communicate same. While great sex is no indicator of potential relationship success, the intimate time will give you clues as to whether this is going to be worth proceeding with. Bad sex, though, is just bad sex; if enthusiastic sex is very important to you, be warned that this doesn't really improve very much under the stresses of moving in together.

D. MAINTENANCE

23. Keep talking. If you can't communicate very well at the beginning, this is very unlikely to improve: you'll keep little easily solvable problems buried until they become big messy problems, if you don't feel safe enough to speak your mind.

24. Have you ever lived with more than one adult? If not, you may be in for a shock. Anyone who's been in a couple that was wonderful right up until moving day will think very, very carefully at this juncture.

25. What are you going to do with all that extra furniture? If she doesn't have extra furniture, what does this say to you? And didn't you talk about the pets?

26. Now, here's all you have to do: the three of you just have to keep growing at the same pace, in the same directions, forever, yet without losing a fascination with and responsibility to the other two; it will ebb and flow, sure, but if it disappears, you're in trouble.

27. I've observed many marriages that spend one to three years as a closed monogamous unit, then, when they're secure with what they have, they become a primary couple in an open marriage. Our threesome opened, and I gather that most closed triads reach a similar point. If this

happens, will you stay together and flow with the changes, or is it all over?

Things to avoid

In my observation, a sexually closed FMF triad is *not* a few disasters waiting to happen – the number is probably closer to twenty. No, make that thirty.

For one thing, it is *impossible* for both members of a dyad to develop a relationship at the same rate with a new person, and one of the dyad *must* fall behind for a while… which is unfortunate, because fast-burning relationships tend to burn out when the NRE burns off. So, about the time the NRE starts to fade, the "third wheel" is getting less attention from *two* than she'd been getting from *one*, and is looking for an apartment. End result: three people who will never speak to each other again.

If you are honest and insightful, you will have spotted some of the risk-points in the previous section, and perhaps even spun out a scenario or two that chilled you just a little. Let me list a handful of the more likely outcomes of ill-conceived FMF triads:

- couple gets bored and/or frustrated with dealing with a human being, and dumps their toy, probably to go looking for a superior replacement;
- husband pairs off with new girl, loses all interest in wife;
- wife gets jealous of not being sole proprietor & boots new girl;
- wife and new girl find that sex drives are more compatible than the five-minute wonder's, and he gets jealous;
- new girl realizes that she really doesn't need this crap, and leaves;
- new girl finds herself alternating care for household, children and/or new baby with being available at whim for sex, so original couple decides she needs some help and recruits another girl.

With the usual heavy-handed irony of the Universe we know and love, the following unfolded while I was attempting to finish the first draft of this book. As I'm occasionally able to grasp a sufficiently large hint, I include it, with only minimal fictionalization.

Lily had been too busy for months to even think about finding a steady lover. After her previous relationship fizzled, she'd found herself so immersed in the busy season at work that she didn't yet feel much of a lack.

Then, while taking a weekend off to visit Seth, an old friend living halfway across the state, she found herself attracted to two of Seth's friends, who were in a polyamorous household. After a couple more weekends, Lily was practically a member herself, with two new lovers who were close friends and housemates.

Polyamory was a completely new concept for Lily. She was amazed at how well the members of the household got along, and that there was no competition over her – in fact, the two men seemed to be supportive of each other's relationship with her. They also had primary relationships, and her visits were a whirl of getting to know the many people associated with this extended family.

Finding herself spending a quiet weekend at home, Lily searched the Internet until she found a poly social group that met monthly a few miles away. She decided that she'd like to learn more about how others handled the lifestyle, and just (as her new friends had suggested) to get out of the house a little more often for some relaxation.

The social group welcomed her warmly, though they seemed much more guarded than the poly household. Lily also noticed that most of the people were either married couples or unattached singles, mostly men.

If only to give you an idea of what an absolute bastard I can be, the following was posted to a polyamory website a few days after the incident described. To cut down on indignant howls, I've changed a few key facts, such as the names of the cities.

Experience makes me very wary of people who say, 'I've decided to become polyamorous.' We carry an extraordinary amount of baggage from the culture that spawned us. It takes years for people to get rid of this garbage, and some never do, because it suits their purposes. My complaint is that it just doesn't have much to do with such minor concepts as openness, honesty, communication, fairness, and so on.

I am also edgy around couples that, with little or no experience, launch into searching for a woman – preferably young and even more inexperienced – to create a closed triad. Though they protest loudly (usually more loudly than anyone else ascribing to nonmonogamy), many of these couples are looking for a plaything, a sexual toy over which they can exercise complete control. Even good people aren't able to deal maturely with the neurotic behaviors that can come to the fore. As a couple, they form a 'front' that bears remarkable resemblance to codependent behaviors. I don't mean to tar all hopeful couples with this brush, but perhaps by the end of this you'll understand my edginess.

People tell me I've got no basis for such feelings; these people typically have far less experience in nonmonogamous living than has accreted to me, but two decades of observation and experience *does* count for more than the prematurely gray hair. Then, something pops up as what follows.

One of the facets of a functioning intimate network is that we talk to each other. Except at the fringier areas, we live under the notion that our various interconnecting relationships are not a sort of extended fling. We stick our noses in each other's business, sometimes without welcome, because we care not only about ourselves, not only about our loved ones, but about the happiness of our loved ones with their loved ones. So, we worry about the well-being of people we may not even particularly like, or know at all well.

With that in mind, I am going to metaphorically slap the living crap out of a couple of people, right before your startled eyes. They are an excellent example of everything that is wrong with an automatically inclusive linking of the words "poly" and "community" – moreso because I deny that either term applies to the accused, and am equally certain that nobody is going to subject them to the sort of scrutiny they so richly deserve.

There's a young woman in Metropolis, Lily, who has found herself drawn into an intimate network of which I'm a part, in Gotham. As all this "poly stuff" was new to Lily, she belatedly started reading up on the subject. She also took a leap of faith, and sought out a local polyamory discussion group.

Lily was soon chatted up by a male about twice her age. He and his wife (call them Fred and Ethel) and maybe one or two members of the discussion group very quickly moved along to telling Lily that the Gotham network **isn't really polyamorous** because Lily couldn't possibly expect to be a primary.

My people said, "Huh?"

I said, "Oh, crap, I can see what's coming next." Sadly, I was right.

Fred suggested that Lily should move in with him and Ethel, where she could be an equal partner, unlike those *other* people. Lily felt that this was at best awkward, since she didn't find Fred (or Ethel, for that matter) particularly attractive. Except, of course, that they were so willing, in the name of True Friendship, to give her so much "attention."

Soon thereafter, Lily decided that Gotham presently has more to offer, even if you leave out of the equation her new community there.

When Lily mentioned this, Fred broke down in tears. Not fair, not fair, not fair.

So, of course, Lily had sex with him, seeing as how she was (after all) the one responsible for Fred being so terribly, terribly upset. We'll set aside the dumbness of this, as I've had dozens of women try to explain the reasoning to me and I still can't figure the progression.

Lily realized that it was probably a mistake. She continued to keep in touch with the, of course, socially, telephonically, and IM-wise. And, when Lily mentioned her relocation plans, Fred started sobbing, and no I'm not kidding.

A few weeks later, getting jitters about putting the plans to move into place, Lily got very upset with the whole damned network. She was feeling like an outsider. Hey, stuff happens. Lacking (for that moment) someone sympathetic at whom to rant and rail, she called up Fred and Ethel, who were very ready to offer tea and sympathy. Or, well, cheap wine and sex.

Lily, of course, *had* to stay the night with Fred and Ethel, who had made sure to drink enough that they had a good excuse to not drive Lily home. Odd how that works out. Similarly for the one bed.

Once again, Lily realized that this whole situation was a large error. Though Fred wanted to continue the sexual escapades well into the night, Lily decided to cut her losses, and pretended to be comatose. Fred and Ethel toddled out to the livingroom to chat. Actually, as it turns out, they reviewed their strategy.

Strategy, you say? Oh, yes. If you thought the tale was pretty much stupid so far (though not totally unfamiliar to some of us), you'll enjoy the next part.

Lily swears that she listened to them (in normal tones, albeit a bit slurred) discussing her (Lily's) menstrual cycle, and calculating if they could get her into having sex with Fred at the peak time of her ovulation.

Yep. They were *planning* to get her pregnant, so that they'd have a hook. Think of all the legalistic fuss that Fred could raise because *the mother of his child* thought that she had any right to move, seek an abortion, end the relationship, etc.

Say hello to two members of "the poly community."

Get the idea? Speaking generally, we would like it a *lot* if you didn't turn out to be like Fred and Ethel. You may also want to avoid becoming like Lily, who now defends Fred and Ethel – they obviously desire her very much to have concocted such a plan, and their degree of fixation makes her feel needed.

Should you be a much better human being than Fred and Ethel, don't forget that they are nevertheless probably thrashing around in your part of the map, teaching everyone what nonmonogamy really looks like – their version, anyhow. You can take steps to counter this, or you can let the world's picture of you be determined by the damage caused by every Fred and Ethel. If you should run into a Fred and/or Ethel of your very own, then call them on their games, and demand either sudden improvements, or distance. Such people do regularly try to attach themselves to poly-related social groups, which affords them HBB opportunities as well as lending their games a tone of political correctness.

Assuming they don't see any reason to wise up, to stop these shenanigans and maybe locate a good therapist, I strongly suggest that you consider forwarding their names and behaviors to every polyamorous person, family, community, and organization you can think of – after all, Fred and Ethel might indeed clean up their act, in which case they deserve the same sort of guidance and support that would be offered any other sincere but clueless novice.

Many such couples are simply trying to recapture youth, or patch up a long-established loving relationship that is nevertheless fading. Sometimes, it reflects many drives that are in conflict, such as sexual curiosity mingled with missing a household full of their now-married kids. I have no desire to impugn people with such perfectly understandable desires and needs; my hope is that, with a sense of true poly *community*, these drives could be channeled so that everyone wins.

However, there is a point at which the search becomes obsession, and clumsy lovers morph into obvious sexual predators. In the story I laid out above, Fred and Ethel have crossed that line.

But for obvious risk of a lawsuit, I would gladly put real names to Fred and Ethel. Leaving them untagged is equivalent (as a farm-raised friend of mine puts it) to "letting the cows crap upstream of the pump," a very apt metaphor in this sort of situation. Even if Fred and Ethel do not hurt you directly, you will eventually have to deal with the messes they leave behind, especially if you are using the Internet to make polyamorous friends around the country. Let me again grant that they may be well-intentioned people, but their actions are nevertheless reprehensible, they present a risk of putting everyone polyamorous into a bad light, and, unless they correct their actions, they are obviously capable of adding regular obstacles to any true sense of community. If there is indeed a polyamorous community, then it ought to be the responsibility of that community to admit to the existence of this sort of behavior, then to examine it, openly discuss it, clear the path for other victims to come forward, openly discuss this behavior, criticize the responsible parties and, if necessary, shun them or even bring legal action. A community is self-policing, and anything less is not community.

Most importantly: do not become Fred and Ethel. If you're as lacking in self-awareness as most of us, then make an effort to have people around you who care enough about you to question your behavior long before you cross that line. Such friends may be incorrect, but sometimes an informed conscience is a very handy thing indeed.

08. Other sides of the coin

The previous chapter largely considered a monogamous (likely married) hetero-sexual couple looking to form a closed triad with another woman. When I look at the majority of people who decide that they are "going to get into polyamory," it appears at first blush that this is accurate, but that is an oversimplification. In reality, there is a great deal of diversity, and such pigeonholing doesn't hold up. Rather than try to categorize everyone so neatly, I will instead address briefly a few other main groups.

Single females

The good news for you is that you are what most people are after. If you are bisexual, or at least possibly interested in bisexuality, or comfortable with the idea of physical and emotional affection with either gender, you are the Grail of polyamory, as well as of swinging and for that matter of the various types of monogamous practice.

The bad news is the impression you'll get that apparently everyone will be after you for these characteristics alone, and you will have to develop a certain amount of skill at fending of some very clueless attempts to woo you, court you, draw your attention, manipulate you, and wangle you into commitments and sexual situations.

In polyamory, especially among people who are new to the concept, there is a strong tone of ownership still present. Many couples (and singles, admittedly) are still holding to the concept of sexually exclusive relating, but want to add a girlfriend, something I refer to as "a typical marriage, just with three people." The actual expansion appears slight, and thus less risky to the core dyad. On one poly-oriented Internet site, I noted that the number of couples specifically searching for a bisexual female outnumber the number of bisexual females looking for a couple by about ten to one. What complicates this is that the couples are largely looking for a closed relationship – if the relationship were open, the ecology could sort itself out a lot more easily.

Such couples pop onto a site, and begin expression frustration within a few weeks – no, I am not exaggerating – if they have not found their ideal "life partner" and convinced her to commit to them. I suppose that, if you are as desperate as they are, this might work out for all parties.

You will need to develop reserves of tact and diplomacy, in order to fend off well-meaning couples who can be in a surprising rush to get things moving now that they've decided to make the leap.

Almost as demanding are single males who want to form a core dyad so that they can quickly add another bisexual female and have a closed triad. The odds for such a fantasy are even lower than for couples, but these guys can be far more pushy; should you encounter this on a website or list, you may find yourself turning one or two over to the gentle ministrations of an administrator who will sympathetically boot them out the nearest airlock. Think of it as a learning experience.

Single males

You, meanwhile, will likely have exactly the opposite experience set. The only controversy is whether a heterosexual male has a more difficult time of it than a bisexual male.

A decade ago, some of us *Loving More* subscribers noticed a pattern in the newsletter's classified ads. The ones that were seeking partners were almost entirely from couples or single males, even though the gender mix among subscribers and readers didn't seem significantly lopsided, and we had an interesting discussion about reasons for this. On the one hand, this makes no particular sense to me, if examined at a simple sexual level. As my wife used to point out, a sexually healthy female is about equally matched to three or four sexually healthy males. The idea of a harem of women assembling themselves around one male might pander to his fantasies, but it may be a rude shock to him when he finally understands how much effort will be involved to keep so many women satisfied on a sexual level alone.

Single males are anathema precisely because so many of them are looking only to fulfill that fantasy. They will satisfy their curiosity and move along, or they will back down from how much interpersonal effort they need to expend, but in either case they will not be able to live up to what they are willing to promise. Two decades ago, we were set upon by a string of males who wanted to join our household, but many of them soon made it clear that they were working from the idea that they were going to replace me, rather than join me. Some wanted to squeeze me out of the household – my partners were turned off by this even faster than I was. Others wanted to use our household as a sort of shopping mall, where they could "test drive" the women and then choose which one they were going to form a closed dyad with; again, that didn't go over at all well.

The nice guys, of course, get buried by all this, and these are the ones I am addressing. Main message: all is not lost. First of all, you will need to have a personality, and be an interesting person in your own right. This is hardly the Herculean task it might appear, nor should it be. I've found that, if you are capable of starting an interesting conversation, a willing listener will quickly encourage you to bring out what you actually are, which is why pick-up lines, even if trite, can nevertheless serve to break the ice; if it's corny enough, and your timing is good, the resultant (shared!) laughter is hardly a bad beginning. That's where the truth lies in an old joke: "What you need is sincerity. When you can fake that, everything else is easy."

Even if you, as a single male, meet up with a compatible single female, you are dealing here with polyamory, which is definitely a two-edged sword. If you want the freedom to become intimate with other women, then you will have to be open to the idea of "your" lovers possibly being intimate with other males. Many polyamorous people have had at least passing experience with harem-minded men, so you've got to understand that they are a little leery of single males for this reason among others. If you are free of that sort of preconception, though, there's nothing much that you have to do besides make clear that you're different, and be a little patient. The more you can get in touch with this flexibility, and communicate your heart-felt desire for open-ended relating, the more you stand apart from the crowd of prowling lone males.

Bisexual males have a very difficult time. Dyads that are open to the possibility of including another male – yes, they do exist – will many times back away if an otherwise interesting man makes clear that he is not entirely straight, because the male of the dyad is not at all interested in physical intimacy with another male. (Once in a while, though this is much rarer, the male of the couple is more gay than straight. Because of this rarity, I'd rather not go into any depth here, but I can advise that a male who joins with them will have to be very comfortable both sexually and emotionally with his own bisexuality.) As one such hapless guy put it, "I hit it off right away with the woman, but her husband didn't want her to get any closer because 'something might happen' between him and me. Hey, he's a very nice guy, and I could even see living comfortably with the two of them, but he's not my type. If it went the other way, and I moved in to be with a married bi man, I wouldn't automatically expect to have sex with his wife!" Another friend told me, "I'm mostly straight, and I would like to have a steady boyfriend too. Most men I meet, though, either want me to 'go gay' and leave my wife, or they show interest in me only because they want to have sex with her. It's irritating. I know it'd be absurd, but I sometimes feel like giving up completely on men."

Stick to your guns. Present what you are, discuss your experiences (good and bad), and be straightforward about your intentions. If you are open to possibilities, and honest with others, you will eventually be recognized for your strengths.

Over 40

Nothing makes you appear "too old" quite so thoroughly as thinking and acting as if you're too old. I'm heading rapidly toward 50 myself, and the laugh lines around my eyes are turning into gulleys, even as various extremities are demonstrating that gravity is not my friend. Nevertheless, I keep in shape, I dance, and I'm up on the current music and technology, so despite the fact that I'm not exactly easy on the eyes, my energy and attitude regularly lead to favorable comparisons with people in their 20s. An added bonus is that the years have brought me a breadth and depth of experience that nobody half my age can possibly offer – not to mention a vast repertoire of funny songs and terrible puns. By contrast, I met a woman, recently divorced at age 26 with two young children, who horrified me by referring to herself as "still young at heart"!

Though our culture denigrates age, "deviant" lifestyles such as polyamory inherently have an iconoclastic streak, so you're not so likely to be seen as over the hill merely because of a few extra years. The main problem with age is that we become set in our ways, where someone on the sunny side of 30 is still thrashing around – but as long as you're not too thoroughly root-bound by your own little orthodoxies, this groundedness is an automatic plus to someone who wants a little steadiness and continuity. If you are in a perpetual state of curiosity about the world, there's only so old you can get. Mature, maybe, but not old.

For that matter, if you're a stay-at-home couch potato, don't lose hope – there are plenty of people in *any* age group that would be happy to share the sofa with you.

Under 20

There *is* a point at which I have to put my foot down. Until we start raising kids from birth to adulthood in polyamorous houses, and marrying them off to each other, the blunt truth is that poly people are products of monogamist indoctrination – period. To be social deviants (and, sociologically speaking, polyamory is indeed deviant), we need to be very aware of how we fit into the world. This awareness comes largely from experience, and one factor of experience is time. Therefore, age does matter.

In the 1980s, almost all nonmonogamous people I knew were over 30. It seemed that, before that milestone, people are either casting around for a marriage partner, or trying to figure out how to get a little space from their spouse (whether via divorce, affairs, or sexually open marriage). When their mid-30s arrive, people seemed more likely to come to the twinned understanding that they wanted to hold onto couplehood yet add to their lives, and found responsible nonmonogamy to at least look like a feasible path.

I'm hardly ageist. My roving eye can occasionally fetch up on a lively and intelligent 19-year-old. I've dated women who at 20 were much more mature and world-wise than some of 50 who'd lived relatively sheltered, "safe" lives.

For the most part, though, until someone has had a few years-long monogamist relationships, they really do not have a basis from which to understand the difficulties inherent in being poly in a mono world. There are exceptions that, from their very novelty, emphasize the rule. I recently met a woman who, at 23, was undergoing her second divorce; her wit and candor in talking about these marriages showed me that she'd learned much about her own unconscious motivations.

If you are under 21, and you are drawn to polyamory, then I strongly advise you to stick to intimacy with people in your immediate age range (two years difference at most). We all screw up in relationships, and you will do better if you make your learning mistakes with people at about your own experience level, rather than be indoctrinated into someone else's long-established patterns. Whatever your gender or orientation, there are always a few people in any definable group who are quite willing to take advantage of your youth, and are drawn to you only because you're young. They will target your inexperience to attempt to mold you into their idealized plaything. It may be flattering at first to feel that you can monopolize the attention of someone older than your parents, but the likely truth is that anybody your age could do the same.

As I indicated above, I personally don't give much of a damn about age, because age isn't necessarily a decent indicator of emotional maturity or intellectual level. I follow my instincts. A certain 17-year-old set her sights on me; I knew her parents, and it was unlikely they'd object. However, she was intending to travel the United States, then look for the ideal college, and hoped to work straight through to her doctorate. I wanted her to experience life, something she couldn't do if she was in a primary relationship with someone like me, at the time locked into a career-oriented path – whether I'd been 25 or 35 or 45 was irrelevant. So, came the day when I took her by the shoulders, looked deep into her eyes, and said, "If you still want me in ten years, I'm yours." If she should actually look me up at the end of that time, I have every confidence that she'll be more attractive for her experiences.

If you're a young adult, enjoy *being* young for a while. Date around or settle into monogamy or start a Tantric sex commune in South Dakota, whatever, but don't be too fast to give up your freedom and autonomy, even if it's to be part of a really cool thing like an established poly household. Becoming "settled" and "serious" is overrated, and life isn't *that* short, so you can always get around to it.

09. The first fatal steps

Signing the social contract

By claiming membership in a particular social class or stratum, you are taking on what is called a *social contract*, which delimits what you are expected to say and do, and even to think. If you don't want to be bothered by that sort of restriction, then you also do not have claim to the rights that a member of that (for lack of a better word) community deserves. For instance, the queer community is not going to rush to the defense of an outspoken homophobe who apparently delights in making life miserable for gays but frequents the bars at night.

When you say, "I am polyamorous," you are saying,

> I hereby declare myself to be part of an ill-defined community, subject to its guidance, though I understand that this will regularly be mutable, changing, and temporary. As well, I declare myself responsible for others in that community, in the sense of supporting their growth and healing, and of providing guidance for them to the best of my ability, and of being aware that my actions reflect upon us all. I will listen with sincere self-evaluation when I am criticized, I will not be merely shouted down when

my considered viewpoint differs, and I will take personal responsibility for my actions as well as to speak out should I see those who claim to ally themselves with me in polyamory acting in a manner that is questionable, reprehensible, or destructive. I will listen to and observe others with humility and calm criticality. I will join with others to the best of my ability in order to better define our community and thus to add to our happiness and productivity.

If you cannot ascribe to all of the foregoing statement, then bless you for your depth of insight into your own motivations, and even more for your honesty. These abilities set you apart from millions. The odds are definitely tilted in favor of you and the people around you.

But you're *not* polyamorous, in that case. That is the social contract that summarizes the here-and-now of polyamory as a pervasive way of life. The fact that you can't agree to it does nothing to prevent you from being actively and responsibly nonmonogamous and receiving praise and support commensurate with your goodness – it's just the "poly" label you have to leave behind.

Bad enough that polyamory is a catch-all for everything that isn't rigidly monogamous – this oversimplification is far from correct, but that's nevertheless the direction the terminology has headed in the past decade.

Like any contract in the real world, it really doesn't much matter if you didn't read the fine print, or don't understand what some article or clause meant. Unless you can demonstrate that you were impaired, misled, or coerced, you have to live up to it. A social contract is a contract, ill-defined though it might be. Ignorance of the law is no excuse.

The two ways to become polyamorous

Though it's widely denigrated as being outdated, I consider *Group Marriage*, by Larry and Joan Constantine, to be necessary reading. While I'd agree that the details are difficult to apply to any specific nonmonogamous situation, many of their points remain as relevant thirty years later.

The Constantines say that there are two general ways in which people get into group marriage. The first, and likely most common in present-moment polyamory, is the **rationalistic** approach. A few couples get together at a social event, and the conversation maybe rolls around to an article about a group marriage or commune or whatever, or maybe a review of a book on that sort of topic. They chat about the pros and cons, and at some point figure that there are some really intellectually interesting reasons to have a more communal approach to intimacy. Being sane, calm, self-aware people, and likely college-educated, they look at the downside and figure that they're superbly equipped to work their way past the rough spots. The next time they're together, the topic comes up again, and they kick around thoughts on the problems that would come up, and how they'd go about solving them – just theoretically, of course. But the idea is fascinating, so it keeps reappearing. Finally, two couples, close friends, are getting together over lunch to talk about this, until the bravest one in the bunch speaks up and, half-jesting, says, "Maybe we ought to give it a try ourselves." Plans are made, rules are drafted, and they talk themselves into actually taking the plunge.

The second approach I like to call **propinquitous**, but **chaotic** is probably more like it. Bob and Sue are very attached to their neighbors, John and Mary. One evening, coming back early from a business trip, Bob accidentally walks in on John and Sue in what we used to call a compromising position. Bob starts to get angry, but then he laughs nervously, and sheepishly he admits that he's been having an affair with Mary. None of them wants to end their respective marriages since, despite the inevitable problems, they still very much love their spouses. While this is uncomfortable all around, they realize quickly that each of them has two lovers, they really don't want to change that, and now they can set aside the guilt from sneaking around. They're forced to communicate, completely and honestly, or it's all over.

The reason that this dichotomy sticks in my head is because the Constantines found something very interesting: the people who sort of stumbled into group marriage actually had a better chance of staying together than the ones who logically "decided" their way into it.

My experience and observation is that relationships that "just happen" tend to far outlast those created by fitting a more-or-less stranger into an ongoing situation. It's not *impossible*, mind you, just much less likely, since there are so many variables involved that cannot be overlooked... but often are. If these speed-bumps can be taken out, examined, and partially resolved beforehand, a "made" trine has a much better chance of lasting more than a year. (Average span of a polyfidelitous relationship is 6 months to 2 years, depending on the study... which, really, isn't much less than the average "life-long" monogamous marriage.)

This significant difference between the two approaches seems counterintuitive at first, but made a lot of sense after I thought about it for a while. See, if you decide you're going to undertake some huge project, you *plan*. The problem is, when you're getting ready to dive into polyamory, you really don't have any idea of what you're planning to do, so you can't know whether you've thought of everything, or what you're going to do when life tosses you an inside breaking curve. If you cling to your carefully worked out agenda – and what else can you do when you're in deep water? – then you're only likely to get deeper and deeper into trouble. But when you find yourself dropped right into the middle of the lake, seemingly very abruptly, the only way you're going to keep your collective head above metaphorical water is to start thinking really fast, and discard useless ideas quickly, rather than quoting theory or logic or good intentions to each other like a mantra to a god that doesn't seem to be paying attention.

It's not about the sex, but it's about the sex

Another way to define the split between the rationalistic approach and the propinquitous is by *utility*. I ask rude questions of people, like, "Did you decide to become polyamorous to fix something, or did you just fall in love?" Apparently that's a little too close to, "Are you just here for the sex?" Couples that a moment before were asking me for help in searching out the woman of their mutual dreams – a woman who would not only pass a whole long shopping list of qualifications as well as practically give up her life as an individual in order to join them – would suddenly swing 180 to deny loudly that they wanted their own private Mary Poppins in a bustier: "Oh, no, not at all! We want love and respect and equality!" Conversation quickly steers away from the sexual side so obviously near the top of their list moments before.

The main problem here with a rationalistic approach is ironically a **fear of practicality**. Being *sane* about creating an intimate loving relationship should not be seen as bad just because the term "love" is featured prominently. There are many perfectly reasonable underlying desires for personally taking on something as demanding as polyamory, and various types of intimacy are valid for examination. The Constantines list 47 reasons to be in a multilateral relationship. By far the most popular (82% chose it as a reason, with 42% calling it a "strong reason") was "More companionship." Coming in second (88%, but only 18% saying "strong") was "Variety of sexual partners." This is funny because the Constantines found (and I've repeatedly rediscovered, as I'll go into in detail a little further on) that most non-swingers who've decided they'd like to have more than one sexual partner won't readily admit that sex is a motivating factor! (Actually, "variety of sexual partners" is more of a masculine answer; the women in the study were more likely to accept it as "avoid having to choose between partners.") This demonstrates that "companionship" was not merely a coy euphemism for sex – they liked the idea of having more people to hang out with as close friends from whom they wouldn't have to hide an important facet of their life.

The Constantines found that people who were in group marriages had been a bit adventurous before they joined the group. About half had experience with extramarital sex, one-third admitted at least one homosexual encounter, and almost two-thirds had some experience with group sex. In short, these people were not entirely naive going into group marriage. In fact, it means that they already had some experience with jealousy, possessiveness, self-image, control and abandonment issues, as well as how to deal with all of these things in such a way as to keep their marriage together.

I should note that many groups located by the Constantines didn't survive long enough for them to reply to the written survey. This suggests that those in shorter-lived groups may have begun with less-tried generalizable relationship skills. Though they may have been more adventurous than most people, they apparently did not have experience with maintaining long-term emotionally intimate complex relationships. The skills they possessed in dealing with the complicating issues (jealousy, etc.) as far as their core dyad did not have sufficient general models with which they could apply to a larger group – society provides many models and mechanisms that are specific to dyads.

While I remain amazed that the people in these group marriages had managed (pre-Internet) to even locate enough like-minded others to just make the attempt, there's something I must call your attention to. Interest in group marriage, communalism, and forms of nonmonogamy such as co-marital relationships did not spring up from whole cloth, but was part of a wider movement to understand human nature. Back in the late 1960s and early 1970s, the word "self" was featured prominently: self-exploration, self-awareness, self-actualization, and so on. Things that have become clichéd phrases of the "New Age movement" were at that time very much alive, especially for the college-educated middle classes. For instance, mainstream Protestant churches were allowing or even sponsoring discussion groups among the devout that led to much earnest and highly educated lay analysis of the underlying structures and assumptions of marriage, couplehood, sexuality, monogamy, and interpersonal relationships in general. This resulted in experiments in community, from regular meetings of social and discussion groups to actual communities, the occasional educational retreat center with buildings and all. (For a small but significant example, go back to Chapter One and note the source of the term *co-marital*.)

One of the books on my "must read" list particularly stands out as a reflection of this impulse. The annotated biography alone for *Honest Sex* by Rustum and Della Roy in only nine pages presents a surprising selection of books dealing with a positive Christian ethical perspective on sexuality, nonmonogamy, and homosexuality. The Roys were instrumental in the Christian Community movement. They published an amazing (and amazingly titled) article, "Is Monogamy Outdated?" in *The Humanist* (March/April 1970). This piece answers the question by demonstrating that the institution of monogamy (as opposed to just dyadic sexual exclusivity) must have its definition expanded if it is not to fall entirely into disrepute, with such startling comments as, "If monogamy is tied inextricably with post-marital restriction of all sexual expression to the spouse, it will ultimately be monogamy which suffers. Instead, monogamy should be tied to the much more basic concepts of fidelity, honesty, and openness, which... do not necessarily exclude deep relationships and possibly including various degrees of sexual intimacy with others."

Contrast this forward-looking attitude with a minor ruckus I created a few years ago. There's a little-known polyamory event that pops up practically at random around the United States and Canada, known as **alt.polycon** (its name derived from the Internet list-server whose membership created the convention). I was at the very first one, in Minneapolis, and greatly enjoyed meeting other polyfolk from around the nation.

The primary organizer, Elise, at one point drew most of us into a large room, formed us into a circle, then went from one to the next asking us to bark out a reason that polyamory was important to us. I was on the far end of the rotation, and felt that I was hearing everything that would occur to me: a sense of community, expansion of love, diverse role-models for children, enhanced economic power, and so on. With every statement, there was a sea of nodding heads and murmurs of agreement.

When Elise pointed to me, there was one thing nobody had mentioned yet. "Multiple sexual partners," I said.

Silence. Absolute, chilly silence. Elise wisely moved along before the heated denials could begin.

Since then, I've found that many people who claim to polyamory, even those who are frankly promiscuous with a longstanding habit of shallow sexual contacts, are stunningly squeamish about claiming sexual variety as a factor motivating them toward responsible nonmonogamy. That people who pepper their conversations with words such as "communication" and "honesty" can shrink away from such an obvious – and positive! – reason for a drastic lifestyle choice, for fear that they will be misperceived at a glance, is not just obviously ridiculous (literally), but unhealthy.

Sure, we are embedded in a culture with attitudes toward sexuality that are prurient at best, and you may not wish to have your responsibly nonmonogamous ways confused with lifestyle choices that could be frowned upon in the larger culture, but that is not a good excuse for falling into the trap of denying something that is actually of prime importance to you. Sex is still a "hot button" issue in the United States. Since sex figures into almost all nonmonogamy at some point, misunderstanding is inevitable. You will need to face up to this fact and be prepared to deal with it straightforwardly. To begin from denial is to make the decision to base your self-perception on lies. Lies multiply, and lying will eventually poison other parts of your life, as well as the relationships that develop therefrom.

You need to defeat lying at every turn, and this should be a habit you establish from the very earliest moment of deciding that you are going to move in a direction other than the rut that has been laid out for you. And if you're going to deny sex as a motive for your nonmonogamy, then unless you're scrupulously celibate, I hope you'll understand if some of us occasionally roll our eyes.

The concept of fidelity

There are many ideas that underlie monogamy. A surprising amount of these are held up as high ideals, yet are largely overlooked, ignored outright, or regularly subverted in monogamy's practice. Adopting polyamory makes it important to go back to these ideals for careful examination, and in many cases for their active resurrection.

"Fidelity" is one of those largely empty "everyone knows what it means" words. (Rule of thumb: when most people say "everybody" as in "everybody knows…" it almost always means "I don't have a clue, and I doubt anyone else does either.") Way back in the olden days – like 1985 – many of us had to work out what that and related words meant for us. For the most part, we decided that "fidelity" does not equate with "sexual exclusivity." Just because a couple is sexually monogamous does not mean that they are joined at the heart – which some of us would argue is a precondition that ought to be at the core of an actually fidelitous relationship.

Now, leaving gender aside, let's address briefly how we go about "allowing" our partners to have sex with others without (as one correspondent put it) "going nuts about it." To tell you the bald truth, many of the discussions at poly-related social groups or on the Internet stem from the fact that – no matter how experienced we are – we most assuredly do go nuts about it. It doesn't happen constantly, or consistently, but it can pop up at the damnedest times. I definitely speak for myself on this one: I get jealous, I get possessive, I get insecure, even if I've got two other steady relationships. (We'll look at this in more depth in Chapter 18.) I really doubt that I'm alone in this reaction.

The next step, though, is to look for the *why*. You cannot communicate clearly and effectively with others if you cannot do so with yourself. I start by assuming (usually correctly) that I'm afraid of abandonment. Something inside of me worries about being unceremoniously dumped for someone who is, if not somehow "better," then at least more novel. Simply bringing that fear up for examination is halfway toward a solution, and I've gotten pretty good at it.

If the apprehension is still there, I go on to the next likely cause: I'm very protective of my loved ones. So, I root around for my specific concerns. However detailed they are – anything from vague doubts to specific reasons for distrusting my partner's lover – I try to do a thorough job of finding it all.

Then, the most critical step: I sit down for a long unhurried talk with my partner. I start by admitting that the problem is mostly within me, then I lay out (as best I can) what's going on in my own head and heart. Sometimes I need specific reassurances, such as that I'm not going to be abandoned for this new person; generally, I only need to know that I'm heard, and have my worries acknowledged.

Actual fidelity is based in this sort of clear, honest communication that grows from a willingness for self-understanding. Fidelity is commitment to truth.

Sex *appears* to be the big bugaboo for most people facing nonexclusivity. This, though, doesn't stand up to even cursory examination, if you set aside the assumptions that come with monogamous expectations. If you were to find yourself in a situation where your partner became enchanted with another person, spending all their free time in the new relationship, changing set-in-stone social obligations in order to be with this new person, talking about them constantly, would it be *okay* as long as they weren't having sex?

In my polyamorous experience, I don't think that sex is a particular threat. I've known many couples who are fine with their partners having sex with others – as long as they never discuss it, and that interaction is limited almost entirely to sex. Many forms of swinging follow variants on this rule; more than a few clubs will still boot a member who tries to make a date with another member outside of sanctioned events.

In short, it's not the sex that's the threat, it's the interpersonal intimacy. So, keep in mind that sexual jealousy may be nothing more than an emotionally loaded smokescreen for underlying fears.

After the leap

To live polyamorously, you will need to make *many* leaps, actually. There's really no "after" involved, just the moments before the next.

You discover that people do indeed live outside of the monogamous enclave. You find that most are very happy doing so. You surprise yourself with empathy toward their choice. You become attracted to more than one person. Then there's courtship, nonsexual intimacy, sex, cohabiting, and commitment. Along the way are misunderstandings, arguments, the occasional attack of sheer panic, breakups, reconciliations, and terminated friendships. Multiply this drama by two (or three, or four, or five), and then factor in your own crises, and you'll get a glimmer of why polyfolk consider themselves exceptional: they usually don't start out that way, but they certainly have to pick up the skills.

There is no magical point at which you know everything you'll ever need to know, and your every minute will be perfection. If you are going to "become polyamorous," you are setting yourself up for disappointment, stress, depression, loneliness, and self-doubt. You'll many times find yourself asking, "What the hell am I doing?"

Then, like many of us, you'll sigh, shrug, and dive right back into the struggle. When it comes down to it, life is pretty much marred by the same problems, whatever your choices. Us poly people might have a lot more drama than anyone in a nice little marriage, but the rewards can be amazing, and often are. We each know a lot about ourselves because we've had to become self-aware just to get through the day. Likewise, we've had to learn vast amounts about interpreting and understanding others. The ones who haven't been able to develop these skills – or have refused to – fall by the wayside all the time, bouncing from one short-lived relationship to another,

It's not just a single leap into polyamory. It's one leap of faith after another. Often enough, that faith is amply rewarded.

10. Prepare your sacrifices

Let's look at some more words and the mudholes they mask.

As with the concept of *gift* (see Chapter 35), that of *sacrifice* has been badly mangled by the culture of the United States.

When you become involved with another person, you give up a degree of autonomy. It doesn't matter if it's a lover, a coworker, a roommate, or a friend. You have to avoid some topics, soft-peddle others, and generally revise your communication style when you're around particular individuals. One friend might detest hearing you speak positively about another. A habit that one doesn't notice, or even approves of, might set another to shouting or crying or angry silence. Whether to be nice to people we love and care about, or just to keep the screaming to a minimum, we sacrifice our freedom of expression to the greater good of interpersonal harmony.

Other words have been lost, widely misdefined, or mangled beyond all possibility of usefulness, *compromise* being one of them. We all have some degree of deep-seated belief that confrontations must be of a "win/lose" form – that is, one faction is right and the other wrong, or one gets all the marbles and the other goes home empty handed. To compromise is seen as a poor improvement upon this, where both or all parties give up victory. In other words, we feel that compromise is a "lose/lose" situation, where the "winners" don't win absolutely and the "losers" aren't entirely impoverished.

So, call it sacrifice, or compromise, or selective communication – to be around any particular person, you've been trained to present an incomplete or distorted version of yourself. It's probably ironic that the closer we feel to someone, the more carefully we present ourselves.

When you're in a crowd, that filtering has to be even more cautious. Either you must drastically restrict your presentation of self, showing only a very limited case, or you must remember exactly what the subgroup in closest proximity to you needs. The former is far less work, and generally safer, but means that you are presented in a fashion that is either very bland or very distorted.

I'm not saying that this is a good thing at all – far from it – but it is inarguably somewhere between a sad necessity and a diplomatic shortcut. In an ideal world, we'd be as complete and seamless as possible, at almost all times, and most especially so when we we're surrounded by our intimates. Misunderstandings would still happen, but they'd be sorted out as quickly as they were communicated, because all parties involved would be working from a base of empathy and trust in the other's inherent goodness of heart, without having any emotional hot-buttons that could be accidentally triggered. That is an *excellent* goal, but isn't yet here as a general case, so the overly cautious presentation of self continues because it makes day-to-day living easier.

Still, dishonesty is dishonesty, even if it's done from a sense of caring.

After years of careful examination, I'm convinced that the root of the problem is simple and (in hindsight) obvious: We've started from a whole raft of incorrect suppositions. Though an entire book – more likely three or four – could be filled with rooting out these underlying mistakes, examining them carefully, and tearing them apart, we ought to take a look at a few of them to get you started.

Down to the ground

Let's begin at the root. Human beings are unique. We each see the world in different ways. When you encounter another person who sees certain things in a manner that seems remarkably similar to your own, you are surprised and gratified, which of itself demonstrates that a significant degree of agreement is hardly commonplace. In short, we start from a ground of disagreement, and that's the way things are. But we insist on holding to flawed thinking, that one point of view is "good" and another "bad."

I'm of the deep-seated belief that a surprising number of situations ought to be win/win. The only trick involved is to choose what I am willing to discard, tokens that may be of little or no value to me but of higher worth to someone with whom I am negotiating. If you play cards (especially bridge or pinochle), you know that every card could be a vital part of a winning hand, so you have to decide which ones can be discarded in relative safety, both without damaging your strategy and not handing your opponent a card vital to their own strategy. Each card is a token, and its actual value shifts wildly from game to game, as well as between players in any given game. Similarly, there are tokens in any argument, disagreement, or negotiation.

Trading tokens

For starters, I don't have a need to humiliate someone with whom I disagree, so you could say I'm "giving up" the token of dealing my opponent a crushing defeat. If I am playing a friendly game, I will often back down my offensive once I'm assured of an easy victory, so that the final score isn't lopsided – overwhelming victory is in fact embarrassing to me. Hundreds of hours of my life have been spent with a billiards cue in my hands; if the game is clearly going my way, I will try for more difficult shots, which gives my opponent a chance to catch up, draws out the game, and sharpens my skills for the moments when I have no choice but difficult shots. (Not that I'm a saint. If an opponent takes an early lead and unfairly ridicules me, I'm known to get very quiet and then stomp their scores into the ground.)

One of the most powerful tokens I've ever found in a negotiation is to indicate that you are hearing what the other person is saying. Miraculous agreement can many times be achieved from simply replying with something like, "What I hear you saying is that..." and repeating back a summary of the person's demands or complaints. We are fragile little beings, and it is very important to us to know that our words aren't falling on deaf ears. Suddenly, our footing is more equal, and we are more willing to let go of a few tokens in compromise.

Recall the movie *Patton*. At one point, General Patton had a very public meeting with his equal from the Soviet Union. Someone proposed that they toast the joint efforts of the two countries. Patton, at his surliest, muttered, "I'm not gonna drink with that son of a bitch." This was repeated to the Soviet general, who replied through his translator, "You, too, are a son of a bitch!" The two men locked eyes. After a nervous silence crashed over the room, Patton harrumphed, then started chuckling. Finally he said, taking a champagne glass, "One son of a bitch to another." The press photos show them drinking the toast with linked arms. Each had had an opportunity to make clear that he wasn't going to back down easily; to put it another way, they had traded tokens, with both giving up on "absolute winner" status yet gaining tokens for strength, forthrightness, and willingness to compromise.

When hammering out an agreement in a polyamorous relationship – which in my experience seems to happen daily if not more often – words like *negotiation* fly by every sixty seconds or so. Well, the word does, anyway. I have rarely seen the sort of serious negotiating session that most folks pretend happens. This is a lot like the omnipresent "communication" that is generally just noise. I'm a stickler for clear, concise contracts, and have used them regularly for poly relationships and households, but I've seen a lot of goofiness go past, with some variant on, "but we **talked** about it...!"

We try to acknowledge that each partner is (hopefully) growing and changing, and so is each relationship (each pair, each trine, and on up to all the people involved in any way), so therefore negotiation is not just something that happens at the outset, but is necessarily recurring, even constant.

Remake the words

Sacrifice is *not* a bad thing – we've just been lured into taking part in making it seem that way. The act of sacrifice, of giving something up in order to curry favor from someone else, has become a token, and I think that this has to stop. Likely, many other words that incorrectly imply coerced loss of control or power or esteem are in the same situation. You can fix that, and you can benefit.

I had been dating Sandra for months. No, that is not in the least a euphemism – we were going out to dinner and chatting for hours, holding hands on the sofa while we watched our favorite science-fiction shows, and generally drawing closer. I can honestly say that I was so enraptured with getting to know her that the thought of throwing her over my shoulder and marching us off to the bedroom never occurred to me.

One evening, as we were making dinner together, Sandra got very quiet. I noticed that she wouldn't look me in the eye. We stayed in that uncomfortable silence awhile as we kept about our duties. Finally, Sandra said, "I'd like to stay the night, if that's okay."

I probably should have been primarily ecstatic, but the baffled part was winning, so I skipped right to the next question. I asked, "What's the matter?"

She drew herself up for the confrontation, and met my eyes. "I need you to use condoms."

Well. I looked at her, and blinked. I blinked again. Finally, the confused thoughts settled down a little and I put my arms around her. What she was actually saying was quite complex: I knew she'd had a few pregnancy false-alarms with her previous boyfriend, who would become sullen when latex was even hinted at, which meant she associated her caring and desire for the guy with anxiety over the potential complications. She wanted to be intimate with me, enough that she was feeling herself drawn to make the same mistakes.

"I have a beautiful woman who wants to make love with me," I told her. "I don't see a problem."

With that statement (followed through diligently), I earned a high degree of trust and respect. My "sacrifice" validated Sandra's boundaries, strengthened our friendship, and allowed a deeper intimacy between us. I also "gave up" the time I could've spent wheedling her out of that "silly" need for condoms.

I encourage you to sacrifice sacrificing, and instead to create your own definition of the word so as to make it a positive and mutually rewarding act, a win/win situation rather than the half-assed alternatives. What you need most to give up is the notion that you're giving up a whole hell of a lot.

Since I appear to have fallen into a fit of self-disclosure, let me tell you another story, about compromise.

I lived in a closed triad for a year. One evening, I looked up from my typewriter to find my partners nervously standing next to me. Lynn, her fingers twined in front of her, said, "There's something we have to talk about." Marie stood off to the side in silent assent.

I've thought about this for years, and for the life of me I cannot remember what the crisis was. Basically, though, I was doing something that was driving my partners nuts. They had talked it over between them, and finally worked up the courage to brace me about it.

I listened to them until they had laid out the problem, succinctly and without being mean to me. Then, without a word, I got up, walked outside, sat down on the porch, and silently lit up one of the expensive cigarettes I smoked back then.

When I was finished, I went back in. Marie and Lynn were sitting in the livingroom, talking quietly, and they went silent and wide-eyed when they saw me. My smile made them even more worried.

I sat down on the floor between them. "I've been thinking about it," I said, "and you're absolutely right. I made a choice that seemed inconsequential to me at the time, and I didn't think it would matter. I can just as easily do it the other way."

They traded glances, looking very surprised, but pleasantly so. Lynn said, "We were really worried when you walked out."

I laughed. "I was caught. I'd done something wrong, without meaning to, but it hurt the two people I love most in the world. I was feeling really, really stupid, and I needed a few minutes to kick myself in private."

Actually, my love for each of them increased markedly because of this event. Lynn was normally the least confrontational person in the household, and Marie tended to run roughshod over everyone, including us. That one had spoken up and the other had curbed her somewhat intemperate nature touched me deeply. They had also worked the issue through together, and agreed on their approach. In all, it was a bonding experience, as we'd all learned how confrontation and compromise *ought* to work.

I hope that you profit from such stories, and readily share your own. Here, my point is that, while you should stand by your principles, there comes a point where you are only defending your shiny little ego, to the detriment of everyone. Intimacy demands sacrifice, but sacrifice *does not* demand loss. You have to know when to let go and work *with* others, when to make "love" and "trust" and "communication" become very real in practice rather than as high-flown and untested theories, or polyamory is guaranteed to suck.

11. You will screw up

Mistakes are inevitable. Fearing them *cannot* and *will not* make them better or prevent them from happening. You *can* minimize the negative consequences, and maximize what you learn from errors, if you approach them honestly.

Certainly, this lifetime is not a dress rehearsal. Everything that you do has consequences, repercussions, fallout. There are no do-overs: once the situation is gone, it is gone permanently, just as certainly as every minute, every second, every beat of a heart is unique. An act in one moment might turn out drastically different if taken but one moment sooner or later.

Though you cannot capture exactly that moment, that mood, or those words, there remains enough similarity that you can glide past similar stumbles – if you can learn to understand why you have made mistakes.

Drop the fear

If you're afraid of making a mistake, then when it happens – and it will – you deny or lie, or you blame (yourself, someone else, the way of the world). That's human nature, but you'll be a lot happier if you recognize it as fact, accept it as true for yourself, and deal with it.

Yes, by all means avoid running off a cliff. Don't go out of your way to do exceedingly stupid things. When you see a steel trap in front of you, try to avoid stepping in it, and restrain yourself from poking it with your fingers to "prove" that it's harmless. Traps and cliffs, though, seem to *follow* us through life and work their way around until they're right in front of us, and we sometimes don't know there's trouble looming until we hear the wind whistling past our ears or that jolly metallic *snap*.

What can you do at that point? Well, saying "Ooops!" is a surprisingly good start, and already puts you ahead of the curve. Recognize that you've walked into trouble, and say something bright like "I think we've just made a mistake."

Then, you work your ass off to avoid blame. See, blaming might give us some sort of satisfaction, but it doesn't get us anywhere. Blame is primarily a very handy way of invalidating any further rational discussion of the problem. If you blame yourself, you get to play at martyrdom, and pretend that the problem is only there because of your innate evil, your poor upbringing, or other personal melodramas. You could blame someone else, and feel vindicated that this other person has tried to tear you down for some hidden, devious, irrational purpose. Or you can blame the world that is so fearful of your potential that you had to be humiliated. Whatever your justification for blame, you've nabbed the culprit, and now life can go on without having to take a good close look at real reasons for why the ugliness happened.

Take responsibility

Oddly, one of the best ways to circumvent blaming is to take responsibility yourself. People with a tendency to act as martyrs can do the "*Mea culpa! Mea culpa maxima!*" gag perpetually, yet never get around to making a simple statement: "I screwed up. I feel bad about that. Now I want to do what I can to fix it." It's far easier for many people to be either be a wimpy martyr – "Beat me! I've been bad again!" – or a self-righteous martyr, than to accept responsibility.

When you seize responsibility, you simultaneously cut yourself off from such superficial retreats as blame and you face the problem squarely, ready to not merely move ahead with your life but to reduce the odds that you're going to easily walk into a similar error in the future. You will never eliminate error from your life, and you shouldn't waste time moping around because you've fallen short of that impossible ideal. Dealing with honestly achieved error as merely another facet of learning, growth, and life means that you regain incredible amounts of energy that would otherwise be spent in pain, recrimination, worry, doubt, and fear.

Taking on responsibility *doesn't* mean that you should beat yourself up for the problem. I'm not talking *fault*, here; I'm talking responsibility, which is not the same thing, and any similarity is merely poor semantics. If I were hit by a car while walking down the street, the fault would obviously lie with the driver. At that point, it is *my* responsibility to get on with my life, and that means getting healed, and not letting my life fall apart while I'm recuperating.

Easily half the serious interpersonal mistakes I've made in my life happened because I let them happen. On the surface, this would probably sound silly to an impartial observer who'd followed the evolution of the problem right up to the precipitating crisis; after all, I'm sharp, but I have a long way to go on getting my godlike omniscience up to speed, and I'm interacting with self-willed people who have their own motivations, agendas, and blind spots. But the fact is that I really want to deny that I'm seeing what I'm seeing. Probably like you, I prefer to avoid pain, and if the only route to avoidance is denial, then I deny, if only a little.

Denial is a human trait, and I fight it regularly. I deny because I am afraid – but fear, and the little tensions that signal its presence, is what usually alerts me to the fact that there's something wrong. As my karate instructor said, "Pain is an alarm that tells you you're broken. But if you let that pain *run* you, when you are in danger, you could lose your life. Don't let the pain run you. Notice it, acknowledge it and what it means, and then set it aside so that you can do what you need to do. When you are safe, then you can find the pain and use it to get strong again."

Like you, if I make a mistake I'm generally long past its clear beginnings when the understanding finally seeps into my consciousness. Rather than get stuck in endless cycles of blame, the first thought that occurs to me is, "Okay, what do I do next?" I talk to the people that would be affected by changes I need to make, which includes whoever else might be at fault. I call up my best friends, lay out the situation as I see it that moment – generally admitting that this could be heavily biased by my viewpoint and the stress of the problem – and ask for their snap judgements. Then I begin to lay out what I need to do to begin getting out of the corner I've walked into. Usually, I keep my advisors apprised, update them, and ask for further input.

In short, taking responsibility for a situation has to be a concept that you keep carefully separate from fault-finding, from blame, and from avoidance of unpleasantness. You're stuck with a problem, and responsible individuals strive to fix the problem, not point fingers.

Learn to love intelligent risk

Robert Anton Wilson proposed dividing people into two groups, *neophobes* and *neophiles*. The former are cautious, taking each step very carefully, hardly ever making a mistake, and being generally comfortable. The latter, by contrast, make a hundred horrible (but sincere!) mistakes for every one of a neophile's successes… and somehow manage to have more ringing successes than a neophile's little cautious steps bring. I know of a man who was a millionaire *three times* before he was 25… and bankrupt twice. Each time he bombed, he learned valuable lessons, and left behind good work, putting support businesses and contractors in the black and training cadres of highly skilled workers who became eminently valuable elsewhere.

The direct analogy in my head is to unconditional love. We – you and me – are out in the desert, making bricks for a city, and we simply don't know what the hell we're doing. So we learn, and we learn to learn. It starts by being willing to make mistakes–excited about it, even – and to learn from the failures.

I've had 30-some sexual partners. I'm still actively intimate with three. Huge "failure" rate, eh? But that includes a 12-year marriage which most folks "knew" wouldn't last six months. And of that 30-some relationships, I still have close friendships with about 25 – whether kissing and cuddling, or sharing problems, consolation, and tough-love. At a large party, it's practically impossible to see a difference in my interaction that would indicate someone is a recent ex, or someone I'm currently practically cohabiting with, or someone I broke up with 16 years ago.

Robert Kiyosaki states in his books that, out of ten business ventures any entrepreneur launches, five will carry their weight but never become particularly great, and three will be abject failures. He suggests that perhaps it would be best to get your failures out of the way early, and pick up some important lessons that will spur your future successes. My experience and observation is that this is not a bad paradigm to follow in relationships in general, and particularly with multilinear intimate relationships. This is very important, so let me be blunt: you may have to go through two or three not-so-great experiences in order to add one person to your family who has the skills at that point in your milieu to both draw strength from and add strength to your family. Even then, you may have to have one or two "almost perfect" relationships before you win big and find someone who could truly be considered a life-partner. Though largely unnoticed, that is as true in monogamy as it is in group marriage. If you are moving from a dyad to a triad, or a triad to a quad, or making the change from a closed relationship to open relating, then you must understand that you are taking on that level of risk.

I observe many neophobic couples who spend years looking for their ideal mate. They do not date outside of their couple bond, even nonsexually, yet they appear to believe that Miss Right will magically appear, and stay forever. At some point, they may forego Miss Right for Miss Right-Now, and if they've guessed far wide of the mark, pay the price in a very un-fun emotional rollercoaster until the whole thing falls apart. The few neophiles understand that they're going to have to go out, meet people, develop flexibility, flirt, date, try out a potential relationship, make mistakes, learn, then try again until they find someone with whom they can form a committed years-long relationship. They accept the misunderstandings that will likely occur, and they are ready to face them as they happen.

Other people

You and everyone else around you will make mistakes. If you have huge difficulties forgiving yourself or other people, then you have no sane reason to believe that you're going to improve this situation by having *more* very-close relationships. If you have no experience with multilinear intimacy, crap *is* gonna happen, and when it does it's going to be sudden and intense. Nothing but experience can teach you flexibility, but if you trip over an opportunity to gain that experience and you are rigid and unyielding and dogmatic in your thinking and interaction with other human beings, then you'll fail. A book has its limits, but we can make a beginning toward eroding such horribly mistaken preconceptions.

First lesson: start thinking about the bad stuff. You need to start this, *right now*. People are far from perfect, and even the best of us slips off the pedestal when we're under stress, or are tempted by an especially juicy-looking reward. Therefore, you ought to be ready for it.

You need to start playing out what Albert Einstein called *thought experiments* – he supposedly developed his theory of relativity from role-playing, by imagining what he'd experience if he were an electron. What I'm suggesting is nowhere near so abstract: you role-play yourself.

I made a brief study of what some call *community-based resolution*. The Hawai'ians have for centuries used what they call *ho'oponopono*, some Native American tribes have resurrected similar methods, and in our modern culture is a rise of addictive interventions. It all comes down to pretty much the same thing, whatever you call it. A group of people affected by someone's malfeasance gets together, including the miscreants. The group is made up of the family members, relatives, and neighbors who feel they've been affected by the antisocial behavior, as well as the victims and their family and friends. Then they lay out their grievances, and the entire group seeks for a combination of apology, restitution, punishment, treatment, and rehabilitation that can solve the problem and thus lessen the burden of the entire community.

The process doesn't have to be so involved. A study of juvenile crime found that young offenders could be very succinct at describing how they ought to be treated. In a typical case, a corrections officer spoke in a friendly manner with a young vandal, and told him a story about a young man who committed a series of acts that frightened and saddened people. The tale was clearly that of the vandal himself. Then the officer asked the boy what should be done with the character in the story. The boy, though hardly a good student, readily suggested a combination of incarceration, restitution, apology, and therapy, a course that all observers agreed was much more strict and comprehensive than likely would have been meted out by a court. Similar findings have been noted for high schools that put their offenders before a jury of their peers.

In *Reality Therapy*, Dr. William Glasser presents many instances where mental patients, even those who are clearly violent and antisocial, prove very capable of providing active and helpful input into their own treatment. In many mental facilities, new patients are put into locked cells and very carefully watched until their potential risk to the staff and other inmates could be assessed. Then, depending on their threat level, they might be kept in such a cell, detained in a heavily guarded ward area with layers of locked doors, or placed in a lower security ward. As a patient showed signs of improvement, he would "graduate" to the less-restricted level, and finally be ready to be released. Glasser noted that some patients were obviously happy and productive in the most restrictive circumstances, and as their diagnosis improved would become more withdrawn and sullen, until they made an outburst or committed an infraction that got them sent back to lockdown, where the process would begin again. One patient in particular was in the middle of this forced climb when Glasser asked him what he needed. The patient said that he was happy at the hospital, but not becoming healthy at the rate the staff appeared to believe, and he was afraid to go home until he was cured. Glasser digested this, then promised the patient he wouldn't be forced out into the world until he agreed that he was better, though he would have to be returned to the locked ward for his most recent infraction. The patient grinned, shook Glasser's hand and thanked him profusely, and his rehabilitation finally proceeded from that point.

Glasser's ultimate point in the book is that, short of actual organic damage to the brain, every human being is capable of readily discerning right from wrong, even if not so great at applying it to themselves and their own behavior. Given the least chance to view their own action objectively, though, they could take an active and effective role in working things out, to everyone's satisfaction. This ought to describe you and the people near you.

Most of the time, the problems you encounter in polyamory will involve and affect other people. There are changes you can freely make all by yourself, but your powers are limited, and you cannot swoop in and single-handedly make it all work. Your ultimate strength is that you can quit; while you shouldn't use this as anything but a last resort, and bringing it up too often as a threat is manipulative and small-minded, you should always consider it.

Aside from such a "cut and run" option, you have to work with others when trouble arises. First and foremost, you must always strive to surround yourself with people who (hopefully) like you are willing to take rapid responsibility and ask the "what must I do now?" sorts of questions. With enough calmness and love and support, you can help the people in your life to increase their capabilities. Some people, though, will take a long time to learn these things, and it may never happen. And even the best will have their weak moments.

Since you are reading these words, you are giving up a degree of naive innocence. Now, you need to help the others in your life, empowering them so that they too can become a little more aware. They then return the favor, and your own awareness expands slightly. The process should never end.

The strong cannot always be carrying the weak. This drags you all down. But you must all be prepared to help each other to overcome the hurdles faced by the individual so that you can all move forward as a community. The more brave (if apprehensive) people that you ally yourself with, the happier you all can be.

Painful thinking

Thought experiments aren't easy at first, and they *will* be profoundly irritating. They're just invaluable, though, so stick with it.

The situations you construct in your head will likely not have much to do with final reality, at a surface level. In fact, if you do it properly, few paths will ever have a chance of occurring, you will actively dodge most of the remainder, you will fix or overcome the tribulations of what's left. Disaster can be largely averted, and damage from the few you didn't avoid is kept to a happy minimum. On a deeper plane, though, a complex crisis, even though imaginary, will have many facets that resemble situations that have hurt you in the past or that frighten you when projected into the future. It's a blessing that people aren't prescient: I can't see where it would be pleasant knowing that a specific disaster awaits me, but I don't know where or when. But, when taking a hard look at the future, that's the very predicament that awaits us all. So, like buying insurance, it's best to prepare diligently even though we secretly pray we'll never have to cash it in.

You have to learn to think about how you might act, the sorts of mistakes you're particularly apt to commit, the potential mistakes of others that would most deeply wound you, the events that would cause you to walk out the door and never look back, and so on. Your partners need to address these same considerations as well. Working together, you have to be unafraid in presenting them to each other. If one person decides to take something as a personal accusation, then it'll need to be clarified with statements such as, "No, I'm not saying that you'd do that. But if someone else in my life, in our life, does that, I am going to need your help, as my friend, in sorting it out."

Until you adapt to performing this exercise in great and gory detail, and it becomes something like second nature or even reflex, you *will* be in a heightened anxiety state. You'll be more emotional, possibly crying once in a while. Your attention span will suffer, you'll be regularly distracted with your thoughts, and you may lose some sleep.

This will suck – in the short term. You're designing an insurance program, remember. Compared to what you're heading off in the future, one hour of nail-biting will save you days, even months, of serious chronic anxiety in the future. Even if the actual situation you encounter is far different from anything you managed to dream up, the fact that you have schooled yourself in dealing with terribly anxiety-causing conflicts will make you less anxious should something such occur, and thus vastly more effective.

Please don't play dumb on this. The first cop-out I hear when I suggest this exercise is, "I don't have any *idea* what could possibly go wrong. As long as I'm involved with good people and we are communicating, no problems will appear. I can't even imagine what something like that would be like." If you've read the book through to this point, you have an inkling of what a sun-baked pile of tripe I consider such thinking to be.

I'll start you off with an easy thought-experiment to practice on.

You have a closed monogamous relationship. You are very happy with your partner – the love, sex, companionship, and cohabitation are all better than you would have hoped. One day, your partner confesses having had an ongoing affair for the previous two years, during lunch hour, two or three times a week. Does that mean that all the love you felt retroactively disappears? Do you decide to end the relationship? If so, how suddenly? Add to this list as occurs to you.

Assuming that you presently have at least one steady partner, or can nab a close friend, take these questions and apply them. Sit and stare at your friend across the table, silently, pondering the way you'd feel if this person took such steps. Better still, ask your partner to join you in a little role-playing exercise, where you ask the questions you would ask in such a situation, and have them respond as if speaking for a person who had indeed been caught out in such an affair. Watch carefully, both yourself and your partner, as the words that you're speaking for an imaginary person in a fictional situation begin to take on an edge – defensiveness, hurt, bullying, triumph, affection, disgust, resignation, exhaustion, pleasure.

Okay, so it's "negative." Why avoid thinking about it, especially if that's your only excuse? Do you *want* to be totally blindsided when it comes to pass?

I've included a few dozen true tales throughout this book demonstrating what a mixed blessing polyamory can be. Take a look at them. Ask yourself how you would have handled each character's situation, or at least give a thought to your snap judgement as to how they ought to have handled it. Should they have seen it coming? Should they have used different words, or presented their feelings in a different order? Where should they have asked questions? What were their vulnerabilities that they acted as they did? What obvious paths did they overlook, and when?

I've probably never met you, but I believe in you. If you're capable of parsing some of the three-syllable words you've encountered in my writing, then I have every reason to believe that you are capable of spinning out more than a few such "what if" stories for yourself. And anyone capable of putting together that sort of scenario is able to shape the ending toward something productive. Heck, you can probably write yourself a few happy endings.

A higher standard for polyfolk

From a stable base, though it should be *easier* to reach out and take emotional chances, I see very little of it in the polyamorous "community." We finally dredge up a little safety, a little stability, and defend it with fangs bared, instead of capitalizing upon the base. It's so easy to forget that happiness is a tent pitched on an escalator – the world has a habit of moving along, no matter how much we happen to like our campsite, and remaining flexible and aware and good-humored is about the only actual long-term solution set.

I don't see hopeless cases – I see incredibly good-hearted people who, if they were willing to actively "court disaster," could hand on a distinctly better world to their grandchildren, and possibly even to their children. If you're sincere about being polyamorous, you can have a role in shaping this world – if you are truly a part of it.

12. Relationship is not security

So far, we've examined myths, the societally ingrained presuppositions and prejudices that color our thoughts about love, relationships, marriage, sex, and likely almost everything else in our lives. We've also dabbled in thinking about how myths that make no sense, and don't work at all well even in the most stable monogamist support structures, have nevertheless managed to attach themselves thoroughly enough to our psyches that they've made the leap to polyamory.

One of the myths that has traveled along from monogamy is that, once you've got an engagement to be married, you're set for life, no more worries or effort. In polyamory, there appears to be the belief that, once you make it past some specific crisis, then it'll be nothing but smooth sailing thereafter. Let me relate a very true story, demonstrating how good people in a near-ideal situation can still fall prey to the ticking time-bombs planted in our heads and hearts by the culture that surrounds us.

Sharon was happy. In fact, it seemed that life got better every time she turned around. Before she and Ralph had married, they'd lived together for eight years, and they had been openly nonmonogamous throughout, augmented by having a wide-ranging social circle that was heavily polyamorous. Three years into the marriage, they developed a steady relationship with another happily married nonmonogamous couple, Liz and Mark. Though they were well along to forming a stable core of four primary dyads, they remained committed to openness, and Mark was involved with Amy.

One day, Mark announced that he was uncomfortable not having a relationship in which he was the sole primary. He was breaking off his contacts with the other three in order to devote himself to Amy. Mark had never brought these things up for discussion with the others; apparently, he had been storing away his doubts and grievances, cutting himself off from his partners, then blaming them for not picking up on his needs.

Sharon was nonplused, but Liz was devastated. Since Sharon and Ralph had a nice large house, there was little problem with moving Liz in with them. During the course of settling in, Liz admitted that, with both women sharing a primary partner, the arrangement would have to be made "more fair."

A few months after Liz moved in, Sharon realized that "more fair" for Liz meant being half of a clearly demarcated couple, specifically with Ralph. His decision to divorce Sharon was another rude shock.

So, here we began with no less than five people with varying degrees of experience in living polyamorously, committed to the lifestyle and to each other, making promises that expanded upon long-term couple-based commitments. Yet, in a year and a half, four of them had precipitously returned to couple-front relating, abandoning their "most important" commitments and connections in order to be a dyad, and completely avoiding any responsibility to bring their doubts and fears forward to their ostensible loved ones so that everyone could participate in seeking out mutually constructive solutions. These people are well-educated and in their 30s, nullifying excuses of either inexperience or midlife crisis. When the dust settled, only Sharon remains committed to something that doesn't resemble marriage with consensual adultery.

Was anyone *lying*? No; they were merely (though tragically) wrong. Basically, they promised something they *thought* they could deliver, and they were mistaken. If you are going to swear allegiance to polyamory, keep this in mind: in the end, good intentions aren't worth squat. If you sign a mortgage for a lovely house based on the income you're going to have from a job you haven't found yet, you're a fool; you're no less foolish if you irrevocably commit to hang your own future on someone else's obvious foolishness. Polyamorous people are absolutely enchanted with good intentions, pleasant fantasies, and trenchant theory, clinging to the assumption that, if all these stones are in their approved places, all the niggling details of practice will fall neatly into place. This is, oddly enough, true. However, it all falls apart when the players discover that their cartload of positive thinking and rationalism doesn't absolve them in the least from occasional Herculean effort, irrational fears, or self-doubt.

When you set out to live your life polyamorously, you should take all your good intentions, and those of everyone involved, and metaphorically frame them and hang them over the fireplace. They are a goal, a worthwhile dream, **not** extant reality. Eric Berne refers to phrases like "he means well" or "she's doing her best" as *tombstones* because that's where they belong, on your tombstone, in the past tense: "He meant well." "She did her best."

Doesn't sound quite so attractive, does it? You have to do better than "good enough" because it's never truly good enough.

Sharon had no particular reason to believe that she was depending on fools, though fools they turned out to be. While they probably all possessed the fundamental intelligence and maturity to present their shifting needs and feelings to each other, four of them ran away, specifically back to the "easier" well-demarcated territory of monogamist living. They talked the good talk, skimmed off the fun stuff, and took the easy way out when confronted with a need for actual determination and problem-solving. I wouldn't be at all surprised if, a few years down the road, some or all of Sharon's ex-partners decide they're really poly after all, and for the good of everyone, I hope that their reliability and depth of commitment, as demonstrated previously, is hauled out into the open.

Having a relationship does nothing to protect you from change. Neither small nor large is inherently more stable. Even if it's a sprawling, well-established intimate network, one crisis can blow the whole thing apart – and crises tend to come in rolling sequences, as the stresses added by just one problem will call attention to further weaknesses. If you are lacking in insight, communication, problem-solving skills, and experience in dealing with lesser crises, only a little shaking will be required to bring down what turns out to be a house of cards.

13. Communication: the big lie

The story goes that Mohandas Gandhi was asked for his opinion on Western civilization. He replied, "I think it's a very nice idea."

Likewise, I say that communication is a great idea, but most people (probably including you) don't have the faintest idea of how to go about it, much less the required determination. The majority of people, in fact, detest unimpeded communication. When you hang out with polyamorous people, you'll read and hear phrases such as "Communicate, communicate, communicate!" and "communication is key" until they become an addition to the background noise of daily life, and you ignore them.

By "communication," most people mean talking. They appear to be working from the assumption that, since they talk to a lot of people, they must be skilled at communication. This is as shallow as calling every person you've ever met a "friend." Talking is noise that may possibly possess meaning, but this is not at all a guarantee.

A little theory

Mathematicians differentiate between *data* and *information*. Everyone else confuses these terms, using them interchangeably, but they're quite different. Everything is data, whether it be a rhinoceros, a quark, a mathematical operator, a sound, a color, existence or nonexistence.

Information cannot exist without an intelligence to process it. Data can become information, if it is sensed or conceived. Information tends to spawn further information. To put it another way, data is raw material, information is finished product (whether one part or a whole system).

Even a quiet-seeming world is packed full of data. When our eyes are open, and we begin shoveling bits and bytes into that poor overworked brain, we are able to quickly overload the front end, the input device. Data that could have had very high significance is lost, drowned out in the overwhelming noise.

I'm no expert in the subject, but I can help you out with a brief overview of the concepts as they apply to complex intimacy.

Polyamory is *terra incognita*, unknown territory, even for those who are experienced with it. In order to map out your corner of the world, you need more **awareness** of what is going on around you and within you. That could quickly lead to gibbering insanity, because there is so much data that *might* be of use to you, and most of it is flying in your face. Even if you hold onto your mind, you'll be expending so much effort on sorting and winnowing the data that you won't be able to do anything useful, or fun.

Hence, the immediately second step: **filtering**. Until you learn a firm grasp of seeking the information you need, you will have to ruthlessly weed the data. The goal here is to achieve a sort of automatic filtering capability. We do this all the time, but very few people are aware of it. If you've ever experienced a strong reaction to a mass-produced product in a television commercial, that's what it's like when your filtering mechanisms have been set. You need to learn how to set them yourself, consciously, so that the messages of most importance to you are the ones most likely to get through.

After filtering comes **questioning**, primarily variations upon that core mystery of the Universe: "Why?" Armed with goals, you can then create less-sweeping questions. Since the questions are simpler, you start looking for the data that will bring you suitable answers. Rather than casting about randomly, or barraging yourself with all the data clamoring for your attention (which is where we started), you are by this point empowered to dive right to the heart of the matter and pull the answers you need right out of the air. You scan the numbers, and the ones you need seem to leap out at you.

You may be surprised that I don't offer some sort of "answering" stage. The simple explanation lies in the beauty of a well-posited and appropriate question: put to an intelligent being, such a question all but answers itself.

I do caution you not to confuse answers with *solutions*. Answers are still part of analysis; they get you closer to your goal, true, but they are part of an interim step.

When you begin getting the answers you need, more questions arise that might lead you to more pertinent (or even more fruitful) queries. I call this **hysteresis**, though the programmers among you might prefer **recursion**. This is not dissimilar from an artist who dabs at the canvas, steps back to survey how the change affects the painting as a whole, then moves forward to dab further.

At some point, maybe even before all the data is in, you will begin guessing at what the message is. The analysis of any bit of information can always be refined, possibly forever; literally, you cannot possibly know everything. You have to have adequate information, surely, but if you wait for perfection, you'll likely wait eternally. The art is in knowing from a combination of skill and intuition when a **decision** probably ought to be made.

Making sense

You're human. Polyamory doesn't exempt you from that. You are occasionally therefore an outright and indisputable pain in the ass. Selfish, vain, irritable, inconsiderate, rude. Bad enough that one of us has to be in the room; when you reach two it's iffy but tolerable. Add more, and the potential for Big Problems begins to expand exponentially. That's why it bugs me when so many people pat themselves on the back for their excellent communication skills when what they're actually saying is, "We have hardly ever fired a gun in anger" – lack of bloodshed doesn't signal clear success so much as lack of suitable opportunity. To say, "We communicate very well" generally means "I am asserting my own highly biased opinion that we have communicated well to this point." There's no reason to believe that this communication exists, much less a guarantee that it will persist into the nearest future.

Actual communication is emotionally risky. To communicate, you have to open yourself up to the possibility of disapprobation, whether from what you say, how you say it, under what circumstances you say it, and so on. If you're not risking, you're not communicating in any deep sense.

Even if the other people possess the patience of saints and a parallel depth of human understanding, each of us carries a critic whose sole purpose is to project our insecurities onto the people around us. If you were to be marooned on a tropical island, years might pass before you began doing away with behaviors intended to curry the approbation of the phantom audience that lurks in your skull. If we are that vulnerable to long-past interactions, then imagine how easy it is for each of us to be manipulated by well-aimed jabs, real or imaginary, in the here-and-now.

People sincerely believe that filling a room with noise is the same as communicating. Sure, we can *say* "communicate!" but the simple fact of our culture and world is that:

- most people don't know *why* they do what they do
- most people are afraid to begin looking
- most people are scared to death of honest self-disclosure, even if they've caught a glimpse of how to do so.

And with all three of these things in place, "communication" per se is probably impossible.

The solution? Root these things out. Kill them with information, the best information that you have at hand. Undermine them at every opportunity. Take emotional risks by being honest, expect and reward honesty from others, and deal directly with hurt feelings.

If you are going to truly communicate, there are a few things that *must* be present. You must be able to present your thoughts and feelings in a manner that is both thorough and honest. You have to choose the words that best fit what you are trying to say, even if that means backing up and offering an explanation of your choice. You must do so with a tone of voice that is relatively far from mocking, deriding, belittling, whining, or accusing. Your body language must be a posture that doesn't suggest either attack or defense. Your word choice must be generally straightforward, without an edge of anger.

To get to these things in the first place, you have to learn to be a very good observer of yourself. You have to spot any tension in your own body and voice, and learn to relax it, preferably gaining this ability as a reflex. You have to be aware of the way your words change when you are under various stresses.

And once you've gained good habits in your own communication style, you must begin to ask for the same from the people with whom you are attempting to communicate.

The very tools with which we attempt to communicate are flawed. Phrases or even mere single words pick up a vast freight of meanings that aren't what we intend when they fall out of our mouths. Leave out tone of voice, body language, complex context, situation, and relational history, and you can still get into heaps of trouble with a poorly chosen word, as many users of the Internet can testify.

Consider one unfortunate *cul de sac* of our language. "I don't care" can as easily mean "great idea!" or "fine with me!" as "well, I suppose so…" or "sure, go off and have fun, I'll just sit here in the dark" or "whatever, but I'll get even" or "yeah, okay, stop blocking the television."

Once, my spouse was going out on a date, and asked me if I was okay with this. I realized that "I don't care" was dishonest. So, I said, "Well, I don't see him as my friend, and I don't think he'll make a long-term relationship, but I can't see where he'd hurt you, and you'll probably have fun. He might try to get between us; if he does, will you tell him to get lost?" She laughed, told me *that* would definitely happen, so I kissed her, told her I'd be home if her date bombed, and shooed her out the door. I had a nice quiet evening, she had fun, and decided he wasn't someone she wanted to be involved with on a regular basis.

So: did I care? Hell, yes. If you have *zero* concerns about losing someone you love, then you maybe don't love them so much after all, or have such a lousy self-image that you don't think you deserve to be happy.

But "caring" doesn't equate with "controlling." Be honest, speak your mind, mention any least little doubt that you have – about yourself, your partner, his/her date, your dyad, their dyad, the odds of getting hit by a meteor while on the date... whatever. Give your partner the full set of data, so that they can judge for themselves, as a responsible adult.

To **trust** does not mean to let someone do whatever the hell they want without consequences. (More thanks to Gandhi.) *Real* trust buds when you don't censor your own thinking, blossoms when you offer these thoughts in an honest, loving, and non-attacking manner, and reaches full bloom when the recipient accepts them in a like manner. When you can manage that (and can do so often, if not always), then you are indeed communicating.

Veto power

In polyamory, some believe that partners in a primary relationship *must* have the right to restrict the activities of their partner; this is commonly called a **veto**. Others work from the theory that they *ought* to have absolute trust in each other, therefore they claim that they already *do* have this level of trust and thus no control over each other's actions.

Both are only extremes. They are each deeply flawed, yet they each have strengths that I would recommend to you. Let's look a little closer, then at all that territory in the middle.

As a brute-force solution, the veto *cannot* work, because there is no practical way to actually control the actions of another human being that couldn't get you sentenced to jail. You can threaten what you will (divorce, abandonment, slander, etc.), but that doesn't physically restrain someone from acting. A veto that isn't backed up with an enforceable threat of sufficient magnitude to make the liable party stop and think carefully before *any* potential boobish behavior is nothing but window dressing; humans being inherently contrary creatures, it practically begs to be defied. A veto with teeth is coercive, a heavy and sharp sword forever suspended over your head by a filament.

Replacing the veto détente with ideal trust is no wiser. A business consultant told me, "A verbal contract isn't worth the paper it's written on." Even if we manage to root out our irrational destructive tendencies, and monitor ourselves closely enough to avoid some of the more egregious behaviors, we are nevertheless imperfect beings: we make honest mistakes. If such an error is perceived by one partner to have violated the trust between them, then trust is indeed dead.

A potential middle ground would be to actually sit down and write up a contract between you. This piece of paper then spells out the rights and responsibilities of each party, including things like behaviors in certain specific situations, penalties for violations, and the means by which these penalties will be enforced if there's a breach. I'm not saying that such a contract would be enforceable in any court, but when two or more people sit down together, define the situation thoroughly and concisely, phrase it in such a way that it can be written, and review the now-mutual understanding in stark black print, they all have a stake in the situation, and are much less likely to misremember or misunderstand it.

What you need is both the trust *and* the veto, and *neither*. Your trust is not so much in the other person's future actions, or even their feelings, but that they will at least listen to your doubts and fears, consider them in a manner that is both judicious and loving, and then act in an appropriate manner.

Our married dyad had a basic rule that we brought to our subsequent relationships: "Talk to me ASAP." It was usual that if one of us met an interesting person at a party, we'd discuss it on the way home, just in case something developed subsequently (most surprises being, by their nature, unpleasant). We had already agreed upon a rule that, unless other plans were made ahead of time, we would go home together from any gathering we attended together, as that was basically a date for us, so attempting to change plans mid-evening was identical to breaking our date – "get their number, make a date" was how we phrased it. The point was not control, but communication. We trusted that we'd get a fair hearing, and each of us held ourselves to timely disclosure, largely to encourage such disclosure from each other.

And we indeed had such dates. Once, I was utterly fascinated by a young woman, who slowly revealed herself to be far wackier than could have been apprehended at first. My partner took me aside, and simply said, "Are you sure that this is what you want?" I stood back, looked at it objectively – and broke off the relationship two days later. I stayed with my partner another 10 years; since I am highly averse to being controlled, I offer this longevity as evidence supporting our respect for each other's opinions. Not veto power, just mutual trust. To this day, it's not unusual for me to get the opinion of three or more current or previous lovers when I'm smitten anew.

The messy parts

In order to communicate, you must rely on *disclosure*, a word that encompasses honesty and completeness and risk-taking. A basic example of this would be where I'm at a party with a date, and one of my close friends takes me aside, saying, "I can't put it into words, but I get an uneasy feeling watching the way she acts around you." Another would be where I have said, "I know you have a date tonight, but I'm feeling really insecure. Could you reschedule, and stay with me instead?" It all comes down to stating facts in a plain and occasionally downright bald fashion, even if the words are less than perfect, rather than waiting for a "perfect" moment or a flawless presentation.

There is a fine line between disclosure and *attack*. For instance, if I tell someone that I've got a primary, and right now I only need one, that's disclosure. If I tell her this every time I see her – maybe hourly – that's attack. If I choose words that seem neutral to others within earshot, but that I ought to know full well are emotionally loaded for someone and will prompt a heated response, that is attack.

Communicative confrontation is necessary, and it doesn't always work out well but it's got to be done. I have a truly **huge** ego, so it's virtually impossible to *not* step on it occasionally. The people I trust are the ones who can present me with a judicious version of the unvarnished truth, and trust that (a) I'll feel stupid, which looks a lot like anger, and (b) I won't be angry at someone who dares to look through the cloud of bullcrap that sometimes accretes around me.

Be loving, but stick to your guns. In the long term, it's a choice between honesty and trust, and stagnation and eventual explosion. Don't ignore truth just to keep the peace – that's practically the definition of abuse and codependence.

14. You don't know what you're saying: language & metalanguage

Throughout this book, I emphasize tightening the precision of your language and the "standard" terms and phrases we use to perform the acts that vaguely resemble interpersonal communication. This isn't some mere pedantic exercise. The words we use are strong indicators of how we think and feel about a subject or situation. Much more importantly, though, the words we choose, and the way in which we use them, all deeply affects how we are *able* to think, a fact that has been proven time and again, yet is widely ignored.

You may have had some exposure to *NLP* (neuro-linguistic programming), or to the *general semantics* of Korzybski or Hayakawa. Advanced students may have read Linebarger's *Psychological Warfare* or Ellul's *Propaganda*, or *Programming and Metaprogramming in the Human Biocomputer*. At the very least, you may have made use of hypnotherapy or affirmations. Similar concepts appear in everything from studies of body language (more properly called *kinesics*, as it's much more than generalized "body" communication, comprising stance, posture, gesture, facial expression, eye movement, voice-stress patterns, word choice, and phrasing) to the branch of social psychology known as *symbolic interactionism*. If you want a good grounding in the subject, you might begin with Suzette Haden Elgin's "Verbal Self-Defense" books.

Symbolic activity is important for two reasons, the classic two-edged sword:
- *what we do* is an important indicator of our mental and emotional state; and
- *what we do* not only reinforces what is inside of us, but can program or reprogram those things.

Basically–for our purposes, at least – it all comes down to the same thing, or rather the same set of things. While a million words *might* make a good dent in the subject, we'll skim briefly over some of the concepts, if only to sketch an explanation of my apparent obsession.

Conscious framing

If you control the language, you control the thinking. That is at the root of George Orwell's *1984*, with such concepts as *newspeak* (and *thoughtcrime*). A semantician will refer to this as *controlling the frame*. As my political science professor put it (likely cribbing from some previous philosopher), "If you give someone a list from which they may choose, you are not granting them freedom of choice."

If you're going to be polyamorous, you're going to have to be as free as you can from "either-or" thinking. The situations you encounter won't fit neatly into little boxes, and can't be solved by running through a checklist. You need to have the soul of an artist and the analytical capabilities of a businessperson. Unless you are in one of the uncommon situations where decisions have to be made quickly, options should only be constrained by things like laws of physics, availability of assets, considerations of legality, and the like.

You can work with frames: modify, edit, emend, expand, redefine, combine, split, or eliminate. Never forget that insoluble problems are usually a symptom of the wrong point of view. Reframing could simplify a problem or even eliminate it altogether.

And therein lies a danger. One of the meanest traps I have seen imported into polyamory is to provoke a situation, then shift the frame, and define the adversary's response in terms of the newly defined frame. Anyone who has worked with codependent chronic victims will know this one: work diligently in private to undermine the adversary, ensuring that one more little well-camouflaged dig (before a relatively neutral audience) will set off a spectacular reaction, thus gaining tons of sympathy for the "victim."

If you are a chronic victim, and self-aware enough to realize it, please seek professional help because, until therapy can help you straighten out a few of your issues, you will be *incapable* of sustaining a relationship with someone emotionally healthy. If you are the adversary, you can attempt to get your partner into therapy – you both likely need it if you have any hope of being together – but otherwise you either need to escape, suddenly and thoroughly, or to start keeping meticulous records of what actually occurs in those "setup" moments that are hidden from the public eye, up to and including secretly recording their own conversations – okay, so it sounds like mere paranoia, but I have observed third parties who had witnessed the *sub rosa* game-playing, and had spoken separately on many occasions to both parties, yet they fell prey to their own tendencies toward victimization and took the side of the "victim" when a crisis had been successfully provoked. When the frame shifts, all bets are off as to who will end up where.

After my wife ended our relationship, I met up with a mutual friend who pulled me aside and asked, "What the hell is going on with you two?" I laughed, and asked, "So, which version did you hear? The one where she threw me out in a fit of righteous indignation for my various sins? Or the one where she was heartbroken because I stormed out of the house for no apparent reason?" His eyes slowly widened as it dawned on him that he had indeed received both tales, and finally he said, in a tone of sheer wonder, "Ohhhh."

Anyone can learn to control the referential frame in a healthy manner, though. You won't do it perfectly all the time, especially the first times out of the blocks, but like so many other crafts, theory can never take the place of a good eye and a steady hand developed from practice and its mistakes. Shaping the frame requires patience, objectivity, tolerance, and lots of love. Do it enough and it becomes so easy that you'll probably stop being aware of it, especially because everyone around you will have it down by then. For instance, when you raise a complaint in a manner you felt was reasonable, and end up being verbally assaulted, you can probably make a huge difference with just a few words. If the shouter hasn't walked away by the end of the tirade, and is simply nursing a steaming scowl, then the chances aren't half bad. Stand back (metaphorically) from your stung pride, become curious and compassionate, look straight at their eyes (even if they refuse to meet your gaze), and ask, "Why does that make you so angry?"

That's called *unpacking*. By addressing the attack in such a manner (especially speaking in the present tense), you are quietly moving the frame of reference, from "Here's how you have hurt me" to "I want to help you to feel better." You redefine the frame from one of accusation and retribution, and turn it into one of openness and risk (yours), which is less accessible to defensive attack. When the topic is especially sensitive, or one or more of the involved people is mostly new to this approach, you might have to go through a few iterations of meeting personalized digs with simple and loving questions (sometimes repeating the same question until the barriers to discussion begin to weaken).

Accidental self-programming

The unconscious is *lousy* at hearing and remembering certain parts of speech–for instance, superlatives. It's best at simple nouns and verbs and objects, and that's about it. Modifiers fade rapidly. So, for example, "I don't want to be fat" gets packed down to just "I … fat." With the mind putting the simplest, most general verb in place of the ellipsis, what your unconscious registers is "I am fat." And verbs derived from *be*, such as *am* or *is*, are dangerous because they are not clearly constrained in time or by circumstance, so "I am fat" then unzips to "I have always been and always will be fat – I am inherently fat." You can see how supposedly "positive" affirmations such as "I don't want to be fat" actually undermine attempts at weight reduction: why fight such a simply-stated universal truth?

You get past this by framing as much of your thinking as you can in simple positive statements, without giving your unconscious mind much room for the equivocation that is turned negative.

While you're at it, learn to own your feelings. If something makes you angry, don't go for mushy thinking and say, "That could make some people feel bad." Equivocation is death. Ditch the "could" and "might" stuff, get rid of the vague label for the feeling, then put yourself into the sentence: "I feel angry." In fact, even that is a half-assed statement: "feel" has been rendered squishy, so what your unconscious mind will be hearing is, "I feel as if I might be angry," and you rapidly cycle away from the feeling! Instead, take a chance and own that feeling implicitly: "I am angry."

Such is the power of words. Such is the power that your words have over you, and over the people around you. The words that you use, whether speaking or thinking, matter. If you practice paying attention to the words you use in thought and speech, your choices will improve, and this will quickly become second nature. As with everything else, you'll backslide and regress occasionally, but changing your relationship to words will make surprising improvements in your life, and in your interactions with other people.

Tone of voice

Many of the people in my life have some experience in theatre or music. Because they've developed their ear for nuances of tone and the emotions that these can communicate, their awareness of tone of voice is greater than most. Though an improvement, the fit is far from perfect, but my own skills have been handy.

There was an increasing tension between my partners, Tara and Marie. I asked each of them what was going on, and they were incapable of telling me; they couldn't nail it down themselves. Their attempts at communicating, so that they could dig out and resolve the elusive problem, just seemed to make things worse. This worried me deeply, as I loved them both, and I knew they loved each other. The frustration could only grow, and didn't bode well for our triad.

As I had no intention of losing a relationship over something so unsatisfying as "irreconcilable differences," I decided to take charge.

I sat both of my partners down, and asked them to tell me what was going on. This devolved quickly into rising voices, interruption, and accusations. I waved them both to silence, the started again. "Marie, tell me your side of it." She did, and I could almost feel the tension radiating from Tara as Marie went on, and soon we were back to dueling interruptions.

Next attempt, I asked that we work together respectfully. I told them both that I would ask questions, that I would stop them when I felt I had enough for that phase, that there would be no interruptions and each would speak only when I asked them to, and that I would restate what I felt each was saying and the other would respond to my words, not what had been said.

This didn't get us a whole lot further, but I finally noticed what my unconscious had been trying to call attention to.

"Marie," I said, "let's start again." She did, and I noted that there was a patronizing tone creeping into her voice. I cut her off mid-word. "Okay, now say that again, but in a neutral tone of voice, as if you're just reading it aloud." I looked at Marie, then Tara. They were both clearly puzzled, but I knew I was on to something.

Still looking baffled, Marie repeated herself, almost word for word, but in a passionless, calm, even tone.

When Marie had stated her complaint, I turned to Tara. "All right, now respond to what she said, in a neutral tone of voice," which she did.

In perhaps five more minutes, we got to the root of the problem, negotiated it, and solved much confusion and anger that had been accreting around the miscommunication.

As it turns out, Marie had been afraid of losing Tara, and this had put a caustic-sounding edge in her tone. Meanwhile, Tara was responding to this as though it was her mother's berating tone, which put angry defensiveness into her own voice. In turn, Marie interpreted this as her own mother's sarcasm. The result was much like putting a microphone directly in front of a high-powered PA speaker: feedback. (Actually, it's called "positive feedback," because the noise builds as it is reamplified, but there's nothing else positive about it.)

The irony here is that both Tara and Marie were conversant in multiple languages, which possibly made them too sensitive on some unconscious, non-English level. At the same time, they were communicating in their tone far more than they consciously intended, via tone, which was then being misinterpreted. A similar phenomenon is what a friend calls "agreeing in rising tones," where the surface communication is very positive, yet the parties end up practically in tears and cannot even understand their own reactions.

Listening to hear, talking to be heard

Zach tells Ariel, "Things seem to be going very well between you and Joel. I know it sounds silly, but I'm really worried that you're going to break up with me to have more time for him." Ariel can reply in a (probably infinite) number of ways. I'd like you to consider some of the more obvious or common, with hopes that you can pick the most effective. Among them:

That won't happen.
That's ridiculous.
If that's the way you feel, then maybe we should end it right now.
I'm tired of you complaining about Joel.
I'm tired of you complaining about me.
I'm tired of you complaining about my relationships.
I'm tired of you complaining about our relationship.
Why would you feel that way?
Why are you feeling that way?
What is making you feel that way?
What can you do to fix that?
What can I do to fix that?
What can we do to fix that?

Zach knows that he's opening up such a can of worms by simply voicing his insecurity, even though he's even-handed in his presentation, and is clearly owning responsibility for these feelings. I hope it's beginning to be clear, though, that if he buries those doubts, he will begin to feel increasingly distant from Ariel. So, while he's prepared for the potential of a reaction from the top of the list, his hope is that they can arrive at something nearer the bottom. He's also aware that the negative reactions signify Ariel's insecurity, and that they possibly stem from his own previous errors in communication. If Ariel is up to Zach's level, she will recognize her own reactions that are leading up to those statements, wonder at their cause, and look for assistance in digging out the insecurity that prodded her to lash out. Zach will be wise to roll with the punch like any good boxer, since such an ugly reflex might have nothing to do with the way Ariel actually thinks or feels.

There we are, back to trust tempered with hope for improvement.

15. It sucks to be secondary

When you have a relationship with someone who's in a productively intertwined dyad, it seems like your good times, though extraordinary, are overshadowed by the potential for priorities elsewhere.

Let's choose a slight stereotype and say you're involved with a career-oriented woman married to an executive. A sizable number of his weekends go to meetings. When one of those merry fetes is canceled, and your lover doesn't have anything actually scheduled, can you blame them for wanting to take advantage of the time to be together? You've got even less cause to feel snubbed if you've been sort of taking it for granted that most of her free weekends (due to the vagaries of trying to mesh their professional schedules) are wide open, and you can usually swoop in if you're in the mood.

Escalate that a little bit. You and your lover have been operating under the assumption that most of the weekends are for the two of you. But, due to the way her husband's office has scheduled their production rollout, the next three months won't require him to be constantly in the office, at an off-site meeting, or in the next state working out details with the software designers. He gets to be home, enjoying most weekends with his spouse.

It's not like he's a total stranger to you; in fact, you both appear to be developing a friendship, when he has time to be social. But you have discovered a lurking fear that you're not going to have any time alone with your partner for the next quarter. He doesn't have a girlfriend, because generally he barely has time to have a wife. You could rationalize that this is his problem, except that, well, you don't have another lover, either, so that line of reasoning could become quickly embarrassing for you if you were to wield it.

Generally, if they encounter a crisis, whether over jobs or children or illness, they will close ranks and face the situation as a couple, leaving you feeling neglected. On the other hand, if you should encounter a similar crisis, the result will be canceling of dates "until you feel better" – and leaving you feeling neglected.

There are many ways to work around this – all small, to be sure, but they can add quickly up into something formidable. Firstly, all of you need to avoid blinding yourselves by clinging to the belief that some sort of equality exists. If you are deeply attached to someone who is in a healthy couple, your position cannot possibly be equated with that of your partner's partner.

With that erroneous assumption held at bay, the three of you are in a position to approach each situation and even moment constructively. Let's take Hank and Morgana, a married couple. Pete, Morgana's boyfriend, has been putting in loads of overtime recently, which makes setting up long romantic evenings impossible; when he does come up with a free evening, it's generally a surprise to him, which makes any degree of planning impossible. Hank might suggest to Morgana that she plan an occasional late dinner with Pete during the high-demand time, the sort of "base-touching" that is important to friendship, and vital to building a strong intimate relationship. In this case, Hank demonstrates understanding that waiting for a "perfect" moment to have time together is a way of keeping distance built into a relationship – sometimes you just have to take advantage of the cards you've been dealt, even as you're working for future betterment.

If you are someone's secondary relationship, or you are maintaining an intimate relationship that has lower priority to others in your life, then facing situations head-on can go far toward defusing sticky situations as they happen, or even before they occur. Left to themselves, secondary relationships can indeed suck, but they don't have to unless you let them.

16. It sucks to be primary

Let's look at the in-built bliss that awaits the partners in a primary dyad.

It's Thursday afternoon, and Ralph is looking forward to spending a few days by himself. He has a very happy marriage with Carol, who is planning a weekend at the lake with her lover of three years, Kevin. Ralph's partner, Ann, is out of town on a work assignment.

Ralph plans to stay up all hours, playing the stereo at high volume, working on an idea for a book, and generally enjoying the freedoms attendant to living alone.

Wednesday evening, Carol is exhausted after work, and falls right into bed after dinner. By Thursday, she's looking less than perfect, and has to cancel her weekend with Kevin. As it develops into a bronchial infection, Ralph spends his spare time caring for Carol, rushing home as soon as he can get free from work, and taking a couple of days off himself to bring her to the hospital for assorted tests and diagnoses.

After two weeks, Carol is recovering nicely, though Ralph is exhausted from his extra duties. Ann has been back in town for days, but Ralph has been tending to Carol, refilling vaporizers, making sure she kept up with fluid intake and antibiotics. Intimate time with Carol has been nonexistent, of course.

One evening, as he's washing dishes, Ralph stretches at a knot in his shoulders, and realizes that there's nothing he would rather do than spend a weekend at the cabin with Carol, relaxing from their shared tribulations and enjoying each other's company. A few minutes later, when Carol steps out of her office, Ralph outlines his plan.

Carol looks at him perplexedly. "I've already made plans for the weekend with Kevin."

"Oh," says Ralph, momentarily taken aback. "But we've been having such a difficult time of it recently. I would really like to have some time with you."

Carol shakes her head. "I don't understand how you can say that – we've had almost two whole weeks together."

When you're a primary, you are first in line for many things, most especially when the unpleasant stuff hits the fan. Yet, in better times, you will find yourself in awkward, frustrating situations where all your years of partnership count for nothing, or even count against you when your partner decides that newer relationships need more of the focus in order to get things up to speed. When NRE takes hold, you may even find yourself on one side or the other of blaming your partner for their self-centeredness or obstinacy.

The primary bonds are what can keep a complex relationship together when difficulty strikes. Even an intimate network is only as strong as the typical dyadic bonds therein.

But these benefits are not some sort of automatically functioning mechanism. They exist as potential, as a resource that can be built and nurtured to be relied upon when necessary. These bonds must be recognized, and given some degree of priority – not because your primary partner is more important than a secondary on an emotional level, or in any way as a reflection upon their worth as a human being, but because your lives as a primary dyad are so much more intertwined on many levels.

If this is not recognized, compensated for, and encouraged, you are sending a large range of signals to the effect that you are happy to put that relationship at risk for the benefit of relational situations that are to some degree speculative. These signals are being picked up by your friends, your children, your other partners (especially those who have cause to believe they are receiving a higher degree of consideration), your primary partner, and yourself. Any of those (including you) may be therefore getting the impression that you are willing to sacrifice your primary relationship should something interesting appear. Whether true or not, this undercuts the strength and resilience of the primary relationship.

As an example, one such signal set is quite common. That is where, by your words or actions, you say, "I am giving this person higher priority than you, because I see you all the time." This overlooks the fact that "all the time" includes the bulk of health and familial crises, for instance. That time might include childcare and household chores, which is difficult to compare directly to time spent with a new lover who is childfree or has an income with few long-term expenses such as a mortgage. In some relationships, the communication is closer to, "I can see you anytime I want, so I won't because I associate so many difficulties with you." The partner making that statement is usually very shocked and hurt when they get a flat demand for change – or a goodbye note.

So, some of the words change, but the reality is as valid: If you are someone's primary relationship, or you are maintaining an intimate relationship that has higher priority to others in your life, then facing situations head-on can go far toward defusing sticky situations as they happen, or even before they occur. Left to themselves, primary relationships can indeed suck, but they don't have to unless you let them.

17. It sucks to be polyamorous

Surprised that I'd say that? You shouldn't be. Sooner or later, however much you might be in love, or find yourself infected with a missionary zeal to change the world with the true light of polyamory, you will hit bottom. Though polyamory is of itself no more complex or demanding than a rich monogamous life filled with friends and family, polyamory has none of the societal supports. Just like people dream of going back to "the good old days" when things were so much better, whether that fantasy is set a few years ago or back in the Middle Ages or even ancient times, the problems of the moment will seem to pale compared to the imagined perfection that was left behind.

This can occur at any time, and there's nothing to prevent it from recurring. Even if you believe yourself to be immune, one of your partners may start to feel this way, and before you know it that person has paired off with someone else to announce that they're moving out – soon.

So, I'm not being sarcastic to say that polyamory sucks. Looked at through the lens of monogamy, it *does* suck. Living polyamorously is a struggle, without nice easy remedies, even illusory ones. When the troubles seem to pile up – and often they do – it is a perfectly natural reaction to want to run away. I'm here to tell you to embrace the feeling, to not beat yourself up for it, but to stand your ground.

First, find the exit

Late one night, my friend Billie called, waking me from a sound sleep. I picked up the telephone to the sound of barely controlled sobbing. Once I had her calmed down, I managed to get out of her that she'd had a huge argument with Zach, her fiancè of two years, over something that had been building since they met.

I gave her the bad news first. "Are you thinking about leaving him, packing your bags and being out by the weekend?"

Billie drew a shaky breath. "Yes."

"Good," I replied. "You have been avoiding facing up to these problems because you were afraid that it would lead to the end of your relationship," a relationship I knew was generally very happy for both of them.

Continuing, I said, "I expect you to calm down, tell him that you will talk this out tomorrow night, then go and sleep on the sofa."

I finished with the good news. "You've been feeling trapped, without realizing it. That's kept you from dealing with what needs to be dealt with. Now that you know there is a way out, an exit, I expect you to go back and see what you can work out. You aren't trapped, so I know that you can do your best. You still love Zach, and with good reason. I'm reasonably sure that he loves you. If you're ready to leave, you have nothing to lose, and everything to gain, for both of you."

This was probably the right tack, as they didn't have significant problems for another two years. Things fell apart again, they separated for six months (again applying my suggestions), then moved together to a new apartment, married a year later, and remained happy for five more years.

There are various degrees of withdrawal or running away. Sure, sometimes you need to make a clean break, or you get one foisted upon you, but that is hardly the only option. More often, you just need to step back for five minutes, or a few days, or even a year, in order to better appreciate where you stand, what you have, and what you can offer.

The form ingrained in our society, though, is poor. You hit a problem, you break up. Or you break up, cool down enough to "forget" about it, return to the status quo, and repeat the cycle. The problem with both of these is that nobody involved really tends to *learn* anything. Much serial monogamy is outright obsessive, refusing to be open to negotiation, to give up some minor irritating habit or being unable to tolerate the same in others. In short, the baggage moves along with you, poisoning relationship after relationship. I pity my friend Bert, who has had seven "serious" long-term relationships in the time I've known him (variously poly, open, and monogamous), because he's not on even cordial speaking terms with any of his ex-lovers – I have current telephone numbers for more than half of mine, and we enjoy seeing each other at social events.

I'm hardly immune to screwing up. What makes me different is that I'm not afraid to admit error, fault, blindnesses, or simple orneriness. Any defensiveness I feel is swamped by chagrin that I played a major part in allowing things to run so badly awry.

The two-way door

No matter that you are incredibly invested in a situation – emotionally, financially, whatever – you might have to abandon ship. That includes the entire lifestyle of polyamory as well.

But: much as you can end up terribly abused by the collapse of a relationship yet still manage to accept love, ditching polyamory after a terrible experience doesn't preclude you in the least from trying again. Burning your bridges would be a bad idea, of course – just because polyamory appears to have let you down is no good reason for, say, putting the name, address, telephone number, and e-mail of members in your local polyamory discussion group onto handbills that suddenly sprout all over your city, with an extra sheaf to each of the more fanatic religious groups in the area. We're none of us perfect, and some of these forcibly outed folks might still carry a little bit of a grudge should you try to rejoin them in a year or two.

Barring such shenanigans, you can always give polyamory another try should your circumstances change (as they certainly appear to). Few polyamorous people blame those of their ranks who, for one reason or another, close down their adventurous nature and settle into closed monogamy. Leaving aside the usual smattering of clueless firebrands, we all know that, in the end, happiness is happiness, and we will not hold it against you if your obvious joy and fulfillment requires that you take another trail.

I know why some might think negatively, though. At the present day, many of those who subscribe to polyamory walked into it thinking that their eyes were open. The rest of us, though, couldn't put a date on our "conversion" if we had to. At some point, possibly by stumbling into two well-founded loving relationships simultaneously, we simply woke up to the fact that this is what we were, this is what we were doing. We most certainly came through the door, but we don't remember the event. That sort of confusion might make a person envious of someone who is capable of not just finding the door, but of using it.

If you're not the kind of person who is willing to do what needs to be done, to do what is best in a given situation, then you shouldn't be taking the risk of polyamory in the first place. I would worry about those who stay grimly poly if it isn't richly rewarding to them! This isn't a particularly well-run cult, and it's a half-assed club at best. If you can find better, or if you need to take a break from the complexity, then by all means do so, go in peace, don't forget your friends, and come back when you know that that is the best thing to do.

Surprise–*life* sucks

In sum, let's just say that polyamory has some inherent degree of suckingness, and there's nothing you can do that will eliminate that, short of being godlike and associating only with others of similar stature. However, if you want to be poly, one of your prime duties is to minimize it.

Sometimes life sucks, but it's still better than the alternative. Since that's how I personally see polyamory in relation to monogamy and promiscuity, I'm content.

18. The jealousy thing

Most "polyamorous" people are clinging to nothing more than an expanded notion of the form of monogamy which even a moment's lucid thought will prove is no longer tenable, and at *best* had a limited usefulness for a mere two centuries, during the rise of the Industrial Revolution – the same old equation, with another variable or two.

A decade ago, I wrote that "polyfidelity is just marriage with more people, and all the same old mistakes." I have lately come to realize that this is far truer than I previously suspected. This is probably why the popular recurring topic for many polyamory discussion groups is jealousy: only a tiny minority of the people want to actually risk open communication, preferring to gloss over their problems with superficial nicety, and patting themselves on the back for being so enlightened.

So, let's talk about jealousy for a moment. Everybody nods and smiles, and the ones who actually figure out how to outmaneuver jealousy would probably have figured it out on their own. (To be fair, at least these groups keep jealousy and similar topics high in awareness, else it likely would be avoided entirely. uncomfortable subjects seem to get that reaction from humans.)

First, we need to differentiate between the concepts of *jealousy* and *envy* (my definitions are at odds with those of other authorities, but I feel them to be accurate, and strive for consistency in my usage). Though widely confused, they can be readily differentiated. **Envy** is a desire for something that I do not – and likely cannot – have. **Jealousy** is a fear of losing that which I already have. Envy is semi-rational and generally deficient in logic, while jealousy is pseudo-rational but rigidly logical.

Even after all of my years of experience with living an openly polyamorous life, I remain ready prey to feelings that could by an observer be called jealous. This is incorrect. The truth is that I am incredibly envious. When there is someone in my life with whom I share deep intellectual connection and emotional bonding and incredible sex, then (despite my human limitations) I am driven to want this all of the time, constantly, excluding boring things like jobs and sleep and food and maybe even air, love without at least a touch of obsession being a little too cold and boring for my tastes. I love her, I desire her, I miss her, and the idea that she's off doing those same wonderful things for which I long with someone else, someone who clearly does not appreciate and treasure her half as much as could I, can irritate the heck out of me.

The fact remain that I am a complicated person, and she is a complicated person. I cannot possibly satisfy all of her wants and needs and desires, sexual and otherwise, however much I may wish to. Neither can she do the same for me, or should she feel that she needs to. Even if I had two lovers who were for all practical purposes identical, who even made love similarly, I'd have no trouble identifying one from the other in the dark. In a hundred subtle but significant ways, they are unique individuals, and one cannot possibly replace the other.

Think of each of us strange human beings as comprising thousands of tiny containers. They are all sorts of different sizes, and each empties out at a different rate. Maybe I have two lovers, one of whom likes to go out dancing far more than do I, and the other hardly at all. By our common socially-ingrained wisdom, I am "incompatible" with both, and perhaps shouldn't pursue a relationship with either. Does this appear silly to you yet? Apply a little more of that "common knowledge," and you'd tend to believe that unless the first is willing to curb her desires and the second to work at bringing her drives closer to my level, then neither of them "really loves me."

Perhaps the absurdity of this is not lost on me. So, with the first, I happily dance until I'm satisfied, and bid her fond farewell as she goes off to continue dancing with her other friends while I pursue my own scattered interests, maybe including resting up so that I can devote myself as thoroughly to our next encounter. Meanwhile, my second partner is now freed from feeling pressured to go dancing with me, and can be a little less guarded when we are together, thus able to more thoroughly enjoy the interests in which we are more compatible, without either of us feeling that I am particularly deprived.

Though it carries far too much of a knee-jerk emotional and territorial charge, sex is really no different from any other activity, or from inattention caused by preoccupied thoughts of someone else, and my experience and observation has borne this out for decades.

All right, I'll admit that this can raise all sorts of interesting conflicts when I like to do something and I have multiple lovers who have about the same level of desire. But face facts: these are usually conflicts over scheduling rather than what people are doing with their body parts. I coined a term: *temporal jealousy*. Let's say that I am a bowling fanatic, and I have a lover who also bowls, but never seems to have much time to do this with me, even though she seems to be bowling all the time with her other friends. This would set off all sorts of internal alarms as I worry whether our communication is deteriorating, or that she might be losing interest in maintaining our relationship. Whether or not she is actually having sex with someone else is a moot point.

For me, jealousy has surprisingly little (as in nothing) to do with being sexually possessive. I have a self-image problem that is hobbled enough to make me rather boringly average. Will my lover find someone who's "better in bed"? Possible, but not likely, as I know from asking my sexual partners. [Okay, not the most objective measure for most of you, but you'll just have to take my word for it that these people don't fudge data merely to protect my ego.] Sometimes, it's really nothing more (or less) than a matter of confidence.

And if she does find someone actually better at things sexual? So what? I trust that she has learned to treasure the differences in *all* her various sexual partners, and that "better" covers such a huge range that it's impossible for one person to be "the best" at everything, if only because some of those "best" things are mutually inclusive. I once had a lover who treasured me for, among other things, making jokes (especially in Yiddish – some of us are kinkier than most) during sex that would reduce her to helpless giggles. From one sexual partner to another, my sexual style varies widely, with perhaps one lover bringing out a near-primal aggressiveness of desire that charmed and flattered her, while another found a loving tenderness that had been lacking in her experience. If they had chanced to talk about their respective lovers, without naming names, they might be very surprised to find that I was both men.

So how do you "fix" jealousy? Trust, and communication. Both of these can be translated as risk-taking, daring to share the chance at rejection and thus encouraging your partner to also take that chance, learning to be honest without attacking or defending.

Fixing the individual occurrences doesn't mean that jealousy is going to fade away forever. Jealousy serves a purpose, uncomfortable though it is. Some people are so talented at grasping the inherent absurdity of jealousy that it doesn't affect them at all. With diligence, and with support, this is something toward which any of us can aspire.

There is nothing inherently wrong or sinful or whatever with either envy or jealousy. The problems arise when you allow them to control you, to blind you to even the possibility of thoughtful mutual examination and creative problem-solving. Should you let this happen, then you are being stupid – and now that you've read these words, if you should allow yourself to be led idiotically around by your fears and doubts, you are being willfully stupid, which is far worse.

19. Swim or die

I held a supervisory job at an organization that assisted people with physical handicaps. I will never forget one of our first pre-launch training sessions, where the board chairman told us how he had gone before a roomful of doctors, and absolutely floored them by saying, "There are assholes in wheelchairs, too." After the stunned gasps had ceased, he went on to tell them how mobility impaired people are still people, mere humans, differently abled but human nonetheless, not "rolling saints" who have somehow automatically transcended their infirmity and thus become superior to the rest of us poor benighted souls stuck stumbling through life on two mere feet.

There's an old Zen saying: "Before enlightenment, chop wood, carry water. After enlightenment, chop wood, carry water."

You've decided that you're polyamorous, whether you've tripped into a multilinear relationship or just decided that it's a good concept. Well, congratulations, and I mean that with something approximating sincerity.

But the boundaries move. Whatever huge leap you take with your life, whether deciding that you can admit to yourself that you're polyamorous, or you've began describing yourself as such to friends, or you've had that first dangerous talk with your lover or partner, or one of you has had your first sexual experience with someone new (and figured out that you still love and desire your previous partnership as much as ever), or you're joining someone else's existing relationship structure or bringing someone into your own….

The title of this chapter is meant to reflect on some core points of polyamory. Sharks must keep moving in order for water to flow over their gills; the concept of "swim" is inherent to that of "shark" – if a shark stops swimming, it ceases to exist. There is very little that defines polyamorous living from any other lifestyle, but the handful contain such things as **honesty**, including absolute ruthless honesty with yourself, and the drive to express that as **self-disclosure**. If you claim to be polyamorous, but you aren't willing to do the work, then you are either *stupid* for glomming onto a trendy-seeming term you don't understand in the least, or *lying*. Neither of these lines up with polyamory. (Stupidity, at least, has a straightforward remedy, and I hope that this book is a step in that curative direction for some.)

Even if you are utterly sincere, and a good person at the outset, you will be presented with opportunities to mess other people around in order to feed your ego. It'd be a good idea if you missed those things, but even if you successfully duck, the people around you are vulnerable to the same temptations. When you make the leap to polyamory, there's a big nasty surprise waiting: sooner or later, you'll find that polyamorous people can be just as stupid, arrogant, pigheaded, selfish, grasping, underhanded, backstabbing, self-serving, and manipulative as anywhere else in the world.

Honesty is a pinnacle that can never be held, only achieved, something to strive for every day, every hour, every moment. You can never be on top at all times; once you manage to get there, you can't sit still. But if you're unwilling to make the constant climb, you cannot be polyamorous.

Nevertheless, polyamory is infested with plenty of people who are floating in the water, dead and bloated. The further upwind you are from the smell, the happier you'll be.

There are assholes in poly, too.

With any luck, and a little warning, you might avoid being an asshole yourself.

Condom cops, one-upmanship & poaching

I got involved with Sami from affection more than love. Her husband, Burt, is a very sweet guy, with a girlfriend or two, but devoted to Sami. His business occupied him for long hours, and he was a little concerned that Sami didn't have much of a personal life. When I first met them, Sami later told Burt that she found me attractive, so he brought this up in subsequent conversation when the three of us were chatting. I admitted that I have strong boundaries about not getting involved with someone who is encoupled, because of all the possible fallout – the last thing I want to do is cause a rift in a couple that is quite capable of solving their little day-to-day problems. Burt assured me that he was adequately experienced in multiple relationships, and that he didn't think I'd be a cause of problems for them. If Sami wanted to explore a relationship with me, he was supportive.

Additionally, they wanted to have a baby. This was a problem for them, as Burt had had a vasectomy before they'd met. They knew my kids, that they were bright, inquisitive, and happy. If Sami ended up pregnant by me, they considered that a bonus.

Then there was Harris. We've known each other on and off for many years. He's one of those people who enjoyed rolling his eyes about the open nonmonogamy of my household. Then he discovered polyfidelity, and proudly declared that he and his wife were polyfidelitous, unlike certain other people (like us) who championed open-form multi-household relating. When the term "polyamory" became politically correct, he leapt to that bandwagon as well.

Harris took every opportunity to speak out in poly-friendly public about how he and his wife had signed a "condom compact" and would impose it very early in the conversation with any prospective sexual partners. This thing is no doubt still circulating in one form or another, a detailed contract between partners to always use condoms with other sexual partners; some of the people who subscribe to this notion like to refer to themselves as "fluid bonded," referring to a ban on "exchange of bodily fluids" with other lovers, except under contractually specified circumstances.

I will admit that I dislike this because having such a contract allows people to easily put their common sense on hold. A piece of paper cannot replace constant thought and communication about the touchy subjects of accidental pregnancy and transmission of sexually communicable diseases, but that certainly appears to be what many people do. There are people like Harris who prey upon AIDS hysteria in order to puff up their egos, and sell themselves as somehow not merely morally superior, but as inherently safer.

Don't get me wrong. I am a diligent user of condoms, as the majority of my lovers have not been able to use other reliable forms of contraception. To me, this reflects my sense of **responsibility**, not "safety." I have caused exactly two pregnancies, which resulted in my children, more or less as planned. Over the years, I've been surprised at how many of my sexual partners expressed amazement when I readily reached for a condom packet, and I won't bore you with the stories I've collected of males who would whine or pout or even become angry at this juncture.

In my observation, some of the "condom cops" who look down their noses at those who aren't interested in their contract are, to be polite, talking through their hats. They go on at length about how "safe" their sexual practices are, yet a little questioning makes them squirm, and persistence will cause them to flee. For one thing, few of them have included clauses in their "condom compact" that cover oral sex, either giving or receiving. If anyone can figure out how to indulge in unprotected oral sex without exchanging bodily fluids, I remain curious. They deny that oral herpes and genital herpes are cross-transmissible – even the American Medical Association has finally admitted that they are the same disease, artificially differentiated only by site of main outbreak. Let's also consider the interesting diseases (herpes, trench mouth, mononucleosis, etc.) that can be quickly passed around via promiscuous kissing.

And I've noticed that, "compact" or no, some of these people will very readily make exceptions for "special occasions" – that is, whenever hunting down a condom would be somewhat inconvenient.

What makes all of this ludicrous is that some of these people complain that my expectations of communication and disclosure, of working out problems promptly and efficiently, is *unromantic*. If by "romance" they mean allowing pleasant thoughts to override common sense, then, yes, I am decidedly unromantic, guilty as charged.

Harris found out that Sami was sexually involved with me. She told me that, at a New Year's Eve party I hadn't been able to attend, Harris had been chatting her up, and soon turned the conversation to how *concerned* he was about the fact that I didn't use condoms with *all* of my sexual partners, every time. He, of course, held himself up as representing some sort of moral pinnacle because of the condom compact – I swear it's true, he used to carry copies of the blank contract with him wherever he went, and pressure people to sign them.

Sami broadly hinted that she was tending to believe Harris's line. Feeling somehow hurt by the distrust this seemed to indicate, I withdrew from the relationship.

By the end of February, Sami was pregnant by Harris. I found this interesting, in light of the "I always use condoms" refrain, and that he'd painted me as irresponsible for not doing the same. As I discovered two years later, the pregnancy came as a complete surprise to Harris's wife – in fact, he hadn't told her about having sex with Sami, which pointed up some fascinating breaches in the much-vaunted contract.

This was not the first time I've gone head-to-head with boobs like Harris, but it was the first time that "safe sex" had been used *against* me.

In one sense, I was happy for Sami and Burt. But when Sami indicated an interest in us being lovers again, I couldn't consider it. Rather than examine my feelings and opinions, or at least to accept our respective opinions as opinions, Sami chose to side with Harris, demonstrably a liar, an adulterer, a slanderer, and a fraud. I saw a perpetuation of the marriage-with-adultery model, the antithesis of how I've always envisioned responsible nonmonogamy. And without Sami understanding the basic wrongness in the situation, I would've been haunted with the question of when it would occur again.

Lesson: Be very wary of people who make a huge case of their moral superiority, especially when they set themselves against someone already in your life.

The poly orthodoxy

You may find this amusing, after having made it this far into the book, but the flat truth is that there are no "experts" on polyamory, me included. Some of us are just thrashing around a little less than others. I have lots of opinions, a fair bit of societally unusual relationship experience, and an ear for stories; I enjoy talking to people, and I'm a writer, so here we are. If I'm an "expert," it's only because there's not much competition yet.

In general, your own feelings are more trustworthy than those of other people. You can listen to others, or read what they have to say, but their opinion tends to be highly biased by their own underlying agendas, stated and otherwise, and sometimes deeply hidden even from themselves.

The semblance between opinion and fact sometimes makes them difficult to discern. Over the long haul, you are quite capable of listening to a wide variety of opinions, applying your own experience and intellect, and setting a course for yourself. Usually, you won't go any further astray than the rest of us. Occasionally, you may need to pull someone aside and suggest they examine their own actions, or even bring someone's questionable activities before a larger group, but that's what community does – you are not making pronouncements from on high.

You *will* run smack into people who pretend to be experts, and polyamory is no exception. I'm okay with that; as a genus, experts are generally harmless, and can be quite entertaining. If you put two economists into a locked room and ask a simple question about inflation, you might end up with blood on the floor, but nobody else will get hurt – and the economy will wobble along as if they'd never been born. To date, experts on polyamory have that same sort of effect on polyfolk.

But every once in a while, you might encounter the ones who make a fetish of power and control, seeking domination over others. They combine their book-learnin' with a little scattered experience, add in some projection of their fantasies and a garnish of paranoia (to keep you from comparing notes with others outside the sacrosanct group), and *voila*! – authority.

Lesson: a fable is a good story, and might contain a valuable moral or two, but experts are rarely good storytellers so feel free to ignore them.

20. Vindication through sabotage

I'm presently very satisfied with my own short list of relationships, and I'm hardly out playing the field (not that I was all that enthusiastic in the first place). Still, I'm active enough in the potential-relationship department that difficulties rear up and bite me on a regular cycle.

You might wonder that, of all people, why would I be having a hard time of it at all? I'm not exceptionally repulsive, my grooming is casual but acceptable, I can hold up my end of a conversation with a fair degree of wit, I'm open, honest, sincere, and I have an established history of polyamorous life, able to maintain most of my lovers as close friends even after the fire dies down and not at all competitive with my lovers' more-primary partners. But, yes, the bizarre difficulties are so regular that I've come to think of them as a regular feature of life, much like mosquitoes

The lesson that I keep re-re-re-re-re-re-re-re-learning is that people – my experience is with women, but I've observed the same behavior in about every possible dyad combination – people *don't* want a sure thing. Oh, they want a risk that they can *tell* themselves – like any other loser at the Kentucky Derby that is life – is a "sure thing". No matter what happens, they can reap positive direct payoffs. If the affair tanks, then it can be trotted out to prove a whole range of preconceptions: "I can't even consider a relationship with you because I once dated a [*insert any vocation, addiction, or physiological characteristic*] and it was terrible." When this little rule collides with a momentary whim, of course, it'll be roundly ignored, then paraded again with renewed vigor and cachet: "See? I *told* you it would be a mistake!" Should they defy the odds and stumble into a healthy relationship with an unsure thing, then they've proven that this sort of risk-taking is justified; when they sabotage the relationship so thoroughly that it finally explodes, they'll use their accidental success as a reason to take another similarly foolhardy chance.

In short, for this sort of a person, a verifiably sure thing doesn't have enough strife to be "real".

I once thought that I was making this up in my usual hyper-cynical frame of mind, until a relationship a few years ago. My lover flabbergasted me regularly in our months together with statements perfectly dovetailing my assessment. "I can't be in love with you because it'd be too easy," she once said. It dawned on me that I've experienced and observed this "too easy" stuff many dozens of times. It's easier (say) to be involved with an unemployed alcoholic who oscillates between neglect and abuse than it is to open up to a relationship with someone who is self-confident and emotionally healthy, because we are raised to believe that strife is *necessary*, a dragon to be slain by True Love. This is such a ridiculous belief that I would feel silly for even bringing it up, except that I've encountered it all too often. You may well be asking yourself, "How in Hell could that sort of programmed self-abuse be easier than something healthy?" (Don't go getting too gloaty on me here: this is a classic land-mine, and even as you can question its sanity, you're all too likely to be carrying it around yourself.)

That's simple enough to answer. It's easier to attach yourself to a foredoomed relationship than a healthy one because, for starters, it makes you feel needed – societally-ingrained caretaking. A greater reason, though, is that you would rather have a pretty lie than homely honesty. You're a dreamer, a sap. If you light onto the aforementioned abusive alcoholic, you can mislead yourself with the vast possibilities, the opportunity to be a Pygmalion, even as you unconsciously understand that all the cards are on the table and it's not likely to change much except to become more of the same (neglect becomes irrational arguing which becomes an "accidental" slap which ends up being beatings of escalating severity). If you look carefully at someone, and you note that the flaws are minimal, society has programmed you to begin worrying: when is The Awful Truth going to come out? The suspense will drive you buggy. So much easier to just go with the abuser and at least eliminate the suspense, because then you know it's only a matter of time before the next trip to the hospital.

To look at it another way, let's say it is somehow possible to have a 100%-perfect relationship. Most people, probably, would be hovering around the 85% level; if you set out your needs and desires clearly, and you actively search for a partner, you could probably find someone who (for you) is 95% perfect. For many, though, there isn't enough room for gain: under the best of circumstances, you could only hope to ever bridge that final five percent. However, if you go out and find yourself an abusive addict with some redeeming qualities, you could start at 40% or even less, and impress yourself and some imaginary audience when you work with your new partner and create a "profit" of up to 60%. Wow! A shame that you can't compare human beings to stocks and bonds in this manner. Yet that is exactly how some people behave when they take up a relationship with the half-hidden hope of "fixing" it.

The ultimate paradox, though, is when people who are playing these little deep-programmed games go out of their way to prompt the very behavior they fear, or to seek out those who are most likely to play those roles. Some of my friends are reformed addicts, and have made themselves very aware of their underlying motivations. One woman told me, "I can walk into a crowded room full of strangers and point out the abusive alcoholics, because they're the men I'm instantly attracted to." Another would do things like crowd her boyfriend into a corner, shouting abuse at him, until he finally shoved past her in order to escape, whereupon she would call her friends (and sometimes the police) to report his "physical abuse" (we had mutual friends who witnessed some of these games in stunned silence). Victims become victimizers. That's nothing more than two sides of the same coin.

The sabotaging of one's own happiness is an expression of what Freudians would call *Thanatos*. This happens because we all possess built-in self-destruct mechanisms, and obey them even as we think they don't exist, or at least that they have no control over us. Motives vary widely but, in many of the people I know, success (sometimes success in general, other times restricted to very well-demarcated areas) frightens them at a very fundamental level, because it would disprove parts of their carefully constructed self-image. We seek secure boundaries, solid fences, yet start picking them apart as soon as we find them, resenting them for being there and restricting our movement, and roundly cursing whoever put them there and whoever maintains or defends them in any way.

Abusive behavior can be very subtle, which only makes it all the more maddening. There was a couple I counseled a few years ago. He had kept telling her, "I'm just not good enough for you" until she was ready to believe it. So, when she went out on an innocent date with an old boyfriend, her husband hit the roof, a full-blown jealous fit. It's as though he pushed her to the edge of the pier, then pulled out a gun – when she quits the relationship, he can tell everyone that she jumped voluntarily. I know it sounds cold-blooded, but if you should encounter a similar phrase, the wielder deserves exactly one warning: "If you say that again, I will believe you."

If you recognize any of these behaviors within yourself, you need to find yourself a good counselor, therapist, psychologist or psychiatrist; if it sounds much like someone in your life, then they need to do the same. You can support each other, but there is a huge and crucial difference between *tolerance of* and *support for* someone's decisions and actions. Don't ever fall into the trap of covering up someone's problems and hoping that they will never recur, that the underlying faults don't exist.

The odds that one of you can actually fix the other are poor to nonexistent. Fixing yourself is admittedly possible, but you may have carefully constructed your relationships to support your problems, not their removal. A concerned stranger, with no emotional ties to you or to anyone in your life, is vital. Learn how to listen and how to be heard, how to deal with fear, anger, rejection, crappy self-image… and how to accept love and approbation. Then say goodbye to the therapist (mostly), and apply what you learned in class.

Until you bring mechanisms and reflexes and strategies into your life that will undercut this sort of self-sabotage, you're building your castles on sand. With all the chaos inherent in polyamory, you are rather literally begging for trouble.

21. **Polyamory or promiscuity?**

The difference between polyamory and promiscuity is simple. Promiscuity is the attitude of, "If it seems like the thing to do at the moment, then go ahead, and to hell with the consequences."

Promiscuity is cynicism papered over with sincerity. Polyamory is the opposite.

Polyamory is far from perfect, if only from being a rather new paradigm, and populated with many flawed and damaged people. Sure, there are some standards of belief and behavior that can be pointed to as defining polyamory. For the most part, though, polyamory is inclusive of many different lifestyle choices, some of which may be completely opposite when comparing two different polyamorous groups. This level of chaos leaves room for people who, frankly, are either deluded or lying. Intentionally or not, these people can cause an impressive amount of damage to existing relationships, and hide behind the all-inclusive cloak of polyamory, aided and abetted by the people who want to see only the best in others, even if this means willfully overlooking the obvious.

In order to differentiate the losers from those with varying degrees of potential, you will need to look closely at three things, for starters. These are the **label** they choose, the long-term **intent** they display, and the **actions** they take. Most people will start with one of these, build up to two as their vocabulary (whether linguistic or interpersonal) improves, then add the third. I am a stickler, and I cannot consider someone truly polyamorous until all three are in place, however shakily.

People who call themselves polyamorous are just that: people calling themselves polyamorous. Whatever their level of sincerity, this has about as much effect in the real world as does pasting Porsche decals onto your old Toyota pickup. You can freely display your interest in such a manner, and it does nothing to turn your truck into a sports car. Adopting the label or taking on the image may be a good first step toward changing your personal reality, but it's not the whole process –for that matter, it is nothing of the process at all, except as signifying an intent to begin.

Someone who is sincerely seeking multiple long-term relationships may go a bit hog-wild in the flush of their new sense of freedom as they discover the huge territory outside of monogamy. An observer might be prone to denounce them as merely promiscuous, when what they're actually seeing is the rediscovered fascination with sex combined with a lack of skills for making sane long-term relational choices. In this sense, their actions are dubious. However, if they put effort into understanding where they went wrong, to making amends and repairing situations, and to avoiding similar mistakes subsequently, then I would have to argue that, overall, their actions are proper.

Many who consider themselves polyamorous are much more forgiving than I. I regularly speak with people who are willing to allow all sorts of lapses, even on a regular basis, because those who exhibit such dubious behavior are "trying" – with which I would certainly agree, though the meanings we each choose for that word are at odds.

Most people who readily whip out "promiscuous" as a pejorative might just as well use "sexual" instead, because that's generally what they mean anyway: "Sex is morally dubious at best, and having *lots* of sex is reprehensible." If you find yourself fighting this line, don't bother with the trite rejoinder that polyamory isn't promiscuity – they are already convinced that the words are interchangeable but that "polyamory" is dressing it over with claims of love and relationship and stability and all that, thus nothing more than delusional thinking. You cannot win such an argument, as the cards are stacked against you. A better answer (or at least holding the thought uppermost while changing the subject) would be, "Yes, I have sex, lots of sex, with many different people, in threes and fours and big sweaty piles. In fact, I'd be doing it *constantly* if it weren't for having a job to keep my bedroom stocked in silk sheets."

More seriously, if you want to go ahead and argue, defuse the whole thing a little by admitting to a potential for sexual variety. Remember: label, intent, action. To people intent on broadcasting their own morality, sex is the action. Define the term "polyamory" for them, lay out the terminology, and thereby demonstrate that this isn't something that you made up in an idle moment in order to justify your personal wanton debauchery. Then tell them a funny or touching story about how nicely your spouse or partner gets along with someone for whom you have a huge, possibly unrequited, and non-secret crush (or even lust).

Then, walk away. If you haven't planted some small seed of doubt, you're not going to get any further. But if you *have*, you might be facing an enraged display at the chink you've put into their nice shiny armor. Your purpose is *not* to proselytize (much less to convert), but to say, "I'm not wrong, you're not wrong." Besides, some of the strongest anti-polyamory arguments I've ever withstood were from people who sincerely wanted to believe in the amazing things I was espousing and I was merely the external target for the argument they were having internally.

The only thing that is truly important is that you have confidence in what you are, and what you choose to do.

22. Pregnancy, disease, legal action, and other distractions

Even if it is something that sneaks up on you, becoming honestly nonmonogamous should worry the heck out of you. If it doesn't, you will have to work to catch up to mere cluelessness. At the same time, I would hope that you don't slide completely into paranoia, however reasonable that may at times appear. For both extremes, let's discuss some of the stickier maybes.

Diseases: incoming, outgoing, unlikely, or imaginary

The "STD question" is valid, and I've been thinking about an uncomfortable countercase. To wit: if we divide the world into "monogamous" and "polyamorous" (and for the moment we're ignoring "other"), which group would you say is more likely to spread STDs?

In 25 years of observing peoples' behaviors (and longer being a popular sounding-board for females of my acquaintance), the number of even boring STDs like yeast infections is vastly lower for openly nonmonogamous people than in the "lifelong couplehood" world. One reason for this is obvious: word gets around faster than infections. When there is actually something resembling a localized polyamorous community, people talk. Sure, there is some residual hangover of the tendency to gossip rather than actually share potentially relevant information, but people learn quickly that sharing information leads to even more sharing. Once the initial flush of discovering polyamory passes, individuals (especially women) might not only recognize their own fleeting doubts about a potential liaison, but will recall someone who was involved with that person in the past, and seek out that partner for questions. Though not as perfect as we could be, polyfolk have a much higher tendency than the monogamous to remain on good terms with their former lovers, so the information they pass along has less of a bias.

This communication level works the other way around as well. I am a lot less likely to ignore the possibility of passing disease along if I know that doing so would result in downgraded status for years beyond my own infectiousness.

With honesty comes a lack of fear over self-disclosure. For instance, I was dating a woman who warned me very early on that she was a potential risk for herpes. Our relationship never progressed to sex, but her disclosure was not the reason – if anything, I found her all the more attractive for being so thoughtful and trusting.

There is another social component that is more prevalent in polyamory, and that is wider opportunity to observe each other's behavior for ourselves. Rick, one of my acquaintances, found himself very enchanted with a married woman, Rose. He also knew her husband Don, and thought of them as a nice, happy couple. After a discussion group meeting, the three of them and a few other members went out to dinner. There, Rick watched as Rose spent the rest of the evening apparently trying to humiliate Don, who mostly shrugged it off. Rick decided that he wasn't comfortable with this, and even less looked forward to the possibility of similar treatment, so he let the relationship quietly expire over the next few months.

Behavior can be even more subtle, and give very strong hints as to potential risk for STDs. Years ago, researchers were trying to determine factors that could be used to predict which groups were at highest risk for sexually transmitted diseases. They were thorough, and looked at educational level, intelligence quotient, financial status, religious upbringing, race, gender, sexual preference, reading material, exercise, diet. At best, they found some vague correlation to education, but nothing reliable in a predictive sense.

As they were finishing up the project, someone had the bright idea to actually look at the "filler" questions that are used as a change of pace in a lengthy questionnaire. They stumbled across some interesting factors, but found one very high correlation:

Seat-belt usage.

Basically, someone who buckles their seat belt every time, as a sort of unconscious reflex, is significantly less like likely to have had or to subsequently contract a venereal disease. The researchers posited two reasons for this: these people are inherently more cautious, and they are more willing to make minor sacrifices for their own well-being. In general, they see this sort of person as *risk-aversive*.

In an ideal world, polyamorous people would all be risk-aversive. However, since polyamory is a "radical" lifestyle, it does attract its share of thrill-seekers–or, to say it another way, risk-seekers. Something so commonplace as driving habits (usage of seatbelts and turn signals, overly aggressive driving, respect for stop signs) can be giving you significant clues from the first.

Be certain to look into *all* risks. The almost gleeful fascination with AIDS and HIV has led to a widespread ignoring of other interesting infections that aren't as glamorous.

HPV won't kill you outright, and it's little more than a nuisance of itself. However, it is hard to diagnose, hard to detect, and hard to get rid of. HPV has been linked to assorted other diseases due to the effects it has on your immune system. Any woman who has ever had pelvic inflammatory disease would prefer to avoid a recurrence, but that's one of the more common results of an HPV infection. It has also been linked to a significantly increased risk of abnormal cervical tissue, which can sometimes indicate imminent cancer. To top it all off, you *can* get HPV from doorknobs and toilet seats. A casual touch is all it apparently takes.

Herpes is with you for life. The "treatments" you see in the ads are little more than palliative: they reduce irritation and swelling, and minimize the duration of an outbreak. Not that this matters because, as long as it's in your system, you can spread herpes, though the chances are significantly lower. There is some research, while still controversial, that suggests anyone who's ever had one form of herpes (cold sores, genital herpes, chicken pox, shingles) can spontaneously develop another form – meaning that an utter virgin might infect you with herpes.

Let's not forget trench mouth, thrush, and oral candidiasis, all transmitted by kissing, as is that old standby, mononucleosis – which *can* have deadly consequences.

Yeast infections are no fun for anyone. However, I am surprised at the number of women (even in monogamy) who don't have the slightest clue that their years-long battle has been hopeless because they are being regularly reinfected by their boyfriend, whose "jock itch" is actually candida, which can live quite well in the urethra.

Short of lifelong celibacy (and liberal use of rubber gloves and disinfectant), there is no absolutely "safe sex." You pays your dollar, you takes your chances – that, in a nutshell, is life. Are people surprised that breathing is a symptom of some degree of risk-taking?

Keep your eyes open, be wary, move slowly, get information, get tested, expect your partners to get tested. Simple, really. If you are capable of finding a good used car, the odds are on your side.

The unwelcome stork

In the heat of passion, the thrill of the moment, or the clutches of NRE, people are stupid. Okay, we're not too terribly bright in the first place, but our tenuous grip certainly gets weaker under stress, especially when it's the sort of stress that's fun and feels nice.

Though this will hopefully be wrong for almost all cases, I ask you to always start from one assumption: when you are first sexually involved with a person, *never* believe that they are using a reliable form of birth control. Either gender can *claim* to have been mechanically sterilized, but unless you walk them into the clinic yourself and have a verifiable fertility evaluation performed, you really cannot be absolutely certain. Once in a while, if follow-up has not been properly performed, the person who has undergone such a procedure may actually be fertile. There are still a few examples where *both* partners were surgically sterilized, yet conceived.

The birth-control pill is a minor miracle, but not yet perfect. Unless you've known a woman for some time, you probably cannot say how reliable she is in taking the pill. It's pretty much impossible for you to tell whether it's working, even if she's dosing meticulously. I knew a woman who discovered that the pills she'd been taking had actually been baby aspirin – her teenage daughter had been stealing the pills themselves to avoid pregnancy, and substituting tablets of a remarkably similar size and color.

I'm a diligent condom user, myself, with exactly two children who were practically scheduled. That's a ground rule. As a statistician, I don't believe that most pregnancies arise from a "one-time oops" but from a pattern of neglectful behavior. Therefore, if such an accident happened, we'd have to look into it together, but I'd bet that either (a) our relationship had been founded upon faulty assumptions, or (b) we had grown far enough apart that the original agreement didn't fit anymore. So, we'd have a choice: start again, or admit that we've got to move along separately.

Coercion, blackmail, lawsuits

There is no way that I can possibly cover these topics in a few hundred words, but a note to the wise should be plenty sufficient.

Here's your notice: if it ends up in court, whoever denounces polyamory first will probably win. To be poly is to be a sexual deviant, and that's a big mark against you even if you are the wronged party.

Years ago, someone said to me, "Wouldn't it be great if magic spells really worked?" I replied, "Oh, *hell* no. If there was evidence that a judge would accept, this damned silly society would start suing each other for literally everything! We'd see people doing hard time for the Evil Eye."

And that's pretty much how polyfolk would look in court. Some localities used to criminalize seduction, interpreted as using promise of marriage (implied or actual) in order to obtain sex or other favors. Having a group marriage (or group sex) could get you raided under local "bawdy house" or "house of assignation" laws. (A house of assignation is roughly the same as the office of an out-call prostitution service – sex doesn't take place in the premises, but arrangements are made. Technically, any dating service could fall under these laws, which could also be used to harass any sex-positive activists.)

How could this sort of thing affect you? Well, let's take a common situation for an example. You go onto the Internet, to look for a young woman so that you and your partner can have your fantasized closed triad. You meet up with a likely candidate and exchange a few telephone calls. She asks if the two of you might be interested in her moving in, and you, of course, say yes. Within the next month, she sells her house for less than market value, quits her job, throws out most of her possessions, and moves 1,700 miles to be with you. Two months after her arrival, you and your partner are facing the undeniable truth that this triad is working out poorly, and ask your HBB to leave.

At that point, there are thousands of hungry lawyers who can already smell your blood in the water. Your sweet young babe has taken substantial and verifiable losses, and might go after you to recover – plus, of course, punitive amounts, mental anguish, pain and suffering, and all that. If you believed that false ID, you've possibly violated the Mann Act (transportation of minors across state lines for immoral purposes), which is a federal crime and gets noticed by the FBI.

Even if the case is entirely baseless in your jurisdiction, you could end up paying your own lawyer thousands of dollars to advise you to pay her lawyer thousands of dollars to lay off.

Are people stupid, greedy, and avaricious? Oh, yes. I recently heard of a woman who is suing her live-in boyfriend for his house, alimony, and support for two teenage boys. The problem is, she moved in with this poor bastard less than six months before filing suit, and they had not even known each other for a year. With a sharp lawyer, she can probably restrict his travel, and possibly have him jailed before the trial even takes place.

Call it a social analog of STDs, because the warning is basically the same. If it looks too good to be true, then it's probably too good to be true. Unless you're really looking forward to that sort of melodrama, then take your time, and check a few references.

Part II

How to actually be polyamorous

Having given you a decent grounding in the concepts that underlie what has come to be known as polyamory, and warned you away from some of the more obvious presumptions and misconceptions, we are going to change the focus to the mundane. In this part of the book, I want to aim the theory more at the actual, practical, daily side of living polyamorously.

Much of my writing on the subject has been called negative. I don't agree, but let's assume for a moment that this is a fair assessment. Why in the name of all goodness don't I focus more on the *positive* side of polyamory?

Well, foremost is the fact that, if your life is running with few unpleasant surprises, there's no particular need for me to come along and pat you on the back. If you have a full and rewarding intimate life, only the occasional stray narcissists would be interested in reading a book that tells them how wonderful they are. That wouldn't make for a satisfying level of book sales.

The other reason for my trademark dour-and-gloomy approach is that I have no interest in presenting polyamory as some sort of glorious, low-cost, easy-to-use and disposable Utopia. This isn't a sales brochure, bubba.

I don't want to be part of a community (however loosely delineated) that is full of tourists. At the same time, I have been very concerned for the many sincere but utterly clueless people who make the dive into polyamory without a clear understanding of the risks involved, and flee screaming into the night, never to be heard from again, when a bit of sympathetic support could have (even if they didn't stay) taught them many useful things about intimate, loving relationships with other human beings, not to mention bunches of ways to find insight into their own motivations, all of which can only improve the world in which we all must live, poly or not.

With that said, what follows is addressed primarily to those readers who find themselves polyamorous, as well as those who plan to imminently walk into the lion's den. Anyone else is welcome to come along for the ride.

23. Core requirements of polyamory

You *could* write your own rules. After all, nonmonogamy comes in an amazing range of shades, hues and flavors.

If you want, you can set things up so that one person or one gender or dyad or clique has all the power, all the freedom, all the control, and can create, amend, modify, break, or eliminate rules and agreements at whim. You could just as readily create a complex relationship that is so studiously egalitarian that you'll spend your time either processing every little concern as a group, or digging for every far-fetched potential problem. Personally, either extreme looks to be far too much work. You'd be perpetually reviewing the litany, which would certainly cut into the positive stuff.

However, polyamory definitely contains some inherent structure. It is a specific case of responsible nonmonogamy, which is itself a specific case of generalized nonmonogamy. As such, if you call yourself polyamorous, you are making a few very specific statements – if you don't like these constraints, and don't intend to be bound by them, then there is likely nothing wrong with your lifestyle choices… but it is not polyamory, and the only way you can apply that label to yourself is if you are a fool or a liar, which all in all both result eventually in people laughing at you. So, let's see what we can do to head off both the need for absolute control and the fear of control.

There is no particular order to the following list, and in fact they all tend to intertwine, so it's unlikely that one is more important than the others.

Future

Adultery is a significant and predictable outgrowth of a monogamistic society. In order to exist, adultery is given at every turn an air of tacitness, treated as if it is clandestine, ephemeral, and an aberration (consider the term "fooling around"), even though it may be a long-term and poorly kept secret that recurs regularly.

Polyamory is differentiable from some other forms of nonmonogamy (including adultery) in that it is *future-oriented*. Poly relationships are not located solely in the moment, but have intentions (though perhaps tacit and vaguely defined) of at least adding to a base of experience possibly so far as signifying a life-long and emotionally attached commitment.

There is nothing inherently wrong with sexual escapades and exploration, and studiously rational followers of nonmonogamous lifestyles are as willing as any other stratum to be a bit self-indulgent. However, such instances do not of themselves constitute polyamorous living.

Honesty

To be polyamorous, you have to deal as honestly as possible with the rest of the people in the world. I do indeed mean everyone; you cannot be at the top of your game if you allow yourself to fall into sloppy thinking patterns (lies being among the sloppiest). Honesty is much more, though, than the mere lack of lying; to be merely honest is to deny that you are seeing situations that you could affect positively.

The closer people are to you, the more honest you have to be about communicating your feelings and actions. You are one of these people, the very closest to yourself. While I don't want you enwrapped in self-doubt and self-criticism, you *must* first of all be ruthlessly honest with yourself about your motivations. Be honest: you have a hidden agenda. We all do. You have baggage that you carry with you, even if you are a virtual candidate for sainthood. All of us odd little humans carry our load of hopes, dreams, and wishes, as well as fears and doubts. Developing the ability to ferret them out, to look at them with both objectivity and sympathy, and deal with them is not only recommended, but necessary to being responsibly nonmonogamous. You can deal with your internalized problems by fixing them, by working around them, or by presenting them calmly as areas you need help with. With the beginnings of this ability, you are in a position to truly deal honestly with others and their baggage.

Disclosure

You cannot be honest with other human beings unless you are honest with yourself. Once you have a grasp of these foibles, you then need to be able to bring them to others, without fear of being utterly devastated by any resulting anger or ridicule. Not that derisive laughter isn't going to happen: if your expressed doubts set off the buried doubts of someone else, they quite possibly will project their internalized discomfort or anger onto you. That's the chance you take, and you take it in trust that you can both work it out, in an atmosphere of mutual respect.

The more that you hide truth from yourself, and the more that you deny what is actually occurring, whether from ill intentions or good, the less able you become to tell truth from lie. To put it another way:

One lie leads to two lies. Avoidance is addictive, because it carries the illusion of avoiding pain or humiliation. In reality, you cannot make something go away by throwing it somewhere else or burying it – all you're doing is buying uncomfortable time, like trying to ignore a hot cinder that is burning its way through the sole of your shoe. You can buy the time, but it's of poor quality. If you hide from a problem, you then likely will have to create a lie to mask the inconsistencies caused by the first mistruth. Then, the lie will cause further inconsistencies, which need another lie. You *must* learn to go after any smallest lapse in truth because, like a splinter imbedded in your skin, it can only get worse, make you more uncomfortable, sap your energy, and make you irritable, when a few minutes of discomfort can remove the splinter and let healing begin. Don't become some macho, stoical martyr when you can be truly brave and fix the problem as early as possible.

Little lies lead to big lies. If one shredding of the truth leads to shelter and support and warmth, then our little hindbrains start getting the idea that pillaging leads to comfort and security. Rather than waste effort with a loose pile of specific, local lies, we come up with big blanket lies. "In for a penny, in for a pound," and laying it on thick begins to look like a practical option. This is nonsense, both logically and empirically, yet the patterns are there and we're stuck with them. If you put effort into avoiding examination of this mechanism, you give it power to play out its drama. We can avoid this by paying attention to the possibility, and defusing the core lies before they can form more-complex webworks of untruth.

Restricted communication further restricts communication. Humans are irritating (and irritable) creatures. Think about the last time someone told you "I don't want to talk about that" when conversation strayed into dangerous territory. If the reaction was especially strong, you likely thenceforward not only avoided the topic itself, but the topics that could lead toward it. Then you avoid the topics that are in the neighborhood of those topics. Less and less becomes safe, until you are running a real danger of not communicating at all. While you probably shouldn't keep poking at something that truly cannot be fixed, this pattern can quickly get out of hand. A basic way to deal with it is to work with the "wounded" party to ensure that nobody (whether from empathy or apprehension) walls off any more territory than absolutely necessary, and that the damage is seen to by some type of counselor.

Truth causes pain, lies cause huge pain. Okay, being truthful is sometimes not the most comfortable thing in the world. Honesty, though, doesn't hurt as much as the alternatives, and it's shorter. As I was putting this book together, my health appeared to be deteriorating. One day, I woke up with an impressive toothache. After an initial denial phase, I went to the dentist and had the offending wisdom teeth removed. For weeks, and possibly months, the low-level pain had been interfering with my sleep and concentration. I'll be honest: even though I was suffering, I was still a little reluctant to go to the dentist. Not only did that mean I would have to admit that I'd been neglecting regular maintenance, but I was *choosing* to have a painful procedure performed – bad enough that I'd been stupid, now I was going to pay someone to remove parts of me. I had a little chat with myself over this, to dig out the various subconscious motivations. First of all, I'd already been stupid, I'd been caught and was paying the penalty, so I needed to admit my fault and give my life a chance to move along. Most important, while I was indeed choosing to have oral surgery performed, I was balancing a pain that would heal against one that not only would get worse, but had been imposed upon me. Once I had a grip on these underlying doubts, I was actually cheery going into the clinic, and the whole procedure was over in less than an hour. After just a few days of recovery, I was already doing much better than recently. When you avoid dealing with a situation, you are doing much the same to yourself. You can try to suffocate it under denial (a particularly popular form of lying), or you can accept responsibility for both the problem and its solution.

Untruth is like taking out a loan against your future: sooner or later, it will come due, and you'll have to pay it off. With interest, compounded.

Was it Benjamin Disraeli or Will Rogers? Anyway, one of them said that telling the truth is simply easier, because then you don't have to carefully remember what exactly you told each person.

Again, you need to start with yourself [unless you happen to be one of those fortunate and amazing individuals who is close to a highly disclosing person and you recognize that they're not merely being mean when they trust you enough to risk honesty]. I won't tell you that it's easy to admit to imperfection–it's merely vital. I have always had problems with phrases that begin "I want…" or "I need…" because I don't want to appear grasping or selfish. After some long deep thought about this, I finally accepted that I do indeed *have* wants and needs, that these are not necessarily invalid, however badly someone else might interpret them, and that these perceived lacks deserved to be heard, if only to be aired to a sympathetic listener. Sometimes this has even led to a much higher degree of understanding, where my friend had never known that I was less than perfect in my self-image – I come across as extremely capable, even if I'm not feeling it – and my improved humanness has led them to be much more forthcoming in return.

When you've begun to deal with the blockages in your self-awareness, and to learn to express them to your intimates, you can then develop the capability of examining other peoples' inconsistencies, and the gaps in your relationships with them. When fears – of appearing stupid, of seeming to attack the people closest to you, of looking ridiculous or reprehensible to outsiders – are put to rest, then the stumbling blocks to disclosure are largely behind you. All you have to do is bring disclosure about when it is needed.

Confrontation

When you have a little understanding of your own baggage, you are immediately in a much better position to bring up problems that are occurring between you and someone else. This is always hardest when, but for a gripe or two, your relationship with this person is going marvelously.

Few emotionally healthy people will want to go out of their way to provoke a fight. When they do, it's usually for a very good but thoroughly hidden reason: the desperate need to communicate, further complicated by fears that honesty could lead to rejection, or that anything gained could then be snatched away. These fears create massive emotional pressure, so even what was intended to be a calm request for communication comes out between clenched teeth, with great tension in the vocal cords and diaphragm; the former causes a tight, sharp tone, and the latter makes slow, even breathing difficult and might require loudness in order to speak at all.

Confrontation resembles attack, I would be the last to deny that. The resemblance, however, is merely superficial. For starters, I have had vicious arguments that a casual observer would assume to be a mild, friendly conversation; I don't have to raise my voice or resort to name-calling in order to be in the thick of flying fur. That's the benefit of a self-imposed regimen of speech therapy in my early years, and regular dabbling in acting, singing, and radio production – I can impose a vocal style that is less layered with angry-seeming emotional cues. If you have (or can learn) these skills, I recommend their application in confrontation.

Your upbringing makes a lot of difference, here, between any two people as to their respective interpretations of a situation. Not tone nor volume nor word-choice necessarily indicates a mood in such a way as someone from another culture, race, ethnicity, or even family could correctly gauge. My roommate was once about to call the police because there was an apparent riot at our neighbor's house. I went outside, listened for a minute, then came back and told her, "Put down the phone. It's a family party." They reminded me of my own family: loud voices, sharp tones, plenty of insults, and lots of jolly laughter. My roommate, by contrast, was from a nice, quiet middle-class suburb full of people who hold politeness and image as the prime social rule.

Confrontation is not a recommended luxury – confrontation is an absolute necessity. If attention isn't called to problems, they cannot be examined, much less fixed. If you cannot confront, or face confrontation with all your skills and best intention, you're doomed when it needs to happen, because you cannot address fundamental problems that will only worsen with neglect.

Trust

In a polyamorous relationship, it is everyone's duty not only to strive to trust relational partners, but also to ensure that they deserve trust themselves.

By *trust* I most certainly do not mean "faith in the perfection of the human soul," but rather in the spirit's *perfectibility*. You know that everyone's got their rough edges, and that they can be fiercely protective of them, just as a wounded animal will snap at someone who tries to clean the damaged area – it's reflex, not judgement. Intellectually, I understand that completely, but it doesn't make such a response any less painful. Knowing the cause of the hurt, and the underlying motivations to that cause, doesn't take the sting away.

I've been blessed to have grown up in a very rude, loud, argumentative, loving family. I've spent most of my life being horrified as I watch other people set themselves up for pain with a purposefully restricted or misleading or outright lying communication style… and they never know they're doing it. It's painful to see. But, since most people from our society grow up blinding themselves to this, they really are unaware of what they're doing, and will even deny that they're doing it. To be forced to acknowledge such a thing scares the crap out of people. You need to be able to see this malign reflex not only in others but in yourself, then be willing to work with it and ultimately undercut it until it no longer has significant power within or over your life.

Good intentions are vital… and not enough. Hope keeps us alive, at least in the sense of not letting setbacks kill off spirit in bite after tiny bite. A life without hope can hardly be properly called living. But basing ourselves entirely in hope, cut off from the cruel, cold winds of intelligent observation and critical analysis, interferes just as surely with living.

I am aware of the limits of order, logic, and so on. It's *not* a matter of order vs. intuition – that is, rules set against True Love. In reality, I desire whopping huge doses of both.

As a culture, we aren't stupid, but we are certainly ignorant. Noam Chomsky is critical of what he calls *willful ignorance,* a kind of self-delusion that empowers us to deny what we are certainly intelligent and informed enough to see. I'd go a step further to say that our culture exhibits symptoms of being somewhere between sociopathy and schizophrenia – neurotic, surely. If you are going to be polyamorous, you are going to have to fight this every step of the way; the complexity of polyamory, even a relatively simple triad, attracts problems much more rapidly than does monogamy, and any attempts to ignore festering problems will catch you very, very quickly.

There's a quote attributed to Mark Twain: "Integrity comes from experience. Experience comes from bad judgement." (It certainly sounds like Twain, but I haven't been able to find a footnote.) Trust is based not upon a record of unerring successes, but upon good-hearted attempts, with the inevitable mistakes tempered by a willingness to learn from what has gone before. In short, to trust anyone (including yourself), you need to pay attention to what is happening, recall what has happened, and then project this forward into current and future situations.

Only when trust is established mutually between the participants in a relationship can the relationship itself said to be trusting. Never forget: The basis of Trust is trust. That is, in order for a relationship to be trusting, then the people in it must be trusting – and, I would argue, trustworthy.

Balance

Polyamory is a two-edged sword. If one person is allowed to have sexual flings, then everyone is. If everyone agrees that it's a closed relationship, then a dissenter has the *right* for her or his displeasure to be heard but the *duty* to leave if that individual's sense of what is right and necessary clashes with the opinion of the group. If one person wants his every little doubt or worry to be fully heard, then he *has* to grant the same right to others. If another wants everyone to respect the flexibility of her schedule, then others have the right to *expect* the same from her.

Once, during a heated exchange with a partner, she demanded of me, "What *do* you want?" Out of my mouth fell the words, "One set of rules, equally applied." That succinct statement has stayed with me for a decade, and neatly summarized what I had felt for a decade previous. You need to treat each other not so much as equals – which is really difficult, if not impossible, given the uniqueness of each human being – but *equitably.* It's a subtle but critical difference: the former would have you trying to somehow divide your life and experience into indistinguishable portions, but the latter only demands that, for the most part, nobody is the clear winner or loser (or "top dog" and "bottom dog," as Fritz Perls called them). In the drive to seek equality (or, occasionally, to avoid it in order to "reassure" a partner of his or her primacy), equability is largely overlooked.

There's no hard-and-fast rule for establishing equability, which is why equality probably appears "easier." That's nonsense, as most people *are* readily able to establish a balance that just "feels right." For instance, let's say that you have two partners that are the most important people in your life. One works long hours and pursues many social obligations, and the other has a small trust fund and a part-time job, and not many interests outside the house. If you schedule almost all of your time with the homebody, that's not fair to any of you; yet, avoiding dates on the off chance that the other would be home early or cancel a planned outing is no more fair. Fairness lies in a *judicious* use of your time, not in measuring with a stopwatch and logging the spans in a notebook.

By "balance" I also mean finding some sort of overall happy medium. Starry-eyed romanticism aside, there is no such thing as a problem-free relationship between any two people who actually have a significant degree of intimacy. Achieving and maintaining that sort of balance is going to mean willingness to compromise or, more generally, to find alternative outcomes that at least satisfy most of the directly affected partners. You may not be able to find equitable balance in every single situation, but you can certainly achieve it in the long run over a variety of circumstances.

Vital miscellanea

There are dozens of points to which I want to bring your attention, and a few are especially important. With (over)due apologies to my editors, these may well be fitted more appropriately in various chapters. However, I feel that they are vital points, though occupying little space. Some of them will probably crop up in passing throughout. Rather than let them be buried by their related topics, I am going to herd them into a single spotlight, so that you don't misplace them.

You need a process orientation.

Western culture has raised us to seek for goals, for ends, for Ultimate Completion. This shows up in all sorts of ways that, if you stop to think about them, are obviously questionable as far as psychological health, most of them what an expert calls *magical thinking*, and us layfolk would tag *superstition*. They're troublesome enough in daily life, but they directly endanger relationships. One is **The Band-Aid**: "If we hide it, it'll heal." There's **The Tiger Charm**: "We've done it all by the book. All we have to do is wait for the fairy-tale ending." And we can't forget **The Silver Bullet**: "I fixed it once, dammit, so I'm immune forever."

You need to look everywhere in your life for examples of *goal-oriented* thinking and replace them whenever possible with a *process-oriented* approach. Any time you find yourself thinking, "If I only had _____, then life would be good," you're stepping toward a big, deep pit of moose-crap. Take an extreme example. If your life sucked, then you were diagnosed with terminal cancer, but achieved a miraculous cure, and you had learned nothing from the experience, your life would likely still suck. In this case, the miracle cure was the goal, but learning something from the experience represents process. I've known hundreds of people who really believed that achieving a goal – graduating college, getting married (or divorced), moving to a new city, job promotion, having a baby, finding another lover, buying a house (or sports car, or Harley, or recording studio), becoming a hermit – would punt their life at least halfway toward perfection. The few who allowed the change to expand their viewpoint did indeed find some degree of improvement. The rest, though, were left hurt, morose, cynical, confused, bitter, angry – poorer, but no wiser.

I have a reputation as a very good lover – and by this I mean that I truly enjoy talking, listening, dancing, holding hands, and so on, and I'm charming, interesting (and interested), and flirtatious. When asked my secret, I say, "All you have to do is enjoy the trip. Get in the car, throw the map out the window, and see where the interesting-looking roads take you." Life ought to be more a dance than a foot-race.

Easy, or simple.

We stroll into deep weeds when we confuse these words, and a note to the wise (which I'm assuming you are) should be sufficient. The *easy* choices can be made without considering potential fallout and long-range consequences. Careful thought, planning, and attention to the details can lead to very *simple* (or even *elegant*) solutions.

The real world is largely not either/or.

As a great physicist once said (Bohr, I think it was), "The opposite of a trivial truth is false. The opposite of a great truth is also true." In our case, there is nothing wrong with the fundamentals of monogamy, and there is nothing wrong with the fundamentals of nonmonogamy – one truth does not supersede or invalidate the other. A closed relationship will probably never work for me, but I do my best to advise those in closed relationships. Someone who steps into the sort of open, network-based polyamory I advocate might find nothing but endless disaster. If you should happen to find something that works extraordinarily well for you, don't assume that it would be ideal for another individual, or in different circumstances. If you admire someone's life, don't get too worked up about copying their methods – the "secret" might, for instance, lie more in their communication style than in how they split the bills. Cut yourself a little slack, and do the same for others you meet, and the world will be a much happier place.

"Good relationships last forever."

In a certain sense, this is true, but it's nowhere near as generalizable as people want to believe. Even the best romances don't last truly forever on this physical plane, and darned few last a lifetime. If you work at it, though, you can surround yourself with deep and abiding friendships that could withstand the tests of time. A solid friendship can roll with the changes.

Intimate relationships are like butterflies: they have distinct stages, they grow, they change – they metamorphose. The "caterpillar" might be kinda ugly, but lead to a "butterfly" that's perfect for both of you. The reverse could be true. You could even find yourself in a relationship that is a metaphorical "pupa," a transition for one or more of you between an outgrown lifestyle and a radically different future. You have to take them for what they are, and that might mean facing up to eventual drastic change. These stages and these patterns have one thing in common: if you force it to be what you want it to be, rather than enjoy what it inherently is, you *will* kill it. Even a "doomed" relational phase might be fantastically rewarding for everyone involved if you don't force it to be what it cannot be.

Getting from knowledge to wisdom.

Knowledge is nothing more than a collection of facts, mere data. Understanding takes reflection, and empathy, and maybe a little experience. Wisdom comes from understanding, not from knowledge.

Count your blessings.

Recall that old song: "Every night before I sleep, I count my blessings instead of sheep." Whether life is good, bad, or indifferent, I do this regularly, looking even at "failed" relationships and blown friendships. No matter how much I wish things had gone better, any sense of longing is soon replaced by gratitude.

Learn from what has passed.

History, like any other natural disaster, is something that happened to someone else. Practice at wondering how you would have handled the situations you hear and read about.

Honestly-won mistakes.

More often than not, an honest mistake demonstrates a willingness to learn. People who live a charmed existence are ultimately like those who don't exercise: when unforeseen difficulties occur, they can only buckle under the load. Anyone who's ever raised a child ought to have learned that the exploration and understanding of the world practically requires a certain amount of breakage. Ideally, error indicates exercise of ability. Don't be too quick to assume that screwups indicate stupidity, treachery, or moral lassitude – at very least, "Never ascribe to treachery what can be adequately explained by stupidity."

Do it now.

Do not wait for the "perfect moment" to show that you care. I don't want to sound fatalistic, but shit does indeed happen. Disasters occur. People die suddenly. Crises pop up that can drive a big wedge into your friendship. I cannot count the number of times when life was wearing me to the bone, and I received a message on my answering machine or e-mail that said something like, "Hi! We haven't talked in far too long. I was just thinking of you today, and how glad I am that you're around." Take thirty seconds and brighten someone's life. If you're feeling expansive, send flowers, especially if you haven't seen each other in months.

Avoid naysayers.

A true friend is someone with the unmitigated gall to tell you when you're about to drown in your own bullshit. However, you can quickly end up with too much of a good thing if they don't know when the hell to shut up. In at least the near future, polyamory involves all sorts of gambles and risks. No matter how frightfully optimistic you are, if you have too many people in your life telling you "it ain't gonna work," unnecessary doubts will begin to creep into your unconscious, which will wear at your problem-solving abilities, and the negativity could eventually overwhelm you. Empty-headed grinning optimism is useless, but reflexive pessimism of pernicious. If you're going to give polyamory a serious try, then make sure you have a few solid friends, the kind who say things like, "I don't know why you'd want to do that to yourself, but I'm behind you all the way." If someone close to you cannot help undercutting you at every turn, then avoid the subjects that set them off.

24. Good theory & $5 will get you a double mocha

Which is another way of saying that "paper polyamory" has surprisingly little to do with living it, every day, every hour. The metaphorical road to Hell is certainly paved with good intentions; nowadays, that road has lovely borders made from good theory.

Getting real

Someone once told me that, to be a cliff diver in Hawai'i, you can study oceanography for years. You can go to the inlet you're going to dive, and watch the water patterns for weeks, even years. You can sonar the rocks below, map out current rhythms, put the whole thing on a computer. Which makes sense: dive at the wrong moment, you hit the surface wrong (or find rocks on the way down or resurfacing).

But when it comes down to it, rationality only takes you so far along in the process. You've still just got to jump off the cliff, maybe praying all the way down, or you're not a cliff diver. Of course, you could still make the wrong choice, and end up quite dead. But at least you'd be a cliff diver.

In the mid-1980s, I got into a tiff with another member of PEP, back in the Olden Days when "poly" meant polyfidelity, period. I was denounced by someone who'd been married monogamously for years, and had recently decided she was really polyfidelitous all along. She took me to task for my "immoral" and "emotionally abusive" lifestyle – meaning that, at the time, I was in a multi-household intimate network, where I had a primary, two secondary, and two tertiary intimate relationships, all out in the open, and all 5-10 years established. So, I brought up that comparing nonmonogamy-as-practice to nonmonogamy-as-philosophy is like comparing walnuts to rollerskates: there's so little commonalty that no valid wide-ranging comparisons can be drawn. The philosophy can survive nicely as dreams and ideals, where the practice is usually inundated with day-to-day processes of being in love, having a life, etc.

It's perfectly possible to have either philosophy or practice – and nothing says that one leads necessarily to the other.

While I understand to a degree where this comes from, I worry about people who make the claim, "I've *always* been polyamorous!" If that statement is based on the idea that, genetically, we are all inherently bisexual and nonmonogamous, then I can go along. Elsewise, it's self-deluding nonsense. After all, if polyamory were so simple and "natural," there wouldn't be much reason to make a big thing about it.

When I was introduced to the concept of nonmonogamy, I just couldn't see why there would be any fuss. It makes perfect sense to me, and always has. But that didn't make me nonmonogamous – I was deeply involved with my first lover, and still a bit shaky at just being gamous!

When I was still a virgin, I knew damned well that my heterosexuality was still entirely theoretical. As I once told a friend, "For all I know, Mister Right could come along any minute."

Blindsided by possibility: real polyamory

The Constantines pointed out that, of the groups they interviewed, the ones that seemed to have lasted longest were where one partner of a close-knit dyad suddenly realized that he also loved another... so everyone *had* to sit down, figure out how to make it work, then maybe find time to work out how in the blue blazes they'd ended up there ("backfilling the history," I've called it). By comparison, the groups that fell apart in a short time, with much screaming, were usually where two couples had intellectualized themselves into it, having read an article somewhere, then decided to embark on a harmless little experiment; see *Bob & Carol & Ted & Alice* and similar.

Don't go getting all full of yourself simply because you've made the leap. As I point up elsewhere, there's nothing more rabidly orthodox than a new convert, or more mean-spiritedly vengeful than someone who's gotten their fingers burned. I'd really like it if you never became one of the latter, and I think we should work together to keep you just as far from the former role.

I was heavily into writing articles about nonexclusive committed relationships back in the 1980s. For this, I was regularly denounced for adamantly living my life outside the One True Way Of Living, called polyfidelity. I cannot count the times since that I've gotten into vicious arguments with people who live in an intellectualized romantic fantasy... then, when they stub a toe against Reality, they start lashing out at "the people that went out of their way to hurt me" rather than sorting out the pieces and learning from the experience.

At some point, you will have to set aside your theorizing, whether it's a few stray thoughts or an entire library, and dive into it. I have some very clear memories of my first attempts ton a two-wheeler, and the parallels are pretty darned obvious to me. Like learning to ride a bicycle without training wheels, you'll likely screw it up, fall off, and end up with various bruises and contusions. If you don't crash on the first ride, you will probably do it soon enough. Being deathly afraid of falling will make you so paranoid and tense that the chances of meeting with disaster increase markedly. There is no amount of reading, theorizing, and visualization that will prevent accidents – which is probably why they're called accidents. If you're going to ride a bike, you need to first accept the risks, then start pedaling.

Cookie-cutters are dangerous

Monogamy is based heavily in unsubstantiated or faulty theory. I don't think there's anything fundamentally wrong with monogamy, but so much nonsense has accreted around it, aided greatly by political and religious strictures that seem to vary wildly depending on which acre of this Earth one is presently occupying.

If we let "polyamory" be defined as "everything but monogamy," we'd find ourselves in the middle of a similar quagmire. This is one of the main reasons that I am such a stickler for some unified base of definitions, and frameworks from which we (especially the people newest to polyamory) can build. As vital as order is, at some point it settles down to being handy when new situations and problems arise, not some carefully engineered template against which you compare your every thought, word, deed, action, or plan. Monogamy generally manages to pretend that it possesses the strengths of both extremes, the "repairs toolkit" and the "construction toolkit," while in reality it cannot access logical structure in either good times or bad.

Even in an ideal world, monogamy is not for me, but I sincerely wish that some of the confusion could be straightened out, so that the people who choose monogamy as their personal right–not the default or only option – could have long, happy, fulfilling relationships.

When difficulties crop up, polyfolk are sometimes tempted to believe that this self-delusion is entirely real. Even if it were, though, the core circumstances are so fundamentally different that the methodology would be at best counterproductive, and likely couldn't be applied at all without reworking the situation so thoroughly that "polyamory" would no longer apply.

At the bottom line, good theory can pull your *tuchus* out of the flames when problems strike and you don't know where to even start. But theory can really be nothing more than the beginning point for common sense, diligence, emotional risk, flexibility, persistence, and all that. Never – never! – fall into the trap of believing that the solution you found in a book, at a discussion group, in a seminar, from friends in approximately similar situations, or even from your own direct experience is going to be a perfect fit to your needs. Even when you're talking the same set of people in a quandary quite evocative of one you've already conquered, time has nevertheless moved on and you may now require a vastly different solution.

25. Lifelong intent, day-to-day attitude

Here we are, products of a society full of high-contrast decision making: you can do *this*, or you can do *that*. From a very early age, we are taught to *not see* where we can do both... or neither... or maybe choose another path entirely – even create a more desirable path, all by yourself.

Responsible nonmonogamy requires a degree of paradox, or at least what we are raised to see as paradox. You will need to let go of thinking in terms of black-or-white, good-or-bad, since there are so many situations that will have consequences both bad and good, and there are so many oversimplified choice-sets that overlook superior courses of action.

Time and again, I have seen polyamorous people (couples and singles) make and accept promises that only the most desperate monogamists would seriously consider. For instance, they exchange telephone numbers the first time they meet in a polyamorous chatroom, spend many hours talking and spinning out their hopes and dreams, and within weeks are making plans to meet so that they can discuss living together (which, at that point, is pretty much a foregone conclusion). You may think that an extreme example, but I have watched it happen three times in the past six months on one Internet site alone. All involved entirely different people, and all fell quickly apart with assorted claims of heartbreak, deceit, and melodrama.

While I could happily spend thousands of words deconstructing these situations, I am going to restrain myself to the present heading. In many of such cases – and definitely in the three mentioned – most of the mistakes could have been headed off in some way if they had not been so narrowly focused on finding a life-partner. This was such a central goal that most of the people involved lost track entirely of looking for a friend with whom they could develop a relationship that might last for years or even until death.

What will happen will happen. You can set your course off toward some glorious future, but the philosopher wasn't kidding around when he insisted that "the journey of a thousand miles begins with a single step." Well, *begins*, hell – a journey is nothing *but* single steps. Along the way is the occasional impassable gorge, requiring alternate routes, a retracing of the path to a potentially more rewarding way, and sometimes complete abandonment of the expedition. Sometimes people quit from disgust or injury or sheer discouragement, or maybe they find a place so beautiful and perfectly suited to their nature that they don't see any good reason to go further. You should always start out with your grand and glorious plans well-conceived, but the world has a way of throwing surprises at you, good and bad, that will require you to revise your itinerary.

Let me bring in another one of those "everyone knows what *that* means" words. That is **commitment**. Likely, you cannot define the term, and chances are little better that you could tell someone in a hundred words or less how to recognize a commitment when they trip over it. We tend anyway to mix it up with **obligation**, and everyone *knows* that obligations are *bad*, anchors that only drag you down, you just have to grit your teeth and take it.

I don't think that obligations are necessarily bad, though they are sometimes burdens foisted upon us. When I sign the paperwork on a new car, or arrange a mortgage to buy a house, I am contracting an obligation. My commitment, though, is much more complex: I am taking on responsibility for the care, upkeep, and repair of my new acquisition, to act as the owner even though I technically do not yet own it. I have to commit to get along with my neighbors, to not unduly upset the health inspectors, and to pay my taxes and insurance. Most of these commitments stand long after the last payment is made. So, too, do you take on a whole shedload of commitments even before (and long after) you establish formal control over the situation.

That's how it goes in polyamory as well. There are nested stacks of commitment, and matching obligations. One simple little choice could contain as many layers as an onion.

First of all, you need to be committed to polyamory. If it simply gets to be too much for you, you can always change, but being poised and ready to jump ship at the first difficulty will not make you many trusting friends who are more dedicated to polyamory. If you waffle enough, people might get the feeling that you're only interested in skimming off the fun times.

Then, you need commitment to your own goals and ideals. You are not merely trying on a costume, but are lining up to join a worldwide community that for the most part treasures the strengths of each of its members. To belong, you must contribute, if only to help provide stability over time.

You have to be committed to the people already in your life. Never forget that your friends might be all that prevents you from making really stupid NRE-driven decisions, or running for the hills just as everything is about to get really good.

After that, you must be committed to the person or persons with whom you intend to form a relationship, and to their needs.

Most importantly, once you've learned how to do all of this, you have to be committed to forever repeating the steps, with established and new and potential relationships alike.

26. Learning to deal with change

Skip this section only at your own peril. No, I'm not exaggerating in the least, and hopefully a few minutes will sufficiently warn you about the major killer of many a solid relationship.

About 1990, I read a study of couples who married after cohabiting. The couples under scrutiny had been living together for widely divergent spans of time, anywhere from a few months up to sixteen years. For you younger readers, premarital cohabitation had been widely seen as scandalous well into the 1970s, but soon thereafter began to gain a cachet as a sort of "test marriage" that weeded out couples most prone to fall apart anyway under the mundane stresses of actually living together, thus minimizing the divorce statistics.

The researchers were interested in finding out how accurate cohabitation was as a predictor of marital success. What they found stunned them, and surprised the heck out of me. Not only was the average time until divorce somewhat less than three years–in other words, pretty much the national average for all marriages – but length of time living together before marriage had no significant correlation with how long the dyad survived after making it official.

A decade later, while examining an excellent book on couple therapy (*You're Not What I Expected*, by Polly Young-Eisendrath), I finally understood the underlying phenomenon. It's simple, really: any significant change has the potential to completely redefine the relationship. Change one relatively large factor, and you might find yourself practically starting over again.

The problem is not the change itself, or the even resultant redefinition, but fallout from what happens when these tremors run smack into prevalent social conditioning.

Job demotions can lead to breakups, but so can promotions. A new house or a new baby can kill a troubled relationship as fast as it can repair one. There are many tales of spouses who filed for divorce soon after their partner quit an addiction, overcame deep-seated mental or emotional problems, or miraculously recovered from cancer. Whether success or failure, change is nevertheless change, and this is even more traumatic if one partner clearly did almost all of the actual struggling – even in failure, that partner has been forced to grow much more than the other. One or both of them will soon feel that the "helping" partner has been left far behind… and this is true enough.

Living happily in crisis

Using the word *never* is absolutely begging for trouble. This thought may have occurred to you in some rather boring niches of daily life. The staunchest atheist will wait for the heavens to rain down fire when they hear someone utter that hallmark of hubris, "Well, *that* could never happen!"

While crisis recurs in simpler lifestyles, it's an inherent facet to polyamory, so you might as well get used to it, and maybe learn to not only enjoy it, but eagerly anticipate that change will come, whether you look for it or not.

Polyamory can best be described as an endless series of changes, many of which are outright crises. Anything you do that is more complex or emotionally loaded than turning on the television set – and sometimes that as well – is at least a change.

If it were just a matter of looking at you as an individual, change would be generally easy to cope with. For the most part, you know your own weaknesses, your blind spots, the areas where you're not so good. Even if you don't, you might know on a semiconscious or conscious level that some things make you uncomfortable, as they press a little close to your comfort margin, or begin to resemble situations that frighten you. Short of neurosis, you get through the days and take change as it happens.

It's very unlikely that any two people possess an identical set of touchy areas, and therefore probably impossible that you react to each stimulus to the same degree, in similar situations. You might both be extremely uncomfortable around bugs, yet it's probable that (for example) one of you can't sleep knowing there's a moth in the house, while the other is frightened only of spiders due to a childhood allergic reaction. You might both have a strong aversion to crunching numbers, yet one of you balances the checkbook without a qualm and the other does the taxes. Usually, such misalignment offers amazing possibilities for the sharing of strengths, as well as for having someone to help you ease around your own weaknesses. In many circumstances, though, it will count against you, because one person is constitutionally incapable of remembering that a particular habit, activity, or phrase sends their partner into absolute panic or rage.

In the days before "no fault" divorce, which is about as uncomplicated as breaking up any other legal partnership by the mutual consent of the partners, you would have had to find a very good reason to convince a judge to approve of your a divorce. One of the more popular reasons was irreconcilable differences; then there was mental cruelty. When I was young, a judge granted a divorce to a couple that had finally disintegrated after the wife proved incapable, despite (one imagines) perpetual nagging, of squeezing the toothpaste tube from the end. The husband filed for divorce after finding the tube crushed yet again in its center. The divorce was granted on the grounds of mental cruelty, which we would nowadays label abuse.

Relationships have ended over many such differences that, to anyone else, would probably seem inconsequential. The family car might be a battered wreck, but perhaps the husband keeps a minute inventory of every dent and ding, and raises thorough hell when any tiny new scratch is discovered during his regular inspections. In the 1970s, a lawyer mentioned that he was increasingly being asked to draw up prenuptial agreements, and said, wonderingly, "If I had my say, I wouldn't allow most of those people to have a joint checking account, much less anything more complicated."

I remember a marriage therapist who said, "I once saved a family with Rubbermaid. She was ready to leave her husband because he regularly forgot to pick up his socks. He'd throw them into a corner or kick them under the bed, and she'd have to crawl around the bedroom before she could do the wash. He was working long shifts, and he'd stumble to bed late at night, dropping his clothing as he went. When they laid out the story to me, it all looked pretty hopeless. For as much as they acknowledged each other, it might as well have been two of us in the room. Knowing that they would probably go right from my office to the courthouse, I ordered them to go out and get a hamper, just for him, then to come back to me in a month. Amazingly, it worked – she didn't have to go hunting down his socks and underwear, and he got multiple rewards from making a game out of diligently using the hamper and pleasing his wife enough that she warmed up to him."

That is how we deal with known, observable habits. The stress level jumps when we are talking about reactions to stimuli that are far less common. When you find something new about a certain person, your view of them changes. Your image of them becomes more detailed, and not necessarily in a good way. You thus treat them differently, or change the way you act around them. Sensing that something is up, and unsure as to the reason, they respond in kind. It strikes me that, for a process that ought to be much like unwrapping a package, things get balled up rapidly: two people who thought they knew each other perfectly suddenly find themselves strangers. If you are prepared for it, this can be an exciting time as you establish a far deeper level of understanding – and a wretched mess if you prefer to pay more attention to the wrapping than to the wonder that is being revealed.

If a mere two people with one bitty little relationship have such rich opportunities for spiraling misunderstanding stemming from their mismatches, then imagine what it's going to be like when you have three people, who represent four interpersonal relationships. (I won't get into the math, but four people have the potential for eleven relationships – six dyads, four triads, and a quad – and five people can have up to 26. Welcome to practical combinatorics.)

Two more words

Some terms, through the way we use them, reflect how inherently fearful we are of change in the established order. You likely will be able to add to these, but I'll get you started.

Chaos

The potential for chaos is inherent in systems, else they wouldn't be complex enough to deserve being called systems. There are many layers as well. The world is full of chaos and chaotic potential. So is Western culture. So is the culture of the United States. So is that of each region, state, area, county, city, district, neighborhood, block, and cluster of houses. Each family is loaded with chaos, as is each household, each relationship. In fact, each level of each and every relationship tends toward chaos.

We look at chaos as inherently bad, and we do the human thing: we ignore it. We pretend not only that chaos isn't possible, but that it doesn't happen to good people, which we (again blindly) tend to believe we are.

Well, we *are* good people. Nevertheless, chaos *is* there.

Most people do not, however, see themselves as creative. They have damped down their curiosity about the world and their place in it, so, even though it sometimes feels as if half the people I meet insist on telling me, "I'm working on my novel," the truth is that the majority are following a formula of putting words down on paper, with no sense of storytelling, or even of the need to develop storytelling skills, much less to love the power of the written word, to express the wonders of poetry and history, and so on. They're not truly creative, because they have not been forced to be creative, and they see no reason to force themselves in that direction.

But the artist and the entrepreneur understand what the mathematician and the ecologist are saying: chaos is potential. You cannot hope to *exploit* chaos in the same way that you can order parts from the warehouse & assemble them – anyone who thinks so is still trapped in their little monkey-brain thinking patterns. Chaos is powerful because of that potential, and we do indeed fear and crave power. Leave both facets aside, and learn to tap into its creative potential.

Since the mathematics of chaos and catastrophe were first brought out in accessible literature, I have been arguing with people who believe they can simply apply mechanistic thinking to the "fuzzy" sciences. Well, bullcrap. If you've ever:

- started a thriving business on a shoestring
- learned to love the nuances of bebop
- learned a little *t'ai chi*
- found ballroom dancing exhilarating
- sparred in a martial art (boxing or karate or kickboxing)
- picked up a guitar once in awhile to jam along with the radio

then and only then are you privy to the truth–

Chaos is a dance, not a machine.

Polyamory has, by definition, more inherent chaotic potential than does monogamy. You cannot hope to be "successfully polyamorous" by reading a book, finding a checklist, attending a certification course, or assigning yourself to a guru. Life can throw all sorts of lessons at you in the course of your poly explorations, but if you don't attend to them, it's not as if they stick to your skin and magically soak into your brain.

One last thought. The opposite of chaos is *entropy*. That's the "force" that drags all energy, all movement, all chance of creativity down toward identity. That is, when the chaotic level in the Universe reaches zero, the whole thing will be nothing but undifferentiated atoms. Go on distrusting chaos in your relationships if you must, but never forget that at the other end of the scale lies predictability. If you would rather have safety than freedom, permanence than the highs and lows of exploration, then it's possible that nonmonogamy would not be the direction you ought to travel.

Drama

A few years ago, I spotted one of the many aphorisms a friend had taped to her wall. This one said, "I will have no drama in my life."

As we'd been discussing the fact that she seemed to go out of her way to create dramatic events from even the most stable of situations, I brought this up to her over dinner. Though nobody changed any minds, the thoughts that surfaced have stayed with me.

There is absolutely nothing wrong with drama – start right this minute to purge such daffy notions from your thinking. The dictionary tells me that a drama is "a story involving conflict of characters." This sounds a little like real life to me... unless you're stuck in denying that conflict has any positive purpose. If you believe *that*, you're a fool.

Desires conflict. Needs conflict. Schedules conflict. If there's a desirable position opening up at work, then there'll be all *sorts* of conflict; even if everyone is

119

totally amicable, this is still a conflict, and there's no way you can talk your way around the fact.

Conflict stems from a couple of simple facts: most supplies are limited, and two people cannot occupy the same space simultaneously. You can minimize the former (though eliminating the fact is impossible), but you're pretty much stuck with the latter. Therefore, q.e.d., conflict is also part of the whole shebang.

Drama is not only inherent, but can be quite invigorating. Problems begin when everyone on the stage doesn't know they're playing. Don't force others to join in your dramatic presentation – at best, that's passive-aggressive behavior, and slides quickly toward resembling codependency.

Grab hold of your own dramatic potential, and start putting it to use. If you're going to work from a script, and interact with others, then make sure you're all on the same page. Find a good storyline. Strive for decent dialogue. Cast people into roles that actually suit them, and rewrite character outlines rather than force your fellow actors into unbelievable situations. Go for a great performance rather than a rote reading of your script.

In other words, drama ain't necessarily a bad thing, but you maybe ought to avoid cheap melodrama. Your audience will thank you, your cast will thank you, and you'll find more enjoyment from life.

27. Figuring out what you are

Not to go all New Age metaphysical on you, but there is a little more bad news I have to share with you.

You don't know yourself.

You don't know what you want.

You don't know why you do things.

You don't know what'll make you happy.

You don't even know how to begin a search that will at least lead you to the right outlook that'll eventually teach you how to ask the necessary questions.

You're clueless. That's okay, it's entirely human. But unless you *face* it, and come to *embrace* it, you'll only have the choice of whether to spend your life thrashing around (likely doing nothing more than damaging yourself and the tiny part of the world closest to you) or sitting in stunned insensibility.

It's not your fault. You were raised this way, in a society that values regularity, predictability, conformity, the assembly-line approach to life. You were brought up to be a good little cog in the machine Leviathan that is the view of the world fed to us by that very machine. If you were especially reliable and useful, you might aspire to someday become a bigger cog.

But still a cog.

There is no sin in that. However, by reading books like this, you demonstrate that you've at least become dissatisfied with the mythos that's been handed to you, inculcated from the moment you first opened your eyes, and while you might not be ready to make any seemingly radical changes, you are at least beginning to understand the terrible truth – there might be options. Options not just imaginable, but potential, even viable, and likely dangerous, exciting, rewarding, and deeply satisfying.

Compared to most people, I'm out on the cutting edge of life, yet not a day goes by that I don't spend at least a few minutes in delighted wonder at how completely clueless I remain. The world that actually exists is so much bigger and more fascinating and outright baffling than the description of the world we are given, where everything falls neatly into place and has a reason and an explanation and a nice simple us-relevant purpose in the scheme.

Someone once said to me, "I don't see what the problem is. All a person has to do is connect the damn dots."

This stopped me. It certainly appeared that they had a point, but something about the idea didn't seem quite right. I thought about it, and I replied, "That is eminently logical, and even obvious, but it's *so* obvious that it overlooks a whole big bunch of reality. To connect the dots, people have to recognize that the dots *need* to be connected. That presupposes that they know the dots are *there*. And *that* is built on the supposition that they understand that the dots could even *be* there. Getting to the point of 'doing the obvious' scares them off on a subconscious level, because putting together that chain of realizations, just to get to the easy part, looks like a lot of work."

It's not really much work, of itself, but we are so conditioned against seeing things as they are, understanding why this is so, and changing the underlying assumptions in order that we can bring betterness into being, that we wander away. The step itself is nothing; taking it is *almost* impossible, because we tell ourselves it is *likely* impossible.

Here's an outline I came up with some years ago, of the steps toward creating a perfect life. [In *The Deviant's Advantage*, Mathews and Wacker call this an **obstacle inventory**.] You should:

- conceive that some person somewhere might have an option, any option at all
- conceive that some person somewhere might realize that he/she *has* an option
- conceive that some person somewhere could analyze that option and see what makes it tick
- conceive that some person somewhere could think about what tools or actions would be necessary to approach that option as a goal
- conceive that some person somewhere could accumulate the resources to acquire the necessary tools
- conceive that some person somewhere could acquire those tools and learn to use them adequately enough to begin
- conceive that some person somewhere could use those tools to move toward realizing the goal
- conceive that some person somewhere could learn in the act of striving toward the goal
- conceive that some person somewhere could avoid giving up in discouragement from the inevitable delays, mistakes, and setbacks
- conceive that some person somewhere could modify and expand the tools they have in order to overcome obstacles and even take advantage of them
- conceive that some person somewhere could achieve that goal

- conceive that some person somewhere could continue the momentum and proceed to one goal after another
- conceive that you therefore probably have options of your own
- conceive that these options are to varying degrees worth possessing
- conceive that these options are therefore worth working toward
- conceive that these options vary widely in how much effort, time, and preparatory groundwork is necessary
- conceive that these options also vary widely in the form and timespan that rewards and payoffs will take
- conceive that even a single goal has many benefits, since each requires polishing a different grouping of skills, and these skills are probably part of the profit
- conceive that this list of options could be pared down to one goal, or a few loosely related goals, or a grouping of closely related goals
- conceive that you could create such a list for yourself
- conceive that you could pare it down to a manageable and immediate size
- conceive of yourself being intelligent and determined enough to tackle this sort of properly focused list
- accept that your life could be better
- accept that you can steer your life in better directions
- accept that resources you currently expend in surviving the moment could be better spent creating the future
- accept that you can learn what you need to get started, and can find the help for what you don't know or can't do yourself
- accept that you will make mistakes, that they are inevitable and do not reflect negatively on you – if you accept and learn from them
- learn to trust yourself
- take the next step
- accept your mistakes and learn from them
- keep moving forward
- keep your eyes open
- keep learning
- stay fascinated with what happens
- feel good about your successes, and about your role in making them real

The reason I felt the need for such an outline is that none of the self-help, motivational, positive-thought books I'd read ever addressed the first steps. The progression is too *obvious*, too simple. In looking through my notes, I found a typical comment I made on this lack: "how do we teach people to dream? to have the simple raw courage to hope?" That thought has been with me for many years, and I still ponder it.

Refer back to the above outline often, and use it as a checklist to see how you're doing. Don't get angry about what you haven't managed yet, or what you've attained then slid back from. Always, let yourself feel proud about what you *have* done. Making it through ten stages in some well-defined project is far better than never having made the attempt.

28. What are *your* motivations?

Here are some not-so-great – but common – reasons that people decide to seek out a so-called intimate relationship. Notice that I do not append the "multiple" modifier, as many of these reasons apply to even the stiffest monogamy. I can court a potential relationship:

- to avoid having to deal with my own self-doubts, perceived failings, and neuroses
- to add excitement to a life that seems boring
- to enliven a sex life that's become routine
- to replace a sex life that's faded, or evaporated
- for the ego-gratification
- to spread myself thinly enough to avoid intimacy

"So," you may be asking, "what's actually wrong with these things?" Inherently, nothing much; in fact, they are all interesting and even rewarding facets to polyamory. However, if they are at the top of your hopefully long list of motivations, then you're likely barking up the wrong tree. These sorts of justifications indicate that you're probably incapable of consolidating your gains – if you can even recognize your gains.

I'm not even going to ask you to stand up in public to admit to your shallowness, if this describes you. But if you cannot at least be brutally honest with yourself, deep within the privacy of your own skull, then you will likely find that the rigors of polyamory will be too much for you.

If you are claiming to be seeking relationships that are more than superficially "intimate," if you ostensibly want commitment and constancy and reliability, then I can tell you the single dumbest reason to take on more sexual partners: because you can. I know this from direct and regular experience.

There is nothing less attractive than desperation, remember. Conversely, I know for a fact that nothing makes me more attractive in general than to appear in public utterly and disgustingly happy with the intimate relationships in my life. I'm not very good-looking, but when my life is running smoothly I am at my absolute best, witty, charming, friendly, affectionate, and unflappable. Many people who meet me in this mood either decide they dislike me, or want to join in on the "wonder drug" that I represent. (Sometimes both.)

Degrees of want

Are there positive, healthy reasons to have multiple intimate relationships in your life? Oh, yes!

Problem-solving is rewarding.

There is more opportunity to share a wide variety of personal interests.

We all need family.

People on our "wavelength" reinforce us.

But when we use the word *reasons*, what we are really saying is, "This is what I want." Such a simple phrase, yet it slides right on up to a word that is far more slippery than you probably realize.

There are many degrees of **want**. They form a sort of continuum, which might be typified as:

- thought
- wish
- "like"
- hope
- desire
- expectation
- need
- lust
- demand
- obsession

I want to look at and compare a few of those specifically; you should be able to deduce the finer points of the remainder.

Want... or need?

I've observed many people over the years who choose to become polyamorous largely because they are lousy at determining their **wants** and their **needs**, differentiating between them, and standing by their varying rights to obtain or at least ask for these things without guilt. Continuing to ignore this will make their foray into polyamory more unlikely, if not impossible. Perhaps fortunately, the wise will find that polyamory offers an excellent opportunity to learn.

Rare is the human who hasn't needed touch or communication, or cuddling or reassurance, and settled for sex instead. Sex is wonderful, sex is perhaps even necessary in some degree for each of us. (One study verified that orgasm improves the functioning of a woman's immune system.) But unless there are other benefits attached, sex is a brief satisfaction. Therefore, sex by itself can only serve as a fleeting substitute for more persistent needs. Outright needs are more akin to hunger in this way, as unless you are outright faint from hunger or low blood sugar, sex can distract you from that as well. But as soon as sex is over, when you've had one or many orgasms, and your racing pulse begins to settle down toward normal, that hunger will return, probably exacerbated. So will any of your other needs, slowly or rapidly.

The object doesn't really matter: To be sanely polyamorous, you need to strive for *better*, more *thorough*, *deeper*, yet many people are still carrying around the myth that all they need is **more**. Should they actually succeed in establishing potentially intimate relationships with more than one person, someone with this presupposition will find themselves dissatisfied – if you have it in your head that you need *more*, then there can never be *enough*. Thereafter, some people lock down to what they have, and assume that more time (without further striving) will make it satisfying. Others decide they've simply got the wrong set of intimates, and expect that they just haven't found "the right ones" yet that will satisfy these cravings. A few believe they just need *more*: more intimates, more sex, more variety, more activity, more melodrama. In my observation, a minority will actually stop and ask the fateful question: "What is it about me that I cannot be satisfied with this person?"

Some poly people do have an actual need for a variety of intimates or sexual partners. There are some relationships where a poly person has two main relationships, one to satisfy most emotional needs and one to satisfy most physical needs, or maybe one to take care of stability (they're fantastic roommates, and both well-employed, with good investment portfolios) and the other for entertainment (together they enjoy a constant round of concerts, plays, exhibitions, creativity, etc.). I've even observed where one was primarily a romantic relationship and another was the primary sexual relationship.

Needs are necessary; wants are optional, but potentially energizing. Nothing is wrong with either group, and generally there is nothing wrong with any of the entries in either category (generally, of course, any specific longing is some combination of want and need, and even for any individual the balance changes depending on circumstances). However, unless you are cursed with an exceedingly poor imagination, or you are suffering under the burden of vast emotional trauma, your wants should always far outstrip your needs. Wanting to have two simultaneous intimate relationships, in hopes for happiness, may ultimately be incorrect, but the desire is not wrong. On the other hand, if you feel that you *need* to have two relationships before you can be happy, then I'd have to say that you are probably wrong.

More about *more*

As many observers of our society have pointed out, we are so often obsessed with sex because we truly don't have enough of it. And I mean much more than orgasms or naked bodies. We are not allowed (by the standard rules) to discuss sex freely, to observe others enjoying it, to ask intelligent questions, to be curious, to assume that others have enjoyed it, to speculate openly at what the thoughts and feelings and experiences of others are about sex. Sex is one of the most pervasive experiences of our existence, yet we treat it as if it's a shameful secret, reasoning that it *must* be icky because that's how everyone else behaves.

Let me back up a little: "we don't have enough of it." The fact is, we are even more obsessed with consuming, with the idea that if we have *more*, then all our problems will vanish. In this case, what we need is to eliminate the **need** for more, which in almost every case should never be greater than a **want**, and generally nothing more than a passive desire or a **like**.

I would *like* to have more money; it would be nice, I know how I would set about enjoying more money and using it to ease my life, explore new facets of the world, and expand my interests. When I'm in a cash crunch, or there's some unexpected crisis or emergency, then I'm likely to be absolutely correct when I say that I *want* more money so that I can get past something that makes me uncomfortable. Very few times in my life has money been an outright *need*, and those were but moments, because I found some sort of solution to each situation.

There are likely many people in our society who do need more sex. However, this is generally true only as long as that obsession remains that stems directly from perceived lack. A woman who dreams of having hours of lovemaking every day, but who feels that she has to settle for ten minutes every week or two, simply has a pleasant fantasy to balance out the neglect she feels. If the same woman were to find herself in a new relationship where hours of daily sex was a *requirement*, she might soon find herself dreaming of leisure time and brief passionate encounters. Though she may never figure it out, what she is desiring is some sort of pleasant average.

On the other side of the coin, I speak with the occasional male who feels that twenty minutes of sex is an oppressive burden. He, of course, wants me to give him the secret of having two, or three, or four regular sexual partners. My current response is something like, "What I hear you saying is that, because you can't handle one frustrated, pissed-off woman, you think having two is going to be better." He usually replies that his scheme is for them to "keep each other happy" until he feels like being attentive. "Dude," I say, "that's a perfect situation for them to decide that they don't need you at all. They might conclude that, if they want a guy, they can find some attentive young stud who is willing to be good in the sack."

Seeking merely for more will get you into far more corners than it gets you out of.

Needs: an inaction list

Any given moment, any act, is either fulfilling a need, or packing down a need. Likely, there are multiple needs involved to some degree, maybe even a dozen, but you can determine which has precedence. As to "packing down a need," this can take many forms: distraction, denial, direct suppression. If what you need most is to rest, then you could find something interesting on television, go out dancing at a crowded nightclub, eat a spicy late-night snack that you know always disagrees with you, guzzle coffee… or go to bed early.

These are called (post-Freud) *slips*. Though we like to think of slips as random accidental missteps, more often than not they are acts of self-sabotage, attempts to prove that we have control over our needs. Sabotage may appear a harsh word in this context, but I assure you that it is a perfectly apt term. While self-discipline is a good trait to master, you can no more banish a need by act of will than you can decide to stop breathing, or to live on a diet with no protein or carbohydrates.

Awareness of your actions and their underlying motivations is a skill-set that is largely lacking in our culture. Over the past 30 years, I've gotten pretty good at observing how my unconscious mind works. Though I'm far from perfect, this has been an excellent tool for examining my own actions and motivations.

Let's set out another obstacle inventory. This one isn't at all pretty. Here are the first steps of what happens inside of me when I say to myself, "I want to be calmer, stronger, better. What do I need to do next?"

- To fix my failings, I would have to find them.
- Looking for them means admitting that they could exist.
- This admission acknowledges my weakness.
- To be weak is to give up advantage by being vulnerable.
- Vulnerability leaves me open to attack.
- If I am attacked, I will lose, because I am weak and imperfect.
- Since I would lose, I had better have something big to gain from fixing even one little failing.
- Though I don't know what "losing" would entail, it must be much worse than problems caused by any given failing.

- Since I stand to lose either way, I should shore up my defenses and hope for the best.
- If I withdraw from the world, just a little, then there will be fewer people who see my vulnerability, fewer situations I might stumble into that would tax me.
- All I have to do is act aggressively, and only the worst will question my talents and reserves.
- I don't need to look for my failings, because I don't have any worth mentioning.
- Life is good, just the way it is. Really.

Again, this is the reflex pattern that remains embedded inside of me, after decades of ruthless introspection! If you are better, and have entirely overcome these self-limiting patterns of thought, then I salute (and envy) you. However, most people in the world, even despite high intelligence, impeccable schooling, saintly intentions, intense meditation, are not even aware of this chain reaction rippling through them when they are confronted with a possibility for growth.

29. Why polyamory?

You will be doing yourself a life-long favor if you begin learning, right *now*, to think deeply about what attracts you enough to a polyamorous lifestyle that you are reading these very words.

Polyamory is developing an increasing cachet of cool, or hip, or politically correct. More and more, I hear people say dumb things like, "I should be poly," rather than, "I would like to be poly." Behind such phrases as "I *am* poly" lurks poor or nonexistent understanding not only of what the term actually entails, but of the underlying motivations (as detailed in the previous chapter).

Nonmonogamy isn't for everyone, especially not the products of our culture. It is a lot of risk and a lot of work, in the middle of a society that whines about physical labor and wants one-pill solutions for every least irritation. It's a drastic choice being made by people who from birth have come to believe that they are in some way protected from their own poor decisions, and who have enough difficulty choosing between the mocha and the latte.

For the most part, we don't have real choice anyway – in a given situation, we get a menu that lists the options someone else has decided to make available to us. If you want your shrimp grilled, and the menu says you can get them broiled or baked, then your choice doesn't matter a whit. (An especially kindly waitron will promise them grilled as ordered, and trust that you won't know the difference anyway.)

It's a false premise to say that most monogamous people have **chosen** monogamy. Most people belong to the religion they were raised in… because that's what's familiar. That's the milieu they grew up in, and, for better or worse, they're just continuing the pattern. Until this traditionalist mindset is shaken loose, you would likely try from reflex to impose notions onto nonmonogamy that are not only untenable in the new context, but spell sudden and messy doom even in situations that otherwise could be worked out.

Similarly, when you dive into generalized polyamory without the slightest conception of the different "flavors," you might be blinded from recognizing a situation that would be ideal for you. Let's say that you are moderately attractive and affluent and emotionally healthy, and thus have no particular impediments to sane relationships. However, you have already decided that you want to be in an open relationship, even though you have no experience with maintaining multiplicity. If you were to meet up with a polyfidelitous triad looking for a fourth partner, very nice non-rigid people, you might automatically reject that possibility without considering that (a) they could be quite willing to be more open in the future, or (b) you might be completely happy with those people for many years to come. Or, if you have glommed onto the idea of having two lovers, you might not pay proper attention to one person with whom you could create a long-term, primary, central relationship from which to grow over a span of years.

First stupid mistake to avoid: putting more effort in looking for "poly" than in looking for "relationship." If not approached cautiously, you could simply be setting yourself up for multi-person melodrama and never quite get around to having one single relationship worth the term. Is your personal desire for polyamory more about open relating, or about multiple sexual partners? I think that this question is central, and it is rarely addressed, or even acknowledged.

No easy cop-outs, okay? I already agree with the rationalizations: "Both – I have a lot of strong nonsexual intimacy, deep interpersonal relationships with a variety of people, and I also have multiple long-term sexual partners." Hey, I'm with you.

But which of them is most important to *you*? What is it that motivates you? Which stood out more when you first considered the concepts that you later identified as "poly"? If forced by situations, which could you most easily eliminate temporarily? How about permanently?

Both factors have come up in the past as primary to the definition of the concept we call "polyamory." While "multiple sexual partners" may be a central tenet, it's not necessary, nor is it defining. Yet, I do know of a few couples and triads who are, well, lousy at interacting with other people, and when I thought about this I started wondering if this wasn't indeed a factor both central and defining to polyamory.

A test case: If an individual (unattached) wanted to learn more about polyamory, would you think it more important that they are willing to be sexually involved with more than one person during a given period of time, or that they seemed to be fascinated with and attracted to deep and interesting people? I know such people, and their interest is sincere, yet they can be very monogamous, and even celibate. Decide for yourself: can you envision a relationship that is undoubtedly polyamorous, yet there is no sex involved?

Words are important: they shape the way we think. This affects the way we act, and thus the way people around us act, and so the way the community turns, and eventually we shape the world by what we say and how we say it.

I'm polyamorous largely because I find that I am at my most creative, my most secure, my most satisfied when I'm surrounded by a dynamic community of like-minded individuals with whom I feel free to express myself without fear. I'm the classic "lone wolf"; I could survive quite well as the proverbial last man on Earth… but my life wouldn't be anywhere as satisfying. The fact that this has led me to deep and abiding intimacy with some truly remarkable people is a welcome side-effect of this seeking for depth.

I'd rather be alone than surrounded on all sides by a society-so-called where people live in fear of spontaneous self-expression and individuality. I find free, honest, open communication to be exciting. Occasionally painful, sometimes outright scary, yes – just like learning to sailboard, free-climb, speak Russian, write a novel, play bouzouki, make a speech, mountain-bike, etc.

But not from fear of loss. The only loss is to die without ever having made the attempt – regret.

Fear (of singlehood, social rejection, forced autonomy) as a motivating factor is misleading. Our relationship choices respond to abject cluelessness more than fear. And I do mean "clueless" in a literal sense: we not only don't know where we are, we can't ask an intelligent question to get directions.

Monogamy is like the fabled official maps of Moscow when there was still a USSR – they're nicely done, and useful, but purposely inaccurate, so that they can't be used by invaders. You hear a lot about what monogamy is "supposed" to be, and after a while you realize that this is used largely to denote the parts that are rare, mythical, or don't really apply generally.

In polyamory, we are quite proud of our one big advantage – we don't have any maps at all. This is good, because we have so much more freedom and power to draw our own maps, each of us, individually, to suit our particular cases, with as much or as little filigree and brightwork as we feel we need or want on our personal map.

The down side is that we *have* to draw our own maps. But even that has an up-side: we might not be able to exchange maps with each other, but we are able to develop a language to trade tips and techniques–a meta-language, as it were.

You will benefit by occasionally asking yourself, "Why am I here? How is it that I have gotten to this point, and why do I stay?" I hope that your answers are mostly happy.

30. Honesty: risking yourself & others

I used to attend a nightly poker game, generally penny-ante, but the stakes could sometimes run up quite high. (I once folded a pat full house, to avoid taking the deed to a guy's home.) For various reasons, I became quite proficient, but happy to take home only a few dollars here and there, or to lose same.

One night, I was winning regularly. I had figured out the habits of the other regular players, and was getting good cards besides. I paid back a few small loans, paid for some beer, and was left with a little more than I'd arrived with.

A few hands later, I was confronted with a solid hand, and I was being raised mercilessly. I wanted the money I'd put in my wallet to stay there, and I was fast running out of chips on the table as the raises went on.

One of the other players, who had already folded, had been enjoying my winning streak, and had apparently seen my eyes widen when I read my cards. He offered to loan me enough to cover whatever the stakes went to, which I declined.

He looked baffled, and a little hurt. "Come on, you're going to take the hand. Why not accept my money until the pot is yours?"

"Because then I wouldn't be gambling. I'd just be messing around with someone else's money, with no emotional stake, so I wouldn't have my edge."

And that's pretty much what love is:

If you're not vulnerable, it's not love.

If you're not at emotional risk, it's not love.

Of course, you shouldn't go backing yourself into the corner of believing that vulnerability or risk automatically signify love. Okay, you're probably one of the sane majority, but there really are people about who will go out of their way to create melodrama, as that represents the degree (if not the direction) of emotionality that they have learned to associate with love. Drama might be part of the process, but it isn't the goal.

Nevertheless, it oughta be part of a standard definition: **If it ain't honest, it ain't polyamory.**

Look both ways

Honesty opens you to risk. For starters, admitting that problems could even exist might easily call into question your self-image – you'd be admitting that you're less than perfect, at least insofar as being in an imperfect situation. But, well, then you'd have to ask yourself exactly how you got into that situation, so maybe the halo has slipped a bit. Besides that, honesty (however vitally necessary) might irritate the other people involved, no matter how diplomatically you handle it. Observers, partial and impartial alike, might decide to take you to task for your method, your approach, your timing, or your cologne. One of them might be a budding novelist, and you will someday be pseudonymously excoriated in a best-seller that leads to a television series.

Well, that's honesty for ya. The simple truth is that most of that flak will never happen to you, most of the rest will blow over in days, and much of what remains will be something you laugh over a year down the road. The risks are rarely life-or-death. In general, the benefits of approaching a difficult subject, with honesty and without attacking, in the spirit of making things better for everyone involved, far outweigh the potential for negative fallout. At very least, this approach brings to light people in your life who are unwilling (or constitutionally unable) to work in a cooperative and constructive fashion to make things better – this is a painful thing to learn, yes, but it must be compared to the potential pain of working around someone who is a major stumbling block to the happiness of everyone. The first is acute and part of a healing process, where the second is chronic and can color your every experience for many years.

Not that "honesty" and "problems" have to be tightly linked concepts. Far from it.

I was involved with a young woman whose parents were emotionally abusive, in an all-too-common manner. When I complemented her, she tensed, waiting for the punchline, the "gotcha" that was attached to praise. If I said, "That's a very nice dress," she was unconsciously waiting for some further comment such as, "It shows how fat you are, though," or "It's a shame that you don't have any sense of color." When I put my hand on her hip, I might be accused of thus telling her that she was overweight. Living in that sort of emotional minefield is no fun for anyone (unless they've got a deep masochistic streak). She was largely not even aware of her own sullen or angry responses.

Many people would tell me I should have just left the whole thing alone, or even left her, because that's the *easier* choice. A fault of my upbringing, though, is that I have never been able to equate *easier* and *better*, as so many appear to. At my insistence, we dug into the damage underlying all these things, and there was a bit of yelling and crying involved, but we stayed on track. As the weeks passed, she became better at noticing that my praise was not a matter of setting her up for an attack.

I bring that up primarily as an extreme example. By taking a series of risks, based from a desire for honesty, I gained the ability to complement someone important to me. Solving an underlying problem was, to me, merely incidental. I am hardly profligate with my praise, and I like it to be taken at face value when it is offered, without wasting time and energy searching out what I "really meant" by it. The result is that we were both freed up to communicate more clearly without digging around for hidden meanings.

Two mantras toward honesty

First of all, practice saying, **I embrace rookie mistakes**. You cannot possibly avoid every error the first time it comes your way, and neither can the fallible people you know. Your task is to minimize repetition, to avoid foreseeable errors, and to deal in a constructive manner with those that sneak through. If you beat yourself up for honest mistakes, and leave the whole episode behind with just that burst of gleeful martyrdom, you're not learning a damned thing, where you ought to be learning how to examine and fix what went wrong, and to avoid doing it again.

In a similar vein, you have to do some coaching, and encourage the people around you to take the same high ground. You start by not resorting to attack (including sarcasm and other deprecating tones) when someone screws up. You also don't let them get away with mere apology, however effusive. You practice phrases like, "Wow, that really sucked. I'd like to not go through it again," which might lead to argument – you may appear to be trying to keep a wound open for your own dubious purposes – but you are quite capable of holding your ground, remaining reasonable, and seeking for solutions. Sometimes, the best you can do is to call attention to the gaffe, make your discomfort clear, then also clarify that, should something similar recur, you will put more effort into repairs then and you desire cooperation. In short, set it aside, but make clear your hopes that this will indeed be a last time.

Not that the people around you are exempt from the coaching requirement. You're the one reading these words, here and now, so I'm picking specifically on you. I've been polyamorous for more than two decades, and the occasional rookie mistake gets by, causing me assorted *tsuris*. When this happens, I have good and caring people in my life, poly and otherwise, to bring stuff to my attention and help me work it through. Chances are that you are not so lucky – yet. Working on honesty in each limited case incrementally expands the amount of honesty in your circle, upon which you can all draw in the future, leading to even more honesty. This expansion ought never to stop.

Give this one a try as well: **I will try to differentiate between fears and risks**. You put yourself at risk every time you get into a car. Giving in to a fear of getting into a car, though, does very little to protect you from harm, while significantly restricting your life. Having a relationship entails risk; fearing problems only increases the likelihood that you'll either avoid relationships that might require effort (which is all of them), or that you'll expend effort in ignoring things that drive you nuts and would easily be remedied.

Fear and risk can exist independently. Like pain, fear can warn you that something is wrong, but otherwise is rather useless and can easily get in the way of enjoying life. Chronic anxiety is something to be rooted out by going after the underlying causes, not by attacking whatever has apparently set off an outburst.

If you shy away from honest expression, then you will need to examine your reactions. The most likely cause is anxiety brought on by a fear of repercussions. For most people, deciding to overlook ("ignore") the problem reduces the anxiety. I'm weird, though: I get anxious from worry about the recurrences. It's easier for me to dredge everything up and sort it out than to allow further accumulation. (Dredging, by the way, is the process of scooping silt and muck out of a river, canal, or harbor before the accumulating sediment brings boat traffic to a halt. This makes for an apt analogy.)

Handy tactics for dodging communication

As with, say, monogamy, we have *communication as fact* opposed to *communication as theory*. When most people use the term "communication," they mean the latter. In that sense, I say that communication is a lie, because people not only don't know how to talk, they hate to do it, unless it's banal chatter or banter in which volume stands as a direct replacement for content, whether intellectual, emotional, or informational.

Even if you can get so far as sitting a loved one down and addressing a sticky or painful issue, it can still, under certain very specific circumstances, be stopped dead with a pseudo-rational statement. For example, the following five phrases have something in common; see if you can figure out what it is before you read the sixth line.

It's never going to happen…
It's unlikely that it'll ever happen…
It's not a done deal – there are still options…
It's happening, so we need to focus on taking care of the problem…
That's old news, in the past, it's all behind us…
… SO WHY SHOULD WE EVEN BOTHER TALKING ABOUT IT?

Used wisely, even a marginally skilled dodger can use a rotation of these five statements to avoid dealing with just about any issue, activity, character flaw, or addiction. While it may not apply to someone who chronically abuses alcohol (drinking to unconsciousness on a daily basis, say), it provides excellent cover for someone who goes on a drunken spree every few weeks and commits assorted questionable acts.

The sequence only works, though, if the dodger can manage to continue appearing to hold to the fiction that each of these steps is wholly independent from the others. That requires that you do some pretending, or to back off the first time the final line is used (probably with an angry snap). Once the pattern becomes obvious, avoiding the reality is much more difficult.

The golem

If you don't present your gripes to the responsible party, you *cannot* humanly bury these complaints–it's just not possible to "forget" about something that has hurt or stung you. Actually, you are probably "testing" these complaints against your experience of the person, trying to figure out what they would say, how they would react. You create a simulacrum in order to argue this all out in your head, and thus to avoid unpleasantness. Certain conclusions are made, which you file away. When another problem comes up, you then test this against your estimates of the person, which have been expanded by your previous guesswork.

Eventually, you will have created this huge complex of estimates and assumptions, which are so far removed from the actual person that they likely have no bearing on the reality. I call this "a golem made of boxes," a warehouse-sized beast that has nothing to do with the simple small human being from which it is supposedly modeled.

When I have had such a golem used against me, I was told by my lover that she had kept a rather ugly situation from me "because I know how you'd react." I described to her exactly what the situation was, as I'd pieced it together very accurately (you *can* do this with the *actions* of humans, not the humans themselves). She was stunned. When I described for her how the root assumptions she had made were largely very wide of the mark, she actually became very angry with me, defending the golem as though it represented the truth, and therefore I must be lying! In the end, she could have better determined my reaction from writing down the possibilities on slips of paper and choosing one out of a hat. While I'm grateful to have come away with such a strong analogy, I would really rather that it hadn't been created in the first place, and I will happily work to avoid ending up in that sort of situation ever again.

The golem is handy, but almost entirely dishonest. It begins from faulty (incomplete, biased) data, and runs rapidly downhill from there. Like the "straw man" argument, you can always vanquish the golem you create, even if this means nothing more than stuffing it back into its box and ignoring it. That's hardly a fair fight, since you are ultimately in control. All in all, recognize your golems, and feel free to test out an occasional hypothesis on this simulacrum, but don't go believing that the results are a reliable model of reality.

31. Friend- vs. family-oriented

The sort of family in which you were raised can tell a lot about how you are going to fare in polyamory. Some families raise their children to be *family-oriented*, with tons of togetherness, game nights, and perpetual family outings. When off to college, the kids return home for every holiday, and they might even select a school largely because they can drive home most weekends. Off and married, the children will still pack up their families to return for regular vacations. The family-oriented family is very protective of its "special times," and discourages others from tagging along.

Meanwhile, *friend-oriented* families let their offspring do largely as they please from a very early age. The kids might opt to stay home from picnics or visits to Grandma. Family outings or camping trips regularly include a friend or two, or even another family. Everyone appears to come and go as they please.

Until quite recently, in the 1970s, it was widely believe that family-oriented families were hands-down healthier. After all, this form produces a higher degree of multigenerational bonding, with the regular mass returns to the nest. Children from a family-oriented background are less likely to wander off with friends, or to even have the opportunity, and thus seem at lower risk of becoming delinquents.

Then it occurred to a few observers that this assumption might be wide of the mark. Friend-oriented families were really no more likely to undermine their children's abilities to form complex attachments than were family-oriented families to perpetuate a kind of institutionalized neurotic attachment, keeping the kids in a state of unease about cutting the apron strings that make them show up time after time out of a sense of obligation, not love. In fact, in an emotionally healthy friend-oriented household, the kids were more self-assured, able to form good bonds with their peers while demonstrating the ability to stand back objectively from an unhealthy relationship, or even to end a negative relationship. These people were more willing to explore the world around them, to travel, to make new friends. As far as juvenile delinquency, children of family-oriented families were somewhat more likely to go overboard with their youthful enthusiasms when they happened, as they had not been so "inoculated" from doing smaller-scale stupid things like the friend-oriented kids.

There were some lovely disagreements I had with my first girlfriend. One of them was over the definition of "home." She felt that the home is the center of the Universe, from which you make forays. As it turns out, I was just the opposite: home is the place you return to after exploration, and you all share your discoveries before making the next excursion. Her family had "family night" every Sunday evening, where my comparable experience was usually spontaneous. In the years since we were involved, she's tended to cycle back into monogamy and open marriage, while I've worked toward large households and open networks. You can probably label our respective familial types accurately.

If you were raised in a family-oriented family, you are probably more drawn toward triads, closed relationships, small households, and maybe one or more steady long-distance relationship. Those of you from friend-oriented families likely enjoy at least the idea of multi-house networks, communal householding, and commitments that could be described as "firm but loose." Recognize the predilections within yourself and nurture them. Be cautious about leaping into situations that conflict too strongly with your previous experiences – given time and support, you can probably fit yourself into practically anything healthy that happens to pop up, but you'll be much happier if you recognize any foreign notes before they become a problem.

32. What will the neighbors think (and should we care)?

That latter is another easy question to answer: no. In an ideal world, you shouldn't have to give a thought to what somebody's opinion is about what you're doing with your own life, much less to worry about the possible existence of such a thought.

But, if we lived in such an ideal world, you wouldn't be reading this book, because you wouldn't have doubts like that in the first place. I probably wouldn't have written it, either.

Until that perfect world happens to come into being, though, we have to make do with the occasionally tawdry inanities that populate and define something we refer to (usually sighing and rolling our eyes) as Real Life.

Nosy neighbors are everywhere. You may be related to these tawdry inanities by blood or marriage, or have to work with them or live next door to them. They lurk, they hover, they pry. Mostly, they don't appear to have much as far as lives, so they need something to fill up the hollows.

For the most part, your best strategy is to stay in the closet, but leave the door open. Actively hiding adds a certain thrill to your life, that sense of secret naughtiness, but in the long run will only lead to shame at what you are and what you have done. Instead, shelter yourself and the people around you, but if someone comes looking for trouble, stand your ground. In other words, unless you are really desirous of being some sort of activist and radical, don't go around picking fights, but face them squarely when they're delivered to your doorstep.

The general problem you stand to encounter is invasion of your privacy. The greatest right (to borrow from the Supreme Court) is the right to be left alone. This takes the form of excoriation (anything from snubbing to attack) or predation (seeing you as a sexual commodity). You might get both from the same person.

Briefly, here are the situations you will have to consider and deal with.

Residence

If you don't want excessive scrutiny, why call attention to yourself? If you're in the kind of neighborhood where everyone knows everyone else's comings and goings, then you'd be better off moving. If the norm is to have two adults (or one) and a couple of children in a six-bedroom house, then having even one long-term guest might cause a flap. If the new vehicle in your driveway is substantially different (better or worse) from the norm, then it's going to draw eyes. If the visitor brings children, then the cat is all but out of the bag, and everyone will be watching. If everyone parks on the street, then spaces might be tight, and an inconvenienced neighbor could cause problems just because there's a strange vehicle in "their" place. I was steadily involved with a woman in such a situation, and I regularly parked two blocks away from her building on a less-crowded street.

Overcrowding a house might cause a few raised eyebrows. Suddenly doubling the occupancy of an apartment will send up big flares. Every door you walk past raises the possibility of drawing attention (don't forget about noisy buzzers and front doors in security buildings). The people downstairs might object to increased sexual activity. If you live in the sort of building where windows are regularly open, your walls to neighboring apartments are effectively a few inches thinner.

Workplace

My partner has photographs all over her desk, including framed pictures of her three boyfriends. Over the years, she's had more than a dozen people stop by to take her to lunch and show some degree of affection. A few of her coworkers know that she's been living with one boyfriend for some time, and one or two might understand that she's bisexual (as she took part in a panel presentation to managers on issues important to non-hetero workers). Mostly, though, they don't ask questions about her private life, because she might answer them.

If you find yourself swearing a coworker to absolute silence before revealing some bit of your life, then you've already shot your mouth off. You've very clearly said, "Here's something really juicy for gossip, and you can beat me senseless with it when you get angry with me."

When someone asks a question about your lifestyle choices, and they're not already in full-on attack mode, answer it with a verbal shrug. As a friend said, "When someone asks you, 'You're black, right?' how can you answer it except with a simple 'Yes'?" They ask a simple question, you give a simple answer. Of course, if they ask a complex question, you probably want to give a simple answer to that, too – your job doesn't require that you educate, inform, or proselytize. When in doubt, tell your querent, "This isn't really appropriate for the workplace."

If you're living in some horrendously backward part of the world, or your employer feels invulnerable to charges of discrimination (for instance, some religious organizations and privately held companies), then unless you want to remodel that closet into something more comfy before you slam the door shut, your options are limited: get a different job, or move somewhere more infested with sanity. For the rest of you, bring your boss in on your secrets at any time. I've been a manager and a supervisor, and I prefer to know this sort of stuff in case I need to step efficiently on a troublemaker. If your locale or company has a history of coming down hard on people who harass gays or lesbians, then tell your boss you're bisexual–a manager who isn't sure what to do with nonmonogamy has probably spent dozens of hours hearing company-sponsored horror tales about the legal Hell awaiting companies with poor reaction curves.

The military is a special case. I have known people whose dogtags read WICCA or even DRUID who were held in high regard, and I've met people who were harassed out for being the wrong flavor of Christian. I know queers who are shielded by their commanding officers because of their skills, and also a straight woman who ultimately left the service because she couldn't convince everyone. Posts around the world have couples cohabiting who are married – but not to each other. Depending on circumstances, just about any action could get you slapped into prison, or promoted. If you're unmarried, brag a little about all the members of the other gender you're dating, but lay off the philosophy, and you shouldn't have any more problems than anyone else. If you're married, play your cards as close as any other "geographical bachelor" in your unit who's dating. If the secrecy will drive you nuts, then you probably shouldn't re-up. (An acquaintance in the Australian Navy tells me that he was commissioned as an officer even though he's been out as poly and bisexual for years. "I introduced my commanding officer to the couple I'm in love with, then I was taken on a tour of the queer officers' barracks! Isn't it great?" If he wasn't totally pulling my leg, I am envious of his society.)

Education

Generally, you're better off at colleges that are state-run, or have a long history of non-mainstream thinking (few compare with Oberlin or Evergreen in this respect). Again, a large and active gay/lesbian community is a good sign.

A few readers are in high school. You know how difficult it is to be out about *anything*. However, before it becomes an issue in the classroom, you ought to be out to your parents, so that you can enlist their active support. Go for image: though polyamory doesn't necessarily equate to wild sexuality, the unwashed immediately equate poly to promiscuity, so being active in programs for sexual responsibility will help your case should anything hit the fan. AIDS-awareness programs, peer contraceptive education, even celibacy clubs are good.

Teachers and administrators resemble real human beings, and are therefore free to hold their own opinions. But their rights to inflict them on you are limited. If wisecracks offend you, a discussion with the PTA, the school board, the principal, or the teachers' union might be necessary. At the college level, your advisor might be able to help, after which you can go to the head of the department. I can't recommend going about trying to save (or educate) the world, though; your goal should be to keep the boneheads at enough of a distance that you can get an education.

Church

Very few religious organizations would be happy finding polyamory in their midst. If you are very lucky, others in your congregation are of the type that recognize individuality, and will rush to your defense on the basis of "By their works shall you know them" and similar statements of faith. (For those of you who don't encounter that particular phrase very much, it's usually interpreted to mean that, if someone is living a good and righteous life, then everything else is mere detail – if God was particularly upset, you'd all know it. Blessings on those Christians who've figured out that God is probably big enough to take care of Himself.)

Some religious groups are very supportive of nonmonogamy. The best that I have observed are the Unitarian-Universalists and the Metropolitan Community Church; the former has been around in various forms for a couple of centuries, and has congregations practically everywhere, as well as an internal organization specifically for its poly members.

On a local level, I've been hearing about individual Episcopalian, Lutheran, and even Baptist churches that are taking firm stands for their gay and lesbian members, usually based on the belief that God wants people to be in loving, stable families. If exposed to long-term responsible nonmonogamy, they might embrace these as well.

I wish that I could give blanket approval to all Wiccan, Neopagan, and New Age groups, but there is no central uniting authority for them. Some are somewhat less liberal than a Fundamentalist church, while others of identical religious belief and practice (and even overlapping membership) are quite promiscuous.

Blood kin

I am surprised at the comparisons that can be drawn between many families and the street gangs in the worst part of the city. It's not inconceivable that you might be in a family where your parents (or even grandparents) would use polyamory as justification for removing your children.

There are many people in the world who still choose to see polyamory as a direct attack on their monogamy. Taking up freedoms that others consider impossible might get you labeled as crazy because an alternative explanation would be that they've been living under an unnecessary and loathed restriction. Being related might only make this worse.

You might feel better moving to another city, or even another state entirely. You might have to curtail or eliminate visits. Correspondence might dwindle to you sending cards for birthdays, Christmas, and anniversaries.

Mostly, though, the only reason to throw your whole lifestyle in the collective face of your family is that you are harboring deep-seated anger at them. There's a thoroughgoing literature of "coming out" stories in the lesbian and gay community. You would likely benefit from a little reading. One common theme, though, is that parents and siblings take the news a little better if you bring home one steady lover a few times to meet everyone. When they're dealing with a loving relationship, and not the entire sociopolitical freight of the ever-expanding queer movement, understanding is made somewhat easier, and acceptance is on the way. Showing up to Thanksgiving dinner with one partner and Christmas dinner with another is a good way to break the ice, especially if you mention the non-attending partner a few times in the present tense, which makes clear that things are out in the open.

Polyfolk

Just because someone claims to ascribe to polyamory doesn't mean that they are poly. They might be correct in their self-assessment, but they might also be willing to pronounce upon your life. After all, we're all pretty much stuck with being human, and anything that differs too sharply with our conception of the world might come across as negative judgement or attack. Exercise a little caution before you hand out all of your theory and methodology. When I'm expounding, I try to remember to mention occasionally that I'm relating what works (or doesn't) for me, or what I've seen elsewhere, not all-encompassing divine wisdom. Not only is this true, but it goes quite far for settling hackles.

Theoretic friends

Unless you're as obsessive as me, most of the people you call friends are actually acquaintances. If they have fallen into a comfortable misassumption of knowing you, the transition from monogamous (or asexual) you to poly you might be a shock. For most of the people in our culture, polyamory is a much bigger step than a complete change in religion – say from Foursquare Baptist to Baha'i. As with family, some of the people around you might take this "leap" as some sort of personal affront. People who've been in your life longer might be surprised, but probably won't attack you – and please note that I say *probably*. Someone might step out of your life, not so much from loathing polyamory, but from finding the "old you" replaced. Don't take it personally, keep in touch, and let them know that things are really pretty much the same, merely assembled better.

General public

A few times a year, I piss someone off just by walking down the street, unaccompanied, minding my own business. Usually, it's some moronic teenager's cry of, "Hey, faggot!" as they drive past me. Since this breaks my train of thought, they soon discover that my vocabulary and vocal tone could make a drunken longshoreman cringe – this is especially entertaining to the populace when they end up trapped at an intersection and I have a full two or three minutes to exercise my irritation.

Now, if little old me gets that sort of crap on a city street, I don't know why you'd want to court public dialogue by strolling around hand in hand in hand. If you want to paint a target on your back, that's your choice. If you insist on expressing your complex affections in public, and don't particularly want trouble, then at least choose your audience responsibly. Displays of affection at a shopping mall or football game will simply go over more poorly than at a Renaissance Faire, a science fiction convention, a Pride Day parade, or a Society for Creative Anachronism campout. The world is improving, but slowly, so figure out what it is that you are actually trying to accomplish, and choose your potential battles with care.

Children

If some busybody takes a dislike to you, they can attack through your kids. Social service agencies, to be on the safe side, can investigate at the drop of a hat, and have the power to break up even a perfect and boringly average family. Their inquiries and evaluations could take months, holding you guilty until proven innocent. Usually, the instigating busybody is protected by the law, even if they have blatantly lied.

This is true for *everyone* with children. Polyamory's present weakness is that it doesn't have the legal and social clout of gay and lesbian families. If your lifestyle ends up before a court of law, you'll want to be sitting with a lawyer experienced at drawing blood from encounters with the courts over these questions. Unless you're fortunate enough to encounter a poly-friendly attorney, you'll want to start networking right this moment to get in touch with the nearest attorney-referral service, and diligent research through gay-rights groups might eventually land you a meeting with a cheery crusader.

Let me emphasize that you *must* do this long before you actually need such an attorney. Giving them absolute confidence in your situation might be that grain of sand to tip the scales in your favor. Though the charges may be nothing but garbage, the central question is whether the safety of children is at stake, and all parties may be fighting harder than they would in a typical murder trial.

Get the lawyer, even if it costs you cash. Think of it as an insurance policy for your family.

33. Communicating with a partner or other life-form

So often, to be "nice" to someone means to withhold the truth. It's an attractive myth, and eventually leads you toward believing that lies are better than truth. After all (the reasoning goes), if truth leads so often to conflict, and conflict hurts, then we ought to be happy in our lives comfortably padded by degrees of mistruth.

There are times when I truly wish that were the case – how much easier it would all just be to gloss *that* over and move along!

Lies, though, are not communication, are in fact the antithesis. Maybe in a better world, avoidance of the truth would indeed be a useful part of a rich and thorough palette of communication that enriches all of the people involved and all those that they will ever touch.

But, as you've no doubt observed, I can't accept that this is the case, or anywhere near it. We're human, therefore we're flawed. We don't communicate very well in the first place, and we are prone to taking seemingly every opportunity for avoiding thoroughgoing communication.

Start with some basic training for yourself. I cannot too-highly recommend reading *The Intimate Enemy*, by Bach and Wyden. This is the book that brought the term "fair fighting" to the public eye. If you can get yourself into some sort of "communication for couples" workshop, all the better. For the moment, we're going to focus on the general communication, and we'll get to serious head-to-head skirmishes later.

Blurt your way to the top

Differences inherently happen in an intimate relationship. That is not something that can be argued with, however much you are presently in love. Familiarity does indeed breed contempt. Glitches occur in any human relationship except the most superficial and, if they are not addressed, will eventually kill it, whether in obvious ways (divorce, spousal abuse) or in a slow and spreading rot that at best means you're eventually living with an amiable stranger.

You might be able to get away with this in monogamy, with its many and varied social supports, but noncommunication is absolute poison to polyamory. The most common occurrence I've seen is when someone neglects their primary relationship while chasing after other opportunities for intimacy, only to one day be awakened to the fact that they've let their most important relationship wither, sometimes beyond hope of reclamation. For some reason, it is exceedingly easy to believe that someone who will "always be there" is going to tolerate perpetual neglect or even abuse.

If you bury a problem, then you're moving backward. You *must* realize, analyze, confront. Then, you *must* elaborate, negotiate, and compromise. Yeah, it sounds like a lot of work. Well, *that's because it is*. If that bothers you, quit now. However, I can assure you that every crisis you successfully surmount, however tiny, eases subsequent solution of problems, however huge. The basis for this is an atmosphere that fosters open, ready communication.

Unless you are about to bite someone's head off, then you need to say *what* you are thinking, *when* you are thinking it. A friend aptly calls this **blurting**. You have to summarize your thoughts, which might mean suddenly dumping vague feelings and even bodily tensions into words. Sometimes you have to provide a very brief preface as to why you've got a particular something in your head. This doesn't have to be Earth-shattering: for instance, I might be scowling silently, lost in thought, while my partner worries that she's somehow upset me, and I sheepishly explain that I'm trying to figure out why my printer has been defying me all afternoon.

You need to encourage the people around you to blurt. When you are doing this properly, the empty little phrase, "What are you thinking?" takes on shocking potential depth.

You have to be tolerant when someone takes a mammoth risk by blurting, because those outbursts may not be fully formed, or perfectly articulated – in fact, since it's blurting, there *will* be rough edges all over the place, and some of them *will* sting a bit. If you react with immediate defensiveness, rather than hear things out, only the most stalwart will repeat the exercise.

To become more flexible at blurting, you may have to dip into other languages. I have had to rely on concepts that do not properly exist in English, calling upon my small linguistic storehouse for assistance in German, Spanish, Latin, Greek, and occasionally French and Chinese. (What, after all, is the English equivalent of *gestalt*? And that's a simple one.) These need brief explanation. When I find myself in a corner, I recast the English, saying, "It's not a perfect fit, but it's sort of like...."

Rules

As much as people dislike limits, they are the basis of social interaction. Your life is a vast webwork of rules for conduct and communication, even though most are unexamined and tacit. Sometimes, though, someone has to say, "I've found a personal boundary, and here is what I need to recognize this." The only question seems to be whether people more dislike making rules from necessity or having them imposed at someone else's insistence.

Part of the problem is that, if someone imposes a rule on me, and I go along with it, then I've accepted it. Okay, the rule might suck, and though it didn't bug me *much* at first, it's finally become enough of an irritant where it's stormed into my consciousness.

So, I've got two basic choices: say "this is driving me nuts, I need to have it changed," or just break the rule. The latter, in many cases, is easier, even better. However, in *both* cases, there's the primary risk: I have to be ready to own the consequences of my action.

In that way, most core rules for a couple that is moving into polyamory can be very one-sided. The husband decides to be poly; the wife goes along. The husband decides that she ought to give bisexuality a go; the wife goes along. The husband decides that no men ought to be considered, and in fact any potential girlfriend shouldn't be involved with another male; the wife goes along.

In short, he decides, she goes along, then they tell me that they have equal decision-making powers.

In one sense, that is true: you can use democracy to sign away your democratic rights, in practice if not in theory. (A basic rule of contract law is that an agreement to give up a Constitutional right cannot be enforced.) If you empower/enable your spouse to make decisions for you, then they become your decisions, too – responsibility without rights, an untenable pairing. If you subsequently take a step toward declaring your autonomy, and your partner absolutely cannot live with that, then the larger contract, the dyad, is done – and you would then have the choice between your individuality and continuing the relationship.

Though this behavior is (in my estimate inarguably) screwed-up, remember my maxim: jealousy is logical. Most importantly, jealousy expresses fear of diminishment, which is a valid underlying concern. If the stereotype husband could let go of some self-doubt, and learn to trust under the changed situation, the relationship can recover (with a few new and hopefully better rules). If not, then nonmonogamy is probably a bad idea, because the unaddressed insecurities will probably crop up anyway with a girlfriend.

There is no divine authority that is going to enforce your rules; even a mere court of law wouldn't touch that job. Don't make a rule that you as an individual cannot or will not enforce. At the bottom line there is exactly one fact that enforces *all* agreements: **Either the rules are respected, or the relationship changes.** Breaking a single clause of a simple contract renders the entire contract void. That might mean ending things entirely, or moving to separate residences, or backing off from the primacy of a relationship (possibly to leave room for someone more willing to consider balance, or at least is more entertaining). This is up for you to decide as an individual: know your limits before you find them the hard way, have some idea of which issues are particularly severe for you and which you are more willing to give ground on, and give plenty of thought as to how (depending upon the severity of the problem) you would need to react, think, and rebuild. This is also up for you as a dyad or group to decide. The more work you put into this sort of thing before you need it, the better you will be able to hash a situation out. Since rules are by their nature (or cussed human nature) begging to be bent, stepped on, and broken, contingency planning is important.

Some guidelines for exploration

Here are a few key elements in top-flight communication.

Define compromise.

If you are having a disagreement with someone, nothing is going to actually be fixed – though one or more of you may make that mistaken assumption – if you do not agree very closely on what exactly "compromise" entails. It (as usual) depends. Sometimes a compromise is where everyone bends a little; sometimes it's where everyone finds a previously missed solution that is preferable all around.

In particularly toxic cases, when someone says "be reasonable," they specifically mean, "a reasonable person would do what I want." Similarly, "Let's compromise" can mean "I'll avoid giving an inch until you come to your sense and do it my way." If someone is basically unwilling to negotiate an actual compromise under any circumstances, then at least you won't waste too much time and energy.

Take the bull by the horns.

Call it confrontation, and maybe grimace a little at the thought, but very few things in life get better with age; if they're negative, they almost never do. You don't have to leap on a gaffe within seconds, and it would probably be better if you didn't. So, close your eyes, count slowly to ten, then speak up. For that matter, if something pleases you, then say so – positive feedback reinforces the behavior, after all. (But don't lay it on thick – overly effusive praise is indistinguishable from sarcasm.)

Have the courage of your convictions.

Believe what you believe, and stand by it – change your mind or compromise as you must, but don't go leaping to the conclusion that your feelings are wrong. Yeah, there'll be mistakes or misinterpretations, but someone who caves or folds under the least little bit of resistance will be taken advantage of even by otherwise good, conscientious, thoughtful people.

Watch your language.

Step back from comments that translate easily into "You're a moron." There are "logical" variants on this that begin with words like, "Any *reasonable* person could see…" that will only raise hackles (and hackles are surprisingly opaque to discussion).

Word is bond.

When someone says they're going to do something, then they either ought to do it or inform those affected by the promise (for that's what it is) that the parameters have changed. However, do it too often, and folks rightly begin to doubt statements right from the beginning: it saves time an effort. If you can't guarantee an outcome, then don't promise it; if there are guessable blockages, then maybe you ought to at least mention them, and discuss an alternative or two. Strive to maximize this "capital."

34. Levels of attraction: define "love"

When you find yourself attracted to someone, whether they're an utter stranger or a long-time partner, the various parts of your interaction are governed by the degree to which you're intermeshed. The word "love" simply can't bear up all of the possibilities by itself. I am going to take a moment to show you how to begin dissecting usage of the word and its underlying concepts.

There are four possible levels of non-unhealthy attraction:

- tolerance
- acceptance
- desire
- lust

You're probably already assuming that I'm talking about just sex, here, but it's much more complex than that, though we've all been conditioned to instantly associate emotionally loaded terms with sexual feelings. Beyond lust is **obsession**, which I cannot see in a light that is at all positive; at the least, the downside outweighs the benefits. (Note also that I am very specific in calling them "non-unhealthy." There are healthy and reasonably neutral instances alike.)

When you **tolerate** someone, you have decided that you can put up with them. They're good enough – and "good enough" should *never* be good enough in an intimate relationship. Though many dyads appear to be built heavily on a basis of tolerance, neither popular acclaim nor historical tradition can cover up that this is a lousy way to interact with others, and I would doubt the accuracy of the term "intimate" being applied, no matter how much sex is involved. Our society is presently based heavily on tolerance, albeit with clenched jaws and much-bitten tongue. I refuse to be in a supposedly intimate relationship that involves primarily tolerance; I will not "put up" with someone in a relationship that is meant to be more than transitory, and I will not for long be merely put up with.

To **accept** someone is to be comfortable with them, calm in knowing that the bond between the two of you is secure and persistent. This isn't a thrill-a-minute life, but when the world seems to alternate between life-or-death crisis and mindless drudgery, there's much to be said for the benefits to the soul provided by quiet acceptance by another human being. Acceptance and friendship are largely the same, for me.

If you **desire** someone, you want to be with them in particular. Though I deeply treasure those unpredictable intimate moments with my friends, I cannot consider someone a lover unless there is ongoing desire – though, when desire fades, I do not turn against someone who is otherwise a friend.

By **lust**, I mean everything from raw sexual desire to simple obsession with someone, such as wanting to hear one particular friendly voice to help lift the weight of a stressful day at work. Lust is not something on which a relationship can be built. It's fun when it recurs, but in excess lust easily becomes superficial and obscures the deeper wonder at the uniqueness of another human being.

When I say that I love someone, I mean all four of these things, intermingled. Oh, yeah, they shift around, shrinking and growing depending on the situation, the stresses of that particular moment, but most of the time a dyad is based around simple acceptance. When we love, we tolerate each other's momentary foibles and imperfections (with, of course, the trust that anything persistent or recurring ought to be dealt with). Once the NRE dies down, you'll start thinking of all the trash that appears when the tide goes out, marring a previously lovely (but much smaller) beach. If the love you feel is real, is a healthy and living thing, it can change and grow to accommodate the shifts in the growing individuals involved, as well as of the world around you. All you need to do is let it, and let go of fears of change. Start from the base of acceptance, deal with the shifting moment, and see where it goes.

35. Love, conditional & otherwise

We live in a culture that has poisoned the concept of "gift" to virtual extinction. Think of birthdays, Christmas, weddings, and so forth: if you give a "gift" to someone, it's because they gave you one, or you expect one from them, or you otherwise somehow owe it to them. In other words, it's a transaction, a purchase perhaps, buying the "respect" or goodwill of others – doing what is expected, following a cultural script. It's a bribe.

If I say, "I love you," and you respond, "But I don't feel that way about you," then, by the widely-held model – that love must be two-way – one of us is lying, or at least deluded.

Let me say: I *detest* the term "unconditional love" not from any argument with its core intent but because of its widespread blatant misuse, especially by perpetual victims who are either justifying their remaining in a clearly abusive situation, or are forever seeking the pity they can get from observers at their ongoing martyrdom. Those who use it to victimize (as in, "If you *really* loved me, you would....") are no better.

At its best, though, unconditional love is simply love without expectations. It's hardly easy, but it's honest, so I hold it as an ideal.

If love is a transaction, then you open up a whole can of worms, namely, how to determine who is providing "more" love in the relationship – that is, whose "gift" is the "best". If it's love, then it's something to which superlatives (like *more* or *better*) cannot be applied.

If I love someone who I believe to be deserving of my love, then it doesn't matter whether they are willing or able to return it – I have nevertheless determined that there is some aspect of this person which would (all other things being equal) deserve my heart. My love does not depend on what the other person is willing to say.

Unconditional love *does not* mean hanging around to be hurt, or forcing yourself to watch this wonderful person melt down in an impressive display of self-immolation. One of my beloveds is a recurring drug abuser. After the last bout with heroin, I told her that I would whittle away my own life if I knew it would make a long-term difference in her own... but I wouldn't so much as give her a cigarette if I felt that it was prolonging her pain, or "paying her to die".

In short, the other side of "unconditional love" is "tough love". We are in a "sink or swim" phase, and my heart lurches every time she slips... but she has to learn some hard lessons, and I can't learn them for her. I'm trusting her to know *when* she can call me for *real* assistance, because I won't be around 24/7 to shield her from every temptation.

Yes, I love her with all my heart. If I'm very, very lucky, she may someday be healthy enough to love me in return. But our lives go on, I don't have to be a martyr for when she lashes out, and I don't have to beat myself up every time she chooses to backslide.

And, finally: unconditional love – the real thing, not the common empty misuse – is the only remedy to phrases that begin, "If you really loved me...."

36. Creating a dyad

Simple enough, right? Two proximate people, ergo dyad, q.e.d.

And if you don't see how dangerously simplistic that statement is, put this book down, right now, and wait at least a month before starting from the very beginning and reading every word, slowly and carefully.

Courting the obvious

You need to understand. The problem with understanding, and (a step earlier) with comprehending, is that there are all sorts of things floating around in the world that my Australian friends would call *somewhat bloody obvious*. That's kind of a mixed-meaning descriptor, though. For instance, there are many things about yourself that almost everyone who interacts with you every day would recognize in a moment, yet of which you are only vaguely aware. Sure, you look at yourself in a mirror from time to time, or even dozens of times a day. Yet, if you were shown a videotape of how you walk, how you move around in public, you would likely not have the faintest recognition of your own distinctive body language, even though every one of your family members and friends could pick you out of a crowd of hundreds of people in a matter of moments. Your gait and gestures are thus obvious, and you are the one performing them, yet you are likely the only person who could not describe them, or even spot them. Obvious, or no?

You have to become consciously aware of some terribly "obvious" things if you're going to be able to adequately handle the complexities that polyamory can throw at you. Therefore, I'm going to describe (here and throughout this book) some things that I'd readily agree are somewhat bloody obvious. Your knowledge is flawed, your understanding carries critical gaps, and you have fallen into habits that make you overlook simple stuff that a stranger would see in seconds. You need to start learning how to fix that. It's as plain as the nose on your face, the nose that sits right between your eyes but which you only really see in reflection. To assist in that process, let me lay out some simple truths.

Simple-seeming terms like "couple" and "two people" and "dyad" are in no way interchangeable, especially near polyamory. With rare exception every complex relational form comes down to the interaction of dyadic relationships. Dyadic relationships are made up of two people. In a relationship that is healthy, dynamic, and flexible, these two are individuals, quite capable of functioning in complete independence.

The synergy of selfishness

Stick two people together, and you have... two individuals, doing whatever the hell each of them decides independently to do. If each of them chooses to do essentially the same thing, then you might be correct in defining them as a couple, since for all intents and purposes they appear to be working together, even if they aren't – change conditions in the right way, and they will each produce a similar response. That's nothing more than a statistical nicety, though one that pervades our thinking.

When they interact in pursuit of their respective goals (be these goals similar or entirely dissimilar), then you have a simple relationship. As their individual needs and goals and rewards begin to intertwine, then they move toward becoming a dyad.

The dyad is the coming together of two essentially selfish organisms to produce some sort of synergy, where giving up a bit of autonomy eases the load for each. In short, the dyad is a means to an end (or more likely a series of ends). Monogamy tells us that the dyad is both a duty and a goal, if not *the* goal. Find someone with whom you can rapidly reach some sort of mutual toleration, and you're set, all good will thenceforth flow.

Nonmonogamy says almost the opposite. You start by "fixing" yourself, by setting yourself on a path toward taking fullest advantage of your personal capabilities and working around or with the inevitable gaps we each carry. Then you are capable of bringing someone into your life whose portfolio of strengths and weaknesses interacts with your own in a mutually beneficial manner. Maintaining this relationship requires understanding that the situation must constantly be watched for necessary redefinitions as each of the partners grows, as the relationship itself grows and changes, as the environment shifts, and as future goals appear and disappear and change likelihood and desirability. The dyad is not a goal, but rather nothing more than a starting point, and possibly a basis from which to achieve desired outcomes.

Notice that romance is not inherent in this. A dyad is capable of functioning in a mutually rewarding fashion without a trace of love, or possibly even respect. Conversely, all possible love and respect does not necessarily mean that two people will prove capable of forming a productive dyad. (In our irrationally romantic society, love might actually *hinder* the formation of that sort of dyad, a phenomenon that is an underlying theme of this book.)

The building block

In many examples of nonmonogamy, there is what could be referred to as a core dyad, who could be a well-established married couple, a young relationship still in the early throes of NRE, or just a couple of very good friends. Their other relationships may come and go with the years (or months), but those two people are pretty much together for the long haul.

Not that the modifier "core" should be interpreted as pointing to some sort of arbiter of Truth. A quad or an intimate network could be constructed from nothing but separate clearly defined primary dyads, each of which considers their dyad to be a core – a healthy level of responsibility as long as it doesn't turn into a power struggle over which couple is in charge.

Let's again trot out triads. A triad is the first step up from simple couplehood. It could be formed in basically one of two ways: as a vee, where one person is intimately involved with the other two, who have some personal distance from each other, or as a full triad made up of three dyadic relationships. The vee actually offers more stability in its flexibility, since the dissolution of one dyad does not necessarily affect the other adversely, where the collapse of one dyad in a full triad effectively ends the overall three-way relationship and reduces it to a vee.

This downside is what made so many group marriages unstable when people were leaping to this relational form in the 1970s. Two couples would decide to embark upon their grand experiment, and create a polyfidelitous relationship containing four mixed-gender dyads and (ideally) two same-gender dyads, all supposedly primary.

The problem here is that, again, we have all been raised to be monogamous. When crisis strikes, be it good or bad, our trained reflex is to retreat to the dyad. But, in group marriage, *which* dyad? Some people, thrown into nonmonogamy, exhibit one of two reactions: confuse NRE with signifying that the newer dyad is "better," or flee from the newness in favor of comfort. This didn't work so well when a partner in a preexisting dyad wanted the old way and the other the new – given human nature, this conflict wasn't uncommon. Typically, such a group marriage would dissolve into a new autonomous dyad and two newly single individuals, or fall apart into its founding dyads.

Polyamory today carries the seeds of these same conflicts, starting from hidden or misunderstood individual agendas. Sooner or later, one of the dyad partners discovers cause to believe that he or she is getting the short end of the stick. Their partner then has to choose between desisting from nonmonogamous activity and minimizing their own resentment at this change of rules, or standing firm and risking anything from accusations of being "unreasonable" to dire warning of the imminent end of the relationship.

Forming an initial dyad from two people already possessing positive experience with nonmonogamy increases to chances for long-term happiness. This is no guarantee, however, since falling into the couple front can bring out those reflexive monogamist habits. Sometimes, one partner will hold for themselves the freedoms of polyamory, yet expect the partner to hew much closer to plain couplehood.

I can't help it: I think of relationships as interlocking plastic building blocks. There's a reason why bricks have the shape they do: just large enough to be interlocked in row after row, yet not so big that a row can't flow or bend a little. (Yeah, it's not the greatest analogy in the world, but it deserves consideration.) Smaller half-sized bricks can shore up the ends of a wall, or openings for doors and windows, and when you need to bridge a gap, a long brick makes more structural sense than a stack of the normal. Generally, though, the big expanses are filled in by the same size of brick repeated over and over.

Turning away from monogamy, or even rejecting it – depending on when you talk to me, I'd claim either for myself – should mean not blithely importing assumptions that failed in the old paradigm because they were inherently flawed and will probably remain flawed when transplanted to the new earth of polyamory. At the same time, good ideas that struggled under the freight of nonsense and myth heaped upon them shouldn't be rejected on the mere basis of their previous misapplication. Couplehood is both strong ("atomic" in the literal sense) and flexible on account of its size. Even if you have no need or desire to hide for the world, you will nevertheless find great benefit if you occasionally clean the grime off any prejudices you may be carrying against dyadic relating. Avoid the seductions proffered by the couple front, and you should be fine.

Power center

An established dyad has the strength of its track record.

That might not sound like much to you, but it is true and vital. Starting out, the most ideal couple in the world is nothing against a long-established dysfunctional relationship, because the oldtimers nevertheless function as a team. They've interacted for long, noisy years, and know each other's responses, reactions, strengths, and weaknesses in minute detail.

The newbies, though, present a much greater potential synergy. One dyad had a big stick, the other will have an even better, bigger stick... someday. In the moment, one has the strength of practice.

We seek for the long term, and therefore we select people who can make such growth faster or broader or more thorough. That's the theory, anyway, and practice skews this sensibility from the early stages. Few couples that seek to form a triad will actively look for someone older than either of them; in fact, I noted while studying a fairly large poly-oriented dating site that about nine percent of the couples looking for a female explicitly specified someone *younger* than either of them. As in monogamy, the male tends to be the elder in a couple, with up to two decades being not unusual (a situation which, if the genders were reversed, is still seen as aberrant in our society), meaning that the female of a couple is probably less experienced in relationships. Adding an even younger female makes a dearth of experience still more likely. The problem here is that weakness is heaped on weakness: if the couple has little or no experience with responsible nonmonogamy, then chances are they will attempt to make a full partner from someone with even less established ability. If the dyadic partners are still thrashing around in attempting to define the details and fine points that will allow them to be polyamorous, then adding someone likely less experienced and more insecure, dependent on their seniority on many levels, multiplies the complexity.

In the rush to form an "absolutely equal" multiple relationship, many people overlook the inescapable facts, with some predictable options for fallout. I'll again illustrate with the triad, though you can elaborate these to describe more complex situations.

- The couple refuses to admit to the control they exercise over their new partner.
- The couple refuses to recognize the responsibility they have to get their new partner up to speed.
- The couple refuses to recognize that they have ceded a large portion of power over to their new partner, without an equal share of responsibility.
- The new partner chooses to believe that the words and philosophy part is more significant than the actions and outcome.

- Things appear to be going relatively well, until one of the dyad feels overwhelmed, and the other decides to cancel the triad in order to preserve the preexisting dyad.

- One of the dyad is essentially promiscuous, explaining their activity as "looking for the right one," when what they're actually doing is having affairs but without the guilt.

Let's look at a few ways of thinking that might steer you away from such traps.

More than likely, you are one of the people who needs to establish a strong dyad from which to grow. No, it doesn't have to last forever as your core dyad (though life-long friendship would seem to be a good initial destination, subject to change), any more than your first house has to be the one you spend the rest of your life in. When you reach the point where you are both convinced that polyamory would be a good idea (in whatever form, but especially when the aim is a closed triad), then what you both need to do is to *not* go rushing headlong and hell-bent into an ill-conceived caricature of what you imagine polyamory *ought* to be. If your dyad is highly important to you, then you need to begin examining its strengths and weaknesses, working together as a couple. This may well appear counterintuitive to you, but it is easier to relax personal need for control with a strong bond than with a weak one. If you are going to add another partner, then you need a high degree of self-awareness as a couple before you will have the confidence to relax the boundaries, the walls that you have formed around your dyad.

Ideally, this would be the point at which a couple would turn to a polyamory-friendly counselor, therapist, or coach – sadly, there are not yet enough of these in the world. So, take full advantage of what *does* exist. Before you make an actual move into living polyamorously, step back from the edge to collect yourselves and strengthen what you already have. Find other polyamorous people, so that you can relax a bit from the burden of feeling as though you're the only deviants in the world. If you aren't within a hundred miles of a poly social group, then look around you for opportunities to form one. Many swinging clubs have social events and dances; I have found many of these to be quite welcoming of truly sympathetic couples, even if you aren't interested in sexual situations. The Internet can help you greatly in finding or creating at least the sense of community, and working up to telephone conversations with supportive people is certainly better than nothing. As a dyad, you need to take some time before embarking on searching for an ideal partner – spending months or even years working out the situation from which the two of you will extend your reach seems like a rather small price to pay if you're truly serious about finding someone with whom you can establish a lifelong relationship.

Only when you have your heads on straight, and the first flush of embarking on the hunt has cooled a little bit, should you actually search for a partner. If you are in too much of a hurry, you will jump at the first opportunity that isn't too far from your standards (which is usually far too far). If you're lucky, you'll pass many irritated weeks and months, loudly cursing the Fates for not sending you your ideal fantasy within minutes of the moment the two of you saw the light. Since you're supposed to be finding a once-in-a-lifetime situation, then you ought to be prepared to spend, if necessary, a significant portion of that lifetime in searching.

Sadly, there may come a day when your dyad is forced to break away from others, or must itself break up. Attitude is everything in these situations, as long as it is positive attitude under the guidance of good sense. Do not abandon the dyad from an unexamined sense of escaping to something better. Relationships tend to be flawed because they are made up of inherently flawed components, mere human beings. It is usually not the flaws that cause the problems, but the inability or unwillingness of the people involved to make intelligent, reasoned, and timely decisions. For instance, when you're in NRE with a relative stranger, you're half-blinded to that person's imperfect humanity, and that illusory perfection makes your existent partner's flaws stand out in high relief, even as you've become so inured to their strengths that you are no longer consciously aware of these.

At the same time, don't be too quick to assume that abandoning a new relationship will magically fix an old one. A new relationship can only damage an established one as much as you let it. If you decide to stay with someone who is needy or grasping, that is a choice you are free to make – but don't level more of the blame on someone else than you do on the members of your dyad. Let's say that I'm proven right, and you have gone out of your way to find someone outright clueless about the risks and insecurities inherent to nonmonogamy. It's easy to say that they could have been better individuals, but the point is that you chose them: you misled yourself, or you participated in allowing them to mislead you. Accept responsibility for having set the mess in motion, then accept responsibility for changing it, and finally accept responsibility for not being too obvious about repeating those mistakes in the future.

The dyad can be your refuge, your strength, the foundation of your life, but using it only as a societally approved fall-back position for thoughtless, shallow dabbling in pseudointimate trysts demands you and everyone around you.

37. Problem-solving: how to fight

All right, fine, so you love each other very much, and have such refined and limber problem-solving skills that you've never had an argument. I've heard that many times, and never found reason to believe it. You will need the occasional direct mutual confrontation.

My friends Steve and Shannon are probably the clearest example. After I'd voiced my observations on the topic, Steve replied laughingly, "Bullshit." He pulled his wife of a year closer to him. "We've never had a fight, and look at us!"

Six months later, Shannon filed for divorce, soon after their first (and last) major disagreement.

Actually, I wanted to title this chapter **Confrontation sucks & it will likely save your sorry ass**, but that ran a little long. Besides, some people though it was too confrontational. Be that as it may, it would've been accurate.

Confrontation is where you bring something up that leaves you vulnerable, or runs a risk of seeming like an attack on someone else's vulnerability – or both. In this sense, confrontation can take place even over inarguably good things: giving or receiving a complement requires some degree of vulnerability.

From this I wish to differentiate fighting, where there is a give-and-take between people on an equal footing. Using the techniques of *fair fighting* (per *The Intimate Enemy*, Bach and Wyden), this can be a very powerful tool for the polyamorous. See, you *will* run into all sorts of difficulties, some predictable, others utterly surprising to any observer. Acquiring the skills of fair fighting, and working with them until they are second nature, you and the people in your life will have the ability to solve crises on the fly: quickly, efficiently, and productively. This kind of drop-of-a-hat process seems brutal to casual observers, yet it too has its own positive uses. You can probably think of plenty of examples where

This chapter will mainly be an adjunct to the work by Bach and Wyden, and their heirs. By all means, study.

Four reasons to talk to me when you're angry

Here are the main reasons I want my loved ones to come to me with their problems:

> you need to blow off some steam and want a sympathetic audience
>
> something has happened to you and you want assistance in finding solutions
>
> something you've done might affect us and you need help
>
> something I've done might affect us and you want me to fix it

Some methodology

Polyamory has a high demand for involved/attached objectivity. You need to care, and care deeply... yet you must have the ability (not always exercised, of course) to take a step back from the situation and ask yourself honestly what you'd advise strangers to do in such a situation. Given that, you might decide that your objective self is entirely full of crap; otherwise, you look at how you can better align the ideal with the real.

Always double-check your assumptions. In our society, it's virtually impossible for you to distinguish an informed leap of faith from guesswork or hopeful denial. Sometimes you can get around this by playing the situation out in your mind as if it were a television show, inserting relevant names and faces. You might be surprised at how rapidly the absurdity becomes apparent in a situation that is quite tender for you personally, and how readily alternatives and solutions can appear.

Where did the idea come from that, once a relationship is established, all argument is supposed to simply cease? Problems and compromise are always going to be there. Disagreement does not signal failure–in fact, many relationships don't really begin to break down until all ability to communicate at all is lost, even arguing. (Two people screeching in each other's direction is *not* argumentation.)

Perhaps part of the misunderstanding lies in definition. For instance, compromise should be win/win, not lose/lose, and I'm not entirely pleased when circumstances force it to come out win/lose. The "all or nothing" mentality is an artifact of our culture's pseudomonogamy, and certainly one that we could all leave behind.

When you sit down to have a fair fight, especially in the first few times you give it a sincere whirl, you might find that the intended point of disagreement isn't the actual problem. It could be something that underlies the initial argument, perhaps very deeply buried, or it could be a completely unrelated problem and the argument was started from the last little straw being added to a massive stack of unresolved complaints. Don't let yourselves be easily led astray from an ugly problem, but don't be so rigid in your thinking that you cannot work together to find the actual disagreement.

At root, *everyone* must be able and willing to lead, and *everyone* must take 100% responsibility.

Learning again how to breathe easy

As with general confrontation, constructive fighting is risky, and feels moreso. The strength of our triad was that we were willing to take the emotional risks and address our doubts, fears, worries. Crying was not unusual – and neither was laughter in the tears. It was frightening, even painful, to take the risk, but it was always worth it. Sometimes, my beloved partner is afraid she's gonna say one wrong word, and I'll never speak to her again – not my fault at all, but I'm the one paying for it. Therefore, I accept responsibility in trying to fix it. For me, the sharp pain of solution is far better than the perpetual dull ache of blocked communication.

The amount of effort you put into effecting repairs on a problem will likely vary with how close a person is to you, and how fixable the situation is. My usual strategy in my non-primary and non-household relationships is to keep touching base, say "I don't support this behavior, but I love you, you can always call," then wait. If it doesn't blow up, then I guess they're happy with the dysfunction, and I get to decide whether to adapt somehow. If it blows up, then I offer a change – I prefer prickly honesty over the ticking timebomb of dishonest comfort.

Trite phrases, even if shouted, don't contribute much more of a message than, "I'm not invested enough in you to say something original." There have been people in my life who appeared to believe sincerely that "I love you" was an appropriate way of curtailing discussion of a touchy subject.

The immediate translation of "I'm sorry you feel that way" is "Stop whining, you idiot." Tone of voice tends to give this one away. When this phrase makes an appearance, communication is on the verge of ending. At that point, you will have to decide whether it is best to ignore this, or call attention to it, or merely end the confrontation with a truce.

As in any other exchange that is both intimate and forward-moving, fair fighting needs trust. You need to give trust – *not* a trust in that other people will be perfect, but that they will try, and that they will learn. You also need to be willing to be trusted, and thus to be worthy of trust. Though mutual trust is necessary before things can move forward, trust can only be truly repaid in kind.

All in all, when you go nose-to-nose with someone, what *can* you do? That's simple, really: take your lumps, accept your responsibility, forgive each other, and get on with your lives.

Useless apologies

Generally, "I'm sorry" is superficial. Apologies are good – don't get me wrong – but they don't fix anything. An apology can as easily mean "I am incredibly mortified – let's see what we can do so that something like this never happens again," as it can, "Okay, I'm eating crow. Happy now, asshole? Let's pretend that none of this ever happened, and never mention it again." Many a flowery, tear-stained *mea culpa* is a dramatic presentation of the latter subtext.

Your task is not to reject apologies or to avoid making them. Your task is to make them an honest and complete expression of feelings, attached to some sort of avenue for corrective or constructive change that will benefit as many people as possible, not the least being the person receiving the apology and the person giving it.

An apology doesn't mean that you are claiming that you could have done anything different, or would do anything different if you'd known the eventual fallout, or even that you could possibly have made a difference if you'd known. If my partner's date turns out to be a complete bastard (of whatever gender) and spends the evening humiliating her until she walks out of the restaurant and takes a cab home, I am truly sorry that she had to have that experience and make that discovery about the nature of some so-called humans.

In a sense, I am apologizing on behalf of the Universe for the random genetic factors that have resulted in me being of the same *genus* as that dumbass. In another, I am not taking blame, but I am taking responsibility for shoring up the feelings of my partner, and possibly for helping her to understand how she might have seen earlier on that the person was such a bozo (not to mention reinforcing the understanding that she's perfectly correct in not putting up with shoddy treatment).

When you screw up, you need to do more than issue an apology: you need to own your role in creating the situation. That means seeking changes that will prevent drearily similar recurrences. Anything less is the opposite of communication, and people who refuse to communicate are not polyamorous.

A brief & familiar fight

I'll walk you through a rather typical sort of problem that I observe in polyamory. Ben mentions to me that, though he and his fiancée Sian have been nonmonogamous for many years, she appears to be jealous that he is showing interest in Kellie. The situation is tense because Ben and Sian have always been very trusting of each other; this has the downside that they aren't at all skilled at dealing with feelings of jealousy, in their partner or in themselves. Up until this point, they haven't had the opportunity to learn. Further tensing the situation is that Sian doesn't know how to explore her own yet-vague attraction toward Kellie.

Let me state the general case of the problem: Does Sian have a right to say "I'm uncomfortable with the idea of you having sex with other people [in general] right now"? Certainly! – and then they should sit down together and explore what her insecurities are. If she just high-handedly insists that she has the *right* to make this demand, then she's manipulating; if Ben leaps into defending *his* inalienable rights, then *he* is manipulating. And in neither case are they able to get anything constructive out of this as a dyad.

So follow along with me here. We bring the reasoning from the general to the specific. If she says "I don't want you becoming intimate with this specific person – ever," they should…

…sit down together and thoroughly examine her insecurities. (You *did* arrive at that answer, didn't you? Good!)

And I think it'd be good for the two of them to discuss *his* insecurities, as far as threats to his autonomy. If this is always going to be a "hot button" for him, then he ought to try to defuse his reflexive counterattack – when people are learning how to "fight fair" in a positive manner, they occasionally lash out in a completely off-topic attack at their opponent's vulnerabilities, in order to make that person blow up and walk away, thus ending the argument. Ben can still hold to his views, but he definitely needs to work on desensitizing them, otherwise it's a really easy target for those irrational attacks.

Now, to explore further. If Sian wants to court Kellie on her own, that's an honest topic for discussion, and perhaps that is what the fight ought to be about. If she already feels second-best to Kellie and doesn't want to risk being compared unfavorably in an intimate way, then that is also a good topic for discussion. If she's saying that she needs a little more reassurance from Ben before he gets involved with **anyone** new, then that is another topic.

Don't get in trouble over words. When someone is trying to express a *feeling*, the first pass is probably going to be a little rough around the edges. When I start a new courtship, I ask the other person to always give me a chance to fully explain my occasionally bizarre word-choices and metaphors. It always feels like I'm forced to use the not-quite-right words that run through my head, and at best express poorly the concept, the feeling, the flavor, the soul.

Bring your insights to bear, and learn to revel in exploring "hot buttons" – your lovers' and your own. Any fool can share the good times and crow about being a superior human being, but how many have the guts – the love – to get down in the steaming fetid muck and start clearing out the swamps each of us carries around in our heads and hearts?

If you can frame the question, you can find the answer.

38. The tyranny of time

In the Universe as we know it, there are three absolutes: energy, intelligence, and time. That's my pet theory, anyway, and I won't bore you with the various metaphysical ramifications of this. However, for our purposes, we're going to talk about time.

While time is largely a construct of the human psyche, and the notion of the clock has only been with us for a scant few centuries, there are a few vital regulating events against which we are powerless. Though the measures are themselves arbitrary, there are only 24 hours in a day and, with the exception of leap years, 365 days in a year – period. Nothing to be done about it. There are other measures that are completely arbitrary, and even a little weird, but so universally recognized as immutable that we're powerless: seven days in a week, two of which are a weekend, and almost 31 days in an average month.

I do believe in the depths of the human soul, and that it's quite possible for a human being to be deeply attached to more than one other person simultaneously, perhaps even dozens.

But any attempts to do so run squarely against the indisputable facts of clock and calendar.

Take a simple case. From your experience, how many hours of "alone time" would you expect to spend with someone you deeply love? Forty? Thirty? For the sake of illustration, let's say twenty a week of uninterrupted couple-time; this is more than just the closed-door intimacy (most couples spend less than an hour a week on sex, remember), and might include dancing or talking or window-shopping, but the emphasis is on the dyad.

There are exactly 168 hours in a week. If you have a standard job, you're there 42.5 hours per week. Your transit time is an hour each way, so that's another ten hours. If you're young and healthy, you spend 42 hours sleeping. So far, the time over which you actually have some control has plummeted from 168 hours to 73.5. Spend twenty with your beloved, and that leaves 53.5 hours in the week for eating, shopping, television, hygiene, visiting family, surfing the Internet, raising your children, and so on. Oh, yeah, and intimate relationships.

When you add another primary-level relationship, who pays? Unless you make cuts elsewhere (which is very risky), your discretionary time drops to 33.5 hours. Actually, this is even less since, given the opportunity, new relationships will occupy far more of your time, or at least bigger blocks of it, than those that are established. Add a third relationship, and your discretionary time is down to absolute necessities. A fourth, and you're into negative numbers.

When it comes to standard blocks of time, I hate weeks. They force us to work too many sequential days, yet they are too short to be useful for complicated scheduling. If you have tennis class Monday evenings, and Thursdays usually find you exhausted from work so you go to sleep early, and you spend Sundays getting the next week's schedule together, and a herd of your friends goes off to the movies most Friday nights, then you're down to three outright available evenings a week. If you start courting someone who has a similar (likely not identical) personal schedule, chances are that you'll be able to line up no more than one evening, maybe two, unless someone is willing to make changes.

Whenever possible, I advise people to take charge of their week. **Don't be any more a slave to the seven-day week than is absolutely necessary.** One approach is addressed later in Chapter 67, "The infamous dishwashing schedule." We left ourselves plenty of flexibility, but the root idea was that not-so-great evenings would be spread around equally. For instance, if my Wednesdays usually involved getting home about 10 pm, leaving a little space for conversation over late dinner before going to bed, then my partners shared these evenings equally, and planned accordingly. If I were to have started dating someone else in addition, then we would have expected that she share these evenings as well, and not simply receive higher priority for the nights that I had totally free. Since I am attracted to people with rich, fulfilling social schedules, and almost all of the people presently in my life work the typical forty-hour, first-shift, Monday-through-Friday schedule, I enjoy having dinner on the table when my date for the night comes home after a long day, or I might provide transportation.

One person cannot impose this sort of scheduling unless the relational network you have is relatively loose and you are all functioning mostly as autonomous individuals. In a tighter group, even a majority is not enough, and everyone might have to surrender a degree of complete autonomy in order to make the whole thing work best for all. You'll probably have to work things out in layers, with successive cycles of negotiation. Fill in the easy things first, of course, as when you and exactly one partner have next Tuesday open – well, there you go. Then you get down to the complicated-looking choices that fall quickly into place, like you *all* have Friday after next free, but you and partner X have had scheduling conflicts for weeks, and partner Y has plenty of other social possibilities. After a few passes, only a few conflicts will remain if you've all been honest about your desires. (If someone hasn't, that's another topic for discussion.)

You do need to leave a certain amount of "alone time" for *yourself*. Anyone who has worked with closest-packing algorithms know how complicated these situations can get, and approaching 100% eats exponentially into your wiggle-room. A bit of unstructured time gives you room to breathe, and provides a buffer for the small surprises that are thrown your way.

39. Hierarchy, whether you like it or not

Most people who are involved in any way with polyamory thoroughly detest the idea of putting their relationships with others into any sort of order of primacy. Well, tough bunnies, I say. You have some choice as to how you care to justify it or apply it situationally, but the fact is that there will be some necessary degree of hierarchal structuring in your relationships.

You may decry this, going into great and emotional detail to describe how the evil that is hierarchy does not affect any of your close interpersonal relationships. I would be the first to agree that you have every right to your feelings. I would also be the first to say that you're wrong. Not merely *incorrect*, mind you, but out-and-out **wrong**. If you behave as though you are right, you are only setting yourself (and the others nearest to you) up for all sorts of heartache.

Maybe you hate labels like "primary" and "secondary." You are entitled to your feelings. But you probably detest taxes, too, yet you also think of the programs they fund as yours by right, and you probably wouldn't deny that taxes exist and that you pay them. Hierarchy is no more an immutable law of nature than is taxation, but it too provides common benefit to the community far in excess of the individual portion.

Hierarchy is the antithesis of chaos. Speaking as an artist, I could go on at great length about the power and beauty of chaos. Speaking as a businessman, I could just as eloquently show you how even tiny bits of chaos can destroy a company that is otherwise able to withstand enormous changes in economic fortune.

We all want, naturally enough, to view affairs of the heart as more closely resembling artistic works than businesses. This sort of autodidactic revisionism is fine if you are intending to have an affair, a fling, or a one-night stand, and antithetical to anything more complex or involved. A work of artistic merit, with very rare exception, reaches a point where it is completed, then it is shown or performed or published. In a word, it is done, even before it has an audience. Art is static, generally, and in that sense dead.

A business, though, follows an organic model. Once a business succeeds, it must keep succeeding, every year, quarter, month, week, day, even hour. It must find its ecological niche (even if self-made), and it must grow and even evolve if it is to have a chance of being viable in the future.

In that sense, a relationship must of necessity more closely resemble a small business than a work of art. This is even more pointedly so if your life involves multiple deeply intimate relationships.

This is not to say that some sort of artistic model doesn't have its place, and may in fact be not only highly apt but enlightening, even inspirational. This book, for instance – even if it were ten times better than it (admittedly) is, it would still be nothing more than, say, an orchestral score. Of itself, it is blatantly dead, lifeless, a collection of marks on biodegradable paper, prone to fire and rot and fungus and ingestion by a horde of assorted vermin and scavengers. Those marks, these very words that you are reading, are nothing more than my notations that are a problem-fraught attempt on my part to show you how to hear the music that is in my head, and thus to bring out (perhaps with the help of others) this poorly communicated glimpse of beauty that I've tried to set down. But without many layers of business and technology, computers and printers and distributors and advertisers, the ideas would go only so far, reaching at most a thousand people.

A dyad is a wonderfully simple thing. There are only two general cases of structure possible: each partner is perfectly equal to the other, or one partner is the (more) dominant, whether in specific circumstances or overall. When the individuals involved are themselves complex, then it's no surprise that so many of these simple constructs don't bear up so well, as reflected by the divorce rate.

Add so much as one other influential person into that equation, and complexity takes off in a sharply nonlinear fashion. Complexity quickly leads to chaos, when tends to equate to disaster in circumstances that require communication, planning, or security to any degree – an intimate relationship, say.

Structure manages complexity. One way of viewing structure is to look at the priorities under which we reason and act. Once we can see these priorities, we can learn to understand them, work with them, and shape them toward the ends we desire, not the least of which is ongoing happiness.

Work the words

Before running too far afield, we ought to consider language again.

Polyamory is a new concept, not for any of the activities it comprises, but as a unique set of concepts we employ to think about the Universe, or at least our place in it.

As such, polyamory and everything it contains is still plastic, and remains extraordinarily malleable. If you are serious about being polyamorous, then you have the ability (and perhaps the duty) to help shape its meaning. That includes the terminology.

Start off with a hypothetical case. Say that I live with a roommate in a nonsexual relationship, and I also have a girlfriend who lives halfway across the city. When I came down with the Martian Death Flu last fall, and spent two weeks sounding like a clogged Hoover, who is it that had to explain to her guests? Who is it who cheers me up when my job goes into heavy overtime? Who has to put up with my dirty dishes for days at a time? Who have I joined on regular shopping trips to decorate the apartment? We look out for each other, and we share the little crises of daily life. The argument could be made that the relationship I have with my roommate is more truly primary than the one with my lover.

Take time to think about what you *want* the words to mean for *you*. Maybe you have only one primary relationship, or three, or none. The word "primary" could mean marriage (or equivalent), or could as easily mean that it's just not quite as shallow as your other dyads. As long as you can be clear to yourself about what you mean by this word, and communicate it to those closest to you, go ahead and be creative.

A primary relationship is not "better" than a secondary, except for as you set the situation up that way – if you want "better" (or "best" or whatever superlatives strike your fancy) to be part of your definition of *primary*, then enjoy. But state it explicitly, and write it down for sharing.

Whatever definition you come up with is probably okay, as long as it is clear, and maintained consistently. The meaning shouldn't easily shift with mood or situation; if it needs caveats and exceptions, then these are spelled out. You could work this out on your own, then present it to your partners, or you could all sit down at the table and create it together. Thinking about it strengthens you, as does putting it into words. Sharing it strengthens your relationship.

Put structure into your life

Without hierarchy, it's damned difficult to have structure. Without structure, you rely on peoples' good intentions merely in order to get anything done in the moment, and the future is likely going to be nothing more than smoke. If you put together a multilinear relationship based solely on peoples' hopes, dreams, and good intentions, you're doomed from the start, and waiting for the end. At best, you'll have all the foresight and direction and ability to maximize the moment as any other bunch of sheep, which live generally between two moods, placid and spooked.

If you have a household set up in this fashion, with nobody leading, nobody in charge, then at best you're a bunch, and at worst a mob. It's unlikely that you can organize a bunch to any purpose, let alone long-term goals; a mob, though, cannot be turned toward any *useful* purpose, though it is exceedingly easy to get destructive things accomplished. Either way, you are more vulnerable to manipulation, and more likely to be panicked into decisions that in more rational moments would seem terribly imprudent.

The word *power* has for some reason taken on a bad flavor in our society. Power (think electricity) is entirely neutral: what's important is how you use it. What is just as commonly overlooked is that with power comes *responsibility*. The two are separable, of course, but when separated they both become malign. If you have power and no responsibility, you become rapacious or decadent, not giving the least little damn about the consequences of your actions, or their effects upon other people and the world around you, destructive of what you can reach. If you have responsibility but no power, then at best you have been set up for depression and self-loathing, unreliable to yourself – your Self – and others.

Let's take this down to concrete cases. If you have a household, someone must write the monthly check for the rent or mortgage payment. Do you merely leave this for whoever gets around to it? Or is it the primary or sole responsibility of one person, month after month? Can you fear giving any one person in your household "too much power" yet allow one to run around and write checks at a whim? If you trust them to spend the household's assets, trusting in their best intentions for everyone involved, then do you allow *everyone* equal access to the accounts?

I'm quite willing to wager that your household has all sorts of tasks and responsibilities that ultimately devolve to one particular person, whether to carry them out or to ensure that some or all of the members band together to accomplish these ends. If so, then, like it or not, you have a hierarchal order, period.

I am no champion of monolithic hierarchy, where all decisions are in the hands of one or two or three people in a community or household or multilinear relationship. In some sense, *everyone* must be in charge to about the same overall degree. If one person clearly has most of the power and most of the responsibility, then they will soon fall into the trap of "knowing" what everyone else wants and how the complex relationship ought to be run. If one person has the bulk of responsibility and a dearth of power, then they are an indentured servant, held prisoner by bonds of economy or emotion, fearful of losing what little they have. If one person has the bulk of power and a dearth of responsibility, then they easily fall into a trap of behaving as though the complex relationship is little more than a projection of their being, their needs, a ruler surrounded by varying degrees of servant. Who would be surprised when such a person becomes a petty, childish tyrant, expecting every whim and change of mood to be indulged instantly by others? Adults can be just as thoroughly spoiled as any child.

As with a child, giving an adult the responsibility for something of importance to the group, supporting their endeavors, and seeing them live up to that commitment lest the group suffer, is empowering. Sure, it's a burden – which merely makes it one instance representative of the burdens we all carry for the good of all.

I don't think what most people damn as "hierarchy" is hierarchal at all. It's a matter of who knows who better, who has the best relevant experience or skill-set, time served in doing the task, needs of the moment, strengths of the moment, and so on – a benchmark for the moment, and subject to change.

I was living with Marie, my fiancée, back in 1983 (a.k.a. The Early Cretaceous, or The Dawn of Time, depending when you talk to me). Marie found a friend of a friend who needed a place to live until she got settled in the city. Tara and my wife became friends the first time they met for lunch.

Marie and I had a talk, and readily agreed that we'd all be happier if the "new girl" and I didn't leap in and complicate things further. Tara was young, bright, gorgeous, and witty, and falling in love with my wife-to-be. I agreed easily because, even if we weren't to be lovers, Tara was someone I definitely thought would add to the productivity and joy of our household.

As it turns out, it was one of the smarter decisions in my life. Two years later, we'd all fallen into a happy routine, each of the three of us very much in love. We each had an intimate friendship outside of the household. Tara and I had never shared a bed, much less anything more intimate, but we were bonded.

One day, Tara told me she was dumping the latest boyfriend, because he expected to get all of her "free time," as in time she'd just as soon spend doing what she wanted, even just reading quietly. So, I laughingly said, "Well, there's always me. We live together, we like each other, and we know each other's boundaries." And we stared at each other, not laughing – yep, we'd left the obvious option behind at some point. So, we called Marie in and asked her opinion. Her reply: "I think it's a good idea – and it's about time *you* two figured it out!"

Did we defer to Marie's primacy? Hardly. Would we have become sexual partners if she'd had *any* doubts? Oh, hell, no.

So: is it hierarchal, or not? Like everything else in polyamory, that mostly depends on how you define the terms. I'd say not; we were trusting Marie's opinion, as our lover and friend and partner. We wanted her empathetically informed objective opinion, and we were ready to listen to any exceptions she would present, which would then inform our decisions and subsequent actions. She, meanwhile, had withheld her opinion to that point, so as not to force us together if we weren't ready. The situation was consciously structured, and negotiated, and we worked at keeping each other highly informed of our thoughts and actions. Hierarchy of a sort was present, but we were not acting on a hierarchal basis.

Freedom versus equality

There are a few concepts that recur regularly in polyamory. They are quite rich, and I want to consider them only briefly here, but you would be wise to discuss them thoroughly.

Though one of the precepts for many people is that all relationships are at the same level of importance – egalitarianism – I hold out for the whole primary/secondary/tertiary thing. Critics cut this attitude down on the basis that each dyad "should be" equally important… but that's like saying that we *should* all be rich, happy, and successful. It's *true*… as far as it goes. Nevertheless, if I'm living with a partner, someone with whom I share kids and debts and mortgage, then that person *is* a primary, however much I might love and/or lust for someone else with a separable life. Our level of engagement reflects our commitment, and the reverse is also true.

When my wife and I were at our strongest, we were also dating others (including sex). We started with the ground rule that our dyad was the first priority, followed by household operations, and jobs. We had one or two experiences with our otherloves trying to crowd into this; I was involved with a fellow student who would pout if I wouldn't call in "sick" to work when she didn't have to be on campus until noon.

More recently, I was dating Bryn, who when we went to our favorite café would spend more time with her friends than with me. I put my foot down, insisted that she'd either curb this or we'd go somewhere else for our dates – if Bryn wants to spend time with these people, that's absolutely fine with me, but they can get their *own* dates. She didn't like it, until we were at a party where I was surrounded by many close friends, and Bryn was the outsider. Early in the evening, she pulled me aside and suggested she could leave early so as not to get in the way. I pointed out to her that, though those people are extremely important in my life, I was her date, and if she wasn't comfortable, I would gladly leave with her. When the shoe was on the other foot, Bryn admitted that the rule was a good thing. We don't have a primary relationship but, in that situation, she held primary status.

Equality and egalitarianism are excellent ideals, but they only go a short distance when pasted on a human being. Their real-world utility gets smaller and smaller as the situation increases in complexity. Many times, you will be faced with a clear choice between getting results and upholding the ideal.

When you begin from the premise "I treat everyone equally," you have already blinkered yourself from seeing where you don't, or can't, or shouldn't. There is no way to treat two people equally, because they are each unique, with respective strengths and weaknesses.

Similarly, you cannot expect a happy outcome if you assign people equal responsibility, because even intelligent, sane, rational adults aren't equally responsible. There are many people in my life who variously shouldn't be allowed to have alcohol, drugs, babies, cash, checkbooks, car keys, sharp objects, firearms, or matches. I have a friend I worry about when she walks to the corner store without an escort, because she has a habit of crossing the street without remembering that there are usually cars there as well.

Utter trustworthiness in one aspect is *never* a good basis for trust in any other. I would make a large cash loan to Mike with complete confidence, but I wouldn't let him within ten feet of a pistol – and I'd readily trust Ted with a loaded gun, but "five bucks until tomorrow" is money that'll never come back.

Then there's egalitarian process, usually called *consensus*. As a friend of mine observed, "Consensus decision-making means that the loudest person gets their way." Consensus-run groups tend to be very vulnerable to domination by a small clique of bullies. Calmer heads will be shouted into silence, derogated, or otherwise undermined. If you've already decided that nobody in your group is a bully or would ever become so, then (again) you have set yourself up for disaster, because this is the equivalent of saying, "I will staunchly refuse to acknowledge controlling, manipulative, even abusive behavior, no matter how bad it gets." People who are first-order bullies can quickly spot such people and situations. (Lower-order bullies stumble into self-blinding situations and, if stopped in time by clear, firm boundaries, can be just as productive and happy as anyone else.)

Freedom, democracy, love, success. What each of these concepts has in common is that, once you've worked and worried and slaved to achieve it, you have not accomplished it once and for all time. You must continue to work in order to maintain it, possibly even harder than you did to achieve it just once. You cannot do this without intent, and will, and planning, and structure. The path may well change, but you cannot be said to be achieving any sort of progress merely because you are constantly walking in a circle; there may be movement, but does the movement actually take you anywhere?

Making your rules

Give some thought as to how you feel about the concept of rules. That's another hot-button area for many people, because they see rules as set in stone, immutable, inflexible, cold, and sometimes downright daffy. Still, many people who would disagree with me about the necessity of rules nevertheless have their own calcified rules that they carry around, rules which they obey like the crack of a drover's whip even as they deny it's there.

The fact is that rules are incredibly useful in self-discipline and communication, yet must be subject to change, emendation, and exception. Putting up a solid fence (whether for protection from wolves or to keep your chickens from straying) does not *prevent* you from moving the boundaries – just from having them moved around casually.

True, rules cannot actually solve problems. That's not what I claim. Sure, I have seen poly relationships toddle along quite happily for years, then one (or more) of the partners is taken over by a pod and changes drastically. Would rules have helped? Not directly, no; but many of these problems stem from a downward spiral of communication, which appropriate rules certainly could have gone a long way toward correcting. Rules can't repair misunderstanding any more than a well-stocked toolbox can fix your car all by itself – but you're not going to get far in either case without appropriate tools.

Implicit rules are okay, but prone to misunderstanding, and to the apparent die-off of peoples' brain cells which edits the words and meaning while in storage. That is why you must keep an eye out for situations that provoke the "everyone knows that" reaction. Such a simple statement usually masks implicit rules that are sloppy, misunderstood, vague, and riddled with loopholes and logical gaps.

That is why rules should be recognized as such, then spelled out and written down. I'm pretty aware of my own persistent foibles, blind spots, and weaknesses.

Experience shows me that having a set of spelled-out rules, and reviewing it occasionally, helps me to keep my foibles to a minimum. Explicit rules don't have to be complicated; the simple act of putting them down on paper clears up a boatload of future misunderstanding. If you can get even that far, you've already freed up huge amounts of time and energy that you would probably rather apply toward the things that reward you and make you happy.

My triad put together a list of rules in order to get past some recurring potholes. I would type them up and pass a copy around, then file it away. Some rules had a "sunset", an automatic expiration. Usually, though, we'd be talking around the table, and decide to kill a rule early because it was no longer needed. The idea was that, if we were to bring someone new into the house or the relationship, we wouldn't overlook something that was a potential critically sensitive issue we'd not thought to call attention to. One rule spelled out that we were devout omnivores, and kept a variety of dead animals in the kitchen. Another was that we had a few small-caliber pistols and were proficient in their use, as we lived in the state's most crime-ridden neighborhood, with infrequent murders nearby. In a few instances, someone who was wild to be considered for inclusion in our household reconsidered after reading the sheet, and I figure that we all were happier for that simple dose of realism.

Not that rules are foolproof! People can agree, then decide that the agreed rules don't apply to a given situation, and so on. In our case, discussion of interpretation was very much a bonding experience, every time. If one person's interpretation vastly changed the purpose of a rule, we would rephrase it, but generally misunderstandings were minor and worked out to everyone's satisfaction by discussion. You may find to your dismay that one of your partners has a habit of interpreting the rules loosely whenever it is to his or her benefit, and possibly enforcing them to (or beyond) the letter when controlling others' behavior. That, though, is an entire can of worms of itself, and you will at least have some warning that common rules of conduct (against theft, outright lying, vandalism) might be actively ignored.

Most people who "don't have rules" are trusting in common sense – that is, an internalized set of "obvious" guidelines rather than a codified external set. As Robert Anton Wilson pointed out, *common sense* is a very popular oxymoron, since good sense seems hardly common, and common beliefs are so often nonsensical: "Common sense is what tells you the Earth is flat."

Be a leader

Be honest. When you first encountered this chapter, your reaction possibly contained a little of, "Well, there he goes. He expects that we're going to choose one of us as the all-high power in our family!"

To this, I can share a few observations:

That *is* likely your reaction.

It's a stupid reaction. Consider yourself thoroughly chided.

Don't feel too bad, because it's probably common, so you're hardly alone.

If you don't overcome that reflex, your relationships *will* suffer.

Decisions need to be made, and will need to be made. Someone has to make them. Someone has to be responsible for them.

As Dan Burne and Alan Morrison point out in *Business @ the Speed of Stupid*, projects appear to be led by two types of people: leaders, and managers. Leaders have followers, which I further divide into leaders and managers. Managers have followers of a sort as well, but they are all of a type, which could be called workers, underlings, employees, or drones; even if those secondaries are themselves managers, they're still nothing more than underlings to the manager further up the ladder. Given a chance, leaders will nurture people who can move on to become leaders in their own right, while managers will fight to prevent others from even becoming managers, because then they're competitors. Leaders deal in moving their projects into the future; managers demand here-and-now stability, and to that end struggle against forward movement and growth. Leaders take responsibility; managers assign blame.

Let's look at an example that is, sadly, drawn from real life.

Jan runs a branch office, though she's only been there a few months. It's a nice enough building, but a bright August afternoon can push the air conditioning a little beyond its capabilities. Jan is no dummy, so her crew is already used to closing the windows and blinds on the sunny side of the building, and, on all but the hottest days, opening up every possible door and window on the coolest side.

One such day, as sometimes occurs, a nice layer of clouds rolls in just after lunchtime. The oppressive heat on half of the building's exterior is quickly replaced by pleasantly balmy breezes. Temperatures inside will be pleasant in an hour or two, making a nice ending for the workday. Tense people relax and smile for the first time that day, and the tired-looking ones perk up.

Edna comes back from lunch a few minutes early. The employees who are at their desks are working, and everyone else is out walking or down the in cafeteria.

Jan walks through the somewhat stuffy office, only to find Edna closing all the windows and doors. Jan is a little miffed at having her orders overridden without being told. "Edna, I had those windows opened for a reason," she says.

Edna says, "I know, but–"

Jan waves her hand. "I do these things for a reason, you know." Glancing up at the clock, she adds, "Your lunch break is almost over. You should get back to that report." She turns her back on Edna, who seems about to say something, then shakes her head and walks back to her desk. Jan presses three of the nearby phone-bank people into reopening the windows.

Half an hour later, the fast-moving thunderstorm, which Edna had heard about on her car radio, arrives. The wall of driving rain slams into the building, immediately shorting out six workstations and a router, and causing a small fire from a previously undetected fault in the electrical supply. This sets off a string of failures in the telephone system, PBX trunk, Internet feed and LAN. It's going to be six figures in damage, and the insurance company might have some questions about negligence. Luckily, just before the system collapsed, Edna sent an e-mail to her friend at corporate headquarters, asking whether she should transfer to get away from that sort of treatment.

Everyone's screwed, to a greater or lesser degree. All that's left is how to assign the blame.

That's Jan the manager. What would Jan the leader look like?

Edna comes back from lunch a few minutes early. The employees who are at their desks are working, and everyone else is out walking or down the in cafeteria.

Jan walks through the somewhat stuffy office, only to find Edna closing all the windows and doors. Jan is a little miffed at having her orders overridden without being told. "Edna, I had those windows opened for a reason," she says.

Edna says, "I know, but all the radio stations are saying there's a huge storm heading this way, and fast."

Jan hesitates all of five seconds, glancing out the windows closest to her. The bank of black clouds is hard to miss. Then she claps her hands for attention. Knowing that some clients can hear, and she's possibly interrupting their transactions, she nevertheless says loudly, "Okay, folks, listen up. There's a storm heading in that might hit us hard. Unless you're on a call, close and lock the windows near you and close the blinds." She points at one of the phone people not currently on a call. "Bill, do me a favor. All-call to the supervisor stations and make sure they do the same."

"You've got it," says Bill, reaching for the phone.

Jan points to Edna. "Walk around to the stations on the north side, just in case they're away from their desk. And thank you for thinking of this." Jan then heads for the far corner to do the same.

With that warning, people back up the files they've been working on.

The storm takes out the voice line, and other than a two cracked windows, there's no damage. A week later, everyone's largely forgotten the event, but the staff is working together more efficiently, internal communication improves marginally, and morale is good. Even if Jan didn't send Edna a basket of Lifesavers candy, Edna would likely come away with the feeling that she'd done right, and that she liked working with Jan.

I decided to go with an example set in the business world because it improves palatability, for no good reason. We are willing to look at these sorts of stories when applied to anything but intimate relationships, which is a big loss for our relationships.

Crises happen all the time. You will need to know how to react when things happen, and how to straighten out the resultant problems. But: **the single best way to deal with a crisis is to avoid having it**. That takes "negative" thinking about bad things that merely *might* happen, and it takes a ready willingness to grab responsibility. Thinking like a manager usually results in ignoring the future, good or bad, and likewise forgetting lessons from the past.

You've probably been blinded by managerial thinking, which I usually label Confucian (recall Chapter 2, Reinventing the wheel, "Where from here?"). As a result, when I stand up and say, "Someone's got to be in charge," most people will equate this to a call for establishing a benevolent dictatorship.

Nonsense.

Authoritarianism basically sucks. It dilutes or eliminates true wisdom that comes from outside the accepted channels, and pumps further hot air into icons that are already overinflated with pompousness. At best, authoritarianism retards forward progress; at worst, it destroys the very system that gives it control, and rapidly. I am antiauthoritarian, and I have every reason to believe that polyamory must largely be as well.

I don't know your situation. It could comprise just you, or your dyad or triad, your household, your family, your tribe, your immediate or extended intimate network. That doesn't matter, even if we're talking a hundred individuals without a touch of leadership ability or desire among you. At some point, a crisis *will* arise, which *will* persist until some one of you steps forward and says, "I'll take care of it."

That person is a leader. Oh, not leader of you all for all time, but inherently demonstrating leadership, though perhaps only for a limited moment and set of circumstances.

The point is not to have a leader, or even a clique of leaders. To be polyamorous, you will all have to follow, and you will all have to lead. (And in case I haven't been clear, note that you will have to have the ability to fill mutually exclusive roles, perhaps simultaneously.)

40. Children

Many people new to polyamory, or giving it serious consideration, are worried about the effect it'll have on their children, and how much they ought to hide their private lives from their children.

The latter is based on myth – in truth, you're not going to pull much of a scam on your children. Kids are frighteningly perceptive little buggers, and adults prefer to forget this. We call them "pre-verbal" then pretend that their comprehension is somewhat less than the cat's (though above the philodendron – usually). The link between babies hearing endless retarded-sounding "baby-talk" from adults has been known for decades to be a major cause of early speech impediments. They comprehend, and they remember.

If two adults who normally feel free to display affection toward each other were to be forcibly restraining themselves when "the children are up," the kids *will* sense it. At best, they'll think you are really weird; at worst, they'll begin to believe on an unconscious level that *they* are the cause of this tension – which is true, if you act that way for that reason – and internalize anxiety and guilt.

In short: if you can't be yourselves around the kids, then don't be together when the kids are around. Everyone'll be happier. However, that's not the best course for anyone involved. I believe that my kids have benefited from having Mom and Dad's lovers/friends/partners as regular guests at the house, and seeing the warmth, friendship, and love we displayed. Therefore, I'd say you ought to be yourselves: don't restrain yourselves from acting spontaneously in simple ongoing demonstration of the love you feel.

Of course, though, we have to go messing around and make things more complex than that idyllic scene. The variables are seemingly endless:

> The children are infants, or toddlers, or gradeschoolers, or teenagers, or young adults, or adults.
>
> I have children and my partner is about to move in with me.
>
> My partner has children and is about to move in with me.
>
> We both have children.
>
> I have joint custody.
>
> I have sole custody.
>
> I have regular visitation days.
>
> My ex hates polyamory.
>
> My ex hates me.
>
> My partner's daughter is pregnant and has been disowned by her father.
>
> We have a baby on the way, and I don't think the relationship is going to last that long.

Each of these situations deserves a book of its own, and there is no way that I can do any of them justice in a smaller space. However, I will slide a few salient guidelines past you.

First of all, don't give the kids more than they can handle. If you've got lots of friends who treat you well, and you bolt your bedroom door at night whether you have company or not, children usually don't dig any further into the details. My family of origin is entirely monogamous, but very physically affectionate and sociable, so holding hands, hugging and cuddling are common; my kids have grown up seeing much the same thing.

Second, don't over-share. The quickest way to nauseate your teenager is to saddle them with the persistent mental image of you having sex. Mostly, they don't want to think about their parents having sex – *ever*. I once horrified a roomful of "sex positive" thirty-something polyfolk when I reminded them, "Your parents must have had sex at least once or you wouldn't be sitting here."

Third, don't think that you're hiding *anything* from them. You *may* be able to do so but I'd bet that you will never be able to guess which parts have been successfully camouflaged and which are well-known.

Fourth, plan for disaster, but don't get all prematurely sweaty about it. If you're panicky about the first time your child refers to his "Mommies" in school, you've already given away some control over the situation. A welcome side-effect of the rising divorce rate is that many teachers just assume that there's been an emotionally healthy changing of the guard, and don't see any reason to inquire further into the details. If the school has become relatively comfortable with children of gay and lesbian couples, then chances of snoopiness drop even further (and you may find yourselves invited to a social group for such families). Your teenager, on the other hand, might spell out the details to friends, or in a paper that's read to the class. Begging them for discretion will work about as well with your poly life as it does for anything else, so I wish you luck in that respect.

Fifth, remember that, without a brace of lawyers and some special circumstances, the courts *will not* recognize you as a parent unless you can prove a genetic basis or provide adoption papers. You could raise your partner's child from birth to college, only to find that you have no rights whatever in (say) a hospital emergency. Find a good attorney if you want to look into possibilities for minimizing this gulf.

Sixth, give some deep consideration to how the primary adults in the lives of the children will handle them. Is control and discipline solely the domain of a biological parent? How are you going to refer to your partner's children – "kids" or "stepkids," for instance? Will there be changing of surnames?

Finally, figure out how you are going to handle further reproduction. Is the relationship largely a means to making more children? Will an unintended pregnancy be treated as a happy accident, a minor problem, or something in between?

41. The mixed-marriage problem

Take two intelligent, perceptive human beings. Bond them together emotionally. Then expect that, because they're so very much in love, they're going to be at the same stages of emotional growth at all times, with the same degree of curiosity about the same things, and identical willingness to explore and take risks.

Okay, it's a stupid idea, but that's where most people start from. I'd like you to try to avoid falling into the trap.

Polyamory and your dyad

Chances are that you already have a partner or spouse. I'll give you the benefit of the doubt by working from the assumption that you're not going to use polyamory as a way of ending that relationship, or have any willingness to screw around behind your partner's back. Leaving aside questions of morality, this would be just A Bad Idea, as it sets a precedent that will eventually reveal you as a two-faced dishonest weasel.

If you are in a couple, both of whom decide that you're going to become polyamorous, then one of you desires it more than the other. You may both be sincere, but there's no way that you can be *equal* beyond that point.

Similarly, one of you was interested first in polyamory. Some of you reading here are in a dyad where your partner isn't particularly interested in nonmonogamy, or even doesn't know of your interest. A few of you are reading this because your partner is tending toward nonmonogamy, and you're trying to get a grasp of what the hell is happening, and what will happen.

Compared to how this transition is handled by many, those little mismatches are easy to deal with.

Weasels using poly as an excuse

Here's a typically lousy way to tell your partner that you want to explore nonmonogamy. A guy gives his wife a "choice" of "I'm going to have other lovers, period, and I can do it secretly, or semi-anonymously, or be up-front about it – you decide." That is *not* discussion, that is *not* compromise, that is *not* constructive synergy. It **is** an ultimatum, especially if he's at all aware that she has insecurities that will not presently allow her to present an equally stern (but potentially constructive) counter-ultimatum: "Let's work out a solution that is equally beneficial to us both, or we go separate ways, because I won't stay with someone willing to jerk me around."

But most people who are venturing into polyamory are clueless, especially at the beginning. They might know, deep down inside, that they want a polyamorous lifestyle, but they have no idea of how to get there. Most people learned to "swim" as poly by jumping into the deep end of the pool, so I can't see throwing rocks at someone just for making mistakes when they allow the situation to get ahead of their learning curve. Diving into polyamory is acceptable, but first secretly shackling someone else to you is rude at best.

What worsens the situation, though, is that most people carry along absolute *tons* of baggage from monogamy, a sampling being: either/or thinking; closed or nothing; male in charge; pseudo-egalitarianism; blind assumption; poor problem-solving skills; no self-disclosure ability.

So, start with the very basics. The husband is thrashing around for another sexual partner. Any sexual partner. He's not particularly fixated on one woman, just sexual variety, though he has the dim impression that there should be more than that.

If he's serious about actually being polyamorous, and doesn't simply want to start his own little harem, this would be a good time to knock off his adventures for a while, sit down with his wife, and work out some ground rules. I'd strongly recommend a reputable therapist for the couple, as well as that she see a therapist to deal with her own self-esteem issues.

If the wife, right this moment, were to have a turnaround, and start spending some of her alone-time having coffee with an attractive man, just to chat and be friends, I'd give 50/50 odds that her husband would throw a jealous fit, anything from threats to end the relationship to pulling a long face for the "you don't really love me" routine. Well, ain't that tough. If the sword can't cut both ways, then it's *not* mutual.

You should have a commitment where neither of you has the unilateral power to change rules that affect you both. Without that as one of your biggest rules, then ventures into polyamory will mostly be cheap melodrama.

Put yourself on the other side of what we've been discussing. You meet up with someone who has a little understanding of polyamory, and would like to explore the possibilities further, specifically with you. Problem is, that person is married, and their spouse is in the dark and will likely be kept there because they "wouldn't understand."

Yes, I have watched it happen.

It's not so difficult to talk a monogamous person into an affair… but a sea-change to long-term lifestyle openness is unlikely. Don't let someone kid you about this.

I'm one of many polyamorous people who, due to vicissitudes of life, goes through long periods of sexual limitation (one partner, or even none), but I haven't "changed" when this has occurred, because I have known since discovering the concept that multiple intimacy is so much more than just sex, and there are many things to be shared, even if it's just mushy e-mails with my ex-lovers. (Oddly, I don't consider myself very "permissive", and feel I'm somewhat stodgy and slow-moving compared to many of my peers.)

A temporary difference

There are times in a polyamorous dyad where one partner is freer than the other. Pregnancy, career demands, health problems, or education can all put a crimp in one's intimate life. Occasionally, one partner will take full advantage of this, then back rapidly away from letting the same freedom apply to the other.

> Andy and Colette had been married for four years, when they decided to have other lovers as well. Well, actually, it had been Andy's idea, and Colette hadn't found much reason to put an absolute veto on the program. Despite this, things had worked out very well, though Colette was putting off anything more than occasional dating until she finished the thesis for her master's degree. The men she went out with accepted this.
>
> In the meantime, Andy spent most nights with his girlfriend, Vera. Colette thought it a little odd that Andy seemed to make a big thing out of being willing to cancel these outings if Colette wanted him to stay in. "Of course not," she'd say, looking up from the computer screen. "I'd be doing the same if it wasn't for this paper." *Besides,* she thought, *I'll finish it all the faster if I can pace around as much as I need, and that's easier when I'm alone.*

Finally, Colette's paper was accepted by her advisor, pending some minor revisions. The end was in sight and, overjoyed, she went out for the evening with one of the boyfriends, and ended up spending the night.

When she got home the next morning, Andy was sitting at the table, looking glum. This surprised Colette, as he almost always went straight to work from Vera's apartment. "What's wrong?" she asked.

"I came back for a different shirt, and you weren't here. I was worried."

Colette beamed. "I'm going to be done with my program by the end of the month!" She bent down and kissed Andy's forehead. "I'll finally have some time to spend with my men," she added, walking toward the bedroom.

As she stripped off her clothing, Andy followed. "I'm concerned about how this is going to affect our relationship."

"School, you mean? But that's almost over."

"No, I mean having other lovers."

Colette, reaching for a fresh towel, stopped. "I haven't *had* much for other lovers. I've hardly had lovers, *period*, even counting you."

Andy nodded. "Yeah, things have changed."

"Not *changed*," Colette said, "gotten *better*. I can take a month or two to check for postings, and that's time that I can start to have *people* in my life again."

Andy looked away, shaking his head. "I'm worried about where this is going."

So am I, Colette thought. Aloud, she said, "You've had all those nights with Vera, days and weekends, even, while I was in the library, or plugged into the computer. And you wanted this polyamory stuff way before I got so busy, so it's not fair to blame my work."

Andy stiffened. "I didn't *have* to go," he said defensively, "but you *wanted* me to."

The upshot from this *contretemps* bothers me, so I'll summarize. Since Colette was pretty much finished with her college work for a few years, Andy wanted to have time with her again.

To that point, things are pretty reasonable. But Andy had decided that the best plan was for Colette to stop seeing anyone else so that scheduling conflicts wouldn't arise. However, since he'd established a solid, regular relationship with Vera, he felt obligated to spend a few nights a week with her, "to be fair." When Colette expressed her feeling that this was hardly *fair* to anyone, Andy offered to end his relationship with Vera. Colette, though, had been looking forward to her own chance to explore, as well as having more time with Andy. After all, her dating partners had been patient, waiting on nothing more than a promise. She felt that Andy was trying to keep her all to himself, yet have a steady girlfriend, and she also felt that he was unilaterally changing some fundamental rules.

I'd agree. Variants on this theme have flitted past me a few times over the years, all damned silly, all underhanded attempts to grab for freedom and flexibility without granting it to others.

The above example was a little unusual, in that Colette and Andy have an open-form relationship. Closed-form relationships, especially people aiming for FMF triads, have their own common variants; I'll address some of these concerns later, in chapter 45, "The doubtful triad."

Different worlds

There is really nothing that actually *prevents* two people with drastically different feelings about polyamory from being intimately involved. But, however close or distant they happen to be as far as their personal approaches, *each must* feel fairly treated. If one of you is monogamous, and the other polyamorous, and the monogamous partner has a satisfying and rewarding life, then I hope neither of you wastes much time trying to poke holes in your happiness. Remember, two people with almost identical approaches to nonmonogamy might nevertheless both be extremely dissatisfied with the interaction of their choices – such is the human condition. Fault does not necessarily lie with monogamy or with those who prefers monogamy for themselves. If you cannot live happily, or even comfortably, with your partner's lifestyle choices, then you must do some serious thinking about the other options, including ending the relationship. Gritting your teeth over bothersome habits is a third-rate sort of love at best, and not emotionally healthy for anyone.

Don't start cozying up to someone with the idea that you're going to change them, and be wary of those who try it with you. Sure, changes will probably happen – if you have a dozen casual, irregular involvements, you might spend more time with someone new who shows every sign of becoming a primary relationship. However, if this is part of your or their agenda, your communication is seriously flawed. I have been forced to end two relationships where I soon discovered that four or five evenings per week was not adequate for them, and I started sensing pressure to move in together and to further cut down on my time with other friends and lovers. Both are wonderful people, and I'm certain that they can each find a husband that fulfills them, but it isn't me. Polyamory is not simply a phase that I am going through, nor is it my way of wife-shopping.

I cannot recommend getting involved with someone who doesn't communicate your existence fully to their partners and receive something like approval. Maybe it's a personal failing, but I do not like the idea of providing a catalyst – or worse, an excuse – for someone to get out of a relationship. I would first have to believe that their communication style is flawed, and would come back to haunt me later. If dishonesty is involved, then I'd have to wonder at what point that deceit will be used against me. Then, once they have broken up their relationship, would I still be useful? Perhaps my position will spark the sort of crisis they need in order to start communicating properly and work out deep-running problems – where would I be then?

42. Dating outside the couple front

Perhaps you could answer a question for me: What is the damn *hurry*, anyway?

There's a certain behavior among monogamists that sets my teeth on edge, though I'm immunized by the years from being actually horrified, or even surprised. They meet at a bar, have sex within three hours, can't remember each other's name on the second date, move in together the next week, get married a few months later, and file for divorce when the NRE wears off, which is about the fourth month of pregnancy.

With such absurdity staring us in the face, and a mandate to make polyamory a vast improvement over the battlefield we call monogamy, we go ahead and commit the same pratfalls. Even that level of absurdity I can understand, albeit in the same way a botanist observes at an ant farm. (I have some understanding of their actions, and from observation I can estimate what the end will be, but there's no way for me to get into their little heads and understand their thought patterns.)

What the heck is wrong with *dating*? I don't understand why couples, so intent on taking on huge risks to their conjoined life, aren't a bit more cautious about slavering at the thought of opening up their relationship. Couldn't they *each* just find a girlfriend, someone to go to movies with, or dinner or coffee or shopping? After all, if going out on no-sex dates sets off all kinds of arguments, then they'd have a better idea of what needs to be worked out between the two of them if they're going to stay together at all. From having a social life as individuals, they could better learn how to have deep friendships, intimate in more than mere sex. Honing their social skills, discovering things within themselves and how to better be fascinated with other attractive human beings, they would be in a much better position to perhaps find one sole individual who is ideally suited for both of them, and they for she.

Triadic sex

Let's get this out of the way. The topic is entirely too prevalent, with a misty air of childish fascination that is so obsessive as to approach the mystical. Folks: threesomes, like triads, can be wonderful. That's *can* as in "it's theoretically possible – but *possible* covers a lot of turf."

A few factors are screwing things up, and I will summarize. If you're chasing after polyamory because you want to fulfill a sexual fantasy, then you're already in the wrong boat. Go out, have fun, maybe join a swing club or something. But don't grasp blindly at highfalutin' words in order to paste a politically correct justification on it. (Not to be picking solely on those who want a closed triad, either. There are many and many "poly" people who are here to get laid, just as there are those promiscuous "monogamous" people.)

There are very few people who are anywhere near perfection. Most of us do not always work and play well with the other children. Put three people together, and chances are that even if one of them is halfway to godlike status, the other two are down around the average for the race.

I'll give you the benefit of the doubt, and admit that you might end up with three wonderful people. Stop and think about that. Have you ever had two friends, or members of your family, each of whom you love and respect and rely upon – and they absolutely *loathe* each other? Even if the feeling isn't mutual, it's hard to have a loving dyad when one is hiding a deep desire to see the other thoroughly humiliated. We are all to some degree complexly flawed little beings, and, just as one person can bring out the best in you, another can bring out the worst under pressure or excitation – and "pressure and excitation" suits the sweaty way that the products of our culture tend to approach physical intimacy.

All in all, if long-term triads or threesomes were particularly easy to arrange, don't you think they'd be a lot more common? And does the fact that they are most assuredly not common pull you up a little short... or have you already convinced yourself that you are one of those half-perfect people I mentioned?

Therefore, let's take a brief moment to discuss sex. Should you perhaps be coming from, say, a culture where sexual self-image is used to sell car wax and watery beer, and sex is therefore something hinted at but never quite achieved, something you sneak around for, something you pretend that no decent human being longs for even as you brag hintingly about your "conquests," then inasmuch as this attitude has blinded you to both reality and possibility, you are (to use a highly appropriate word) fucked. As one or two of my readers might indeed be products of such a culture, let's look at how you should speak with such an unfortunate.

First of all, if everything is centered around "real" sex, intercourse, then things depend entirely upon the "staying power" of the involved male(s). If you want things to go that way, more power to ya, but I think the penis-centric worldview is seriously restricted.

I've only had a couple of dozen FMF encounters, and even that label is wrong, because nobody was the center of attention for large bits of time. It's not unusual that one of us will drop out for a few minutes (getting water for us all, visiting the bathroom, answering the phone, stretching, catching breath…). Or one of us will be nuzzling someone's belly as the third is rubbing their shoulders. Or each is fondling the genitalia of the other two (and you always wondered why God gave us *two* hands). Or a nice little ring of oral play. Or… well, I can't magically give someone an imagination; if you're creative, there's plenty of opportunity to spend a pleasant three or four hours.

It *helps* if males are long-lasting, not too penis-centric, and/or can "recover" quickly; and if the females like to touch and be touched, don't get too sensitive after orgasm, and are at least bisexual enough to accept attention.

If someone feels they're the "odd person out", then either the other two have to be a bit less couple-centered, or the third has to try to be a little more active. If it's just not "clicking" for me, I've been known to warmly kiss my partners, then go and make snacks (and it's surprising how often, after a little break and a nosh, the energies have changed and we're back to a proper three-way exchange). Unless your personalities have that sort of flexibility, then your best bet would be to stop everything right there and have a very serious discussion.

If you go into a three-or-moresome with rigid expectations, intent upon fulfilling your preconceptions exactly like the two-dimensional people in your head, this kinda defeats the purpose of doing something new and unique. Relax, explore, have fun. If it's a pleasant encounter, then you're doing okay. If the three of you still want to go out for coffee next week and next month and next year, that is something to be treasured.

Reasons to go slow (reprise)

Whatever your own level of experience, be very wary of getting involved with two sorts of people: those who are already encoupled and have little or no experience with ongoing sexually open relating, and those who have few or no apparent attachments.

With the former, there is always some degree of risk that you will end up damaging their relationship because, again, the couple-front is very strong right up to the second that it shatters. Should that happen, then it's likely you or your new partner will feel this responsibility deeply, and you've participated in electing yourself to be one of the prime parties who gets to clean up the mess. Do you really *want* to spend almost all of your time together processing feelings about the breakup? How many weeks – or months – are you willing to do this?

You may even find that you have been chosen to become the straw that broke the camel's back – in short, you're an excuse to break up the relationship. In which case, when that dyad is dead, your usefulness may well have ended.

You might discover all sorts of unpleasant reasons why that couple didn't survive your intrusion. There may be similar reasons to explain why a person you find so attractive is single and entirely unattached – sociopathy, perhaps. Heartbreak is unpleasant; moving a fascinating stranger into your life, before you even begin to know them, may be more trouble than the whole thing could possibly be worth. A few months of caution would certainly be of high worth, if not invaluable.

Fighting the Society in your heads

At present, only a minority of people exploring nonmonogamy have successfully set aside the standard mode. You can call that mode marriage, or monogamy, or the couple-front – in this context, they're all the same.

I think of myself as one of the early sports. I did not leap away from monogamy as some sort of rebellion, or based upon some philosophical premise. Nonmonogamy is not and has never been my way of biding time until my "soul mate" comes along. Neither was I interested in writing myself a ticket for unlimited sexual explorations. I had years remaining in my virginity when I first encountered a passing reference to group marriage; my thought at the time was, "That makes sense." Then, for the most part, I forgot about it.

My first intimate relationship, though lasting five years, was a suite of variations on getting burned in monogamy. Finally, I shrugged, told my fiancée that I had decided to claim similar freedoms to hers, and started dating. Up until that point, she'd been telling me in many ways that, if her actions bothered me, we ought to end the relationship; I called her bluff, and I was not in the least bluffing.

Increasingly, I am meeting people who are free of the influence of idealized couplehood. They aren't afraid of commitment and deep intimacy – one of the more common "explanations" of all nonmonogamy, even that attached to monoamory – but they cannot even pretend to believe that this could only be possible with one person at a time. For them, the number of people to whom they are connected is limited by measurable physical limits of time and proximity, not some undefined maximal divisibility of one human heart.

They are fighting an uphill battle. True, it appears that the critics they carry buried in their brains, the self-censors, the self-saboteurs, have been successfully suppressed, or have never been able to grow larger than to make a feeble protest. People such as these are at the forefront of change, but they are still a minority. Dating outside of the couple-front, mere simple dating, is still something that sets most of the members of our society a-twitter.

Though it takes time and effort, the best way to offset the learned societal pressures that will interfere with your happiness is by having as many people in your life as you can who are at least supportive of your beliefs and practices, and preferably who follow a similar course to yours. You also have to spot your self-defeating reflexes as they occur, and examine them thoroughly asking what they are, why they are there, and what possible good they are supposed to be doing for you. That is, you have to act as your own best friend. Once thoroughly examined, these reflexes lose much of their power, and you'll find that they fade with time and experience.

Remember, too, that each of your partners is carrying around a head full of Society. You need to help them with all your heart – within reason. I add that last caveat because there are always people who will be willing to take a huge leap of faith into nonmonogamy, but will find the experience frightening, or threatening to their sense of control, or possibly even panic them by demanding that they redefine their self-image in a way they are not yet ready to face. Given such an impasse, there is little other than therapy that can make a long-lasting change. Don't try to fix or convert them. Give yourself distance as you must in your particular circumstances, remain open, and keep talking – if polyamory is really the way that they are meant to go, then eventually they may reach a place from which they can learn.

Dating outside your new species

My wife Marie was a rude bitch, for which I loved her dearly. When a male would start sidling up to her and making overtures, she'd say, "I'm married, and I'm not going to leave my husband for anyone. Still interested?" It's surprising how often they'd slink away.

Over the years, I've grown increasingly leery of getting intimately involved with someone who has no experience in nonmonogamy; I'm willing to compromise if she's had the experience of regularly dating two people simultaneously. More often than not, if I don't take that precaution, a woman will progress rapidly from "yes, I fully understand that you are committed to that lifestyle" to "what's wrong with you/me that we can't do everything together?"

When you decide upon polyamory, you are giving up potential for refuge in many illusions. This can make you an uncomfortable or even unpleasant companion for someone who depends upon unquestioning belief in those same illusions. Compare it to politics or religion if you must, but let's at least say that your worldview would easily trample all over theirs, because polyamory accepts iconoclasm, while orthodoxy cannot tolerate it.

I will start from the assumption that you are intelligent, observant, giving, and caring, and even that you have had some happy experience with responsible nonmonogamy. In fact, I'll go out on a limb and assume that you have at least one solid partner who is that way, too.

The problem is, most of the people in the world aren't. They are missing at least one of those crucial elements, the most common probably being that they have no experience with nonmonogamy, and may never have considered the concept at all except for a few passing thoughts about adultery. Someday we may have a saner society, in which people are more familiar with responsible nonmonogamy, encountering an example or three in their daily life and thus having the opportunity to observe extended families that function in a healthy manner over the long haul. Here and now, I doubt that one person in a hundred could define "polyamory" in a manner that even caricatures what it's actually all about.

Someone with that degree of inexperience might as well be from another species, as far as experienced polyfolk ought to be concerned. As "interested" as they might be in you, they are working from ignorance and, even with a pure heart, they really have no idea how to go about being intimately involved with you.

As a sincerely polyamorous person, you run a constant risk of not being taken seriously. Monogamists will be more than happy to have an affair with you, and have no interest in maintaining anything like a friendship. In such an instance, you're a passing entertainment, an affair – because that is the only model of "extramarital sex" that they've had any exposure to. If you have a clearly delineated dyad, then (they reason) you're looking for a little action on the side, nothing serious or long-term. They might end up horribly shocked and offended to find out that you've told others about your liaison, even though they gave you every assurance at the outset that the involvement was above-board, and not sneaking around; some might even think that this was a bit of playful fantasy on your part, and therefore were simply going along with the game, speaking the lines they imagined you wanted.

Even if you should be especially cautious, you might find that someone else's dyad ends up not being so open as they'd told you. Sometimes a couple will be smitten with a sort of NRE about the whole polyamory experience, charge headlong into sexual exploration long before they are emotionally, intellectually, and relationally ready, then one or both of them will be floored by doubt or guilt. If one has a strongly positive experience and the other doesn't, this disparity could pull a couple apart when both refuse to compromise their respective self-discovery.

Again, be cautious. You could literally end up with all of your neighbors turned against you if word gets around that you're being held responsible for breaking up a relationship. Unless you're a particularly polished liar, you could find yourself clinching your own public damnation by stammering through a denial of guilt. You might cut them both out of your life, but that doesn't go very far toward making you appear innocent, and you've lost not just one but both, and turned yet more people against you for abandoning your friends during a crisis.

In general, I think it best to find someone of approximately your own level of experience. This should be true not only as far as nonmonogamy, but more widely: sexual experience, social life, committed relationships, group-living situations, and so on. Those who are more experienced might have a desire to "mentor" beginners, and people new to the concepts might be overly impressed with the presumed wisdom of the old-timers. However, each situation is so new in and of itself that, no matter how you approach it, everyone will probably have a lot of very specific new knowledge they will have to acquire, and quickly. Therefore, I recommend that you all be relatively equal in other things, and that you set out to learn as a group rather than hand over authority (consciously or not) on the basis of some irrelevant seniority.

The risks are always there. It's up to you (individually and collectively) to make those risks as intelligent as you possibly can.

The mechanics of dating

I didn't date. It's another fault of my upbringing, combined with not wanting to show interest in any girl in my small hometown, lest one or both of us become fodder for gossip and ribbing. When I went off to college, I pursued one young woman for a month or two, then became fascinated with Cindy. We lasted five years through an amazing range of tribulations, coming within hailing distance of marriage more than a few times. After having my metaphorical fingers burned enough times, I started dating, including the woman who ended up as my partner two years later and my wife two after that. All told, Marie and I stayed together in various flavors for twelve years.

After a bitter divorce, I awoke one day to a startling fact. There I was in my mid-thirties, and I had not been truly single for even a year in total since I'd moved out of my parents' house. I'd almost always had at least one primary relationship, however rocky. I had only been monogamous for a few years at the beginning of my sexual life, yet I had been so affected by society despite my iconoclastic family that I'd never been loose in the world as an individual adult. And there I sat, just me and my cat, scrabbling to make the occasional date with women who were important to me. This pathetic situation had to change, so I began consciously observing my own habits, and the effects that I have on other people, and discovered a few things about flirting and courting.

I didn't have more than a glimmer about dating. And, as most people would define the word, I still don't. However, I have picked some thing up along the way. Much of this is scattered throughout the book, of course, but there are a few pointers I want to pass along.

Foremost, be yourself. If you're just out to get laid, no strings attached, then you can put on a big show, only reveal your best side and your talents and your strengths. Who's to know? As time goes on, and polyamorous nodes pop up increasingly, word gets around that your initial appearance is only a thin, artificially constructed coating, a veneer that won't stand up to time or scrutiny. If you put too much work into it, then only those who are seeking the veneer, nothing else, will be drawn to you, which you might find a bit painful when they walk back out of your life without looking any deeper. Should you duck that particular bullet, and you find someone you'd like to possibly spend a few years or more with, then you've got another major problem: Keeping up the act is draining, and you'll eventually need to come clean about who you really are.

Rather than waste all that effort (and, ultimately, time) in putting on a good show to impress others, try to enjoy being yourself. If there's something about you that you're worried may offend someone in whom you're interested, then work to change it, rather than to hide it. If you're pretty much stuck, then you might be surprised at how a humorous story you tell about your foibles will eliminate that potential landmine – that's just the way you are and, if someone is going to get bent out of shape about it, then better for everyone that you know where you stand from the start.

When you are dating, you must keep your eyes open for situations in which your habits will impinge on others' self-image. For instance, be *very* wary of buying affection – it's an easy trap to fall into, and usually one that can be avoided (or extricated from). If you are normally a bit free with your cash, and your new partner goes home with a friendship ring more opulent than their wedding band (worse, competing for space on the same finger), then their partner might not properly appreciate this symbolic gesture. Going out for a night on the town, or a weekend at a resort, is a not-uncommon risk, especially if your date's extant partner does not have the same sort of disposable income. (I see this most often when a single non-parent is dating someone whose dyad has children.)

All you have to do is say that you're feeling a little "snug" in the pocketbook; after all, if you're bothered by the potential fallout, it will diminish not only your enjoyment of the show, but will make you begin to question what the motivations are of the involved parties, which hardly makes for a perfect relationship. Besides, the impression you make shouldn't have the price tag still attached. As the relationship progresses, and everyone involved has a chance to feel comfortable with each other's underlying motivations, gifts can begin to move a little more freely. I've lived half my life in the low-pay bracket, so my sympathies are with my partners who can't even drop $16 on a great show. I know how to live frugally, but I've also been known to casually spend $200 on an evening for two.

On the other side, don't be bought. Can your date truly afford the sort of cash they're flinging about, or are they draining their retirement account? Are they flush enough to keep it up, or is it only a short flourish? If they can afford it, then is this the way they live – and the way that you want to live – or could they be doing something better with their resources? These are the sorts of questions that help differentiate an affair from a relationship.

If *anything* bothers you, it should be addressed. Period. A long-term partner would gladly discuss your feelings, even early in the relationship, and even if it momentarily makes them uncomfortable. If you want to see the show, you're paying for your fun; if you need to see the show with a particular person, then you're paying the freight on that, too. But if you're doubting the motivations of one (or both) of you, then it's something that *must* be discussed – that'd be one way to tell it's a possible partnership, not just someone you happen to be dating.

Self-image, self-doubt

Most of us harbor the belief that, if someone we are very attracted to actually likes us, this will change once they see what is *really* deep down inside. The less experienced you are with revealing yourself to others, the more likely it is that these feelings will surface and sabotage you. If someone you are attracted to has had few intimate relationships, then these doubts are even more likely to become crucial.

I admit, it lurks inside of me. When an attractive woman chats me up, my first reaction is panic; I'm thinking, "Ohmigod, this person is *incredible* – why would she be talking to someone like *me*?" It fades out pretty quickly, especially after I dated a former fashion model who admitted that she felt the same way: she couldn't figure out why someone as brainy as me would ever give her a chance! Self-doubt affects us all.

I spent months flirting with her. She is stunning and, to this day, I have no idea how I ever worked up the nerve. Half a year along, we went out on our first date, finally ending up back at her place. She went off to get ready for bed: scrubbed off the makeup, put her flame-red hair up in pigtails, took off her contacts and put on plastic-frame glasses, and peeled herself out of the silk dress for a flannel robe.

And when she came back, she was so beautiful that tears came to my eyes. The transition from high-fashion to perfect raw honesty was a shock bordering on ecstasy that, eight years on, still gives me chills.

That sort of revelation is what I wish for everyone who enters sincere and emotionally vulnerable into nonmonogamy. We were both well into adulthood, both widely experienced in nonmonogamy. Both she and I stand out in a crowd, and the force of our respective personalities draws people to us. Yet we both began from a vast self-doubt, a gulf made still wider by the attraction we each felt.

As ever, begin by trying to be as aware of your own reactions as you can. Bring it up, examine it, question it, then set it aside and let it fade. From there, you are in an excellent position to help others to do the same.

43. The sexual credit bureau

In his wonderfully funny book, *Sex from Aah to Zipper*, Roger Libby suggested that, in order to be more happily nonmonogamous, we need something like a "sexual credit bureau," where prospective partners could call up an individual's record and read a thumbnail sketch of what it's like to be involved with that person. Believe me, if there were a way to work around confidentiality issues and to filter out unreasonable biases and outright propaganda (good and bad), I'd have founded this long ago. Without it, anyone who makes the right noises, says the right words, or hangs around with the right people is accepted as polyamorous based only on their simple claim.

While this likely cannot ever exist in any actual formal state, such as a dating service, you can find the next-best thing, or put it together for yourself. Communities do exist that have a high degree of open polyamory, though it varies by region. If you are affiliated with the Society for Creative Anachronism, certain religions (such as Wicca, or the Unitarian Universalists), your local Renaissance Faire, or the larger fan-run science fiction conventions, you likely know someone who knows someone.

I've played about every possible role in this sort of tacit reference service. I have begun some wonderful relationships because a mutual lover or friend felt that the potential dyad would be a good match, and put in a suggestion or recommendation to one or both of us.

I've also done a little matchmaking myself, though I don't fool myself into thinking that I'm going to be the catalyst of a lifelong partnership. Happiness, after all, is happiness, and can't be properly measured in terms of years, mostly determined only retrospectively and therefore hardly the sort of thing amenable to spreadsheet projection.

A young woman I was briefly acquainted with came up to me at a convention, and asked, "What do you know about this Mark guy?" "Well," I replied, surprisingly unsurprised, "he's very socially gregarious, a lot of fun to talk to though he can be exhausting, he's extremely intelligent and loves to dance. He's trying to figure out long-term relationships, but I know a few of his previous lovers, they all still like him, and I've heard no complaints about his attentiveness." She looked thoughtful, thanked me, then went off and had a mutually delightful fling with Mark.

Open communication presents something of a "bootstrap" problem: in order for members of a group to be able to communicate, they need to be able to communicate in the first place. If you're going to have enough of a community-type collection of people for any of you to benefit from sharing information, then it's probably best if you start as soon as you can. Give trust to get trust and, for heaven's sake, don't go stomping all over someone if you find they've give you a less-than-perfect profile – not only *are* you imperfect (unless, of course, you're an alien being disguised as human, in which case I offer my abject apologies), but your friend may have frightened someone away that you'll eventually be thankful to have not gotten involved with.

When you ask around about someone, what you are looking for is not absolute authority, but a wider range of input. Each individual has biases, and the limits of their objectivity may swing wildly depending upon mood, context, and circumstance. The recipient can look at the positives and negatives, and rank them in an entirely different order from that of the source. Trusting someone's advice does not mean necessarily taking it at face value or hanging on every word – what you are trusting is that the opinion is honest and more-or-less complete. This also gives a general idea of what the people closest to you would think about having your proposed paramour possibly included in your social circle.

Without this sort of "credit bureau" function, there is no way that there can be in any real sense a larger poly community. There are some true communities that I have met, and they do indeed function more or less as communities, so I am certain that the function is indeed possible and workable. However, these are usually limited by region (or even neighborhood), and become tenuous as geography intrudes. The problem, as ever, remains to produce a sort of nation-(and eventually world-) wide basis for passing such information around between us, in an atmosphere of trust.

44. Then, the sex starts...

Sex is a fundamentally simple transaction between emotionally mature individuals. Motivations largely stem from a desire to exchange affection and pleasure. Sexual interaction inherently expands the range of possible communication between the individuals involved. The deep intimacy afforded by sex allows us to grow emotionally. Even though this interaction might not result in a long-term intimate relationship, the sex brings us closer together as human beings, and thus forms the basis for life-long friendship.

Yeah, we'd like that, wouldn't we.

In reality, we're a bunch of flawed beings. We project our self-doubt and insecurity onto others, we force them into roles that fit poorly and get upset when our expectations don't work out, and what little ability we have to learn and adapt usually goes completely out the window when other people are involved.

Usually, we work around our character flaws. This generally means that we pretend those flaws don't exist or are caused by external factors, though we sometimes acknowledge our weak spots and devise strategies to prevent them from undermining our lives.

In circumstances that are stressful or anxiety-producing or insecurity-provoking, the haphazard structure we've built to get us through the day is dealt a series of sharp kicks. Since a new relationship is all of those things, and especially so as NRE begins to wane, the result is that we readily fall into a loop, as we project our fears and blemishes alike onto the people nearest us, onto one or more relationships, the physical or social situation we are in at the time, and so on. The loop is completed when these behaviors put distance between us and our friends and loved ones.

The risk is always there, whatever your circumstance happens to be. The difference lies not so much in degree, but form. Let's say that you have a closed, monogamous dyad, and you decide that you're going to turn it into a triad. If your dyad isn't solid, this strategy puts your relationship at high risk. On the other hand, if you've got a solid dyad, emotionally healthy and mutually productive, then becoming a triad will likely put your relationship at high risk. Finding an ideal candidate can break you apart; becoming involved with a not-ideal candidate can as well. Of course, merely *pursuing* a potential candidate or three puts your dyad at risk, as does discussing the possibility between the two of you.

The more thoughtful and good-hearted among you will have already considered this, at least briefly. You trust in the better parts respectively of yourself and your partner, and as well of your relationship, and the situation in which you live. Really, though, you cannot even say how you as an individual are going to react in any given situation until you are actually in that situation. For instance, if you and your partner have already had some experience with intimacy outside of the dyad, you may be correct in assuming that moving into intimacy yet again – and I'll assume that this next situation doesn't involve a person or persons any more demanding or less wonderful than that bygone experience – you may be baffled at how this unique situation (at least, I hope that all your relationships are at least deep enough to be unique) sets of all sorts of insecurities within you. It is uncomfortable to find two or more voices fighting for control over your head and heart, with your rational, sensible, loving self slugging it out with your fearful, insecure, irrational side.

When one partner in a dyad begins a new intimate relationship, the individuals in the new dyad can experience all sorts of awakenings, while the left-out partner from the original dyad can easily fall prey to fear that their relationship is over – in the usual structure of "monogamous" society, that's pretty much how things work, and to varying degrees we are each stuck with this legacy. There can develop a *huge* gulf between the wariness brought by this (all too accurate) fear to the first dyad and the emotional heights produced by the second, with the result being that, in a sort of self-fulfilling prophecy, the first dyad breaks up, or the second dyad is ended to protect the first.

In most cases, the crisis begins to form at the first sexual experience. Until that point, our ensocialization typically allows us to keep doubt and fear at bay because the incursion appears more symbolic than actual, and thus more vulnerable to rationalization. This can happen even among those very experienced with polyamory – again, a particular person, at a particular moment, in a particular situation. Though it may be a not-so-pleasant surprise at such a late date, most will have already experienced similar feelings in the past, and have developed strategies to deal appropriately with them.

Dyads that are new to polyamory, though, may be quite shaken by the reaction, knowing little about how to deal with or interpret these feelings, whether in self or their partner. A given individual might swing wildly between abject denial, hoping it'll just fade if ignored, and being totally swept away by hysteria. This is redoubled when one of the members (or both) had little experience with a steady, reliable relationship before the formation of the dyad.

For many people, especially established couples, it is with the first sexual experience outside of that dyad, in the context of assumed polyamory, that a major and possibly relationship-threatening crisis occurs. Up until then, it's been an exciting little fantasy, with sanctioned flirtation, and a huge feeling (usually premature) that communication between the two has vastly increased. Then, the sex starts, and things become really real, really fast.

The newer you are to intimacy, and especially to multilinear relating, the more caution I urge. Don't just go diving face-first into a situation, assuming that you're going to dip only briefly into the poly pool and come up with the person or couple with whom you're going to spend the rest of your life. The likelihood is *very* low that you'd find such on the first try, or even the first few. After all, you don't yet have the experience to know how to search for or recognize an ideal person. Once you actually experience nonmonogamy (even if it's something as compact as a closed triad), you will probably find that some of your initial assumptions were incorrect and have proven unworkable. This presents all sorts of problems if you've moved in together by that point.

For every step forward that you take into nonmonogamy, you may have to retreat a step, or more. This doesn't mean that you are dabbling, or even that it isn't ultimately right for you. The fact of the matter is that, in order to examine your feelings, and then to determine what parts have worked nicely for you and which haven't, you need to be in relatively safe, known territory. A few of us old-timers are familiar with this dance, and do not take it as a personal affront when a new dating partner or lover has to have some alone time – possibly weeks or months – before they can sincerely say whether the experience represents a direction they'd like to explore further. As polyamory matures, I am reasonably certain that this part of the learning process will not only be tolerated, but supported, perhaps encouraged.

People with polyamorous experience, whether solo or single, ought to move slowly as well. Courtship has its place in responsible nonmonogamy, and life isn't so short as to justify taking one foolish, unthinking leap after another. The first sexual experience will tend to lock down the relationship, unless you take action to keep things moving and growing. Again, we're carrying a not-so-great legacy, part of which is that sex is a main goal. Once you've gotten laid, what else is there but to go on to the next experience? There's no sane reason that courtship cannot go on after or even begin from a spontaneous sexual encounter, but the products of this society carry many quirks that can militate against that process-oriented approach.

Another of those artifacts is the belief that sex is always intimate (which relates to the belief that intimacy requires sex). Such is hardly true, and sexual thrills can quite easily be used to turn off emotions and create interpersonal distance. I created a term: *nonintimate sex*. Many people do use sex as a way of shutting down communication, of cutting themselves off from connection with another human being. For example, many dyads, monogamous and otherwise, agree that there are times when an argument that could have been very productive was short-circuited by "make-up sex." With all those good feelings (or, some would say, a working out of aggressions in sexual form), it is easy to make the mistaken assumption that the situation was settled, only to find the same situation appear again.

If you're going to be polyamorous for life, then you've got a lifetime to be polyamorous. Why rush?

45. The doubtful triad

Threesomes and triads are not the actual subject of this book, though the reader might find reason to doubt that statement. I believe, however, that any intelligent and insightful person (that, hopefully, would be you) is capable of reading about the members of another culture and finding relevance to their own life, however dissimilar the circumstances – we are, after all, more or less all human. But many of the people who "logic" their way into nonmonogamy are operating as a couple; this may even be a majority, so large is the portion. Couples also make up the majority of those I observe who get badly burned by foreseeable (to the experienced) errors. Since most couples blithely entering into polyamory or its vague equivalent are leaping with skittish caution, they mostly are looking for a triad; most of these are looking for a closed triad, most of *these* are looking for a closed triad with a female, and most of these want a closed triad with a *bisexual* female.

So, I talk about threesomes and triads a lot.

I will be blunt: anyone who goes *looking* to start a triad is a fool. Anyone who *wants* to start a *closed* triad is a loon. Anyone who has no experience with ongoing nonmonogamy and wants to start a closed triad is an idiot and should be kept away from anything more dangerous than a well-worn telephone directory for a small rural town.

I don't like to impugn sincere people, but facts are facts. Those who are fixated on threesomes tend to have an inability to be self-entertaining. A need for a closed triad – nothing more, ever – indicates a higher degree of neurotic togetherness. And tons of vital questions go unasked at the outset; for instance, what happens in a "one bed" household when only two of the triad want to have sex?

Superficial agreement

Most couples who decide to seek out their (yes, you do encounter that possessive) bisexual female claim to be in complete harmony as to what they're after. Just below the surface, though, they can diverge wildly as far as motivation. Here are a few (referring to "husband" and "wife" only for the sake of consistency) that I've observed:

- The wife thinks that her husband is becoming restless or dissatisfied with her. Rather than risk losing him entirely, she considers finding him a live-in girlfriend. This has advantages, such as putting the girlfriend under obligation to the majority – that is, to the couple. If the democratic form should ever turn against the wife, she can threaten divorce, yet also hint at finding another girlfriend who is more *compatible*, though an observer might conclude that *malleable* is more accurate.

- The emotional/sexual side of the marriage is dead, so they need to find someone who'll "fix" it. This suggests that either their sensibility was skewed in the first place, or that they are refusing to recognize the relationship's decline – in short, the same thing will likely happen when the NRE wears off.

- The wife wants to explore her own bisexual curiosity, but is worried about being labeled a lesbian.

- The husband has had an affair or two, which led to some vicious arguments when discovered. He isn't at all proud of the secrecy.

- The husband isn't particularly interested in attempting to keep up with his wife's sexual desires. He concludes that having a girlfriend will not only make him more interested in sex, but that the two women will regularly indulge his fantasies, and also keep each other satisfied when he wants to spend all of his free time watching television.

- Heck, if they really get along well, maybe he can even slip out and have a girlfriend on the side, too.

- The husband has considered finding someone else entirely, but doesn't want to put the marriage at risk until he's got something solid lined up. He is (symptomatically) very uncomfortable with the idea of "his women" having other sexual partners. If this works, he can use it again later.

Happytalk about community and family won't cut it, here. You've got to start by taking a long, hard look at the motivations that each of you has for seeking a third.

There's nothing at all wrong with planning to make your sex life more adventurous–as long as you don't pretend that this is the same as searching for a live-in life-partner. Bad enough if you *expect* that to happen, but you're walking toward a very rude reality-check if you *assume* that outcome. Just about all the time, you *can* shop for a plaything, but you *cannot* effectively shop for a long-term partner – I guess it all depends on where your personal definition of "lover" would fit between those two extremes.

Troubled waters

Really, there are only two situations in which I wouldn't recommend that a couple go looking for a third member: when things are going very well, and when things aren't going very well. The second route is ill advised for (hopefully) obvious reasons, though it occurs regularly. We'll get to that momentarily.

But I'm not being altogether facetious about that first one. Two people stumble into each other, and manage to survive into courtship. The NRE hits, then, at its peak, they may think it's a good idea to involve another person in their sexual and emotional intimacies. The problem is, at that point they think that giving all their worldly goods to charity and living on the beach in Barbados seems like a really good idea, too.

At this point in the relationship, it'd be a horrible mistake for two to go searching for a mutual lover. Until they are both a bit more comfortable with themselves, their newly expanded relationship, and the level of communication they will *need* to maintain, then there's a high probability that it'll bomb quickly and spectacularly.

Don't let the word "love" blind you into thinking that you must therefore be irrational: you can and must go about planning how you are going to handle this. Look at how much unlikeliness underlies some of the phases if only one of you seeks an additional lover. You have to *find* someone you're attracted to… then arrange a date… then determine that you want to see her again… then determine that there's a mutual attraction… then see if you're compatible talking about books and going on long walks… then find out if you both want to be lovers… and are sexually compatible….

Throw your SO into this at *any* point, and things get really complicated.

Though the energies are diametrically opposite NRE, the struggling relationship makes similar decisions not merely hoping for a positive outcome but expecting (pronounced "demanding from the Universe as a right") one. Oh, "one," hell! – whether you're on top of the world and feeling utterly invincible, or falling into a fatalist's spiral and down to your last few dollars, you're prone to spend it all, bet the house, go for broke. Motivations might be wildly different, but the actions are directly comparable, as are the disastrous consequences of the ill-considered risk.

The diminishing odds

Because this is so important to so many people who "decided to get into polyamory," I'm going to say it again.

In this big blurry world, it's kinda unlikely that one single sole individual person is going to meet one other who is *compatible* enough to even be constitutionally *able* to negotiate the possibility of future possibilities as far as relationship. And that's just monogamy I'm talking about.

Now, extend the case in one specific dimension. Let's say that I am in a bonded couple, and we decide that, at pretty much the same exact time, we are *each* going to find a compatible candidate for Significant Other... that our respective relationships with these two individuals are going to develop at approximately the same rate... and deepen at approximately the same rate... and maintain pretty much the same level of intimacy at all times... and so forth.

We're getting into the realm of "wow, you have some really stratospheric expectations about other human beings, here" area, aren't we?

So, extend the analogy further: those two new OSOs have to be one person.

Improving the odds

Notice:

I am **not** saying it's impossible.

I am **not** saying that people who want this are fudging their desires.

I am **not** saying anything negative, period.

What I **am** saying is: I believe and trust that the vast majority of established couples who are searching the world for a bisexual female have set themselves one hell of a Herculean task. I sincerely believe that just having the "poly gene" makes them exceptional people, and therefore I would like them to be happy and fulfilled. I sincerely worry that they will instead end up feeling bereft and lonely and undesirable because they've chosen such long odds, and they thus run a huge risk of sooner or later choosing someone who is "good enough" and is *nothing* of the sort, an experience that will leave them not only hurt but more cynical when what the world needs is people who can be trusting.

So, to such good-hearted people, a basic first-step suggestion. For all the couples who want a closed or mostly-closed relationship with a biF: state your respective goals up-front, take a few deep breaths, and let the woman of the couple look for her own darn girlfriend. Face up to the fact that there is indeed the possibility that she'll find someone she likes who just doesn't "click" with the male. Both of you trust that you'll each make the right decisions when the time comes.

Locking the search down to the "both or nothing!" paradigm if you can't even get serious interest is *waaay* premature. I lived with my fiancée and her girlfriend for more than a year before it occurred to *any* of us that the latter and I could be lovers, too. I can't say as the "waiting period" hurt us any; in fact, while I'm barely on speaking terms with the (now) ex-wife, our former lover is still a good friend of mine.

Much the same holds true even if it's one of a dyad's partners who is looking for an additional lover, and the other is content with just one. (Let's assume that the monoamorous partner is being entirely honest.) While the *goal* may be to eventually have a third partner in a vee-type relationship as a member of the household – and there really is nothing wrong that I can see with that goal – anyone who expects they can *start* at the goal is, well, stupid. Even given ideal people in an ideal situation, every major change is to some degree traumatic by definition, and will require one or more of those involved to undergo some fundamental changes of habit at least. (The next chapter will cover a bit more on this.) Rare individuals can thrive in situations where everything is just sort of thrown together, the crises are accepted and dealt with efficiently, and the dust settles in a short time. Most people won't even wish to think about such a catastrophic approach, but they go so far in the opposite direction that they avoid recognizing and repairing small problems until the collected grievances overwhelm everyone.

Success is rare

Let me go into a little detail. I have been in exactly one closed triad. Sheer stupid luck. My fiancée met a young woman, they were fascinated with each other, the latter moved in with us when our household included my other lover and another roommate. After more than a year of intense partnership and deep friendship, my fiancée's lover and I became lovers. When the other roomies moved on, the three of us had busy lives and were happy to spend the rest of the times together. After about six months, we opened it up again. At no time did any of us say, "Let's start a triad." To take a solid dyad and try to force it into a triad configuration sounds to me like trying to bend cold glass: it *might* flex, but maybe you'd be happier if you didn't try.

How likely is it that an ideally matched, unshakable couple is going to find the one person who can form a life-long perfect three-way bond? Not very; that is why the long-term successes stand out so clearly. Experience is the only teacher we have, and experience is a field littered with mistakes. Humans are emotionally messy creatures.

Am I the only one who thinks that, in holding out for a fabulously unlikely 10 on a scale of 10, a whole bigger pool of 8s and 9s is going to be overlooked? That sounds a little like the "all-or-nothing" clause in monogamy. If a couple stumbles across a fabulously perfect third partner, but has not yet had the particular experiences that it needs in order that necessary lessons could have been learned, then that opportunity may be lost forever. The same couple, though, can accept the mistakes that will come, enjoy imperfect relationships for what they are (rather than what they *ought* to be), and thus be more ready to recognize and accept the appearance of a truly ideal partner – or they may find that the same effort actually empowers them to perfect a less-than-perfect (at the beginning) relationship.

Many relationships can have fantastic, mind-altering NRE, yet be totally lacking in a basis for long-term *anything*. The reverse is also true: oftentimes, the very best relationships are slow to develop. If you are in too much of a damn hurry to get on out and establish your polyamorous credentials, then I can pretty much guarantee that you are capable of ignoring the best partners that Fate could ever possibly throw at you, in the rush to scope out hot babes and have some fun. Enjoy, but don't be angry if you burn through one "partner" after another, none of whom will return your calls after the initial thrill – if that's what happens, then that's probably what you were asking for.

Planning a triad

The more you plan it, the less likely it's gonna work out. There's nothing wrong with logic, and in fact more ought to be applied in relationships (especially the new ones), but there's such a thing as overthinking what's going to happen. To play out any scenario in your head, you have to guess at a few variables; the more complicated a situation you posit, or the further you spin a story out in time, the more guesswork you have to do, and likelihood that your well-laid plan will shortly have nothing at all to do with reality is quite high. If your logical abilities are restricted to rationalization, then you will tend to explain away rather than analyze, to create excuses instead of avoiding getting into situations where excuses would become necessary. If you're going to plan, then plan for things to work out and don't rely on assumptions, however logic-based they may be.

I have difficulty accepting the claim that a closed triad is polyamorous. Even less can I accept that a tight dyad seeking to form a tight triad is polyamorous. My reasoning (*post hoc*, admittedly) runs something as follows. Let's say that a truly poly couple (by my biased definition) sets out to find a female partner, with the big-picture intent of finding The Right One with whom they can settle down, probably "for life." How would they do that? Unless they're neurotic, or blinded by Society's expectations for a monogamous couple (yes, they're roughly the same thing), I assume that they would develop a pool of pro-poly friends, some of whom they would date, a few they would actively court, a handful they would become sexually involved with, and one or two would share living space. Most of their courtship up to that point would be "failures" – and their ultimate success is built upon the learning they've experienced.

On the other hand, if this couple fit into the aforementioned non-polyamorous "neurotic or blinded" slot, the only model they have is monogamy, so they have given themselves no choice but to figure out some way to cram a third person into a two-passenger vehicle. They are going to make one and only one foray out into the big, scary world, then drag their prize home and bar the door again, forever. As their desires collide again and again with the limits of the paradigm to which they cling, they would thrash wildly about. The situation would look a whole lot like swinging, but without the finesse or the vestiges of community. Every remotely available female they meet will be scoped out for an hour or two at some social event, then she'll get a tag-team crash-course lecture on the wonders of polyamory, delivered with the sort of sweaty nervousness and strained laughter that convinces a typical adult female her blouse has come undone and her nipple is peeking out. The encounter will end with a few requests (more than thirty per hour is slightly gauche, though) for a date.

Nowadays, thanks to the wonders of the Internet, this couple can jog all across the virtual world, joining e-clubs and message sites, haunting a dozen chatrooms simultaneously while they scan online diaries and weblogs for keywords. (This becomes a bonding activity for them.) If such wacky couples actually existed, they would complain (whether angry, hurt, mystified, or accusatory), "We found this site a whole month ago and we don't have a girlfriend yet. What's wrong with people here?" They would attempt to contact every woman on the site, and express frustration at being constantly rebuffed. Finally, though, they'd locate a woman who doesn't fit their expectations (or their hopes, or even the entirety of their minimum vital qualifications) very closely at all, but at least she's willing to trade messages. Then would ensue long nights of electronic communication via voice and the imp Qwerty. After a week, or perhaps even two if they are especially cautious, arrangements will be made to meet, but even before they've set eyes on each other, they're using words like "life partner," "love," "soul mate," "true love," "sweetie," and "sister-wife" to refer to each other.

Somehow, they never stop to ask themselves if the reason for a desirable-seeming woman's "unpartnered" status has a particular cause – divorce, school, job… or psychosis, restraining order, federal warrant. The Internet has already demonstrated a small but growing popularity for gainful employment by scam artists, confidence tricksters, blackmailers, runaway children, and plain-vanilla thieves and thugs, and the impossible couple I'm hypothesizing has seen exactly one grainy photograph of their mail-order babe when they send her plane tickets and keys to the house and the cars – after all, True Love cannot be wrong.

Giving it a proper chance

The best relationships I've had (dyadic or whatever) were entirely accidental at first; the most wonderful threesomes I've had were spontaneous, usually with years-long friends. Logic alone would not have gotten me into those situations, but the new relationships benefited, as did those extant, because we had thought carefully about some general cases.

The less experience that two partners have outside of monogamy (and I consider affairs, adultery, and promiscuity to be offshoots of monogamy), the more vital it is that those two people get some experience before they even start shopping for their HBB.

I don't mean sex: they need to gain experience as individuals and as a couple with things like dating and social outings and deep friendships. Only when they have a fully primed first-hand feel for the complexity and potential of interpersonal interaction will they be in a position to formulate and state their own desires, and from there to define roughly their ideal third partner. At minimum, learning to interact deeply with others will cut down on how much the couple radiates desperation, which tends to frighten away the better candidates and leave those who are either too vapid to notice, or who thrive on the neediness of others – I cannot say as I recommend either of these.

46. Changing gears

You think that, once you've got your ideal triad or quad, everything is peaches and you'll just be able to chug merrily along forever. Think again, because you're likely wrong. You will save yourself a whole passel of headaches and heartbreaks if you give this some serious thought. You may never need it but, if you do, you had better have the plans in place long before it becomes necessary.

Think of it as insurance, and by that I mean the sort of thing where you set aside cash every month. Nobody in their right mind would ever want to actually take advantage of an insurance policy, because to do so means that something has broken, someone has taken ill or, heaven forefend, croaked. In short you pay thousands of dollars for something that a perfect world would promise would be eventually wasted. Yet, we do it, and people around the world and throughout the past couple of centuries have been very thankful for this small but vital buffer against the vicissitudes of Fate.

I've mentioned the post-Jungian therapeutic paradigm of Polly Young-Eisendrath (*You're Not What I Expected*) in Chapter XXX, "Learning to Deal With Change" – you remember, the one that begins, "Skip this section only at your own peril." I don't want you to go away with the idea, once you get up to speed on this whole polyamory thing, and your life is moving along very well with only nominal, expected problems, that the hassles are over.

Being surprised by the foreseeable: pleasant or unpleasant?

You ought to have picked up a little basic ecological thinking by now, so I'm going to flash some truisms past you, all of them immediately relevant to polyamory:

If it's not growing, it's dying. *Change* and *disruption* are largely interchangeable concepts. A large change can sometimes be taken at a single leap by the same people who will be defeated by an endless series of random minuscule hops. A change that is beneath one person's notice will traumatize their twin. You can change without growing, but you can't grow without changing.

> Gina has been living with her boyfriend of ten years for almost half that time. Julian is a very fun, bright individual, but also a little reclusive, and enjoys having many of his evenings to work on serious Java programming for his friends' websites. Though they'd both been polyamorous since before they met, Julian hadn't had another steady lover in two years. About that time, Gina began filling a few of her own evenings with Andy, an old friend she'd gotten closer to, and had a couple of more sporadic relationships besides.
>
> Now, enter Leann. She and Andy met through a mutual friend at a software convention, and quickly became romantically involved. When Leann came to the city for an extended visit, both Julian and Gina found her utterly charming. Soon, Julian and Leann were steady lovers, and then Gina and Leann.
>
> On one visit, Leann said that her company was going through layoffs, and she was considering the option of relocating to follow a slight change of careers. As Julian and Gina had an unused bedroom, Leann put forward the idea that she could move in with them for a few months, perhaps longer.
>
> I suggested that this had vast potential for problems, because of all the "gear changing" that had occurred, and wasn't being discussed enough.
>
> First of all, Gina, though not in the least possessive, had been "the girlfriend" for both men for two years. She had been able to largely arrange the social schedules for all three of them, choosing pretty much at whim which evenings and weekends she wanted to spend with Andy or Julian, what social events would be attended (possibly with both men), and allotment of public and private times. When Leann joined the circle, Gina accepted as reasonable that Andy was spending about half of his weekends pursuing the new relationship – on a conscious, rational level, that is. On a more emotional level, Gina found that this unsettled her a little, not from any desire to control Andy, but (somewhat to her chagrin) she found she'd been enjoying the assumption that Andy was almost always available.
>
> As Julian became involved with Leann, Gina found that scheduling increased markedly in complexity. In fact, Gina felt that, when Julian left the city for a weekend with Leann, or Leann drove in to be with Julian, she was obligated to spend that time with Andy, even if she wanted to concentrate on her own projects, hang out with friends, or just curl up with a book, so that he didn't feel neglected. When Andy had time with Leann, Gina felt that she ought to be with Julian.
>
> This began to reach a crisis when Gina and Leann became lovers. On those otherwise lovely occasions, Gina felt that she was neglecting both men.
>
> To say the least, multiple changes of pace had occurred by that point. As all four were in varying stages of NRE, the upsets were minimal, but cracks were certainly appearing.
>
> Let's not overlook the fourth party either. Though Leann (new to the concept of polyamory) was greatly enjoying the attention, it was a drastic reversal from a life that had alternated monogamy with virtual celibacy. When all four of them went to a party, Leann found a quiet room and fell into a sobbing fit. Her experience to that point with more than one lover was nonexistent, and finding herself with three very

attentive and caring intimate relationships, all of whom were established in their interactions, had finally overwhelmed her. Leann felt like an outsider, and also that there was no way for her to live up to the sort of casual closeness the other three had established.

I encouraged them to talk, in twos and threes and as a group. I warned that it's not unusual for someone to experience the definitely heady rush of polyamory, then to dive back into monogamy with all of its flaws because the simplicity appeared so much easier, so this had to be made an explicit topic for discussion. Though polyamory was far more complex than Leann's experience, this does not make it worse than monogamy. She needed to ensure that she had time for her own pursuits, and to not fall into the trap of feeling that she somehow owed the others a debt for their "kindness" – it's not as though they were going out of their way from pity: they were each spending time with Leann because they enjoyed spending time with Leann, finding it rewarding.

Similarly, Gina needed to have time for herself, too. It was in no way her job to provide some sort of balance for the occasional evenings that Julian or Andy would spend alone, a responsibility she hadn't felt before Leann.

Details you shoulda noticed

For illustration, let me list a few of the "gear changes" through which Leann alone was going.

- new intimacy after a long "dry spell"
- more than one intimate relationship
- losing her job
- giving up her apartment
- leaving her social circle behind
- leaving familiar surroundings
- moving to another state
- finding a new apartment
- getting another job
- fitting into an established intimate network
- facing the new possibility that she could add relationships without losing those that already existed

Some good, some frightening; some a threat to self-image, others to sense of stability. However, the quotient of "good" or "bad," of "positive" or "negative" has absolutely no bearing on how scary each could turn out to be. They each also impose some degree of stress, whether short- or long-term. Though "positive stress" is no oxymoron, stress is stress, and depletes an individual's reserves. In much the same way, *enervation* covers both excitement and excitation and the huge gray areas between.

Growth and new experience are worth the effort, but they drain energy and cause distraction. One depleted individual drags down the available time and energy of those around them. In the previous example, Gina and Andy and Julian could (and perhaps should) support Leann in the changes she was experiencing. At the same time, they need to protect their own reserves, in case of a serious crisis. Furthermore, Leann needs to learn new skills, and too much support prevents her from recognizing and internalizing these. There is a vast difference between giving someone a shoulder to lean on and becoming their crutch, possibly permanently.

47. Jealousy sucks, get used to it

Jealousy happens, even to those of us who have extensive experience in nonmonogamy.

Jealousy... or envy?

Let's differentiate between two commonly confused terms. *Envy* is the desire for something that someone else has. *Jealousy* springs from the fear that something you have will be taken away.

For the most part, I have little problem with jealous experiences. However, as I told one partner, "I am horribly envious. When you're off with someone else, I am completely aware of what they have. You are beautiful, fascinating, bright, funny, and an incredible lover. I wish that I had the time and energy to take up your every waking moment. But I don't. There aren't enough hours in the day, or minutes in a lifetime, to experience you as fully and completely as I have wanted to from the first moment our eyes met. But jealous? No. I trust implicitly that you will love me, and you won't desire me any less just because someone else is in your life, however wonderful. Take sex. If he's not as good a lover as me, you'll be all the more glad when we are together again. And if he's very good, there is no way that we can be identical, so you'll be refreshed and energized, and better able to appreciate the things that make me unique."

And jealousy sometimes happens anyway, even though I have spent most of my life working at being both mercilessly self-aware and understanding of other human beings.

Have you ever developed a vicious cramp (thigh, foot, ankle, buttock) while making love? Do you believe that this is a negative reflection on your sexual partner of the moment, or on yourself or your relationship? Really, that's about how significant (for a relatively sane person) a jealous attack is.

When jealousy rears up, it indicates that something inside of you is afraid. It's an alarm, nothing less and nothing more. Treat it as such. Maybe it's a false alarm, something said or done resembling a past situation that hurt you.

First-hand insecurity

Presently, my two major relationships are a thousand miles apart. In order to chase employment opportunities, I relocated from one household to the other.

Distance introduces doubts, and magnifies those that were quelled by regularity of interaction. Over the holidays, I was back with Suzy. Since the last time we were together, she'd found a new lover, and made some very strong positive changes in her life. I felt as if I'd stood beside her through some incredibly difficult times, and now here was this "freshman" getting all the good times.

She had a date with the new lover, and was bouncing around, primping and fussing. It had taken me days to figure out I was bothered that it felt like it had been a couple of lifetimes since I had that effect on her.

I'm no tin saint. I tried to ignore these feelings as entirely unworthy of her, me, and our relationship. Finally, hard though it was, I owned up to my insecurities, and Suzy and I unpacked them together: I didn't feel appreciated for my loyalty... I was going to lose out to someone who's not as much a "lone wolf" as me (being a writer and musician can kinda limit my attention span)... I want our relationship to continue growing beyond the otherwise comfortable plateau we've reached....

I was feeling replaced in her heart, and told her how I'd seen her acting and talking, and how much I missed that. Once she realized that I wasn't *attacking* this behavior, she agreed with my observations, and we decided that nothing was stopping *us* from being a little more romantic. So, we did. We worked out a lot of miscommunications, and I felt much better.

And the next time she had a date with "the new guy," I made sure I had a date with an ex-partner with whom I chatted happily until late into the night.

It's never easy. I'm not holding a contract on anyone, and I don't think I'd want to, so I guess that means I *can* be replaced in a moment. That's where the trust and the faith and the love is supposed to come in.

Recognize the fear of loss. Own the fear. Then put it on the shelf and do something nice for yourself. Massage sounds like a wonderful idea. There's a coffee shop with some wonderful ice cream that I sometimes treat myself to.

If someone's heart can easily stray, then they're already lost to you, even before an opportunity exists. If the feelings are true, and you will always be friends, and you can always talk and be heard, then their (or your!) wildest adventures will never change it.

Be sure to talk out these feelings with your lover afterwards! Neither of you should squeam away from it. After all, the thing about polyamory is, the shoe eventually ends up on the other foot.

48. Surviving the radical reversal

Humans are insane. They are so amazingly screwed up that many times they cannot remember what they said moments before, yet at the same time they will be able to quote you extensively, perhaps going back years. They will pillory you if shifting situations force you to change your mind, yet heatedly demand their right to change complex long-term plans and promises to suit the whim of the moment. Worse, they will not see where this presents any lack of fairness (or logic).

Another way you (I'm assuming that, once warned, you won't exhibit the behavior yourself)might run into this is when you are presented with absolute, unbending rules, then ignore them entirely for someone else. I was at a music party at a friend's house, and eventually found myself chatting animatedly with an attractive woman I'd just met. After about twenty minutes, I realized that we were surrounded by many dozens of our friends and were entirely ignoring them, so I called her attention to this. "I'm enjoying this conversation," I said, "but we really should join the party. Maybe we could get together sometime and pick this up again over coffee." Her smile rapidly faded to an introspective frown. She replied, "No, I don't think I could get involved with someone who smokes." At the time, I did indeed smoke – less than a pack of cigarettes a month – but that wasn't the point. I was taken aback, so I said, "You seem very nice, but I was only talking about continuing the topic." "Yeah, I know," she told me, "but I don't think it would be a good idea for me to get involved with a smoker."

With that, many of my self-protection alarms were whooping away. Clearly, she did not hear me at all, and the connection I thought we had vanished like smoke in a gale. Things could clearly get much, much worse, and I knew I didn't want to be there when they did. We never spoke again. A few months later, she moved in with her new boyfriend, who smokes two packs a day. This is one manifestation of the *radical reversal*, the sudden turning away from an absolute and inviolable rule.

That example is a bit of a caricature, but you will probably have a few of your own that are just as silly on the surface. I still count myself as lucky that my reflexes kept me from getting more deeply involved with that woman, and that I had enough objective distance to be able to easily turn away. Chances are that you can't match me in experience, training, or skill.

The radical reversal can pop up at literally any point in a relationship. There is really no way to argue it out in a constructive fashion. Whatever your feelings for such a person, however much you want to care, all you can realistically do is step back, withdraw your support, not be quite so thick a cushion, and let them take on all or most of the responsibility for their actions. Neurosis is contagious, in a rather literal sense – if a centered person remains enmeshed with a neurotic person, then almost invariably the result will be two neurotic people.

Consequences as a learning tool

The term that some of us use for warning someone thoroughly (and lovingly) enough that they can make as informed a stupid decision as possible is to thereby empower them to accept *logical consequences*. I don't have space to go properly into depth on this, and instead refer you to a fine little book on the subject, which you can find in the bibliography as *The New Approach to Discipline*.

There's another one of those handy words, *discipline*, that has been mangled by misuse. Hopefully, you or one of your partners has been formally trained in some martial art, so you will have access to the beginnings of a proper understanding of the concept.

You likely will have to retrain yourself to think about discipline in a non-destructive manner. Most importantly, discipline comes from within. It can be *taught*, but it cannot be *imposed* from the outside. Don't confuse discipline with punishment. As one of my teachers said, you can show someone how to break a board with his hand, and you can motivate him to do it, but to break a board with someone's hand only means that you're a bully.

Logical consequences is a way of teaching discipline. You let your "student" know that, if they take a certain action, there are likely outcomes, for which they will be responsible. Then, if they choose to ignore you, you allow them to be responsible for the outcome. There are limits, of course, and you ought to continue to keep others from serious injury. But, in the long run, the best way to do this is to teach them how to avoid harm themselves.

When my daughter was a toddler, she soon discovered that she could climb up onto furniture, which empowered her. In fact, she could then stand up on the cushions, and even jump around, both of which empowered her even further. And when she learned that straight-backed chairs gave her a secure handhold, she was beside herself. The problem with this is that, when these chairs sit on padded carpeting, they rock, and can fall over quite easily. Showing off her new skill to me, I was of course as horrified about the possible outcomes as any other new parent would be. Taking her off the chair, I told her that it wasn't a good thing to do, as she could get hurt, and I didn't want that to happen. Of course, as soon as my attention was elsewhere, she was doing it again, grinning broadly at me as I walked back into the room.

That set me to thinking. There was no human way that I could prevent her from doing this, short of removing all that sort of furniture from the house until such time as she would no longer perform in such a manner – her teen years, say. But how could I help to steer her away from such cavalier risk-taking behaviors? After all, kids are ingenious, and will find some way to get around any simple rules. If the chairs were gone, she'd likely find some similar activity. Call me lazy, but I couldn't look forward to an inevitable afternoon of searching for stray teeth while we waited for the ambulance.

We want to protect our children. In that moment, I had to face up to the fact that I couldn't possibly be there to keep her from all possible harm. I needed to begin showing my daughter how to make intelligent decisions on her own, and how to be responsible for the risks she decided to take.

I took her down from the chair, knelt, looked her in the eye, and said, "Honey, if you do that, the chair will fall over, and you will get hurt. If you do, it will be what you wanted to do, and I can't make you feel better. Okay?" She grinned at me, nodding.

Under the guise of straightening up the room, I made sure that the only available chair was set far away from any other objects or hard corners, safely in the middle of the padded carpet. She wandered around the room, playing busily as normal, but not going near the chair. The next time I went to the kitchen, though, within moments I heard her bouncing on the chair.

After only a few seconds, there was a brief pause, then a muffled thud. Silence. A short whimper. I restrained myself, reasoning that the difference between running in panicked and strolling casually into the room was inconsequential.

When I rounded the corner, she was sitting quietly by her toys. The chair lay on its back a few yards away. "The chair fell over," I said, matter-of-factly. She didn't look at me. I asked, "Are you okay?" She met my eyes briefly, then looked sheepishly away and nodded.

Then I said, "So, how about something to eat before nap-time?" which brightened her up. I picked her up for the trip to her highchair, which gave me a moment to perform a cursory inspection for any obvious damage, and we chattered happily over carrot sticks in the kitchen.

She never did try bouncing on the furniture again, but not out of fear. My daughter learned two important lessons. She has significant control over her destiny, for good or bad. And, sometimes, Dad knows what he's talking about.

The hardest part you'll likely have with instilling the logical-consequences method of teaching discipline is to control your own emotions. Most parents shout, yell, shriek, threaten, and can hardly make a statement of simple fact to a child without a "stern" edge coming into their voice. All of these things are counterproductive. Worse, we not only tend to absorb these failed tactics from our parents, but we then try to apply them to other adults. This stuff works pretty well in extremely limited circumstances, such as warning my cat away from the smoked salmon, but creatures with a better understanding of English consider it patronizing. When you raise your voice or speak through clenched teeth, you are signaling your listeners to step back emotionally and to apply heavier filtering to the content.

In applying logical consequences to rational adults, there is a further step that isn't taken with small children. You need to ask the other person for their side of it, phrased on the order of, "What is *your* understanding of what happened?"

Backing out of the relationship

There's no good way to head it off: It's sooo easy to think that "new and exciting" is the same thing as "good long-term investment." That's why NRE can be such a problem, blinding you to the negatives of a new target of infatuation or lust even as it clouds your memory of the wonderful side of your existing relationship.

I've had a few experiences where a lover said, "I've found my One True Love, and though I care very much about you, I know that this is the person I am destined to spend the rest of my life with." I smile, and nod, until they run down. Then I say, "I love you, and I will likely always love you. I'm not so sure that this person is a good idea; I could be wrong. You will always have a large place in my life, though, so if you should change your mind, I will gladly start again, so don't forget about me."

As often as not, the "honeymoon period" runs out, the NRE wears off, and we get back in touch.

Just as I'm not the type to go chasing after every "new best thing," I also have largely avoided saying anything to anyone that sounds like a spiteful "Hah! Told you so!! Shoulda listened to me!!"

That does *not* mean that I chronically clean up the messes for someone who goes chasing off after one True Love after another. But the fact that we can give it another try far outweighs any glee from being proven correct.

When my closed triad opened up some years ago, I told my partners, "Have fun, and maybe find someone to add to your life. But if you have any doubts whatsoever, remember that I'm at home, and then decide whether you want to put up with their baggage." Many times, they'd drop a relationship, or even cut a date short, because they already had a better offer – me.

The rude awakening

The radical reversal lurks inside of us all, at least as a potential strategy for survival or preservation. This also applies to your partner(s), your network of friends and intimates, and the other people around you.

There are times when extreme changes in life suddenly sneak up on you, and your first reflex will be a tendency to fall into abject panic. You then run for shelter, for safety, for calm and quiet. Humans are not at their best when they're panicked, and their judgment is normally foggy in the *best* moments. When we're in full flight, we grab for what is *supposed to be* stable, for what is *supposed to be* safe and nurturing. Advertising and propaganda work very well when the audience is hurt or frightened because we then accept slogans as enforceable promises – we need the soothing words even more than we need the proffered reward.

Things will be going along rather well, about as well as any average human being hopes for. One of your partners (or, for that matter, you) appears to be getting a little edgy. Everyone may notice, but it doesn't seem to be a major crisis brewing. Then the agitated person suddenly seems to blow up at every least little nuisance; in extreme cases, they've already started packing their bags.

Actually, I've noticed that this sort of panic is *more* likely to set in when thing are going exceptionally well. Perhaps it's another variation of "this is too good to be real," or possibly "I don't deserve this," or a variation like "I don't want to enjoy this, because I'd feel terrible if it stopped." I call it the "too good to be true" syndrome. This is usually the point where someone who's been burned too many times, and has retreated into blessed solitude, simply disappears. Hope is too painful, faith only opens doors to attack. Without dreams, there can be no disappointment.

I get the feeling that the world is full of people like that, who want so much to believe in the possibilities, yet have been told all their lives that it's impossible, and have been so thoroughly hurt by their own forays into creative living that even thinking about it is too painful.

You need to start setting boundaries long before you need them. If the horses have spent much of their lives running freely across the plains, you are going to spend a lot of time extricating them from fences that you decide to put up. Someone may decide that you're letting yourself be spooked by shadows, fears of things that will likely never have even the possibility of occurring. However, feelings are always valid, even if baseless. Therefore, they deserve to be addressed reasonably, and whatever guarantees you need should be put into place. In the future, you may discover that those doubts no longer haunt you, in which case maybe you have something to celebrate.

In this sense, "communication" and "boundaries" overlap heavily. Communication has to flow in all possible directions, as close to constantly as you can manage. Communication is much more than words: it means noticing body language, tone of voice, speaking style, and changes in behavior.

When momentum is building toward a radical reversal, the primary victim may be totally unaware of the symptoms and warning signs they are throwing off. This could be because their feelings are so foreign that they don't have enough experience to recognize them, or because they're in deep denial of their "negative" feelings. If you truly have built good intrarelational tactics for communication, then the others near this person will have to risk being at the epicenter of an explosion by addressing these apparent anomalies; sometimes, pointing them out will be used as an excuse to accelerate the degradation. More often than not, though, a premature explosion releases dangerous pressures. After the initial blowup, creative work can begin. Ignoring the symptoms does nothing more than guarantee a much more final explosion a little further down the pike.

Hearts do change, & change again

We'll examine this in Chapter 54, "Falling In & Out of Poly," but I want to touch on it a bit in this context.

Polyamory might be a good – and possibly temporary – way of exploring beyond monogamy. Couples come and go all the time, casting around for their personal hot bi babe until they've scared away all the likely possibilities and, having explored the remainder, return to monogamy. For people like this, a triad is an attempt to balance the romance of a "perfect" relationship with someone new against the reality that they have together.

There is nothing inherently *wrong* with this impulse, but it's best to begin by looking at it realistically. Getting involved with someone else is like buying a different car: all you can think about is the problems you've had with the old one and how nice and shiny the new one is. Then the muffler falls off.

Sometimes, the first foray into a complicated way of life such as polyamory is not destined to be a final change. An individual or couple might venture into polyamory, then suddenly flee the scene. This does not mean that they are gone for good, or that they made a mistake, or that they were dabbling in a bit of extracurricular naughtiness. Though I'm not enough of an optimist to give so much credit to all (or even most) such instances, I do know of people who were sincerely drawn to responsible nonmonogamy, but were not quite fully ready to commit to it. Face it: we can't truly know that something is workable until we actually attempt it. They scared themselves a little, and found the paradigm shift overwhelming… but they didn't go back empty-handed. The overall experience left them better-skilled at self-exploration, their communication skills were markedly improved, and they had a previously unsuspected set of resources they could draw upon. The ones who come back do so in a much more grounded state.

The lesson, I suppose, is that the radical reversal might be, considering human frailty, the best thing that could happen in a given situation.

49. NRE: when "common sense" is an oxymoron

I remembered a study I'd heard mentioned in the early 1980s. The researchers had located a few people whose intimate lives strongly resembled the behavior of addicts who go on periodic benders – you might not find "bender" in your dictionary, by the way, so I illustrate briefly by referring to author Raymond Chandler, legendary for occasionally disappearing for a couple of weeks of drinking that would've been literally nonstop except for his need for sleep.

The subjects of this study would meet up with a new and interesting stranger, and devote so much time to them that all other phases of their lives were neglected. In one case, a woman abandoned her executive-level job for up to two months at a time, draining her bank account while living at a resort in the Bahamas with her new flame, then return and be quite surprised that her position had been filled, her apartment padlocked, and the police combing the city for her body (though they were probably not so concerned after the first three times). Though this was more extreme than most of the subjects, she exhibited typical behavior by returning as soon as the fascination began to wane, whereupon she lost all interest in a very short period. The researchers found that the initial fascination produced effects that were directly comparable to those reported by some cocaine users: high energy, lack of need for sleep, imperviousness to pain, little need for food, and so on. There was some preliminary support for the hypothesis that forming a new attraction released such a flood of endorphins that the subjects would, in fact, functionally be coked to the eyeballs on their own body chemistry. When their reserves of these endorphins were depleted, they would suddenly "fall out of love" and attempt to drop back into their daily lives, as if waking up from a dream-state.

Nowadays, us polyfolk would readily recognize an extreme case of NRE, or new relationship energy. Most of us will never get anywhere near that sort of insanity even once, and we likely ought to offer up prayers and incense for that. Nevertheless, you should always keep an eye on the effects of NRE upon yourself and the people in your life – NRE can be continued to obsession.

The six-month lobotomy

For the most part, NRE is thrilling and amusing and utterly harmless. About 1986, writing an article for *Loving More* (back when it was a newsletter), I complained about NRE, likening it to a recent experience of drinking two pots of very good dark-roast coffee while working on a story: it's really nice to get there, and I cannot wait for it to pass. Someone asked me what to do if their feelings for a new lover should suddenly turn into full-blown NRE. I recommended not doing anything that involved suitcases, binding legal contracts, entertainments containing the word "extreme," or firearms, but otherwise to relax and enjoy. Notice that these are all things kept away from children and the chemically impaired – that's NRE.

Sooner or later, even if you think that your little closed triad is going to lock the world out, NRE is going to blindside you and cause you to consider Tibetan retreats and vows of celibacy. There are three basic ways that NRE can affect you: it takes over your brain, or that of an established partner, or that of some new intimate in your life. By definition, it's going to be very hard for you to take a step back toward objectivity if it's your own madness, but unless you are one of those people planning to drastically restrict the intimate possibilities of your life, you can definitely learn a touch more objectivity, if only to avoid looking like an utter (and predictable) gullible moron.

Getting swept up in NRE can be a bit rocky. I've seen people, eyes-open and polyamorously experienced, still throw over an extant relationship for an NRE experience. Dumb. To treat NRE as if it's an immediate (or even unique) potential experience that you've got to jump on *now* before it's gone for good is just silly. You need to let at least half a year pass (and possibly two or three) before you can be relatively sure of enough objectivity to examine your own motivations and actions.

My happiest, longest-lasting relationships took months or years of regular interaction to go beyond friendship. With very rare exception, I am only interested in people who I've known for a while. If they haven't seen me with a few of my intimates (past, present, future), or are close friends with one or more of same, or have heard me tell stories where the cast of characters includes such, then they're strangers – barely friends, arguably lovers, and certainly not yet partners.

Not the "L" word

You *do not* "fall in love right away." NRE has no relation to love – it can fuel it, assist it, hinder it, or prevent it. And NRE is at best a poor indicator of relational success. None of us is being flippant when we say that NRE is capable of overriding every grain of common sense. NRE is that wonderful and dangerous combination of lust and fascination that turns off major portions of the brain and makes us do stuff that's occasionally really stupid. And it wears off, commonly leaving something like the classic "cheap red wine" hangover, but more expensive. The only way to "slow down" NRE is like a lycanthrope who chains himself to the cellar floor every full moon. You risk being swept away, or you back off warily.

It's partially chemical, partially cultural. The endorphins released have been compared by researchers to an I.V. drip of cocaine – you feel physically strong, hyper-aware, and impervious to pain. As for the culture, we're taught that "true love" will appear to us, and will make everything good, and no harm can come from expressing it. Combine the biochemistry and the ensocialization and you've got the emotional equivalent of nitroglycerine.

A real relationship doesn't properly *begin* until the NRE burns away. That's when you have to start dealing with this person as an all-around human being, replete with irritating little habits. When disillusion sets in, love can begin.

To plunge, or not to plunge

That's not to say that the initial reaction *won't* turn out to be absolutely correct. My own experience, though, is that the best relationships I've had generally began from initial enmity that any Klingon would recognize immediately; we approached slowly, cautiously, step-by-step, then did an emotional "I will if you will" and dove in.

Conversely, I've had a few hard-hitting beginnings (once dubbed the "Simple Zap" by PEP), and they've led to exciting but short relationships, though usually good close friendships. I wouldn't recommend signing a marriage license *just* because of the "click"… but sometimes the radar actually indicates something very important.

There is no "solution to NRE," per se. Of itself, there's nothing to be fixed. As for the potential fallout, though, no checklist or guidebook will ever replace wide experience. Train yourself, create good instincts based upon experience and observation, then learn to trust your intuitions about possible effects upon yourself and the people in your life. If you're still somewhat new to this whole polyamory thing, then rely on people with wider experience; don't hesitate to put things on hold for a day or a week with your new flame until you gather some input from those who've both been burned and have had some successes in poly relating. Remember that you're not entirely sane, and listen to that input, weighing it carefully. If you're certain that you are emotionally (and economically, and perhaps even physically) prepared to deal with what could happen should the honeymoon go terribly wrong, then do as you see fit and be prepared to accept the responsibilities and the joys alike.

50. Finding poly friends

I've never had much of a problem finding polyamorous people. (Yes, I *am* exceedingly thankful for this fact.)

First, don't set up poly as a "dark secret" you have to hide, but don't go out of your way to "out" yourself either. I've been lucky in that most of my jobs of the past 15 years have had a large gay/lesbian percentage, which my experience says is somewhat more willing to accept a person at face value. My queer friends set me an amazing example of how to live my life, and trust that others would recognize me for what I am.

Second, some of the people you associate with may drop out of your life when they find out. Funny thing is, most of them will be the ones affected by secret affairs. That's just the way it is.

Third (and this seems to be slightly worse with males), if you make clear that you're a semi-autonomous individual, some people will decide you're cruising for your Next True Love, and actively try to interfere with your primary relationship. Drop them like a hot rock – they'll never learn. I've had at least one almost-relationship who accused me of "betraying" her because I had no intention of "forsaking all others" to be with her. The advantage of being completely up-front as poly is that it minimizes these confrontations.

Finally, enjoy the thrill of any new relationships… but don't confuse that thrill with a deep, abiding, on-going, warts-and-all love.

We had an incredible little poly household, long about 1984. People'd show up for a party, and want to join us. So, we decided on a simple procedure. First, they'd pack a few things and spend the weekend on our couch–no sex, just getting to know us on a new level. Cooking meals, cleaning the bathroom, doing yardwork, or maybe sitting around reading… in other words, our usual household dynamic. If they passed a couple of weekends, we reasoned, we'd invite them to spend a full week, then two.

Oddly enough, only three or four ever made it past one weekend. Mainly, it kinda sucks all the superficial "romance" out when you have to look at each other first thing in the morning as you're queuing at the bathroom. No matter how many parties you've seen a person at, nothing is more *real* than trying to harmonize sloppiness levels, sleep cycles, noise tolerance, and so forth.

In much the same way, you need to be pretty much freed up from any overly romantic notions about polyamory – save the romance for expressions of affection with those few people who deserve it. Those who get all misty-eyed about poly are not in a proper place to actually experience it (per the previous chapter), and you might want to think twice about confusing this happy philosophy with daily life, or getting involved with someone who is holding such exceedingly high expectations. There are many good reasons to learn how to make "friends first."

Playing the Personals

The denser the population you live in, the more likely it is that you can find like-minded individuals who will at least accept your polyamorous interest as a facet of a person they like.

Many cities now have at least one polyamorous social group, who get together at restaurants. This allows a degree of anonymity for those who remain fearful, whether of losing their jobs or children, or being stalked by weirdoes.

Another option is to ask of the nearest Unitarian-Universalist congregation whether they have social groups for polyamorous, bisexual, or Wiccan people. Don't fear rejection; they're very nice people. At worst, you'll probably get an apology and some suggestions for similar groups in your area.

Then there's the computer revolution. Most options here offer a resource much more powerful (if not larger) than the newspaper, even if you're fortunate enough to have a daily paper with a "personals" section. There is a particular website on which I spend a disproportionate amount of my Internet ration. Part of the reason I have (apparently) had much more fun than most members is that… well, I'm having fun. I'm not particularly looking for a lover, relationship, sexual partner, etc. – I'm really just leaving myself open to chatting up people with similar interests. So, if I get bored and comb through the bios at random, I look for:

- people who live in parts of the country (or Canada, or Australia) that I have visited and enjoyed, or would like to visit, or have thought about moving to. I started one correspondence by saying something like, "Hi!! You know that little coffee shop down by the college? Is that still open?" Bread on the waters: maybe all I'll find out is if an interesting joint still exists, but maybe she scans my bio, likes my note, and throws in a bunch of related comments, so we've at least got a basis to continue. As I'm helping some people with small-business plans, I could ask relevant questions about their area.

- people who mention similar interests in their bios. If I stumble across, say, a science fiction reader, I can ask if they're familiar with an author who lives in their region. The reply might be a terse, "Oh, yes," but that's a hint that it probably wouldn't be much of a conversation anyway. Another good one for me is music, as I am heavily influenced by ethnic/worldbeat musical forms, so I can ask bellydance students about schools in their area.

- people who look familiar. This might sound silly at first, but I've been all over the country, and I'm great at remembering faces, but truly terrible at names. I dropped a note to a young woman in Australia who I would've sworn was one of my best friends (if not for the fact I know she's still on this continent), and told her I enjoyed the bio picture very much.

When sending notes, brevity is important, at least at first. Being an editor, I can say that a rule of thumb is that you've got a hundred words to hook a reader – if they are bored (or confused) by the time they reach that point, they won't stick around until it gets better. For "personals" it's probably more like 20.

Also, don't drop a note (even a short one) that looks to a stranger as if it's the same note you've sent to hundreds of others. Ever placed an ad in the personals and received a photocopied letter? (Yep – been there.) It's hard to get interested in someone who appears as if he's taking a shotgun approach, i.e., spamming. Even if it's not spam, and a careful reading reveals this… well, the reader has already been prejudiced.

And, for heaven's sake – and this is specifically addressed to non-gay males – don't assume a woman will change her mind about her preferences if she'd only meet you! An amazing number of bi and gay women looking specifically for a girlfriend get baldly propositioned by clueless men. Same goes for couples looking for a couple or a female (or, for that matter, for a bi male). If you ain't, then don't wheedle; it's repulsive.

On the other hand, if you can honestly say that the person sounds interesting, though you're completely incompatible for sex/love/living together, and you can present yourself in an open, friendly manner to an utter stranger (who may well remain that way), then by all means: say hello, already.

Risk rejection, maybe make a friend. Lightning won't strike unless you make yourself a prominent target.

I think of finding serious partners as akin to flycasting. You stand there in the water. You cast; you reel. You cast; you reel. You cast; you reel. Every once in a while, you might feel a tiny tug… then nothing. You cast; you reel. Maybe after hours, you finally land yourself a beautiful trout. Then you carefully unhook it and toss it back into the water.

The point of trout-fishing isn't to get dinner. It's to achieve a Zen-like moment of being part of the rhythms of Nature, of being a perfectly meshed component in an ongoing process.

I guess what I'm saying is, don't sound desperate. Nothing makes a man or woman more unattractive than the smell of fear. If it doesn't bias your writing, it'll be in your voice on the phone; if you make it past that, it'll be obvious in your body language when you're face-to-face.

Play the long odds, sure… but don't bet the farm (emotionally or otherwise) on "success." Explore your options.

Soulmates are made, not born.

Step back for the view

Desperation is a bigger turn-off than any physical deformity. Giving up is sometimes the best way to handle it.

Maybe six or seven years ago, I was having communication problems with the two most important people in my life with a partial cause/effect of I rarely saw either of them more than one evening every week or two. I was reaching for the phone, yet again, when I said "Oh, to hell with it – I need a little time for me." So, I packed up a small stack of books and notebooks, and went down to listen to music at my favorite coffee shop. Within three hours, I was joined by a lovely 19-year-old, who proceeded to chat me up for a couple hours until I figured out that she wanted to go home with me. She moved in with me the next week, and remained a recurring relationship for five years. Before she left town the most recent time, she introduced me to her friend, who is both gorgeous and highly intelligent, which became a year-long relationship I'll never forget.

A few years before that, I was at a convention, about to leave my spouse for perpetual emotional abuse, and in the middle of a lovely case of walking pneumonia. I figured, life couldn't get much worse… and it suddenly just seemed absurd, and funny. I lightened up, a gorgeous redhead met me in this devil-may-care mood, and we ended up being lovers for three years, which really helped get me through the divorce.

How do I do this? It still beats the heck out of me… except that I manage to be serious and emotionally open, without acting as if I'm scoping out a wife-candidate.

When loneliness or self-doubt get us down, we become unattractive. It's real, but it's not pretty. You can't consciously give-up-to-get (not without lots of practice, anyway), but maybe it's easier to say, "Oh, to hell with it – it'll happen if and when it's gonna happen." Then go do something fun, just for yourself. You might be surprised at how attractive you become in this sort of mood, with a spring in your step and a devil-may-care smile.

In short: give it up, or you might as well give it up. Things happen as they happen. If you relax, be yourself, make friends, it's amazing how often they can turn into something more serious. Take a class, join social clubs, pick up a new hobby – be interesting by being yourself.

51. Searching for your true new love

If you're playing along at home, and taking these chapters in order, and only reading them as you actually accomplish goals based upon my glowing wisdom, then by this point you're comfortable about being polyamorous, but aren't sure whether you're going to ever meet someone else who's serious about finding a long-term relationship with some significant depth.

No quick fixes

There's a huge difference between looking for intimacy and leaving yourself open to it. This dichotomy has been noted by everyone from the Constantines to the editor of *Loving More*. Still, it gets overlooked all the time.

You cannot shop for a partner. You *can* shop for a sexual partner, and you might even be able to find a lover that way, but partnership is much more complex than that. It's possible to have partnership without love, or even without friendship, but the glue that makes a partnership is either a higher goal or a deeper interpersonal connection.

Chances are that you won't dabble in polyamory and come up lucky. Oh, it happens, but it's highly unlikely. You ought to work on developing your ideals in great detail, of course, and have regular long, hard looks at what it is that you want from life, otherwise you won't know a good opportunity when it's sitting right in front of you. But when you first venture forth into polyamory, you're being blinded by your fantasies and your projections.

To get around this, you need to be able to explore a scattered sample of the vast variety that the human race contains. It's not going to happen from dreaming, and neither is it going to happen from watching television. You have to go out into the world in some way or other, and meet up with bunches of other like-minded folks, ideally those who are polyamorous, or at least wouldn't call the police over someone else's budding polyamory.

Join the virtual community

The Internet has its drawbacks – primarily that people think on-line discussions and chatrooms will reflect an individual in a manner that is complete, deep, and accurate – but it's a darned good place to start from, and has the advantage of putting you in touch with thousands of more-or-less-real people across the continent and around the world. From virtual interaction with a subset of those many thousands, you will gain a better idea of what works and what doesn't, which of your expectations are far too high and which far too low, which of your concerns you obsess over are trivial and easily solved while others you've overlooked entirely are vital to happiness. This range of thought and experience, while flawed, is invaluable.

Then comes the hard part: patience. If at this point you still believe that you're going to dive in just long enough to find a life-partner for your closed triad, or that you can sort of graze around sexually and soon lightning will strike limning your new long-term lover, then you ought to stick with swinger-oriented sites. You won't be any more disappointed than you would by the poly sites. And, who knows, lightning *might* strike.

The majority of poly sites, though, house a core of people who regularly trade messages, post their thoughts and comments for everyone else to see and respond to, they form cliques, they have messy arguments, and all in all behave much like a family or a community.

You're trying to be part of that. If you're not, and you don't see any reason to expend the effort, then give up right this second on having any claim to polyamory: you've just said that it's too much like work. You can still go ahead and be nonmonogamous, but avoiding community sucks just about all the "poly" out of your amory.

Impatience is common among the polyamorous, especially those who are relatively new to the concept. This restlessness is aggravated by the impression of instantness that pervades the Internet, where we go huffing away if we're left staring at empty space for much more than twenty seconds. Topping off those pressures are all the glowing stories. Few of us stop and analyze the self-congratulatory tales of "we found our soul-mate on this site!" long enough to note that many of these "successes" suddenly drop out of conversation after a few weeks, or the celebrants themselves vanish overnight without a trace.

Virtual pitfalls

Remind yourself occasionally that regular posters on such sites are a highly self-selected minority, and are not typical of the entire membership of that tiny corner of the world, much less of polyfolk. One such site has about 1,000 listed members. I've estimated, with some accuracy, that fewer than 100 even irregularly rake through the "bulletin board" area of the site to see who's saying what this week. Of that 100, perhaps 10 add to the fray more than once a week. Someone isn't representative merely because they're verbose.

I regularly hang out on a couple of poly-oriented Internet sites. Many of the people appear impatient. (I'm not talking about the desperate-sounding ones, though any "personals" site accumulates its share.) So, to them and others of like mind, I'd like to address a few words, out of a sense of kinship, if not family.

Even if you live in an MMA (major metropolitan area – another TLA for your collection), you're surrounded by strangers. I don't just mean people you haven't met or don't know personally. I mean people who might be in the house next door to you, but live in a completely different world from the polyamorous. (Most of the following covers just about any other lifestyle choice, or even factors such as handicaps and ethnicity, but I'll stick to the case at hand.) The vast majority of people in the U.S. are heterosexual, Christian, and monogamous; perhaps these labels are superficial, but most would be mortally insulted if you hinted they weren't sincere, even if you caught them in flagrant violation.

They are also, for the most part, frightened and powerless. Look at sex: they snicker about "kinky" sex, but that is pretty much anything other than a heterosexual missionary position (with the lights off). Males fantasize about having two women in bed, but hardly know what to do with one at a time; women fantasize about lovemaking that involves human contact and lasts more than five minutes. These people defend lifelong monogamy as the "natural" order, even as they fool around in an endless string of affairs. And, most of all, they are frightened by people who openly flout convention.

When primates are frightened on their own territory, they tend to destroy the strangeness. No matter how openly we wish to live our lives, we sense this. We may not be closet polys, but it doesn't come up in casual conversation at work.

I have homes with my primary partners in both an MMA and in one of the least-populated states. In both, other than my family, if I were to say I'm gay, I'd likely find at least immediate tolerance, if not acceptance, and probably a few dates. But if I say that I've got more than one lover, and have for some years (including while married), very few people would have any empathy, or even a clue what I was talking about. At best, I'd be assumed to be a womanizer, and the odds of getting a co-worker to so much as go out for coffee with me would be minimal.

What I'm leading around to is that I've heard many stories about the problems of finding partners. I've been exceedingly lucky, though it's taken work. I wanted group marriage when I was still a virgin; I discussed the possibility with my first lover, early on. Four years later, I stood my ground and said I was tired of pretending to monogamy: I'd been faithful, she'd had at least five affairs. Since then, I've been nonmonogamous openly in my social circles. My household spent years setting an example, with the result that people could see us acting with open affection and a pronounced lack of jealousy. Most, of course, didn't become sexually intimate with any of us, but absorbed important lessons on communication and honesty – it was no longer a choice between rigid monogamy and adulterous promiscuity.

I get the feeling I've already disappointed one or two women I've met on those websites. The biggest problem appears to be distance. We seem to have some compatibility, but I live hundreds of miles away, and am not in an immediate position to move.

Start slow & local

Don't go leaping into situations. Sure, talk on the phone, meet up at some sort of a socially neutral location. But also make sure you know their name, where they work, the names of their various partners, how long they've lived there, and so on. When you make plans to meet someone, keeping a friend or two posted on where you'll be and who you'll be with is common sense that many desperate polyfolk ignore. Frankly, if I was chatting someone up, and she said, "You sound nice. We should meet. How about Thursday? I can call in sick and fly out," I would be completely creeped out – moreso if I was a female talking to a male. I watched with growing trepidation as a ladyfriend met a guy online, he flew in two weeks later, and a month after that quit his job and moved halfway across the country. I asked, "How can you move in with a near-stranger, who can quit his job, break his lease, and say goodbye to his friends in a couple of weeks?" The question answered itself when he later turned out to be an active closet alcoholic.

One big reason for polyamory is a need for variety. Not merely sexual, but emotional, sensual, intellectual, with people who show signs of becoming life-long friends, and doing so almost in spite of physical intimacy. It still amazes me that I can have two or three lovers, any of whom I probably could happily be exclusive to, yet my curiosity about other intimate friends only seems to abate when I simply run out of hours in the week. It's not that I'm bored with what I have, or that there's some serious lack in my life, or that I'm distracting myself to avoid dealing with extant problems. I am complex and unique, as are each of my lovers and friends. Objectively, it'd be ludicrous to expect that I could possibly be 100%

compatible with any one other human being. Even if it happened, we grow only when challenged–where is the challenge in perfect compatibility? And if there's no growth, how can a loving relationship survive, much less progress? Therefore, some degree of difference is not merely inevitable, but vital.

But, we are creatures of our culture. We meet a stranger and, if they don't appear outright psychotic, we end up in bed with them. Then we tell ourselves that there must be "something there" or we wouldn't have acted so rashly. So, we give away months or years of our lives trying to fix something that has never existed: a relationship. When it's finally over, we withdraw, and actively ignore all potential relationships, even the near-ideal ones. When we recover, we start the process all over again, a little more cynical, but little wiser.

In short, the greatest advantage over preferring nearby candidates is that it's easier to weed them out (if we happened to be closer together, we could make a day-trip of it, and meet at some neutral territory like Starbuck's). For comparison, the biggest problem with LDRs is not the big gaps in time, but that so many of these sporadic relationships seem to eventually meet up with a "one and only" and your first hint is a wedding invitation.

So, a little advice. Relax. You're not filling a job position. You're looking for a pleasant acquaintance… who might become a good friend… who turns out to be attractive to your senses… and a rewarding lover… then a committed partner whose heart will not stray. If you don't see those signposts and in that order, then you're probably on the wrong road and getting more lost with every step.

52. We sleep together, therefore we're partners

Back to the terminology that befogs polyamory, with a few examples of how simple little words can eventually get you into deep weeds. Notice, for instance, in the title of this chapter there is a slippery euphemism, an extremely vague noun, and a sweeping assumption – in a seven-word sentence.

You cannot force permanence or perpetuity upon another person by force of will. Choosing a good-sounding word, and repeating it as a mantra, doesn't bring forever any closer, and really tends to push it farther away.

Soulmate

Half the people I know of who referred to a partner regularly and publicly as a "soulmate" ended up their relationship in a sticky, vengeful divorce. The concept is hopeful and positive, but it may readily obscure very real problems that fester until they explode, where a somewhat less romanticized approach would have led to productive confrontation.

The word suffers from being both ill-defined and overworked. It certainly can have valid usage, and a whole lot of meaning, but "I don't think that word means what you think it means." A soulmate is something you can really only judge in hindsight, at the very least after the initial giddiness of NRE has worn off and you have actually faced a few crises side-by-side. Two of my friends declared themselves soulmates after discovering on their first date that they both liked a layer of Parmesan cheese on their pizza. (They said that this was only one example of how "right for each other" they were, but couldn't come up with anything else when I asked.)

The word must be used with great caution, as it is an artifact of the overly romantic culture we come from, and as such tied in many peoples' minds to one-and-only monogamist thinking. With monogamous couples, soulmate status exempts the relationship from criticism as a mere fallible dyad. When the relationship collapses, this calls the whole concept into question: were the individuals' sensibilities so wrong that they misapplied the word (and therefore should their next use also be doubted that much more), or is it possible that each of us has not merely one soulmate, but two or three or a dozen? If soulmates are so rare, then why do they almost always seem to be living a few miles apart when they meet?

It's "soulmate" in the "only person I should ever be with" sense that worries me. This is far too limiting to everyone involved, and becomes a sort of circularly self-fulfilling prophecy. You find someone who really turns you on, at many levels, from the first time your eyes meet. You seek out further proofs for this being some sort of rarefied bond, using the hope as reason to overlook contraindications. Every minor similarity is inflated to massive significance; every point of disagreement is buried as insignificant. When the initial thrill begins to wane, you accuse your erstwhile partner of misleading you. Then, alone and lonely, you start the process again. The reality of imperfection, recognized and accepted from the start, isn't as much of a candyfloss fairy tale, but it can last a lot longer. And maybe, if you're not stuck in the rut of trying to force every good candidate to be a one-and-only, you'll find more decent people to add to your life.

Soulmates are hardly impossible. My best soulmate is a woman whose been my friend for almost 20 years, been my roommate twice, we have interests and worldviews that are similar and complementary, I used to delight in massaging her for hours every few days, we both use the word "love" very cautiously in general but freely admit we love each other, we've slept together dozens of times… yet we've never shared a single sexual experience. I've had lovers, and even long-term partners, with whom I've never felt as close as I do with her. We provide each other that safe-but-challenged feeling that leads to such incredible personal growth. It's likely that we will remain deeply attached to each other for the rest of this lifetime. Yet, unless there are some fundamental changes in our psyches, there is no way that we will ever become partners.

Partner

I get a little worried when someone refers to a new relationship as a "life partner" for much the same reason. If it's a statement of intent, that seems to be a very good thing… as long as it implies that "we will care enough about each other to not let ourselves base our interaction on BS." In all my open-hearted honesty, I cannot say to someone "I will love you forever," any more than I can say "I will live past age 93," or "I will love you no matter how abusive you become."

Part of the problem is that we distort the heck out of the word "partner." There is no responsible way to make "sexual partner" and "life partner" have a whole lot in common, yet they're used almost interchangeably, especially when the effects of NRE are evident.

I tend to take my relationships in stages, which might have irreparably skewed my outlook. I make an acquaintance (which most folks call "friendship"), then it goes to companionship, new friendship, sexual partner, established friendship, primary, roommate. (After this, it'd be fiancée, spouse, co-parent. I've only gotten that far twice.)

I've been told that having a progression like this both makes me "too serious" and "not serious"–both extremes representing the fear that structure is somehow supposed to replace emotion–but, at least, when the NRE is long gone, and the eddies of life have rolled over, I've still got some darn good friends.

Such a stepwise approach is a reliable guideline... but, yeah, things happen (though, by definition, extraordinary exceptions shouldn't happen almost every time). I've had some incredible relationships that basically started in bed, and it was the pillow-talk that surprised us with how much we were actually on the same wavelength, which resulted in becoming friends (even if we gave up on the sex). The feeling of partnership, verified by objective study, will happen when it is going to happen, not when you want it to. Slapping a "partner" label on a person does little to reflect the truth.

In fact, being a little too ready with the stamp can go a long way toward preventing it from becoming reality. Partnership can either represent an objective estimate of the summit that has been achieved, or the long-range intent of those involved. Ideally, it ought to be both, retrospective as well as a guideline for future effort. Too often, though, it is an entirely empty word, a sort of glib catch-all empty solution employed like "love" to simultaneously gloss over and invalidate past experience and to eliminate any need for future effort.

I've participated in various small businesses. The word "partner" is not to be taken lightly, as it explicitly implies all sorts of sharing of rights and responsibilities. Any concern that takes on a new partner, or elevates an employee to that status, gains strength and knowledge and resources, even as it opens itself up to wider dissent and potential risk.

That is exactly how you ought to view partnership in your personal relationships. You have to be very clear, in your own head and to the people involved and to everyone who knows about your plans, what partnership means. You have to hold yourself and your partners to certain standards of ethics and "corporate" responsibility. Relationships can come and go without being failures, but a partnership that goes bad likely shouldn't have started in the first place. When a partnership bombs, it can drag everyone down and destroy the group– unless, of course, it wasn't a partnership to begin with.

53. Care and feeding: relationship maintenance

One of the best points about living nonmonogamously is that there isn't the "either/or" problem, where you're expected to kill one relationship in order to learn via The Hard Way that *all* real relationships have problems. In responsible nonmonogamy, you have the option of exploring a new relationship with the support of your loved one(s), and it's no longer part of the rules to destroy goodness in order to leap into a mistake – in fact, if everyone's communicating, it's much easier to fix a new relationship that's a little rocky at the beginning: I had a couple of lovers who consulted my wife-of-record when they found me irritating.

Relationships take effort & attention, *period*

In order to have that sort of relationship to fall back on, you're going to have to not merely have one, but you will have to *actively* keep it going. Sounds pretty damned obvious, right? Yet it is so often one of the first things to go flying right out the nearest window when one or both members of a couple discover that, yes indeedy-do, they can actually find more than one person in the world who finds them desirable. Relationships are not some sort of perpetual-motion machine – you need to get them moving and forever *keep* them moving. A relationship that stops moving ceases to be a relationship. If you don't want it to die, than you have to keep it alive. That takes effort; that takes conscious will; and before that, it takes a little attention-paying.

Start with the basics: no matter what happens, you should put every effort into dating your preexisting spouse, partner, or multiple thereof. Dating is absolutely essential for maintaining the dyad. This is even more true if you enter into polyamory with a dyad that you intend to keep as primary, or at least to maintain. If it's not going to be worth the effort when you're being happily suffocated by NRE, then the only reason you're holding on to it right now is because you're acting and thinking monogamistically, the First Law of Wing-Walking: "Never let go of something until you've got hold of something else." Nonmonogamy messes severely with this, asking a question: why are you clinging to something not worth having in the first place? And if it *is* worth having, then maybe you ought to expend a little effort into keeping it viable – before, during, *and* after you go haring off in search of multiplicity. Don't be a weasel: clinging to a relationship primarily (or solely) as a "fall-back" position, a safety net, is repulsive. (Any sane and experienced poly person would also tend to say to themselves, "Wow! If they treat someone with so much history so poorly, how long until *I* get the same – or worse?")

Equal is equal

A new relationship requires just as much maintenance as an established relationship. If this appears obvious to you at the moment, I nevertheless guarantee that it won't seem so obvious when you find yourself in relevant circumstances.

Firstly, when you are in the throes (or, rather, clutches) of NRE, the demands of the new relationship will not seem so obvious. This phase is intensely mutual, and the amount of time and energy and worry that you are investing will not seem so much like a universe of demands at all. NRE feeds on itself for a time, and you are actually experiencing a biochemical high akin to endorphins and adrenaline. With an established relationship, though, the rush is muted or even gone. It's the difference between speed and good coffee.

Conversely, the bloom is off the rose in an established relationship. A new demand is fresh and exciting and a little scary, and rewarding because you are exploring mutual boundaries with a new human being. Maintaining an ongoing relationship, though, has some degree of repetition – you've been here before, perhaps hundreds or even thousands of times. It's old, you're a little tired of the pattern, you wish it would have gotten solved long ago and been put to rest.

The work is the same. The only difference is in your attitude, your outlook.

Let's say I have a lover who detests getting out of bed before noon on Saturday. I figure it's no big loss, though I would like to get in a nice brunch on occasion, or maybe a little shopping on a pleasant spring morning. She develops a new relationship, and suddenly she bounces out of bed almost every Saturday morning a little after sunrise to join in his twenty-mile bicycling regimen.

I have a choice. I can bite back any resentment that I have, rationalizing that this is one of their special times together, and that I therefore don't have any right to interfere, and assuming that I cannot even point out this significant shift in behavior without looking jealous or possessive or whatever.

That's an unfortunate artifact of our upbringing, though, needlessly imported from our cultural background.

Instead, I take a long hard look at what it is that I want, in light of the changed parameters. I then sit down and have a talk with my lover. Likely, I say something on the order of, "I'm glad that this is working out for you. I don't have a problem with this, really, because I don't like to roll out of bed before 9 if I don't have to work. But I would like to have the same sort of time to do things with you on a Saturday morning." Notice that I am not giving her the impression that she is doing something wrong or in some way hurting me. We push this around a little, and agree that, if it's raining, she'll try to shift her emphasis to spending the morning with me instead. We'll see how this works out for everyone involved, and decide that we can follow our whims of the moment, maybe including her lover or my lover, or both, though this will generally be time for us to be together as a couple, so that we can catch up a little without pending obligations hanging over our heads.

Stepping into the obvious

No matter how inexperienced you are with polyamory, you can take heart in the utter cluelessness of good people everywhere, sincere and thoughtful and experienced people who still manage to walk face-first into doing something farcical. Sometimes we all fall into the easy trap of assuming that things, once figured out, are going to continue whizzing merrily along all by themselves. That's why we treasure the people closest to us who have the guts to pull us up short when we need it the most, because they care about us.

Sean and Emily had been working long hours, getting through crunch-time projects at their respective jobs. They each had a regular secondary partner. At the moment, Emily's Jack was out of town for a couple of months setting up a new facility for his company, but they kept in regular contact on the Internet, and she mostly felt that their time would be curtailed for about that period anyway due to her own obligations. She spent most of her evenings and weekends with Sean, and when he was out with Melissa, Emily was happy to spend an hour or two before bed polishing her fiction. When Sean checked with her, she told him with a smile that she was treating this phase like a series of small vacations, and enjoying it.

Melissa enjoyed staying out late, and appeared to function best on five hours of sleep. While this baffled the early-rising Emily, it suited Sean's moods rather well, for a few nights a week, anyway. Jack was an up-at-dawn type, and he and Emily regularly met up for some running and a light breakfast before work.

Emily and Sean would usually go out Thursday evenings to see Albatross, a band they both enjoyed, and to hang out with a familiar crowd. This was a nice break from their concerns, and a good excuse to get them out of the house for a few hours to relax.

One Thursday, as the current project neared its end, Sean came home from work, looking exhausted. Noting this, Emily asked, "Are you still up for Albatross?"

Sean sighed. "I don't think so, hon. I might end up falling asleep by the end of the first set, or I'd start having a good time and not be able to get to sleep when we get back. I think I ought to cancel."

"Maybe it would be nicer to have an evening with you. I'm sure that Albatross will get by without us." Emily laughed. "We go to most of their nights, we can always go next week."

"No, that's okay, hon," Sean replied. "You've been working hard, too, and a night out would do you good. I ought to just go to bed after dinner, so I won't be very good company."

They decided to put together a simple dinner of pasta and salad, and continued the conversation during preparations. They agreed that Emily might as well go out for part of the evening, and let Sean rest. The dishes could wait until the next day.

As they were chopping basil and garlic for the pesto, the phone rang.

"Could you get that?" Emily said, brushing a stray lock of hair out of her eyes with the back of her hand. "If that's Jack, give him a kiss and I'll call later."

"I'm sure that'll make his day."

By the time she'd set the pesto to simmer, Sean still hadn't returned. Wiping her hands, Emily went out to look for him.

As she walked into the livingroom, she heard Sean say, "No, ten-thirty will be fine. I'll be looking for you."

When Sean hung up, Emily looked at him curiously. "Melissa?"

He nodded. "Yeah. She was teasing me about how we haven't seen each other in a couple of weeks. Since you're going out anyway, I figured tonight would be good."

Emily considered this for a moment. She walked over to the sofa and sat. Patting the cushion beside her, she said to Sean, "Sit."

This was Sean's cue to look puzzled. Sitting beside her, he asked, "Is there something wrong?"

Emily laughed. "Yes, and no," she said with a smile, shaking her head.

When he was sitting, she held up her hand, holding her thumb and forefinger an inch apart. "Sean, you're about this far from having an affair with Melissa."

He looked shocked. "But you know all about her!"

"Yes, I do. And generally, I approve of her being in your life. But don't you see what you're doing? You're not far from sneaking around behind my back."

"What do you mean?" he asked, guardedly.

"We usually run off on Thursdays together. That's not carved in stone, and we've both made dates on Thursdays before.

"Lately, though," she continued, "it's been a quiet madhouse around here. Except for a little time in the evenings, we come home and wind down, then go to sleep, with maybe a little lovemaking if one of us isn't already falling asleep. You and I haven't had a whole lot of time in the past two weeks either, and we not only live together but sleep in the same bed."

Sean frowned. "So what am I supposed to do? Just call Melissa back and cancel?"

"I think I'd be within my rights to expect something like that. Not because we had plans, or because I particularly need to have your attention, but because you completely precluded any plans. Not an hour ago, you were dead on your feet, remember? Now, it sounds like you're ready to stay up all hours."

"Are you saying I don't have a right to change my mind?" Sean was beginning to sound angry.

Emily held her ground, quietly but firmly. "Sean, you can always change your mind. You know that. But we made a mutual decision based on a certain set of information. If you can now run off on a spontaneous evening with Melissa, that is telling me that I don't have any right to change my mind, too. You've preempted my part of the discussion, and used the result of the miscommunication to justify your decision."

"I don't know what you mean. We talk about everything. I'm not sure I like it when you're being so high-handed."

"This is no more high-handed than usual. I already know what our options are. I could drop the subject entirely, go and see Albatross without you, and maybe get some dancing in. I could demand that you cancel your date and come along with me, because you now seem to have more energy than you were letting on. Or we could stay home together and catch up a little on our own shortage of intimate moments.

"You just don't like Melissa."

"I like Melissa plenty. She's not the problem. I know her well enough that she'd probably look plenty stung if she knew the circumstances. She likes you, sometimes I even think she loves you, but it would bother her to think that she might have walked a little close to getting between us."

After a moment of uncomfortable silence, Sean stood and walked toward the bedroom.

Sighing, Emily checked her watch, and noted that the pasta would be about done.

As she was spooning pesto over the pasta, Sean entered the kitchen, a sheepish grin on his face. Setting out salad for them both, he sat down. "I called Melissa back, and told her what an idiot I can be. She said that this is no big surprise." They both laughed.

"She wants to see me," he explained, "but tonight she was mostly interested in my company, no overwhelming desire or anything. There's a play her friend is in on Saturday, and she asked if we wanted to go along, then maybe she could run off with me for loud music and late dinner." He looked at Emily questioningly.

"That sounds like fun, but I was thinking of having a long phone call with Jack. The regional manager is driving him insane, and he said it'd be nice to hear a voice that was either intelligent or friendly."

"It was only for a moment, but I want to apologize for forgetting about you."

"We're partners. We're together so much that it's sometimes easy to forget about the important little romantic things. You sometimes have to remind me, too. Now – what are we doing about tonight?"

For those who might be curious: Emily and Sean looked at the options, and created another one, deciding that trading massage for an hour or two would be ideal, giving them both some sensual time, alone together, and celebrating their willingness to communicate.

I'm going to assume that you're up to speed, and leave it to you as an exercise to parse out from that tale where things went wrong, where they could've easily gone a whole lot wronger, and where they went right in a manner that clearly sets this outside the realm of monogamistic reflex-thinking.

54. Falling in & out of poly

We get into occasional snarls over throwing "polyamory" into a conversation as if we all mean the same thing across a huge variety of circumstances. A few people each represent an established couple looking for another unattached woman, and make clear that none of the resultant three will be involved with anyone outside of the triad. Then again, there are a few who, due to various circumstances, have multiple intimate encounters, some of them intended to be on-going, but do not presently have and/or are not looking for a primary partner. We get into arguments here if we start from a faulty premise: "it's all polyamory, therefore it's all the same thing."

Another important concept is *intent*. Obvious-seeming words like "polyamory" can get slippery and lead to all kinds of disagreements if past, present, and future aren't the same. Let's say I've never had a non-monogamous primary relationship... but I want to – so, am I polyamorous? Look at the counter-case: I'm widely experienced in nonmonogamy, but I do not presently have a primary, and I am steadily dating four women, hoping that I will eventually end up monogamous with one of them – am I monogamous? Third case: though I've experienced the whole range, I'm not obsessed with any of the alternatives, and will adapt to the circumstances and the people in my life – am I mono or poly, open or closed?

In the latter, let's say I settle down with a lover, and we decide that, what with a young child and jobs and evening classes and social groups, we have just enough time and energy to maintain exactly one intimate relationship. But, a couple of years down the road, the baby is off to school, the classes are done, the job schedules are flexible, we've dropped a couple of social groups... and maybe we have the time and stability to start dating others. Have we always been poly, and in denial? Are we really mono, and looking for adventure? Have we in some way "changed our minds"?

Polyamory is not a permanent state of being. It's something we become, or discover within ourselves, when the situation is right.

There's a strong possibility that you, whether as an individual or a dyad, will attempt nonmonogamy, then find that it overwhelms you. The experience could be good, or bad, or indifferent, but you're a little stunned. You retreat back to the comforts of couplehood to regroup and talk it over and ponder. You might have to throw yourself back into monogamy awhile, in order to finish sorting out some issues that you'd thought laid to rest before your experience. You might decide that polyamory is too much for you to handle. Or, the communication skills you pick up might renew the feelings you have for your partner, and you find that you are now completely satisfied with what you have already established and aren't so much filled with the need to go out and explore the world.

What I'm saying is, don't feel as if you've signed your soul away because you've found polyamory. This isn't a one-time offer that has to be taken at the first opportunity or lost forever. Whether you stay or not, take every opportunity to better understand yourself and your deeper motivations. Be true to yourself, and the good people among the polyamorous will respect you for your honesty, and the door to their friendship and their community will remain open to you. All you have to do is make your needs clear, and let folks know where you stand. Don't be hasty in abandoning those who have opened their hearts to you, but don't blame them for your culture shock, and don't force yourself to stay in a situation that runs contrary to your nature.

55. Empower everyone

I want to expand on my comments on hierarchy within polyamory, so that you don't misunderstand.

There is no way that everyone can be perfectly equal. Yet it is no paradox that I say there should be no "top dog" – peoples' strengths should be brought to the fore, and their weaknesses balanced by the group working in concert.

Consider something we once came up with in our triad: the freedom to conscientiously explore in an atmosphere of support. Meaning that, if one partner had a habit of getting into trysts that got his/her heart stomped regularly, then the partners had a responsibility to not only be loving but to point out the inherent and recurring dumbness involved. At the same time, honest mistakes were encouraged, as long as the stumbles resulted in forward progress for everyone.

I told my partners, "I don't want apologies. Accidents happen once, or there's reason to doubt they're accidental – the more times something happens, the less an accident it is. If it's truly an accident, I don't see why you should beg forgiveness; if it's a repetition, then an apology doesn't do anything for me."

In the real world, decisions need to be made. Whether you have a dyad or a triad or a group marriage or an intimate network, decisions will have to be made that affect you all. Some of these choices will need to be made on the spot, by one or two people. You will need to know that you can trust your own abilities and motivations, that the others who might be affected by these choices have every good reason to trust you, and that you can trust that your partners would act as much with both their hearts and their intelligence.

When good-hearted people come together in a bunch, they usually end up with some form of consensus decision-making. In the dictionary, consensus has two primary meanings: where everyone agrees unanimously, or where most agree and the rest go readily along. Like so many things in life, this is a wonderful ideal, and will rapidly fall apart when it meets up with a particularly complex situation, of which there are many. To function at all, consensus is supposed to be based upon a deep trust in the reasoning abilities of all participants, by all participants. In other words, even if you don't specifically get your way, you believe that the "winners" will behave consistently, and will admit mistaken judgment and correct course if the group decision appears to have been made in error.

Face facts. We come from a culture that to some degree significantly disempowers people even as it insulates them from the consequences of their own decisions. Many times, the result is that people let their good intentions (or those of others), their hope, their wishes override common sense. They avoid putting in "what if" considerations, insurance, or safety nets because they don't want to expend too much effort in considering the possibility of failure.

By that point, you are already in big potential trouble on three counts. You've stopped looking at the world as it really is, preferring the very limited case that is in front of you. You have moved on to attenuating or even ignoring the reality of the situation in favor of being further blinded by a glorious outcome that may actually be no more than one path in a few million. Then you took steps to eliminate the alternative possibilities so that you could focus your energy and attention toward hewing to that exceptionally narrow path.

This is built into monogamy, where it does little good for anyone. But how does something so obviously weird get dragged along by hyperrational people into polyamory? There are a few main mechanisms.

Groupthink

First, if you don't think about failure, you won't be able to see that you're sinking in it, much less take steps to head it off when it looms on the horizon. Thinking about failure does not mean becoming obsessed with it, but that's exactly how most folks act – they are so fearful of being perceived as "negative," as reflexive naysayers, that they shy away from looking at how the situations could go bad.

Another name for this problem is *groupthink*, where the collective need for unanimity overrides all common sense. I'm relatively certain that "groupthink" is indeed an intentional oxymoron. We treat a committee as though its intelligence is the sum of that of its component parts. In reality, I find that a group tends to be as smart as its stupidest member – at best. Further down the evolutionary ladder, for instance, a mob exhibits intelligence that is a fraction of the average of the individuals it contains, and in my more cynical moments I suggest it's about the square root. A herd of highly intelligent people has a difficult enough time deciding where to have lunch.

You can be forgiven – well, a little, anyway – for being reluctant to speak out in apparent opposition to an entire roomful of people you have reason to respect. Nevertheless, I advocate it, especially among the polyamorous, and the newer you are to being actively poly, the more you should question your own unacknowledged motivations, as well as those of your loved ones.

I'm lucky in that I was encouraged by my parents to not apparent consensus at face value. Many times, I have raised a calm disagreement, only to find that there was actually strong opposition in the room, sometimes by well more than half, but each of these dissenters had looked around at the sea of nodding heads, and decided that they were the only troublemaker, and were all set to go along until I opened my mouth. (When I did my time on jury duty, I was the only one to vote against conviction the first time around. If I'd said nothing and gone along, the defendant would have been sent to jail with less than five minutes' deliberation. I held out, not to be obstinate, but merely to give the other jurors time to relax, then I presented my doubts. If they'd held firm, I probably would have gone their way. As it happened, most of them shared at least one of those nagging doubts, and we decided soon after dinner that there was no way we could convict this guy on the evidence presented.) Among other blots in history, groupthink led directly to the failed Bay of Pigs invasion and the explosion of the Challenger space shuttle. For a very good analysis of groupthink's role in the operation (and collapse) of Kerista, you might locate a copy of "What Happened to Kerista?" by Eve Furchgott.

Gatekeeping

Once in a while, a dissenter will raise doubts or objections, and someone in the group will take the troublemaker aside and apply quiet pressure to "bring them on board." This is *gatekeeping*, a concept strongly interrelated with groupthink. Gatekeepers are usually self-appointed, not of any particular position or even prestige within the group. A gatekeeper will likely have no obvious personal stake in controlling the outcome, which would at least be identifiable as avarice. What they are concerned about is *image*, something that is insubstantial yet controls much of our thought and action.

There are primarily two reasons to maintain a group's image: impression and morale. Impression is image turned outward, in order to impress, reassure, or intimidate others. Morale is image turned inward, to inspire confidence in the group, its leadership, its processes, and its goals and the means used to achieve them.

The gatekeepers are not selfish, per se. The dissent they work to curb may point up obvious problems that will in fact damage the gatekeepers directly, yet their faith that the success of "the team" will reward their sacrifice is strong – it's a gamble, and one that offers great general reward for small personal risk. Or, at least, that's what they believe.

In that respect, the mechanism formed by groupthink and gatekeeping begins to resemble religious (or at least cult) forms. A group thus taken over falls into a self-perpetuating cycle, where less and less outside opinion is accepted, or even acknowledged. As objectivity withers, the group spends its time and energy increasingly in reinforcing its narrowing scope. Everyone accepts this as a rising tide of validation, and the spiral tightens. Finally, as the group becomes heavily committed to an incredibly narrow sequence of choices, the real world rears its none-too-pretty head. I have sat with planning committees that actually wasted hours and days making plans that anyone with the least grain of objectivity would have seen to depend largely or entirely from assumptions that defied the laws of physics or arithmetic.

The only blessing when the cruel awakening comes is that such groups are composed entirely from individuals who are heavily invested, each and every one. Blame and finger-pointing are kept to a minimum. Penalties and losses are divided in a relatively equitable – though sheepishly quiet – manner. Basically, the self-hypnosis (for that is what it is) has been broken, the self-made subjects are embarrassed by their binge of orgiastic self-delusion, and they simply want to get away from the scene of the debauchery and never mention it again.

Misassumption & denial

Then there's the often unconscious plan for a "built-in" fallback position that doesn't exist. Toddlers go through something like this, where they push at boundaries meant to keep them from danger; the attitude reappears during adolescence. Yet, really, the only way to keep someone from putting themselves in harm's way is for them to somehow understand that pain and suffering can result from disobeying – that the abstract rule has a concrete function – and as long as that pain remains in the realm of theory, unattached to the suffering of the recipient (or the empathic equivalent, at least), they might not believe, on a visceral level, that this is a cause-and-effect situation. Bad stuff is what happens to other people.

Monogamy has a variety of tacit and societal protections available to compensate for its inherent flaws. Nonmonogamy has really *none* of the safety nets of monogamy. Broadly, multiple partners have no claim to property, or to legal rights to stay with children that are for all intents and purposes extralegally adopted, or to monetary support.

> You move in with a married couple, who have three children less than five years old, including a baby. The wife has established a good career track, and you thrive around

small children, so the three of you soon agree that you should take care of the kids and the house while your high-paid partners bring home the bacon. Plans are made to provide for you from a sort of household pooling of funds – but, since the relationship is going to last forever, nobody feels rushed to get this down on paper.

Two years later, the baby is in daycare, the other kids are in school, the house has increased in value due to your diligence, and the glow has worn off your triad. One day, you have a difference of opinion over your choice of tree-care companies. Shortly thereafter, the couple requests that you be out of *their* house by the end of the month.

You now have to find a job, and explain to potential employers why that big gap in your employment history doesn't reflect on your abilities. You have to find your own apartment, even though there are parts of the country where you cannot hope to sign a lease without proof of established employment. You could move in with a friend, except that your life has been so devoted to your supposed family that you've lost touch with most of your friends, and the couple's friends won't return your calls anymore.

There's no sense taking your situation before a court: you'd be fighting a well-heeled and happy married couple who have great children and a nice house. You have nothing to show for two years of indentured servitude; to top it off, you have no right at all to visit the children that you raised to school age largely by yourself.

It's so easy to believe that we've left behind the need for outward show, for "putting on a happy face" and presenting an idealized façade of our family, but that is exactly what many polyamorous people do, because ignoring some very real problems is initially so much less bruising to the ego than admitting to problems, bringing them out into the light, seeking professional help, and so on. After you've made a big show about introducing your brace of life-partners to your whole family over Thanksgiving dinner, you may be a little reluctant to call Mom for support and sympathy when they walk permanently out of your life a few days after Christmas.

Penny wise and pound foolish, we prefer to live in complete denial that problems will have to be dealt with, and our only real choice is whether that will be now or later. If you forget about a debt, it accrues interest, damages your credit rating, and all that sort of fun stuff. Sure, it'd sting a bit if you had to pay off all your lines of credit right this instant, but the money is going to be due in the future, and it's going to cost you more to buy that time. Relationship problems work in exactly the same manner. Rather than deal with a problem as it occurs, or even soon after, we tell ourselves that it was an aberration and can be overlooked, preferring to risk a chance of future punishment in order to avoid the short-lived pain of confrontation, even if that pain is both minimal and unlikely.

The co-dependent mindset

In the common model, a co-dependent is seen as the yin to the yang of an addict or abuser. I believe that to be incorrect, or at least incomplete. Someone using "co-dependent" in that sense likely means to refer to such a person as a *facilitator*, who draws satisfaction from an overt intent to "fix" the negative behavior and thus redeem them from their damaged acting-out and allow the goodness within to shine forth, while in actuality supporting, making up for, and camouflaging that behavior and thus allowing it to continue, or even to flourish. In short, the world has a population of self-made (or self-perpetuating) victims. For instance, a child raised by an abusive addict will seek out relationships with abusive addicts, in a simultaneous attempt to rewrite their past yet also to recreate the situation they associate with home, family, and love, without having to question the warped values on which those concepts have been defined for them. Such "victims" can actually be undermining their damaged partner's attempts at therapy and reform by applying a combination of positive and negative reinforcements.

This isn't limited to such hot-button issues. A less recognized version of the phenomenon is where a chronically ill partner recovers, whereupon the caretaking partner refuses to accept being cast in the role of equal, and leaves. An addict can be pushed off the temperance wagon, an abuser can be goaded into a blatant display, but it's considered bad form to arrange to put a formerly disabled partner back into chronic dependence.

Even farther from the popular conception is where two people leave the yin-yang model entirely, yet maintain a mutually co-dependent relationship. The dyad is conflict habituated to a high degree, and would not survive without a regular cycle of relational breakdown followed by superficial repairs, then a period of "gliding" until insecurity pops up again to cause another vicious phase so that the bond can be renewed.

Such a person may be fundamentally unable to maintain a relationship with a healthy individual, especially someone who is unwilling to deny observing the "victim" behavior. Unless the emotional or mental well-being of the healthy person can be dragged down, the relationship is doomed. Self-perpetuating victims and co-dependent partners can be fixed by therapy, but that entails a fundamental desire to fix the problem, followed by strong-willed support from friends and family. Most polyamorous people are unable or unwilling to provide that sort of rigidity; a problematic partner is either supported in their (let's face it) abusive or self-destructive activities, or booted for same, neither of which is therapeutic. Unless you *are* attempting to use polyamory as a form of therapy, and *everyone* around you is explicitly agreeing to that, you all need to set and maintain firm boundaries, or everyone will eventually suffer.

Empower your way out

It's really no easier to give someone power than it is to give them discipline: it comes from within, or it's illusion.

You can, however, give someone the *opportunity* to *become* empowered. That "someone" can include yourself.

Consensus decision-making is fine, and I encourage you to apply it often, perhaps even as your primary method. However, there are two groups of situation in which centralized or individual leadership is imperative: when you require the best expertise you have at hand (whether this is specialist or generalist) [the group can still vote on the action, either before or after the situation is approached], or during a crisis when key decisions need to be made immediately.

In general, there is a simple rule to keep in mind: **You all need to be leaders.** Otherwise, you will soon enough find yourself being led around by the nose, whether by circumstances or by a bully or three. Choose now.

56. How open, how closed?

A cautionary note

Let's say you find yourself with two incredibly compatible lovers. You are very busy people, and almost all your free time goes to being SOs in what is for all practical intents a closed triad (we've called them "situationally closed") because none of you has time or energy, or even desire, to join up with one more person right at that moment.

But there's this new person who just transferred to your area, and she's really cute. You're shocked to find that she's familiar with the poly concept. When you present this to your SOs, they have their doubts. They're perfectly happy with the triad, and would like to make it officially closed.

You respect their reasons, but you disagree, and would like to ask your coworker out to coffee, and maybe home to meet the family. Said family doesn't think you should even get started, because it "might go somewhere".

So: do you suggest that you're not at all happy with the brakes being put on your exploration with other people? or is the stability of the "known" more important to you than exploring something that likely will go no further than close friendship, but risk the trust of your SOs?

More than one closed triad has broken up because a partner stated an interest, a mere curiosity in someone outside the trine which caused all sorts of jealousy – in other words, just like a monogamous dyad, only with more people. The theory is that poly people, even if they get all bristly at first, are better skilled to be able to set those feelings aside for a moment, and say, "Okay, what's really going on here? Are they expressing a desire to escape, or just saying that they find another person really hot? If the former, what is it, and how can we fix it? If the latter, what will that mean to *our* relationship? Would it cause more problems if it lasted a long time, or if it bombed quickly?" and so on.

Those questions are what sets polyamory apart from monogamy: We might not be entirely "outside the box" – but we have the freedom and power and knowledge that gives us a bigger box (and the ability to expand and reshape it at will).

However, such reshaping is never going to be even considered if folks are working overtime to pretend it'll never be necessary.

While there is nothing *wrong* with enforced-closed relationships, the form can't help but carry over some of the taint of ownership that caused more than a few people to question monogamy in the first place. Thus there is the risk of a closed triad becoming nothing but "a typical marriage, just with more people" – and that means risk of importing the failed roles, myths, expectations, etc. If marriage has a hard time containing just two people in this day and age, packing another into the box seems like (at best) a short-term distraction, and likely will result rather quickly in transitioning back to couplehood, or even singlehood all around.

Someone who is in a closed relationship has more in common with my parents than with me. The more closed a relationship is, and the smaller a closed group, the more easily it will fall to mimicking the failed pattern set by stereotyped monogamy. It might be nonmonogamous, but it is straying to the far end of the spectrum from polyamory.

Closed & healthy

I wish to emphasize that there are distinct differences between relationships that are *intentionally* limited and those *situationally* so.

I go through periods where my life has to be rigorously scheduled, and I tend to be involved with people who are as constrained. I have therefore had times in my life when the situation was such that I found myself in a functionally closed triad or dyad, and even celibate. In none of these cases did I feel particularly confined – generally, I was too damned busy to think about it much at all.

Though I have railed for years against people claiming polyamory while avoiding the sort of individual and relational growth that would make polyamory a viable reality for them, what is most important here is your *intent*.

Let's say you find yourself in a successful and growing triad, then the three of you agree that it would be best all around to maintain it as a closed relationship. Well, there's some of that conscious volition, taking charge and making a change that all of you agree heartily to. Compare this to a single person or dyad who set out to create a closed triad. The former tend to be superior to the latter at social skills, emotional connections outside the group, and interpersonal communication. The former type will be much more resilient, much better at seeking advice when problems occur, and more capable of noticing and analyzing and solving problems before they blow up into something big. The latter turn inward when crisis strikes, and are more likely to end in messy explosions when their stunted skills prove inadequate.

Therefore, if your final goal is indeed a closed triad, you'll be far better off in the long run if you take your time and explore some of the other options. If you think this means that I'm advising you to run off onto a hog-wild promiscuous binge, then it'd be a good idea for you to give up on applying the term "polyamory" to yourself. What I *am* recommending is that you spend some time (years, preferably) building your interpersonal skills, renewing your acquaintance with dating, for instance. The skills that you develop and nurture will provide the strength and flexibility you will need, sooner rather than later, to maintain a closed relationship – if, in the end, you come to the informed decision that this is still what you want from your primary relationship.

57. Reaching the end

Breaking up may be (as the song says) hard to do. It's also inevitable. Relationships rarely last forever, and likely shouldn't.

I've put this chapter so far up, rather than nearer the final pages of the book, because the simple fact of the matter is that the number of relationships you attempt will always exceed the number that last for any amount of time, and I'd wager that the number of "failures" – really too harsh a word for many short-lived intimate relationships – you embark upon will always outnumber the ones that at least end amicably. To be blunt, you really do need to think about the end as more than some rare event, because it's a major feature of polyamory.

Increased braking power

The vast majority of people – even monogamous people – have had at least one experience where one day the relationship was just done, suddenly, disastrously. The two people involved have grown apart, and have possibly been denying it for so long that the change looked quite radical.

Sooner our later, even in a nice simple dyad, one of you is going to have to move along. There are four possibilities: you boot him, she boots you, you reach an amicable parting, or one of you dies. That's about it. One of them *will* eventually occur, and there's *nothing* you can do about it.

If you're willing to stick with good ol' monogamous marriage, because that's where life-long relationships happen, think again: half of the people getting married right this very minute will be divorced within three years. Half the remainder will be divorced before four more years pass. Increasingly, many of the people who get into these short-lived marriages have made the trip to the altar previously, and maybe multiple times.

Well, we have it even worse. This is another of those ways in which polyamory can expansively suck. To begin with, polyamory functions on "Internet time," distinctly more accelerated than monogamy. For instance, people on poly-related websites are fidgety (including cranky, accusing, whiny, etc.) if they don't find a "life partner" within two or three weeks of joining.

Time has orders of magnitude. Instead of neat powers of ten, we have a handful that delineate human life. At the outside is the century – likely, it'll be a long time before any human sees the high side of age 200. Moving inward, after the century comes the score of years (twenty), the decade (ten), the year, the quarter (three months, approximately the same as a season), the month (slightly longer than a full Lunar cycle), the week, the day, the hour, the minute, and the second; we're lousy at perceiving shorter segments (though my favorite is the jiffy).

The advent of high-speed global communication for the common citizen has shifted our perceptions by at least one order of magnitude, possibly two. So, if a typical marriage has an even chance of breaking up by three years, I'd say that polyamorous dyads have about the same odds of lasting three quarters, or nine months; I wouldn't be surprised if the average was more like three months, though, as that would coincide with the typical span of NRE. The Constantines noted (*circa* 1970) that the average lifespan for group marriages was six months. This seems completely reasonable to me.

While I hold out great hopes for the future, there is no way anyone will be able to convince me that polyamory will ever have any *higher* a longevity rate than sacrosanct marriage. Sure, some bright day in the Utopia that like a brakeless Peterbilt is bearing down on us right this very minute, polyamorous people will be totally honest, blunt, well-spoken, living each day in full and total mutual disclosure. With all that honesty around, many unsuitable relationships will never begin, and the good ones that do will last for decades, maybe eventually even a century, though they grow and mutate as they echo the changes and growth that are taking place inside the people they comprise.

Until that comes to pass, we're all stuck with frumpy reality. Therefore, let's make the best of it and love while we can.

The dangerous two-step

A few years ago, I had a friend whose husband had pushed her to "try polyamory." When she found someone she was attracted to, and that someone happened to be male, the husband did an about-face and declared that she ought to again follow his whim back to monogamy. Having gone through some serious reevaluation of herself in order to even *consider* nonmonogamy, she wasn't ready to write off all that insight so easily, and she was standing her ground (albeit shakily) in the brunt of a lot of bluster. Here's what I told her:

> You've reached the point where you know that you have to choose between your heart – not in the romantic sense, more the "true self" kind – and someone else's. It's painful; if it wasn't, neither your love nor your belief in the rightness of your own desires would be credible. You do sense that you're the more emotionally mature of the two, evinced by the fact that you haven't resorted to the "go to hell!" attitude yourself.
>
> It could still happen that he figures things out. With experience, he may realize that life's better with you – even if he's not sole "owner" of your heart – than without you at all. At the same time, maybe he also needs to learn that he can stand alone, without you or anyone else… but that it's simply better with a companion. In both cases, he can't learn if you're right there.
>
> I won't soft-peddle it: this sucks. But I'm glad that I've bowed out of a few relationships before we actively hated each other, and that others have found their strengths without me and we've had a chance to make a proper go of it. I'm presently living with one of the latter – we once didn't even speak for two years! – and using this time to heal/repair/upgrade another long-term relationship I treasure.
>
> As the dumb old song goes, "Let's not say goodbye – let's just say *au revoir.*" Don't say "get lost" – say "I love you"… then leave.

I feel that I ought to warn you: polyamory is nothing something to be "tried out" lightly. You aren't signing anything away, but you'll never be able to see your old world with the same childish naïveté again. Once you step outside the fence, you introduce all sorts of questionmarks if you try to claim privileges inherent in monogamy. Most especially, if you have to drag your partner into this experiment, don't expect that they're going to come back with you once you've shown them how to dream.

Early end: when NRE runs out

I once studied the history of the computer. A term that stayed with me is *mean time between failures*, or MTBF. One of the 1950s machines was based around vacuum tubes, each of which had an MTBF of about 10,000 hours. Yet, the computer kept breaking down after approximately twenty minutes, and they counted themselves fortunate to be able to complete a solid hour of work. Someone finally pointed out the simple synergy they'd been overlooking: as the machine had about 50,000 tubes, then five were likely to fail ever hour; since specifications for electronic parts tend to be on the pessimistic side, the actual three-per-hour failure rate was a cause for celebration.

Polyamory works the same way, and I suggest that MTBF applies. Each intimate relationship you have affects the others, if only by messing with your energy, moods, concentration, and time. One rocky relationship could cut so deeply into these resources that, once you avert the crisis, you find that you no longer have those other people in your life.

The "typical" end of NRE appears to be a very real thing, even if there's no hard-and-fast number that is going to apply to everyone. Someone asked me, "How do I know when a relationship is getting serious?" By rights, I should have been stopped by the dubious nature of most of the words in that question. It reminds me of the more typical, "How many times should we go out before we have sex?" Everything depends.

Instead, I said something, almost by reflex, that makes more sense every time I think about it. And it's simple on the surface:

"Wait a thousand hours."

I call it **the thousand-hour rule** (though creative renaming is welcome). The thousand hours starts at the first experience of emotion-risking bonding, which is not always the first sexual experience. I first started trying to formulate it a few years before the above question because we were pondering the span of initial NRE, trying to figure out how long NRE lasts. Answer: six months, give or take three. This range seemed interesting, as it is a rather wide swing. As well, its length is a poor indicator of how long the relationship will continue – I've observed long-lasting deep relationships that began from virtually no NRE, and some that barely outlasted NRE of two years or more. To refine our rule of thumb, we brought in a few other factors. When we finally gave up, the half-year and thousand-hour rules seemed about as close as we were going to get to precision. I think you'll find that they're all you ever need, though.

This is the point at which things get messy. See, there is not just the simple "thousand-hour clock" ticking away. As those sands are running down, a dyad is being given the opportunity to build an actual relationship. If the focus during that period is entirely upon fun, with no effort put toward establishing a communication base upon which to create breadth and depth, then the tide of NRE will recede like the sea, leaving pretty much what you would expect: a long, flat stretch of nothing much.

The endless heartbreak

How many monogamous people will ever experience the exquisite *thrill* of ending two years-long relationships in a two-month period?

Poly relationships are not only shorter-lived, but we can have more than one of them at a time. Oh, the joy! To go from the confining struggle of hitting a rocky patch with only one relationship, to having the incredible opportunity to be hassling simultaneously with two or three, or more.

Is it worth the massively multiplied risk? Oh, yes. But let's be honest that it is indeed a risk, and that polyamory is hardly a Sybaritic playground.

During one of the best periods of my life, I was living with two primaries, and also had two steady secondaries, and got dumped by my newest lover before the relationship had a proper chance to get started.

And it hurt. Despite all the love I had in my life, it hurt greatly that things had bombed with this one person.

I've come to the conclusion that, if breaking up doesn't hurt, then there wasn't much attachment anyway. Cold comfort, I know, but there it is.

The pain fades, as it should. Time is the only true healer (as opposed to, say, hardening your heart so that nobody else can ever get quite that close to you again).

Having another person (or three) in your life who can be both lover and friend is invaluable. Most times, it's helpful just to hear someone else say, "Nothing's wrong with you – it just wasn't the right time."

It's happened a few times that this was proven literally true. Someone with whom I'd had a "failed" relationship comes back into my life – our social circles overlap or whatever. We chat about the Good Old Days, reminisce about the nice things we shared, then dredge up the potholes. Suddenly, it occurs to both of us that there was indeed some kind of connection, and that maybe circumstances have changed so that we can start over again.

I have had exactly that experience on no less than five occasions – and that's quite an admission, coming from such a horrible cynic as myself. One of my primaries is, in fact, my lover from more than a decade ago, after which we both ran into personal problems that pulled us far apart, and there were year-long gaps where we never spoke. A few years later, she called me, out of the blue, for input on why her then-relationship was going down in flames – she knew she could count on our friendship. I gave her my input. We kept talking, started to hang out when we were in the same city, then finally admitted that we both wanted to give the relationship a proper try. Sometimes things have to end so that they can start anew.

Now, practicalities – the pain is real. Treat it like a passing illness: eat properly, get the sleep you need (adding naps as necessary), pamper yourself (whether going to a movie alone or sitting on the porch with a good book), don't overdo or binge (avoiding alcohol and drugs entirely is a Good Idea until the hurt passes), and don't dive into a new "relationship" to "replace" the old one (hanging out with old friends is another Good Idea).

Monogamous timelines

My aphorism: "Longevity is not a hallmark of success." I've seen too many marriages that were a long, slow walk through Hell… for the couple and everyone around them. If I have an intense, loving, productive six-month relationship with someone, and then we decide we are done with it, what is there about that that doesn't spell "success"?

We can get into some interesting corners talking about "how long our relationship has lasted." Here's a stray example: I lusted after someone for two years, enjoyed her friendship, and finally figured out that there was just no way she was going to be interested, and I was okay with that. Circumstances separated us for two more years. We got back together again, and she practically tore my clothes off. It was incredible, we became very emotionally attached, but then the world turned and after a great year we had to part to deal with respective life-crises. Now we've been "just friends" for a few years, occasionally have sex when we're both in town and not exhausted, yet on other levels we're practically soul-mates.

Question: how long have we "had a relationship"?

Yes, this will be on the test.

Polyamory is not suited to simplistic, linear timelines. It's impossible to directly compare one relationship that mostly consists of a romantic evening every few weeks with one that involves living together and sharing a bed, even if they both began the same day – and at what point does a relationship "begin," anyway?

If we have difficulty deciding when the darned things begin, and how much duration they've had despite what the calendar says, then ending is no less a problem. You could hold on to monogamistic habits, and make sure that each of your dyads ends in a dramatic explosion ensuring that neither of you will ever again want to speak to the other, in which case most observers would agree that, yep, it's over alright. Of course, that habit might also call the uncomfortable question as to whether what you're doing is actually polyamory, as that hardly seems the sort of action you'd take with someone who had ever truly been your friend, and doing it more than once or twice suggests flawed reasoning.

Ending is always a possibility. We humans are still mortal little creatures, leaving aside the whole area of souls and eternal spirits and all that. Ethereal portions notwithstanding, our bodies stop developing, then they degrade until they can no longer be sustained. Illness happens to even the healthiest of us. We drive very rapidly in motor vehicles that aren't half as safe as we'd prefer to think, piloted by lunatics alternately trimming their toenails and shrieking obscenities.

Life is fragile, something we rarely appreciate until a crisis, after which we rapidly cease to remember until the next time our attention is appropriated.

And thus go our relationships as well. Sometimes they die, and die permanently. Until that point is reached, though, relationships grow and shift and mutate and mature. Change is a ruthless teacher, and its negative effects can be mitigated by acceptance of that fact.

The "graceful distancing"

Part of the extensive Kerista legacy is the concept of easing someone out of a complex relational situation, which they called *graceful distancing*. I rather liked the idea when it was mentioned in passing, but even a brief glance showed that this is a bit of a "weasel word."

There are many situations in which we find ourselves where a little bit of distance is good for everyone involved. We're too enmeshed in the situation and the personalities that are clashing to see clearly and thus make the best decisions. In a moment of lucidity, backing off a little presents itself. That might mean going to visit a friend, taking a vacation, changing routine, or perhaps just taking on a little more objectivity about the situation. From there, we can take the next steps, which might include walking completely away, or throwing ourselves wholeheartedly back into the fray armed with understanding.

In the Keristan sense, though, graceful distancing essentially meant that your affiliation had been marked for execution, without margin for appeal. In that sense, it was about as "graceful" as the stroll to the electric chair.

As some of the members later remarked, graceful distancing was a tool for keeping people from straying too far from accepted dogma. Excessive questioning of the precepts, or a tendency to present thoughts that made key members uncomfortable, could result in this sudden expulsion. Those who remained were thus put on notice as to the penalties that awaited troublemakers, and the lack of clearly defined boundaries maintained Truth as a narrowly defined area of safety.

This is a tactic popular with cults of various forms, whether the guardians of Truth are an autocratic inner circle or an illusory consensus – it's the same thing, really, but the appearance of group decision appeals to intellectuals. Polyamory tends to be chaotic and messy, and inherently requires a high degree of communication as well as that any rules must be clearly (even bluntly) laid out, with well-demarcated borders that have a certain freedom to shift with time and situation. Even the founding dyad of a closed triad ought to be able to do far better than to fall back on "Because I said so, that's why!"

Constructive collapse

Before we married, Marie and I made a deal: we'd get a divorce for our tenth anniversary. I know that sounds cold, but we figured that (a) the changes in our lives are generally so drastic that putting up with each other for *that* long would be a wonderful accomplishment, and (b) there was still the option of being roommates, sharing the kids, etc.

Insurance policies suck because they cost you money, and you make every payment simultaneously griping about the premium and thanking various deities that you haven't had to use it for one more month. Insurance is the only form of gambling where the punter prays to never win the lotto. That, basically, is what I encourage you to do: plan for the end of your relationship, but feel free to pray that you'll never have to avail yourself of that contingency.

Every time you make allowances for the worst, you suck some of the energy out of that possibility and thus make it less likely to happen. A well-made prenuptial agreement (something that, admittedly, is the exception) can have exactly this effect.

Start with the basics. Who gets the house? How would you go about dividing up the CDs? Speaking of CDs, do you have any investments, Savings Bonds, bank accounts? How about debts like loans and credit cards? Where will the children live, and what sort of visitation would make everyone happy? Who gets which car?

Keep digging until you've worked your way down to minutiae. Work out a deal so thorough and mutually satisfying that, if some weird twist of fate were to occur right this minute, you could pull out the sheets of paper containing the agreement and begin putting it into effect instantly.

Once you get the hang of this process, start branching out into other options. How will you handle it if the love should fade, and you or a primary partner feels a deep-seated need for change? What is the first thing you'll do if one of you should get a fantastic job offer that will take you a thousand miles away for a year or two? What effects might long-term debilitating illness have on your relationship and living situation? Make up lists of changes that could happen, and give some serious thought as to how you might handle them.

Whether we like it or not, change happens, and sometimes at the most inconvenient of moments. We crave permanence. To be "always moving" is something we're taught to fear. We're all looking for purpose, for something to which we can devote ourselves, for permanence, for guarantees, for security.

Security comes from within. Permanence comes from devotion to creating a better world, even if that world is the little community immediately at hand. Relationships may come and go, but instead of looking at that as loss, work to create a community that allows for change rather than fighting it. Face up to the fact that any given situation might end, and try to make that ending friendly and productive.

58. The balancing act: multiplicity

Even if you begin by envisioning your goal to be a life-long triad, excluding everyone else, you'll likely end up attached to more people. That's simply the way it is, and this differentiates polyamory from mere nonmonogamy. The partners in your threesome are very unlikely, once introduced to the sheer amazing possibilities of multiplicity, to all be forever completely satisfied with only two partners. One or more of you will eventually stumble across another very attractive candidate. Assuming that the partner most desiring this candidate has completely learned the lesson to not readily burn bridges just because another true love wanders along, and also assuming that the other partners know that they've got it pretty darned good and don't think that this is an adequate reason to vote their "straying" partner off the island, then your thought processes will necessarily have to change and grow yet again.

By that point, you will likely have forgotten most or all of the lessons you learned at the first go-round. Just as you had to make some serious internal and relational changes in order to expand from a dyad to a triad, you will have to begin again when the situation becomes more complex. There you are, right back where you started from. That is why you must truly *learn from*, not merely *cope with*, the changes that come your way.

Relationships rarely last a lifetime. Even if you remain deeply attached to someone, a full life practically ensures that you will change, your partner will change, the relationship between you will change, and the world around you will change. One or two of those factors might be held constant for an extended amount of time… but stopping *all* of them is impossible. And when these major factors change, the relationship must become something new.

When you venture out into nonmonogamy, the variables do not merely add up–that is, having two lovers is, in some critical ways, far more than twice as complicated as being monogamous.

Yes, nonmonogamy *is* like juggling

Maintaining some sort of balance between your relationships is not something you can learn from a book, any more than a detailed description of juggling will have much use. Sure, a thorough text could give you some idea of the mindset you ought to have for best results, and a few technical hints here and there, but none of it will be of actual use until you get up and give it a try. And, like juggling, you're going to spend vastly more time at the beginning chasing after what you've dropped (or trying to replace what you've broken) than you ever possibly could actually performing the feat you've set yourself.

Some of us are lucky. I come from a loud, loving, expressive family, and spent many happily chaotic times in mobs of relatives and the extended family. Many of you are not so fortunate. As with the juggling analogy, I may be a bit of a klutz, but I know in my bones how to go about learning to handle a new situation, based on experience, and then how to optimize the interaction of this new situation for the unique set of variables.

Keeping relationships in balance is not a technical endeavor, but an artistic expression, much like dance. In order to have a happily nonmonogamous life, you will need to have practiced so thoroughly that your efforts are an expression of a highly controlled set of finely honed reflexes. A person who manages to keep multiple deep, complex relationships chugging merrily along seems to be doing no work at all. If you intend to emulate them by expending no effort, though, you're going to be blindsided regularly until you either come to your senses, or slink away convinced that someone is withholding "the secrets of success" from you.

You have to accept your mistakes, learn from them, and improve with every attempt. At the same time, you cannot fool yourself into believing that the occasional stroke of good fortune (whether based on your budding intuitions or sheer stupid luck) proves that you've achieved any sort of final mastery of the subject. A good juggler is continually expanding upon skills that are beginning to come together, and adds regularly to their repertoire – most of them may never make it into a public performance, but the constant cycle of learning keeps the senses and reflexes finely tuned.

This book is a text on juggling. I throw hints and history at you in hope that you will be encouraged to actually try them out in your own situations, and sometimes will know where to turn for a little immediate advice on some crisis or collapse.

There is no equality in love

I don't try to "make it even" in the affection I show to each of the people in my life, whatever degree of interaction we are currently at. When I once got worried about this, we'd recently had a party at which seven of my current or former lovers were in attendance, so I asked them, and the majority said they were surprised they got so *much* attention from me. So I stopped worrying. Don't get too self-conscious about "even-handedness," else you'll either stop being publicly affectionate in general, or you'll just come across as a stiff. And if you thoroughly scan your "audience" before a PDA, you'll just kill the spontaneity as you get more paranoid – not worth it.

Local culture is a factor. In Minneapolis, and especially in certain social whirls, I'll openly mention my loves by name, and usually greet three or four warmly. (One was surprised at my question, and when I asked her for an opinion on my own handling of such situations, called me an "equal opportunity flirt," adding, "I couldn't tell who you were just friends with from who you were involved with." This helped, as she had big issues about relationships that start out open and suddenly veer toward possession.)

The good thing about having a sprawling social community is to be able to demonstrate, rather than waste energy trying to figure how to bring the concept up in conversation. I mean, very-warm hugs with my ex-boyfriend in public, when we're both with our girlfriends, kinda says a few thousand words.

Time isn't linear, either

You *cannot* measure "relationship time" with a stopwatch. For example, I'm living in a strong primary, not involved with anyone else within a thousand miles, and happy that way. There are indeed 168 hours in a week, so let's look at my schedule. I sleep 56 hours, bathe 2-4, read 10-20, write 20-40, use the toilet 4-6, work on business 10-30, take job contracts 20-30, and so on. Let's say, at minimum, that means I'm focused elsewhere and/or occupied for 123 hours in a typical week, leaving 45. For my partner and me, it's a big jump to assume that our leisure moments line up more than 50% of that free time. If one of us were to start up a new relationship, or rekindle an old one, that would cut drastically into the time we have that overlaps, even if the actual time spent with the other person was only a dozen hours per week.

One of my relationships has been with a woman who also happens to be one of the best friends I've ever had. When we started out, she had her usual crowd that she'd run around and party with, and I'd be with her maybe 2 evenings/week. While I treasured this time, I am also a very responsible person, and about half our dates would center around getting her laundry done, grocery shopping, etc. I finally had to point out to her that I'm a good partner, but a lousy caretaker, and I was feeling like I was making up for the energy her regular buddies took out of her. That was more than ten years ago, and we're still working on it, but she knows what I mean, and now expects her lovers to not just swoop in and scoop up all the "fun" times, but also that they share each other's chores, ill times, and so forth.

You've got to think *quality*, not quantity. Would you rather have ten hours a week of alone-together time, with romance, lovemaking, *no* discussions of work crises or finances... or fifty hours of not-talking, sleeping, balancing the checkbook, etc., with none of the passion or tenderness?

That's not a rhetorical question.

If you want quality-time, you're *not* gonna get it by sending out thought-waves – **talk**. *Ask* for some kind of parity – *don't* start doing a minute-by-minute log, because you'll be lucky if all that happens is she gives you the time but not the *presence*. If she goes out on a regular basis with another guy for dinner, one-on-one, then you two should be able to get about the same number of evenings. And so on.

As for being "selfish," face facts: if you don't think of yourself, nobody else will. That's just human nature. The good folks are the ones that spend every day working to not be *merely* self-centered. Don't sell yourself cheap. A big step comes in saying "This is what I need", but first you have to sit down and figure out what your needs actually are.

Poly doesn't mean you're scrupulous or smart

People do not necessarily behave in a manner any casual observer would label "sane." Measurable intelligence appears to have little to do with it – some people just insist upon acting stupidly, selfishly, short-sightedly, etc.

I was happily married, and had recently started a relationship with Jean. Jean was also involved elsewhere, with Ben, a highschool friend. When she told Ben about our relationship, he went into an extended snit over her being involved with a married man. The fact that my wife was happy with the situation seemed to bother him more.

What made this ludicrous is that Ben's also married... to another of Jean's highschool friends. In fact, they're all part of a social circle that's been together all this time. And Ben's wife was completely in the dark.

Polyamory demands that you learn, and offers you even more opportunities to benignly pick up intelligence, empathy, and self-understanding.

In order to be polyamorous, you cannot maintain a neatly compartmentalized life. Never again is Dyad M wholly separate from Triad N if one member from each pod has a friend in common and everyone is poly. If a significant portion of the chain is merely screwing around and having affairs, mistruth can flourish. Elsewise, you're probably setting off a chain of events that will eventually bite you, causing assorted pain and suffering for you, your relationships, and the people you supposedly love.

I wouldn't say that being as honest and truthful and straightforward as you possibly can with everyone is *easier* than lying... but it is definitely easier than remembering what version of the story you told to each particular person and bunch, especially when they (usually from a random casual remark) begin comparing notes. Lying begins easy, and then absorbs complication like an ideal sponge. If Mervin cancels a Wednesday date with Zelda, claiming exhaustion, then

Helga innocently mentions to her friend Zelda that Mervin didn't look so good when he picked her up Wednesday evening, Mervin is going to have some explaining to do, and both Zelda and Helga might begin to wonder what else he's putting a "nice" spin on.

When people in a social network are working diligently to avoid secrecy and other faults in their communication, I suppose that there's always the danger of overshare, but there are a few simple facts that tend to deflate this. For starters, *anyone* can ramble or blurt, whatever the topic or situation. Polyamory hardly has a corner on this market, or even a significant holding. You will learn soon enough that dredging up dirt on each other is a pernicious form of communication that begs the definition, and rapidly gets sidetracked not from the glut of gossip, but because the motivations of the gossipers begins to look like a much more amusing deconstruction. And, of course, a bore is still a bore, even when relating juicy details of someone else's life – not that prattling about their own makes it any more tolerable.

While I'm expounding on holes in the "communicate! communicate! communicate!" mantra, I'll add a few words on an NRE variant that people mistakenly give too high a value.

There have been a few times when someone in my social circle expressed (without going into any detail) "doubts" about a new intimate of theirs. Only in hindsight did I figure out that a request for confirmation of these doubts was rhetorical, not meant to be answered, so my specific amplifications weren't exactly taken well. But once in a while, my speaking up will draw someone else into voicing their own questions. This is invaluable for examining potential problems before they occur and laying in backup plans for other secondarily involved people – which, in an actual community, can mean everyone.

When introducing new people into your group or network, initial happy-talk has *zero* relation to actual closeness. In fact, edginess at the beginning, if people are actually allowed to communicate without fear, might be more reliable in leading to real, long-term and deep bonding, since overcoming this hurdle in a mutual manner makes it a shared accomplishment. Should an individual prove to have some rough edges, they now directly face the questions of a group, rather than one or two members of that group with whom they interact most directly. In too many cases, though, everyone has a stake in participating in the NRE at second hand, and so actively avoid expressing their own concerns.

Surround yourself with people who will not shut you up or slap you down for an honest question. Embrace paradox, and yet never cease looking for better from yourself as well as from the people around you.

The unanswerable questions of nonmonogamy

Polyamory has more than its share of paradoxes that resemble Zen *koans*, unanswerable riddles that, if contemplated correctly and thoroughly, bring their own understanding of the Universe. The answer you get is more a feeling than a solution like you would get to an algebra problem. This chapter is more about those sorts of questions than their answers, so I'll end with my favorites:

How I can be so completely satisfied, yet want more?

How I can love and treasure and derive both passion and joy from my life, yet still so curious about what lies beyond?

59. Firm but flexible: to the future, right?

Your multilinear relationship has gotten far past its launch, and things appear to be going quite well. You've evolved methods for working out the inevitable disagreements, you've all given up subterfuge in favor of truth and open communication, and you have every objective reason to continue the path you've chosen.

Have you locked the relationship into being only what it *is*, or have you given it the strength and flexibility to grow and adapt?

If at any point you say something like "We'll see how it goes," you're steering toward doom. That's sort of like, "Let's keep driving in the dark until we hit something, then turn the headlights on to see whether it's good." Yet, if you stick with clueless confidence, "It'll last forever so I'll ignore the little problems," you're even more surely killing it. Work on today, aim for a future. You need to learn how to handle problems *and* evolve a problem-solving strategy.

Extreme crises

The more people that you add into a given situation, the greater the chances that something is going to occur that will tear you all apart. At the same time, as a community becomes larger it becomes more capable of absorbing the occasionally nasty tricks that the Universe will deal. This isn't as paradoxical as it may appear: there are two separate sets of variables involved, one declining as the other increases. By this point you can probably parse it out for yourself but, briefly, larger groupings that are just on the verge of gaining benefits of scale are also acquiring the risks associated with snarled communication, with the result that even a small crisis can split everyone into warring cliques more focused on protecting their symbolic turf than on working to preserve the community.

Over the years, I've noted that dyads and triads begin with far more structure than they need, and this trips them up. They discard these as they expand, streamlining with more hindsight than foresight. They end up with a larger household or network that truly needs these skills and rules, but they've gotten so slack that a troublemaker or a "drama queen" easily breezes in and divides the energies or disrupts communication and trust.

An intimate network is closer to the community model. People come and go, relationships break up or shift around, dyads wax and wane, but for the most part the network does not change drastically. Closed relationships are less able to handle high-level stresses, and therefore need to be more prepared for serious problems than do their more amorphous cousins.

In any case, your relationships will benefit if each individual and various twos and threes and fours ask some hard questions, honestly assess strengths and weaknesses, and consider reactions to the situation ranging from how it would be handled if it occurred right this second to projects you could start right now to minimize the damage (wills, insurance, or financial planning, for instance). Since your personalities vary so widely, as do your resources, I will only provide you with some brief scenarios that you absolutely must consider.

Your partner dies suddenly.

You are diagnosed with cancer.

Your child is hospitalized with a raging fever.

You require extensive surgery.

Your job requires you to move 500 miles away for three years or so.

Rumors come around that your partner's newest lover probably has genital herpes.

Your partner's employer goes bankrupt.

Your child dies.

Your underinsured house burns down in the middle of the night, leaving you with your car and your pajamas.

Each of these has probably caused the collapse of a million marriages. None is pleasant to think about. You must learn that the squeamishness you feel is a very good warning that a particular subject must therefore be examined. In fact, you ought to sit down and see how many things you can add to the list that reflect your particular situation. Then, by all means, "rehearse" them until they aren't so frightening, come up with contingency plans and protective paperwork, and keep at it until you're relatively certain that you've got most of your vulnerabilities covered. Should something terrible occur, and you've thoroughly inspected a similar situation from every likely angle, I guarantee that the rest of your life won't so easily fall apart while you deal with matters at hand. In fact, steady practice with this sort of "negative thinking" will make you more calm and efficient in a crisis, which might save not just stress, but perhaps a life.

Stop crisis, stop stress

The problems you encounter occur as either *acute* or *chronic*. This book has been an extended argument against chronic problems. Excepting physical illness and the occasional attack from outside by a mean-spirited person (an ex-spouse, perhaps), chronic problems should be neither overlooked nor supported, and doing either will only exacerbate the inherent chaos of polyamory and lead to relational collapse far sooner than need be. (In a sane world, a term like "chronic crisis" would be instantly seen by anyone as an oxymoron. Nevertheless, that's the state that many of us Western Worlders live in, provoking crisis after crisis so that we can justify our dis-ease rather than addressing that directly.)

But I am no friend of acute problems either. For the most part these can be headed off, minimized, or controlled as long as people are willing to put forth the effort of considering unlikely situations.

Most crises do not simply drop out of thin air. There are early rumblings, vague clues that something isn't quite right. These precursors usually only become clear after the crisis is fully revealed. However, given enough attentive people, and a desire to know the cause for this disquiet, many problems can be headed off far in advance of reaching crisis proportions.

Crisis control consists of much more than just damage control. Putting out a fire is generally easy. That statement, though, assumes that the people nearest the fire comprehend that this is a significant problem, that they know how to deal with it and how to obtain the best tools for the task, and, with a demeanor that combines calm and urgency, see that the fire is extinguished. To follow those few simple steps requires some combination of training, thought experiments, real-world drills, and knowing what readily available methods could do the job.

The part that most people overlook is the post-crisis work. We're all human, and our tendency is to "let past things pass." That, though, requires that the crisis be *finished*. Burying a situation before it is fully resolved is a lot like digging out a particularly troublesome weed, only to carefully preserve the seed and plant it, out of sight and ready to pop up whenever it damned well pleases.

Though not always a fully adequate solution, a good post-crisis discussion can quickly clear the air and make "moving along" much simpler. You will need to look back and pull together all of the warning signs that went unheeded or unnoticed. You will need to catalogue how the crisis progressed and grew, who (if anyone) was asleep at the switch, and how you are going to clean up any hard feelings within your household or network. Then you must examine changes that need to be made to avert recurrence of the problem. If something causes you grief (or even simple irritation), and the same sort of thing keeps happening, then you're a fool for accepting the stress all over again at each occurrence rather than investing a little more time to straighten out the underlying causal factors.

If all you really want is an open relationship, where you have many of the social façades of a "normal" relationship but the freedom (within limits) to roam romantically and sexually, then be honest about it and receive my sincere best wishes. But if you want the right to claim polyamory, then you take on responsibility to see that your particular pod persists into the future. Learn from the past – don't ignore it, and don't live in it, but keep it fresh and alive. Whether any part of that past is good or bad or indifferent, use it as the basis from which to face the moment so that you can grow into the future.

60. Giving up your freedom

Once in a while, someone will tell me that, what with all of the communication and problem-solving going on, and the need for scheduling and confronting and negotiating, polyamory sounds like a complete resignation of individuality. This is actually funny, because sometimes the same person who presents me with such an interpretation will also express the opinion that polyamory is nothing but rule-free hedonistic anarchy, where nobody gives a damn about anyone else's feelings. Neither extreme is at all accurate.

Is it true that "polyamory" equates to "no strings attached"? My experience, I guess, is quite the opposite. Yes, there is restriction and control, and the more people we are involved with (intended to be more than short-term, anyway), the more restriction is involved. However, the restriction is *of one's self*.

Discipline.

I smoke. I have a lover who is violently allergic to cigarette effluvium. She wants to be close to me, and I to her. She doesn't give me a hard time about it, but I can spot the physical reaction, and it's not something I want to do to a sexual partner, much less to a friend. So, I don't smoke before I go to her place. If I have the time, I might also shower and change clothes.

I have another lover who is allergic to most artificial scents. I've changed my shampoo and soap and deodorant and laundry detergent, and I stopped wearing cologne. I don't even wear dry-cleaned clothing when we've got a date.

I have another lover who adores the pale ale I drink, but is pregnant. Instead of cracking a beer in front of her, we linger over ginger ale and ice cream.

In each of these cases, I am restricted, I am controlled. Who is "doing this to me"? My lovers? I'm *certainly* free to do whatever the hell I desire... which is to be with a person who happens to be a close friend, an incredible lover, and a heartmate.

I had a lover a few years ago who hit it square on the head: "So, what's the difference between this polyamory stuff and just fucking around with whoever?"

My answer: "The strings."

The heart-strings.

It isn't so much that I disagree with the "no strings attached concept" as that I'm very aware of the vast difference in meaning when the phrase is used by someone who is actively nonmonogamous and someone who thinks polyamory is reprehensible deviance. To the latter group, I'm promiscuous to the point of abusive; to the former, I'm kinda boring. (A friend says that the phrase becomes useful when recast: "No strings assumed." I like it.)

I'm a musician. It's been an important facet for more than half my life. Suppose I'm doing two shows a week, essentially a paying hobby. I hook up with a lover, all goes well, we're maybe even living together. Then, one night, she says, "I think you should stop spending so much time away from me."

Even if said playfully, my emotions will temporarily lock up, because I need to know *why* this has become significant. Perhaps she simply wants more time with me. Okay, if my schedule's so tight that those two gigs *are* my only free time, then maybe I *should* cut back. It's unlikely, though: I enjoy my "puttering" time too much to be so heavily booked. So, it probably comes down to her feeling insecure for some reason – a reasonable topic.

But if she denies that it's her insecurity, and refuses to go further than "you should stop playing gigs" because "it would be better" and so on, and refuses to accept ownership of doubts and fears... at that point, I have been a doofus and have just discovered that I've walked into a corner: I am presented with a strong indication that I'm in a relationship that is different than the one I *thought* I had.

No blaming, but there's probably some serious rework to be done, and that may require taking it completely down to the foundation, and saying goodbye. It's like having a really good relationship, then discovering one day that your partner's been a closet addict for quite some time. Even if it hadn't been notable in Really Big Ways (though it probably explains a lot of little oddnesses that had been piling up), the relationship is irreparably changed from the moment of discovery, and even going backward.

So, there *are* things you will have to give up, but that's a poor way to think of it. Short of coercion by violence or threat thereof, there's really very little that someone can do to *force* you into some course of action – you might do things reluctantly, but you do them willfully. If it's not healthy (mentally, physically, emotionally) for you to be in a particular situation, then it is your duty as a responsible adult to withdraw, or to accept the consequences of staying.

Should you have a healthy relationship, then compromise is a mundane necessity. What you are doing is trading, dropping (say) a little autonomy in order to gain a partnership that strengthens you. You have to look at healthy compromise as a mutually beneficial situation, not sacrifice. What one person calls freedom or autonomy might only reflect a mood of defensiveness, when those same qualities could be better expressed as loneliness or isolation, neither of which would be much of a sacrifice to give up.

If you would rather have a safe, secure little box containing two adults at most, then I suppose I could see where adding another person or making the box bigger might be perceived as loss, but I can't say I would want to live that sort of life. Cast in that light, I'd guess that it's just as unappealing to you. If you find yourself having these sorts of doubts, then you will be happier for careful consideration of the appropriateness of the filters you are applying to your viewpoint.

61. Scheduling: jobs and other nuisances

Real-world polyamory throws more curveballs at you than merely trying to organize your social and sexual life between multiple partners. There's the work you probably have to do to pay the rent, your hobbies and avocations, chasing the children around and keeping them from creative ways of turning your house into a scrapyard, visiting Mom and Dad, organizing holiday visits, watching television (some people would rather admit felonious activity than a nightly viewing habit), taking classes, reading trashy novels, or whatever.

Flexibility, hah!

Sooner or later, polyfolk discover the dubious joys of the scheduling *trainwreck*. You'll find yourself clutching the telephone almost nonstop for hours at a time. You want to arrange a date for some event with one particular partner, Jill. You've probably been leaving messages for days, and now really need to know whether or not you ought to buy tickets. Meanwhile, another lover who has been extraordinarily busy of late will call and want catch up. This is cut short when a friend calls with a crisis. Someone else interrupts this with an offer of going out to dinner.

And that's just the first hour after you've gotten home from work.

By the time you've sorted out various problems, touched base with a few of the people in your life, and made a promise or two to make plans *real soon*, you notice that it's almost ten o'clock. You still haven't had dinner (your friend's offer having no doubt expired), your housemate is taking the steam rising from your head as a reason to avoid impinging further on your consciousness, and you've avoided making concrete plans for the next few evenings because the portion of your brain labeled Scheduling was fully occupied in trying to work out that evening with Jill. By the time you finally give up in disgust and go to bed, Jill still hasn't called, or answered any of the messages you've left, or replied to your e-mails. Your wrist and neck hurt, you're tired, cranky, and hungry, you've blown an entire free evening, and now you're feeling lonely besides.

Make friends with your calendars

Start with some simple mechanics. Buy a calendar – in fact, buy five or six. Carry a small one with you, have a day-planner at the ready, place a few more near your various work-spaces. If you need extreme measures, go for it: my partner tore out the big leaves of a blotter-style monthly calendar and taped them to the office wall, so that she can put notes and stickers and big colorful circles all over them, and see the major details of the terrain from her desk. This has reduced her work-related stress in a small but significant fashion. We also use a floor-to-ceiling poster-type calendar.

I don't know of anyone doing this yet, but it would make perfect sense to me if some individual, couple, pod, node, or network fragment should put their calendars onto a private webpage. The less computer-literate could get a brief lesson in how to examine this page with one click of a button – while not perfectly egalitarian, it's certainly better than what most people presently can access.

(Mostly, though, I would avoid technology. PDAs are a cute idea, and I am certain that my children will find them indispensable, but I doubt they'll be of any help to my generation–every time I meet someone over age 35 who has never used the Internet, and wouldn't know where to begin searching for a "control key," I'm all the more certain that toys fancier than a pocket calculator ought to be left as a legacy to young people and the older obsessives (lawyers, consultants, doctors, car dealers). People who don't back their files up obsessively or automatically probably shouldn't be keeping critical data on pocket PCs.)

Once you have a calendar, then *use* it: consult it often, and keep it fresh.

Launch a new calendar by filling in the obvious – your job. Make sure to allow whatever preparation, travel, and "cool down" time you feel you need; some of us are not at our best as soon as we walk out of the office. If you have kids, put down the various regular commitments. Make sure that your social schedule is taken into account. If you have a favorite television show, note that – like many other items that will appear on your calendar, you may be willing to share this. If you have a regular time set aside for a particular friend, then put it in the appropriate days. Perhaps you have a lover who has every Wednesday evening free until midnight, unless work is tough that day. You could maybe fill it in, but develop some sort of color-coding to indicate that this entry leaves you with most or all of the night free about half the time. If you have a system that is easy for you to use and interpret, then use it. Don't forget to copy changes, additions, and deletions promptly across all of your calendars.

Take a few minutes every day or three, find a free moment with someone, and do some mutual updating. Remember, time is what keeps everything in the Universe from happening simultaneously – which is probably as good a description as any for what you'll encounter in polyamory.

Every time that you try to tell yourself that spontaneity is so much *easier* than mapping out plans with times and dates and all, remind yourself about the last time that spontaneity bit you on the ass. I had a lover who complained that I wasn't putting any effort into being with her. I pointed out that her schedule was set a month in advance, and that I couldn't put all my other relationships, obligations, and projects on hold in order to wait by the phone, hoping that one of her less-reliable friends would overbook yet again and cancel. I'm averse to turning down a dinner date with someone I haven't seen in a month on the small chance that I could have an evening with someone else – that doesn't strike me as much in the way of friendship.

When you make a date, honor it. Stick to your commitments, or don't make them. Avoid "maybe" dates: there are few clearer ways to tell someone that "I'll find time for you unless something *interesting* comes up." You can get away with this for group outings and public events – "We're all going to meet up at the club. Stop by if you get a little time free!"–but the more one-to-one the occasion, then the more you should be clear about your intentions, and expect the same sense of priority in return. Calling up on a whim and discovering that someone happens to be home can be turned into a spontaneous evening, but don't reduce others to social conveniences, especially if you're also protesting how important they are in your life. This claim would actually be more convincing if you didn't make any promises in the first place. If you end up as the other player in such situations, then you ought to make clear where you stand on being someone else's social convenience.

By the way, it's extremely gauche to announce at the last minute – or, worse, at the beginning of the date – that you have invited someone else along. When you (say) agree to meet up at a movie theater, I don't know whether it's more stupidly arrogant to have another lover in tow or a dozen high-spirited friends – that depends on the person, and is pretty insensitive in any case. It's only slightly less rude when you call and say that you want to do this (or have already extended the invitation), and ask if it's okay. If I've been looking forward to a bit of hand-holding strolling, whether through the mall or around the park, I have been known to make a counter-offer of either staying one-on-one or canceling the date. Larger social outings are fine, and I enjoy them, but not if I've been hoping for something resembling private time. When I show up at someone's house for a quiet evening, I have some not-unreasonable expectations of being the only guest, and that telephone calls will not be noticed unless there is good reason to think that loss of life or limb is involved. (Does any of this sound obvious? Perhaps it is, but I've seen or heard it all – please try to avoid being a stereotype.)

Scheduling is an important way of demonstrating someone's importance. Use it wisely, and with plenty of forethought.

Coordinate individualism

I imagine that this sort of suggestion has motivated some of you to begin leaping around the room screeching about the erosion of the rights of the individual. In response to such a charge, I'd have to say that this observation would be one of those "well, *duh*" moments. Since the opposite of individualism tends to almost always be community and cooperation and related concepts, then *of course* I'm recommending you get a clue. If your purpose in nonmonogamy is to get your own way and to Hell with other people, then you've walked in the wrong door, bye-bye – have fun and all that, but don't call it polyamory, or even responsible nonmonogamy because there's that tricky adjective.

The point is to maintain your individuality in such a way that everyone isn't constantly tripping over each other's priorities. That sort of slapstick will only breed a morass of hurt feelings, sadness, and resentment.

Don't forget that you have the right to your own time as well. Maybe it appears counterintuitive, but there's nothing wrong with setting aside some nonspecific time to indulge yourself. If you can happily spend a whole evening at the model railroad shop, and know from experience that this bores your partners to tears, then block it out once in a while. (My own passion is used-guitar and antiquarian book stores.) You don't even have to be that specific: there's nothing wrong (much less weird) with some entry like "2:00 - 5:00: strolling." Take it for yourself, or bring a companion if the mood and opportunity seizes you.

It helps if you enjoy puzzles. Fitting everyone's desires into a nice pattern is a pleasant reward of itself if you're so inclined. Let's say that I have two functionally primary relationships. I live with neither, and it is about as easy for me to travel to one as to the other. However I work a first-shift job, as does one of my lovers, while the other works on the second shift, though we're all on the same five-day workweek. Should we attempt to give the more-restricted dyad some sort of priority on weekends? I would say exactly that, though perhaps not every weekend, all weekend.

There is no single perfect answer, if you have more than one or two intimate friends in your life. Stuff happens, weather goes bad, in-laws appear suddenly on your doorstep. The rest of the time, though, foresightful attention to detail doesn't take much time or effort, and you'll soon enough fall to planning and structuring your schedule with hardly a thought. Coordinating calendars will take moments, not hours. You'll all be much happier, and life will be more readily enjoyed.

62. Creating & using a network

There are two major drives built into every human being: to belong, and to share. As the concept of family has been whittled away, and sense of community fragmented and disrupted, these drives have become less and less fulfilled.

Singlehood is lonely. Couplehood is less lonely, but merely transfers expectations that should be spread over an entire village and complex multigenerational familial structure onto a spouse and perhaps a few children, a burden that can become rapidly oppressive even as it cannot meet all of one's needs. By itself, a triad is really not much more sturdy than a dyad because it apes so many of the very failings of the autonomous dyad and tries to repair or upgrade them rather than replacing them entirely.

Whether or not your relationship is sexually open, you need community. Therefore, an intimate network offers empowerment for everyone involved, as well as vastly increased strength and flexibility.

Defining the network

An intimate network is a loose and somewhat amorphous construct of multiple intimate relationships. The connections are primarily of friendship and affection, which sets them apart from networks of profession. Some swing clubs are this form of intimate network, others more closely resemble a user group for a particular type of software; what differentiates them is the degree of friendship outside of the sanctioned official events.

In a context of nonmonogamous sexuality, the various nodes or pods of a network are not necessarily connected by sex, whether previous or current or potential. To look at it the other way around, having sex with someone doesn't make you part of the family. Some members of an intimate network are extremely monogamous themselves, but comfortable being around close friends who live in multiplicity – getting out of the house for pleasant socializing with interesting people is enough of a draw. In short, the connections that make a network are of friendship and kinship than of interlocking body parts.

You probably like to think that you don't categorize your friends. You're probably wrong. Either you're wrong, or you don't have very many parties. Sooner or later, you'll find yourself as one of the lucky people in charge of inviting friends to a get-together. Then you get to decide which of your two friends, mythic-level enemies over some incomprehensible grudge you are going to invite. Or two of the people dearest to you have just launched into an acrimonious divorce. When the divisive point has resulted in multiple factions, planning a pleasant dinner with more than just yourself begins to resemble logistic considerations for the landing at Normandy. (I'm lazy: I've been known to invite all sides, tell each of them I did so, then let *them* sort it out. Most were reluctant to skip the party, lest others think they were being bad sports about it, or holding others in our social circle responsible somehow. If your house is of a decent size, six people can spend the entire evening successfully avoiding each other, and you can keep the canapés flowing without a single twinge of guilty conscience, which your other guests will appreciate.)

I'm not saying that you *need* to sort your friends into boxes, just that you *do*. Our little minds are wired that way. Knowing that you are doing this allows you to both consider changing the categories around and to work at not letting the likely artificial or happenstance boundaries overly influence your actions. The good news is that things shift around, which is healthy – people and situations ought to be fluid to an extent – but you need to have some degree of skill at watching what your brain is doing.

Networks are somewhat amorphous. They change, they flow. An intimate network is a different creature from an extended group marriage. With a network, there may not be any edges at all, just a point at which you have no idea who the hell these people are except that they're somehow associated with people you know somewhat less poorly. I once sat down and mapped out our network, only to find that at that moment it contained exactly 27 people – I knew who was involved with who, all the way out to the edges. Soon enough, two divorces and a secret affair restored a workable level of chaos. When the borders begin to close down, the group begins to take on the problems of any closed marriage. Networks seem to be at their best when there are a few recurring strangers about (whether as cause or symptom I cannot properly speculate).

"Friend" is a category

Maybe we ought to take a stab at defining *friend*. Contrary to common usage, a "friend" is not "someone I happen to see at the bowling alley once in a while." That's someone who has maybe made her or his way up to being an acquaintance. There are people in my social circle who I cannot say that I like, yet the relationship is warmer than mere teeth-gritting toleration – I accept their company willingly in certain social contexts. I am known at sight by literally thousands of people, out of which I number less than a hundred as proper acquaintances and a couple dozen as friends.

My partner once asked me about my terminology. I created working definition on the spot: Friends are people who love you enough to risk your friendship by questioning your motives to your face. Actually, I think I also said something like, "A friend is someone who will try to keep you from drowning in your own bullshit." You can likely come up with a definition that is more suitable to your own persona, but you get the idea.

Making family

Be wary of referring to "the polyamorous community" – there really is no such thing. There may be discernible community-type groupings that happen to be polyamorous, but these are local (in an interpersonal sense); you could move from a circle of polyamorous friends in one city to another part of the country, and find that you feel like an outcast among the polyamorous social circle there. I've heard third-hand references to a study indicating that a community can actually contain no more than 150 people before it falls into factional struggles; this seems fundamentally to fit my own observations, though perhaps a little on the optimistic side. To think of everyone who is polyamorous as belonging to part of the same amorphous mass can only lead you into assumptions that largely don't hold air.

With that said, an intimate network is what I referred to a couple of decades ago as a *made family*. As with a good family, they are largely people who support you yet challenge you, capable of giving and receiving honest criticism that is made from deep caring. And, like any other family, this will probably lead to your association with individuals and cliques you don't really favor, but whose presence is strengthening to other people with whom you do like to associate. You interact with larger or smaller clusters for social events, you rely on each other for support and advice, and you count some of them as among your closest friends.

I'm part of a sprawling community of more-or-less poly folk. It's so out in the open that those who choose to be bothered by it can get the hint early on and opt to not socialize with us. Generally, I won't even develop an attraction to someone unless she's had plenty of opportunity to observe our interaction, and I know that her own situation wouldn't be threatened by my interest.

Sometimes, when someone is simply "not getting it," having a community around is handy. There was one time where I was at a party, enjoying a flirtation with a woman (not for the first time). After about the third time she batted her lashes at me and said coyly, "You know, if you weren't married...," I couldn't stand it any more. I called out to my wife, chatting with a bunch of people across the room, and said, "Is it okay if I go home with her tonight?" pointing to the woman in front of me. Marie shrugged, said, "Fine with me," and went back to her conversation. The woman in question hasn't spoken to me since, and I can't say as I feel like I've missed much.

When I'm interested in someone, the best route I've found is to invite her over to one of our parties. Hang out, meet my friends, listen to music, talk until the wee hours. The most reliable way I've found to broach the "poly" subject was for them to meet my primary partner or partners, and also to note that I was openly affectionate with a few other people as well. The point, after all, is not to "recruit her to the poly lifestyle," but to discover whether (a) she can believe that I'm worth the effort, and (b) that she won't run screaming from the mere thought of a nonexclusive relationship.

This chapter can serve merely as an introduction to the complexity and power of intimate networks. Someday, maybe someone will write an entire book on the subject, crammed with checklists and step-by-step plans. If you keep your eyes open for the possibilities, you might be the author.

63. Talk to each other

Recall what I said about polyamory being uncharted territory, and that you don't even have a map. It falls to us–as a subculture, as part of a social network, and as individuals – to draw that map, not only for those who arrive after us, but for those awkward moments when we end up lost with a vague certainty that we've been here before.

Write it down

Let's start with some basics. Keeping a diary is a *very* good idea. By this I mean an actual, tangible private journal, something you don't trot out on a regular basis for the whole world to see – this, therefore, excludes "Internet diaries" or *weblogs*. (Blogs are, more often than not, the worst possible combination of self-serving propaganda and audience-driven dreck. As an almost totally open public forum, screeching nutballs with no other purpose in life draw larger audiences than the thoughtful and the concise, an effect that is the nature of the medium.) Even if you merely use the blogger facilities, and keep your heartfelt ramblings locked and never to be viewed by or even repeated to another human being, the context in which you create affects your viewpoint – you're still writing a blog, and thus acting in alliance with a seemingly endless cohort of semiliterate wackos.

Keeping your diary as a locked and hidden file on your home computer would be good, but even better is to find yourself a notebook or bound journal of convenient size and shape. (Speaking as a writer, I will suggest that you might even choose a specific writing instrument for the job. I keep a bin nearby that holds anything from fountain pens to pencil stubs, to suit my mood, but you may want a special pen, or even a specific color of ink.) For our purposes here, limit yourself to thoughts about nonmonogamy – don't rail about the existential unfairness of your grocery's lettuce prices unless you can tie your thoughts directly to your poly experience.

If you go into polyamory as a couple, or have formed a larger group, it is an excellent idea to write down the problems that you encounter together, as close to "real time" as you can, including individual takes on the situation, a few comments on what you've determined to be the key difficulties, how you proposed to go about remedying them, and the degree of success you achieve.

Should you keep such logs, eventually get around to editing them down for general consumption, then share them with other polyamorous people. If you thereafter decide to add someone to your group, household, or network, letting them read these logs is not only a fast way of getting them up to speed on the territory you've covered, but provides a unique bonding experience.

Everyone talks to (and about) everyone

One of the rules I have insisted on in my own life is that my partners be able to speak with my partners – and do they ever. If I was neglecting a lover, it wasn't unusual for her to take it to my wife and ask for advice. (Usually, Marie simply came to me and said, "Hey, bozo....") Once or twice, I have handed a new lover a list of telephone numbers and e-mail addresses to make it clear that there were plenty of avenues by which to address doubts or concerns.

If you're not in a closed relationship, you don't have to *like* everyone, but you have to be able to talk to them, and I mean more than emotionally reserved pleasantries. A common myth in open relating is expressed something like, "My relationship with one person doesn't affect my other relationships." What a common load of crap: everything affects everything else, period. It's an ecology, and *cannot* exist as a bunch of nicely organized little boxes. If you have two lovers, it doesn't matter whether you're all living together and having sex in a tight trine, or you're maintaining them both as LDRs. When things are going very well with one lover, your optimism and enthusiasm spills over and benefits the other relationship, unless you've still got some of that "perfect relationship" tendency hanging around, in which case the positives of one dyad lead you to blow the lacks of the other out of proportion. When one dyad encounters a rough patch, you can maybe manage to keep this from making you pick nits about the other, but the fact is that your other lover is a suitably placed friend to offer advice, and it'd be foolish for you to avoid their counsel, but that also means that the two relationships are not entirely separate. At the very least, you are a common factor, and there's no way around that fact.

There's a lot of talk in polyamory about trust, but too little example to back it up. What trust does exist is usually misplaced as mere ungrounded hope: many couples will place more trust in a stranger being courted for their triad than either does in their partner.

Sure, we all need to learn a few lessons about making statements in a form that take personal responsibility. I'm still imperfect at remembering that "I feel..." statements are far superior to the "You're making me feel..." version. If my skills need work, yours likely do too.

In order to bring these statements and their underlying modes of thought more fully into our lives, we have to have practice. That means bringing them to bear on suitable situations.

However, the suitable situations are taboo. Say something like, "I'm feeling a little neglected because of all the time you're spending with her," and the whole conversation can rapidly devolve into defensiveness: you don't really trust me, you just don't like her, you're being jealous, and so on, all of these beginning from the premise, "You don't really feel that way," with underlying judgements of "You don't really know what you feel" (or "I know what you feel better than you do") and "If you can't trust me absolutely then maybe I shouldn't trust you at all."

When doubts are expressed, the more advanced game-players will say something like, "If you're having a problem with her, then that's something that you have to talk to *her* about." This neat, utter denial of responsibility also allows the utterer to become angry if such a conversation should actually take place, as it's "talking behind my back" or "cutting me out of the loop." The third party can become angry and defensive in her turn, for being "attacked" and for not including the other player.

As a matter of fact, I've watched people who take advantage of this inherent dissonance, playing one rule against the other at their convenience, alternating between "I don't want to know" or "I don't need to know everything" and "You didn't tell me everything." This gives them great leeway to shrug off someone else's concerns with an added air of moral and intellectual superiority.

From the very beginning – preferably before your relationship grows to include others, and ideally as an expectation you have as an individual previously – you need to demand total communication between and about people. Everyone has to feel free to speak their mind and express feelings. With that right, of course, goes the conjoined responsibility to speak as even-handedly as possible, minimizing attacks and the irrational "just blowing off steam" or "venting" that is so attractive to some.

Generally, you don't need to like your lover's lover – but you'd better be able to talk to them. One way to do this is to start your polyamorous life with the ground rule that there will be an hours-long family meeting every month or two. These get-togethers hardly have to be grim affairs, and can be a house party, an outing at the park, or a pot-luck dinner. Casual dating partners and friends can be exempt from attending, but anyone who is granted high priority by a core member, or appears to expect such priority, must attend for a mutual airing of grievances. Before you ask, I don't recommend any explicit penalties for non-attendance, but everyone who does show up is thereby made aware that perhaps that person isn't very serious about being part of the family.

I think it's vital that new dating partners, especially those expressing an interest in becoming a primary partner or joining the household, attend these meetings immediately, for multiple reasons:

- the new person gets an idea of the nature of the group, especially that people are serious about their interrelationships and committed to maintaining them.

- everyone can attach a face to the name.

- avenues for communication might not be expressed explicitly, but they are not implicitly closed off.

- if there is a basis for a personality conflict, this is discovered early.

- concerns and grievances can be aired while they are still easily corrected.

If this familial grouping is part of a multi-household intimate network, each central group ought to have its own cycle of meetings, since there will be peripheral members of one node that are not otherwise affiliated with another. Besides, more opportunities for socializing benefits everyone, right down to the dyad and individual. The variety of approaches is enriching to all; the concept of family is expanded further, alliances are formed, and the widespread sense of isolation felt by many nonmonogamous people is weakened.

Discuss the difficult

For all the repetition about communicating, you'll probably find it difficult to actually talk about sensitive areas. In fact, you'll probably talk your way around them. Talk and communication are not the same thing, and endlessly discussing the same harmless stuff can be very useful in avoidance of certain topics. Some groups process endlessly rather than running the risk of forward movement.

I came up with yet another analogy to consider this. Let's say that you all share a piece of property, a nice rolling meadow with tall grass and a few trees Wyeth would have adored. You all enjoy this meadow, and you'd like to share it with other people who are important to you, except that there's a problem. There's a hole, about a foot across, and apparently running down to an underground rivulet, because it seems to be at least a few feet deep.

Due to some trick of the land, people who walk around the meadow regularly stumble into the hole. Over the years, there have been many sprained ankles, and even a broken leg. One evening at dinner, you say that you're going to go out the next day, put a sturdy piece of plywood over the hole, and cover it over with plenty of soil. The grasses will fill in, and everyone can enjoy the meadow more safely.

To your surprise, your partners seem very uncomfortable with the topic. They discourage your line of thinking:

"Well, it doesn't take up much space, really."

"It's not like people step into it very often."

"People just ought to pay more attention."

"Sure, there are a few injuries, but they aren't usually very bad."

You persist, asking why everyone is so bothered by this – after all, you're volunteering to do all the work. One of your partners gets hostile: "Why can't you leave this alone!" He acts as though you've accused him of putting the hole there himself in order to hurt people.

Every relationship has at least one hole of its own. Even though fixing it might be relatively simple, people are made so uncomfortable by its presence that they want to ignore it rather than deal with it. Some will even go so far as to ignore the problem's entire existence, wiping the history from the common consciousness.

1. Someone has to admit that the hole is there.
2. Someone has to say that the hole is a problem.
3. The hole must be located and marked off to reduce incidents.
4. The hole must be filled in.

In a perfect world, none of these would be a big step, and would probably happen so spontaneously and automatically that making a such a list would be absurd. Here and now, each stage requires focus, drive, guts, and determination, a trust that this is the right thing to do.

You can't get anywhere unless you start out by having both the ability and the willingness to talk – and I mean talk freely and constantly and spontaneously and with great emotion and no fear of being made to look or feel stupid. Other forms of communication are just dandy, but each has a limited dictionary (albeit with each entry capable of amazing depth and subtlety).

Some processes

Communication is overrated, and the "poly mantra" mostly adds another layer of thick paint to the woodwork, obscuring the richness of detail inherent in the naked surface. Sure, people ought to learn how to really have depth in interpersonal communication, and stop raising mere mouth-noise to some sacramental level. At the same time, I hope that you will do more than your share to ensure that the rich art of conversation does not die under all the weight that sometimes seems to be piled upon it by us polyfolk.

Entire volumes have been written about conversation, and a few more could stand to appear that addressed the subject in the context of complex relating. Presently inadequate to a subject of such wonderful possibility, I will leave that for others. In such a context, however, a few thoughts that you might find to be useful.

In general, watch yourself for phrases that flit into your head telling you to make a good impression. If the person is someone important to you, then why censor yourself? If they're of little or no importance, then are you doing entirely too much work for no purpose? If you are overly concerned with how things will look to intimate others, then not only do you need to examine very critically the impaired communication in your relationship, but you're in danger of letting someone walk all over you in all innocence when they are of the impression that you're both communicating honestly and fully.

Conversely, spend a little time listening to the words you say. Be curious about why you presented something in a particular manner, and wonder at the effect a different approach might have had. Play back conversations in your head, and allow yourself to wonder at the dynamic. This isn't something that ought to be done constantly or even regularly, but it's an excellent aid over the long term in understanding yourself and others and how you interact.

Challenge is one thing, and can be quite good; cornering someone is not good. When you talk to your loved ones, avoid letting things slide into the common corner where the choice offered is to agree or to shut up. We long ago labeled these *conversation killers* for a reason. This is hardly an abstract concept, especially among the nonmonogamous. For example, we worked to avoid statements like "you can't be intimate with that person" – though it probably would stem from an entirely valid personal concern, it comes across as a veiled threat, an ultimatum that short-circuits the dynamic and practically begs for a retaliatory attack. On the other hand, we *were* free and encouraged to say, "here's why I'm getting a bad feeling from so-and-so" or "right now, I'm not doing so well, could you focus with me instead?" Meaning, I suppose, that we created a rule of safe communication of risky feelings. Discussion could actually proceed, perhaps including some sort of negotiation.

Above all, a good conversation is one that leaves you both stimulated and a little tired, with something like a sense of accomplishment, the sort of feeling you would expect from a brisk walk or a short workout. Recognize this feeling when it happens, and see what you can do to help it recur.

64. Sex vs. communication

Check out these statements:

"We are having sex, therefore we are communicating."

"We are having sex, therefore we are not communicating."

"We are not having sex, therefore we are communicating."

"We are not having sex, therefore we are not communicating."

Any of those statements has potential for being true at a particular moment, but overall they are all four fallacious.

Communication, as we all use the term, actually means parallel multichannel interchanging of information. That is, we do not merely communicate: we communicate in many different ways simultaneously. Many times, the channels do not all point in the same direction. You can say "I love you," and perform many of the outward rituals (making dinner, sending flowers, always remembering anniversaries), yet act neglectfully in other ways or otherwise drop broad hints of dissatisfaction, revenge, and so on.

I was once talking with a former lover, who had decided to return to monogamy. I said, "So, how's married life been treating you?" "Oh, it's wonderful," she said, "we've been very happy together." Her tone of voice told me this was absolutely true. But there was a pregnant pause, and she added, in a chilly, angry tone I'd never heard before, "Except for our sex life."

When they came to visit two months later, they appeared an ideal couple, relaxed and affectionate. I'd never met him before, and found that he seemed to be a very nice guy, not trying to impress me or prove that he was superior to me for having married my girlfriend. One evening, the hour was getting on quite late, and he excused himself to go off and get some sleep. She looked up at him and said, "Why don't you do that then, *dear*?" The emphasis on that last word actually chilled me, a flash of bitter anger I'd never heard from her; if it had been directed at me, I probably would've started sleeping alone and locking the door for good measure. (I still have no idea what was going on. She has never volunteered the details, and I didn't ask as I'm not sure I want to know – there is already too much about monogamy that still utterly puzzles me.)

My point is that communication is hardly a simple little chain of events, rather a whole literal bunch of streams that may be mutually contradictory. Sex is another channel for this complex interaction, nothing less and nothing more. For two human beings to communicate, all channels have to be available as much as possible, and regularly, and point in approximately the same direction.

Look again at those four hypothetical statements. The middle two will regularly appear tied to such clichés as, "If we got involved, we couldn't be friends anymore." The first is the common fallacy of a "good" relationship; the fourth, of the "failing" relationship.

None of them is, in any minutely reliable sense, true. However, each of them can take on a great deal of mass if someone insists on treating them as if true. If more than one person is in the game, such a belief can begin to take on the weight of Truth. Such is the power of groupthink and society.

I have long maintained that sexual intimacy presents an opportunity for deep interpersonal communication. I have no reason to change my mind about that. But that statement of belief is also quite glib, in a manner you may not even comprehend. Therefore, I need to clarify.

An *opportunity* for communication has little to do with proving that communication has taken place. Think of a telephone. You have one, your partner has one. Does that mean you are communicating? One of you calls while the other is out shopping; is that communication? Does leaving a message on the answering machine suffice? How intimate or relationship-specific does a message have to be to count as communication? In some ways, any passing of unexpected data is communication, but the word is supposedly used to mean much more than that.

Sex *is* a form of communication. It is also, of itself, overwhelming. Unless you are suffering from the effects of some sort of emotional trauma, and can remain coolly detached from what your body is experiencing, sex can easily be the equivalent of shouting into a microphone and producing nothing but ill-defined noise. This is not communication, any more than random static is a television program just because it's on your screen.

For the moment, let's separate sex from all other communication modes. There are a few ways that these two categories (sex vs. everything else) can interact:

- sex is a catalyst for communication, an enhancer, a multiplier or exponentiator
- sex adds to communication, contributing to the range of expressible feelings, like learning a little of another language
- sex is an alternate form of communication, but prone to misinterpretation
- sex is a substitute for communication, a means of avoiding interpersonal contact

I created those four theses in a completely different context quite some time apart from the four that began this chapter, and am presently surprised to see their similarities, but it makes perfect sense. Sex can expand upon, or extend, or continue, or subvert, or eliminate communication. Being a complex portion of a complex system, sex can be acting on various levels at the same time and in different ways.

We run into big problems when we assume that all sexual interaction, because of its vast *possibilities*, is inherently exponentiation, with a little fallout here and there. This overly sunny estimate is mislabeled as trust, or as love. In my experience and observation, though, sexual interaction more commonly fits into the latter part of the list, and few people regularly experience a catalytic enhancement to their sex lives.

While I would gladly agree that sex inherently brings two souls closer together, there's a problem with that assessment: It just ain't so. Sex stems from selfish motivations and animal drives. Various intellectual justifications can be pasted over those causal roots, but the fact remains. Once that is both acknowledged and recognized by the individuals involved, then things like communication and bonding *can* happen – but until that mutual understanding is reached, the more complex interactions are very, very unlikely. It is far easier for sex to be a method for blocking or undermining communication than for enhancing it. For sex to add to communication at all, there must be an underlying level of communication – sex cannot be the foundation.

65. Having a social life out of bed

There comes a point in a new relationship where the NRE starts to fall off. Oh, probably just the tiniest little bit, but when you've been on a peak plateau for so long – weeks, even months – the smallest decline can be very unnerving.

Polyamory is centered largely around dealing with freer sexual expression. That's an inescapable fact. Secondarily, it deals with deep interpersonal connection in intellectual and emotional manners. The primacy of sex can be decried if that's what you want, but it has to be accepted and dealt with, not merely stuffed into a box and ignored as if that's going to do anyone (like you) any good.

Western culture has a strong undercurrent of repression of the erotic. When two otherwise sane adults get together, they begin posturing about sex and dominance and status. The dynamic is intense but shallow, and short-lived in any given dyad, as is the case with NRE.

Altruistic rationalizations aside, most people are drawn to explore responsible nonmonogamy by the sex, whether to explore a greater variety or to obtain an advance in quality, quantity, or frequency. This is a logical response to the suppression of erotic expression that you've probably experienced for most of your life.

Aesthetic pacing

I hate to sound like I'm advocating that you ration your sexual opportunities. I suppose that's *exactly* what I'm saying, but that kind of self-willed pacing has gotten an unduly bad rap in our instant-gratification society. I've seen many polyamorous people whose intimate lifestyle is closer to poorly structured swinging than to (protestations aside) a conscious attempt to form deep, long-lasting connections to other people. They leap at every opportunity, experience the overwhelming rush of sexual exploration with a functional stranger, then go away from the experience feeling that they've missed something, and so repeat the error endlessly.

My own life experience is from the aesthetics of poverty. I never knew that my family was, by most measures, poor. We always had plenty of food on the table, the bills managed to get paid, and gifts abounded. I learned to spot a bargain, and to repair any number of items that others had discarded mostly out of inconvenience, such as lamps and televisions alike that ended up in the trash because of a broken cord.

Wherever I go, I seek out thrift shops and garage sales. People are clearing out some of the clutter from their lives, and taking a small fee to allow other folks to keep their trash bins from overflowing. I've always had a difficult time at passing up a grocery bag of beat-up paperbacks for half a buck, even if I don't know what they are or, on examination, don't recognize half the titles. Now, thanks to the Internet, I've discovered that my childlike joy at finding a cache of such cheap books, combined with a good sense of their potential value to others, has led to a nice steady profit. You could do the same thing but, unless you've got that same sort of sense, you'd probably not do half so well in the electronic marketplace.

Because of that upbringing, I have a deep respect for the value of small things, one variation of which is usually called presentation. Again, I was surprised to find that this has value in business. An excellent product can fail miserably because of poor packaging or flawed marketing – an ad campaign can more easily kill a company than make it wealthy. Conversely, second-rate crap, marketed imaginatively, can become a market force and push out far-superior products; a skilled marketer understands that it is the image that is being traded for dollars.

Just think of what image and imagination can do for a truly superior product.

I also understand the value of timing and patience. Every time that, for instance, a new vampire movie or television series makes it big, every half-assed beginning author in the world is writing vampire fiction, glutting the market and driving down the chances that any given submission will ever see the light of day (sorry; I couldn't resist). When the "Harry Potter" series became a big-ticket item, suddenly thousands of hopeful dreamers began cranking out their own pastiches. Some of them are probably decent bits of writing, but such qualities are entirely overshadowed by the realities of the market, not to mention some very well-paid corporate lawyers. In a decade, when the furore has evaporated, these novels might be sellable on their own merits, but not a moment before. Some authors have a touch for selling a book for an underserved market, and for riding the crest when a vaguely similar movie becomes hugely popular. Following a trend usually means you've already been left behind before you even get out of your recliner.

Defeated by fun

Leaving aside pointless moralizing, there's really nothing wrong with sex for the sake of sex. Where we get into a bind is in assuming that casual sex is any more significant than... well, than casual sex. At a deep human level, such encounters are more enervating (look it up) than what we normally think of as exciting. Sex can be stimulating as in giving a sense of accomplishment and satisfaction, and sex can be stimulating as in overdosing on amphetamines or narrowly avoiding a high-speed automobile collision.

As well, we are taught to put *fun* and *serious* pursuits on a continuum as opposed extremes, when this dichotomy is entirely false, made even worse when we act as though we can instantly exchange one for the other. (You could spend the same amount of cash on either a Ferrari or a Hummer, yet that is probably the only point of similarity (other than their fuel consumption), and not even a child would confuse the two.) Exerting yourself at a task that is serious and rewarding can still be quite fun, but doing something fun because you have a neurotic need to pack your life full of fun is pretty much a guarantee that any long-term benefits you derive will be entirely happenstance.

Fun is possibly one of the important fuels to a rich human nature. The problem is, Western society has a persistent tendency toward addiction to instant gratification. A case of fine Scotch will be treated very differently if given to a connoisseur than to a deeply disturbed alcoholic, yet it's the same chemical solution, and the two recipients are remarkably similar organisms. The difference is between short-term and long-term gratification, between wringing every little drop of narcotic experience out of the moment and pacing the enjoyment out in order to appreciate the potential enjoyment for as long as possible.

With this reflex of nowness that infects our culture, fun pushes out the possibility of other words: pleasure, joy, satisfaction. You can have *fun* within an established relationship, or instead of one – fun, though, will more than likely short-circuit the actual creation and development of relationship. Merely assuming that "fun" is perfectly interchangeable with those other words, which at least imply a sort of depth and continuity, doesn't do anything to make that interchangeability a reality, and is actually very handy for glossing over the more common opposite. Fun is thrill, and a thrill is something that passes over you, and is gone. You can stimulate it again and again, but its novelty pales each time, so you have to seek out a new batch of novelty. Real joy and satisfaction and pleasure are much longer lived, and self-sustaining when you're in the right mental and emotional state, carrying some ability to recreate themselves, where fun is of the moment, and is gone forever when that moment passes.

So, yes: I advocate that you ration your sexual expression. A better term for this is *delayed gratification*, avoiding activities that are thrillingly superficial, if you are at all serious about building a future with the excitement-causing people in your life.

Build with patience

The erotic side of life is certainly a good thing, but you need to have more of a range developed before the thrill begins to settle, otherwise it's by then probably too late to hold onto anything like an ongoing relationship. NRE is thrill, and perhaps ought to be enjoyed for what it is, with a simple-enough caveat: don't assume that it's going to continue, and don't pretend that it's significant of anything more than itself. The experience will wear off after a certain amount of interaction.

Polyamory, whether as philosophy or practice, demands depth and continuity. The beginning can be fun and games, but that must be relegated to being a minor part of an honest *beginning*. Once this game-playing phase passes, there had better be a *next* phase, or it's not polyamory.

That means patience, or pacing, or delayed gratification, or whatever you want to label it. Give it a term that sneers or glows, I don't care, but the inescapable fact is that if you don't develop a relationship that could withstand a gap in your sexual interaction, then it will fall apart easily (and probably messily) when some similar stumbling block appears. Just filling time between sexual encounters is doing nothing to build relationship; staring dreamily into each other's eyes is (to swipe a term from Zen) mindless, as opposed to mindful.

Mindful: that is probably as good a word as any for the goal I am advocating. Living in the mindless moment is anti-community, a thrill that has multiple participants but is not truly shared, much like a crowd of people watching a movie, each in their own little world despite the common stimulus.

You ought to be striving with your supposed intimates for mutuality, not merely settling for commonality of stimuli. Sexual compatibility is a good thing, and can potentially result in a happy long-term interaction by itself. But without further, much more complicated connection, that sort of relationship is exceedingly fragile. It can be easily replaced by someone else with a little more to offer, if only the novelty afforded by a new sexual partner.

There is much more to making love than sex. Be good in bed... but put far more effort into being a good lover non-erotically and you're on the path to building an actual relationship.

66. Creating a household: living together as a method of suicide

Don't get me wrong–I'm a huge proponent of householding, and hope someday to again pack fourteen adults into a sprawling Victorian. However, like any other complex intimate relationship, it's hardly as simple as signing the mortgage papers and deciding who gets which room. There are many missteps that, if taken, will result in the place becoming nothing more than a rooming house filled with hostile boarders. At best.

Long odds

I noted many years ago that one of the surest ways to kill an intimate relationship that is happy, loving, and rewarding is to have them move in together. No grand theory behind this, just observation.

Even with something as simple as a monogamous dyad, the pitfalls are many, and potentially devastating. Most times, one person moves into the other's domicile. Very few people are skilled at sharing, and those abilities are even less impressive when you are being expected to share something that, up to that point, has been entirely under your whimsical control. You've settled into your routines. You either like having the furniture where it is (and has been for years) or being able to move things around at whim. When you can't sleep, you like to turn on all the lights and watch bad "reality" television. Unless you're expecting company, you stack your dirty laundry next to the front door. You have plenty of bookshelf space, but prefer to make orderly stacks of books in the middle of the floor until you get around to filing them. Your clean dishes sit in the dishwasher for a week, until you either need to make room for another load or you run out of forks. You set the timer on the stereo so that lively Caribbean music is playing when you walk in at night. Maybe you even indulge in the ultimate sin of squeezing your toothpaste tube in the middle.

Okay, they're all silly. They're also all very real, and I wouldn't be surprised to find that each has killed a few thousand otherwise happy marriages. That is to say, if you say "silly" and brush something off without paying attention, it may well come back to bite you. Hard.

Then you start living with your sexual partner. Even if you don't remember the horde of tiny tribulations, you've worked out hundreds of them if you're still sharing space after a year. Your buddy puts up with the occasional used plate on top of the television, but draws the line somewhere before the herds of escaped socks (clean or not) roaming the bedroom; meanwhile, as long as the doors are properly locked before bedtime, you can put up with crumpled towels wedged into corners of the bathroom floor. The two of you have a nice give-and-take rhythm going.

Whoever was there first will probably at some point defend as a right these habits "because it's my house," which is not likely to be accepted amicably at face value. You might as well say, "If you don't like it, you can always leave." Contrast this thinking pattern with such romantic sentiments as, "There is nothing that I would not do for you." Except perhaps occasionally scrubbing the toilet until the porcelain makes a reappearance.

Throw another person into your happy little snakepit, and you're asking for trouble. Especially if she (or he, for that matter) sees you as a perfect pair who make Teflon appear sticky. Even if they can overlook your idiosyncrasies, guess what – you have to discover *theirs*. Each little infraction will appear a challenge to your satisfaction, and even to your self-image as individuals and as a couple.

Think for a moment what it must be like when a couple with children moves in with a couple with children. Factor pets into that; even if both families truly "love animals," what happens when one faction has two dogs and the other two cats? (This is, in my observation, a huge mistake anyway. Cat-oriented people are inherently different from dog-oriented people, having even a different worldview. I like living with a dog, maybe two, but I think nothing of living with a half-dozen or more well-behaved cats. Someone with a neurotic Pekinese is fundamentally different from me, and any chance of romance is probably doomed.)

Step up to the plate(s)

With the right people, the "looking for boundaries" part can actually be quite fun, and a great bonding experience. Living together, even if you're not sexually involved, offers lessons and skills that apply directly to sexual intimacy and therefore polyamory, and the reverse is true as well.

When I first had a household with three and four roommates (the situation varied), they seemed to believe I was the guy in charge. Rather than get in the middle of a potentially ugly fight, or becoming the patriarch, I used it as a way to help them learn to think. When two of them came to me yet again, proposing an Official Rule that would settle some complaint about a third, they had even written it up for me. So, I read it, nodding, and told them it seemed well-thought, with penalties and everything, and that I would agree to it... but "you do know that it will apply to *all* of us."

They looked baffled. I told them it was a *good* rule, if strict, but house rules apply to everyone, because that's what defines a household. So, if any of *us* started slacking off in the same way that drove them batty when *she* did it....

They looked disappointed, took the paper back, and never mentioned it again. They did, however, start actively working with the "troublemaker" to hash out their differences.

With that little roadblock removed, our household situation was of course lightened a little, but the increased level of communication went much farther. Rather than burying some little complaint and allowing it to fester into outright resentment, addressing stumbles became a bit more like second nature for all of us.

We were less afraid to bring stuff up, we were less fearful and defensive when a complaint was addressed to us, and compromise could be reached in minutes rather than hours.

Communication is communication, no matter how you slice it. Likewise, problem-solving skills are rarely limited to some tiny area of your life. If you figure out a new way of straightening things out with your housemates, you'll probably find that things improve with your sexual partners and your co-workers as well – who knows, you might even find yourself getting along better with your blood kin.

A few hints toward householding

All right, so you're going to go ahead and try it anyway. Though walking you through this ought to be another book entirely, let's look at a consideration or two that will point you in the right direction.

Let's start out by defining "poly households" as those where all resident adults (who aren't offspring of members) are polyamorous. I would estimate that more than three-fourths of these households contain two adults. Perhaps a bit more than half the remainder have one poly adult. Only a few percent actually have three adult partners, and those with four or more are even fewer. There's probably a reason for this minority, and I can assume that it has to do with the sheer weight of complexity.

The best poly householding arrangement I've yet encountered was where a big chunk of an intimate network had rented the two-bedroom apartments in a four-plex. The landlord had been suitably impressed with one couple as being better than her previous renters, so when they recommended their friends as potential tenants, she gladly put them at the front of the line. They are presently looking at the possibility of setting up a formal partnership to offer their landlord a years-long lease (with discounted rent), with an eye toward buying the building outright. They are all living together under one roof, but have much more flexibility for the vagaries of their individual lifestyles without crowding their "roommates," an option that couldn't exist in a single-family house smaller than a mansion.

Similarly, two side-by-side houses allow you to pack more adults into a single definable chunk of property without asking for zoning problems. One house can be a "quiet space," or primarily for the kids, or whatever. And you then have two yards, so that one can hold the gardens while the other has the hot tub and other more recreational uses.

But don't limit yourself so easily. Why, for instance, do you need all that much togetherness? I spent almost three years working at a very good job, but it was 26 miles away from the house I loved, via a chunk of freeway I affectionately dubbed "The Corridor of Death" since, even in the best conditions, I would be stuck in traffic about once every two weeks, sometimes with an hour-long delay, as we crawled past yet another major collision. I sometimes worked twelve-hour days and six-day weeks, and couldn't look forward to this sort of time-wasting aggravation either at the beginning or the end of the day. When winter rolled around again, I seriously considered renting a small apartment within walking distance, estimating that it would save me between one and four hours of travel every day I used it – as well as all that meditation upon imminent mortality due to icy roads and twenty-foot visibility.

Your network could have, say, two houses an hour apart, one near a lake and one near a ski area. Or, a condo close to an area where most of you work, and a house in a nice neighborhood with a huge yard. We once looked into the possibility of renting a comfortably run-down farmhouse in a semi-rural area with good schools while maintaining the house in the city for us working stiffs.

While you take time to consider such possibilities, do some searching for two books that I cannot possibly improve upon, *Housemates* by Lorre Sintetos, and *Shared Houses, Shared Lives* by Eric Raimy. In all my bookstore browsing, I've seen exactly one copy of the former and two of the latter, and they're long out of print, but consider them textbooks and pay thirty or forty bucks on Amazon if they appear. The focus of *Housemates* is more toward the search for a suitable roommate (or being such a person yourself), and *Shared Houses* turns your attention toward the philosophical and problem-solving underpinnings. You could also dig up a newer book, *The Share-House Survival Guide*, by Liz Poole and Amanda McKenzie, which has the advantages of being substantially newer and hilariously blunt. The writing is specific to Australia, but the tales they tell are universal.

Here's a hard question for you. Think about one of your partners, and ask yourself, "If I wasn't having sex with this person, would I live with them even on a substantial bet?" Answering in the negative is not a deal-breaker, but you really do need to be conscious of any such reservations before you go into it. If you presently have (or are considering) multiple partners, ask this question about each of them. It probably couldn't hurt to consider it for all your other potential housemates as well. If you're especially blessed (as I have occasionally been), you're involved with someone who is truly your best friend for life, and you'd both move mountains to live together even though you never have been nor ever will be lovers.

(This is an example of why I rankle at the limitations imposed by language upon our thinking processes. There is far more to "love" and "partnership" than sex. While we all hope for a handful of people who can *each* be a best friend **and** a housemate **and** a partner **and** a lover **and** a co-parent, finding someone in this world with whom we can manage three of these is pretty good, and four is a minor miracle. Don't think of this as "settling for good enough" if you should be so fortunate – why spend a lonely and likely half-assed life waiting for god-like perfection if you could belong to a household of mere saints?)

67. The infamous dishwashing schedule

Here's something unusual: funny, eminently logical, and entirely true.

I was living in a quad household. My wife, Marie, and I had moved in her girlfriend, Tara, and my girlfriend, Grace. A few months later, we packed everyone up and moved to a decent-sized three-bedroom duplex. Shortly after finally getting the place painted and beginning to settle our belongings, I became sexually involved with Tara.

One Friday evening, finished with work and looking forward to getting a little writing done, I was whistling a happy tune as I stepped up on the porch.

The previous month, Grace had confronted me. Because of all the hassles of moving, I'd been spending my free time on the new house, then collapsing unromantically into bed with Marie. Grace pointed out (pointedly, I might add) that she and I had not even slept together for two weeks, and she was getting a little worried. As the number of truly free evenings any of us had had was minimal, a little conversation settled the matter to everyone's satisfaction.

But when Tara and I became lovers, things became complicated. I was working on my degree again, and holding down an evening job that regularly kept me out after midnight. Tara's new job started at a point midway between insanely late and insanely early, as in three in the morning. The four of us agreed that lining up our schedules was going to be a challenge, and we took some time to think it over.

When I walked in the door that fateful evening, my partners were seated around the kitchen table. They all smiled triumphantly up at me, and Marie said brightly, "We worked out a schedule!"

We'd been keeping up with Kerista's publications. In one article, they'd talked about how difficult it was to get some points across to people who apparently wanted to join the commune, but didn't seem to be grasping certain key points, and they gave a wonderful example. Kerista scheduled their sleeping arrangements on a strict rotation, one boy and one girl per bed (with, of course, an occasional "alone night" when the gender membership wasn't equal). To drive the point home, they drew out two circles, one with numbers around the edge, and a smaller one with the same number of letters, then put them together with a brad through the center. We'd though it interesting, but not a match for our needs as we also had, among other things, disparate schedules, other relationships, and persistent bisexuality to contend with.

Somehow, I knew instantly, these three surprising women had hammered out modifications that had not even occurred to the Keristan elect. I briefly considered running for cover, as I suddenly had an idea how Chicago felt when Al Capone divided it into territories. This passed after a moment, and I was very proud to have partners who could work out such an elegant solution to a complex and emotionally touchy set of problems.

Marie enjoyed sharing a bed with me as often as possible, while Tara felt that something on the order of a night or two every week suited her best, with Grace falling between these frequencies. The schedule itself was also agreed to be strictly an assignments of priority for the evenings and for bedmates – as some of you are probably a little curious, I will say that we still had many nights where nothing went on other than sleeping. This also left Marie and Tara with clear evenings they could spend together.

In the long run, this meant that no situation was particularly "better" for me, since I was more or less equally affected by each of my partners' schedules, and they by mine. For instance, my wife had about half the week's mornings where she could rummage freely about in the bedroom before work without disturbing me, and my own required late nights affected each of my partners in direct proportion to the frequency we were together. If I happened to be home at a decent hour, and my partner of the night was off to a class or workshop, I might be seduced by one of the others, as long as I shifted beds as appropriate. If I had an evening to myself, then I was free to dawdle on the way home from work, but any other changes had to be agreed to by my bed-partner, else I made every effort to be prompt once my obligations elsewhere were finished.

As an added bit of flexibility, we were all free to "trade" days to compensate for shifts in our personal schedules, as long as everyone was informed and notations were made to the calendar. If, say, Tara wanted to go out dancing with friends on one of "our" nights, but attend a concert with me when Grace's initial was on the schedule, then she broached the relevant offers. As far as my own schedule, I liked to have occasional time to write until sunrise, and I would make arrangements for a place to sleep when I was finally exhausted. I might go to a social event with two or three of my partners, but whoever was on the calendar had me for the night, before and after.

In order to ensure that everyone was kept informed, we posted the schedule on the refrigerator, right below the shopping list and the store coupons.

One day when I was out, Tara's mother was visiting. Being of an analytic mind, she saw this grid of letters, and asked her daughter what it was.

There was a rapid panic-stricken look exchanged between my partners, and Marie recovered first. "Oh, that's the dishwashing schedule," she said.

Mom accepted this. Well, until the next visit anyway, when she asked, "Why don't I see Tony's name on this schedule?" Some excuse was offered to the effect that I hated doing the dishes – which, considering the actual underlying concept, resulted in hastily stifled guffaws from my partners. The subject was successfully changed, and the topic never arose again.

The name, however, stuck. There were regular references thereafter to the dishwashing schedule that undoubtedly confused casual listeners who couldn't apprehend why washing the dishes appeared to have such a large bearing on our social lives.

When you start piling up this level of complexity in your own life, such scheduling becomes very important. Many misunderstandings and conflicts are straightened out before they have a chance to happen. Plus, it forces a greater degree of communication to draw the schedule up for each month, which improves even more as modification and negotiation ensue.

Just as my partners took Kerista's ideas and expanded them to fit our particular circumstances, you will have to determine your needs, your own goals, and a methodology for giving everyone both as much flexibility and input as possible. If one or more of you, though, is prone to guessing at what someone else "really wants," rather than negotiating their own desires into the available resources, you will run directly into problems, either when making up the schedule or as soon as you begin following it – but that is a basic problem that will affect you more globally, and needs to be addressed in any case.

68. Be nice to you

When you're running around taking care of your corner of the world and all the people in it, you sometimes lose track of the most important one.

Yourself.

Since I want as many sincere yourselves as possible to succeed at their explorations of responsible nonmonogamy, I'm going to briefly put in a good word to you about you.

Polyamory is a high-stress lifestyle, at least at the beginning. Perhaps a better way to put it, though, is that the stresses are regularly quite different from those encountered in any of the various shades and degrees of monogamy. This foreignness makes polyamory seem like a far more scary place than it actually is.

Nevertheless, you need to take breaks from it.

Big & small

I've collected many stories over the years of households and communes and closed relationships. Somewhat paradoxically, the problem with all of these forms is that they can work very, very well on a day-to-day basis. The group is resistant to many of the jolts from daily life that would rattle a monogamous couple. Hassles pop up and are dealt with by the coalition of unique individuals of which you are a part. You float through each day surrounded by your best friends in the whole world, and I would probably agree (horrible cynic though I may be) that impression is much closer to reality than to illusion. By way of comparison, a network of intimate relationships is much more fluid and flowing, with the flexibility you'd expect from an amoeboid shape, but takes more constant maintenance energy if only in communication and base-touching since very little can be done by rote.

The in-built regularity of a smaller or closed relationship is a *problem* because such a relationship is so often incapable of actually handling a large crisis – something at about the seriousness level of the diagnosis of a chronic illness in one of the members, or your household's major breadwinner being summarily terminated. It is very easy to develop a "playbook," a set of reactions tied in a rote manner to familiar stimuli. If a novel stimulus cannot be parsed into the rules, then the playbook is applied in a hodgepodge manner until either some minor relief is stumbled across or the crisis gets bored and moves on. (Remember that old joke: a doctor can cure in fourteen days what would otherwise linger for two weeks.) If a crisis lingers, though, the entire relationship can disintegrate quickly into recrimination, cliques, and purges, seeking for a culprit.

When a crisis strikes a smaller group, you might find yourself feeling as though these people, who form the center of your emotional and intellectual world, are suddenly abandoning you when you need them most, or even turning against you in hostility. You're probably wrong, of course (or at least I would hope so), but it can certainly at least feel that way until everyone buckles down and begins rebuilding in the changed situation.

When you feel cut loose from the regularity and reliability of your group, you need to be able to start that rebuilding from the very beginning – you turn to yourself, of course. If you cannot love yourself, care about your well-being and growth, and generally respect yourself, then you've got no good reason to believe that someone else is going to treat you any better. Even as a member of an amorphous network, you will probably have to withdraw for brief period, days or hours, to refresh your autonomy, and renew those things that make you a vital and contributing part.

Chronic or acute

You're possibly one of those "I'd fight and die for the good of my family" kind of people. That's all well and good, but if you are sacrificing yourself on a daily basis, then something is terribly wrong, even though a typical day "only" takes a gram of your flesh rather than a proverbial pound. Givingness and self-sacrifice and related tendencies are (in a healthy context) highly laudable, and likely vital to the larger group's well-being. However, few human beings really have a need for such devotion over any extended amount of time, and demands for such devotion are possibly more a matter of ego-feeding than of any actual constructive repairs – as such, they could go on forever. That's hardly healthy, no matter how you want to look at it.

A good response to an acute situation is generally *wrong* for a chronic problem (and vice versa) – not just "not the best way," but actually counterproductive: when you need surgery, a bandage won't do, and when you just need a bandage, then surgery creates more problems than it solves. At the very least, the confusing of long-term and short-term problems likely leads to waste of energy, and you're so busy pouring water on illusory flames that you never notice the real embers smoldering all around your feet. A long-term problem that spikes up in occasional acute moments leads to people stomping down the outcroppings, treating the symptoms without addressing the underlying perpetuating causes. Conversely, an emergency is, by definition, acute; if it continues, then it's a chronic problem, not a crisis. All that effort would be better spent finding a new boat than perpetually plugging leaks in the old one.

True, sometimes corrective changes can only happen when they *can* happen, and you must keep plugging away until that time. Nevertheless, there's almost never a good reason for you to work yourself into the rest home or the poorhouse unless you particularly want to be a martyr and guilt other people into caring for you in turn – if so, you might want to have a leg or eye removed right this minute and save everyone including you the suspense.

If you put too much effort into sacrifice, the end result is that you will give all of yourself away... and then what? If the people you were supporting are truly in need, then they're kinda screwed without you to keep their heads above water – and if you were buying a bill of goods they were selling, and they get along just fine without your generous contributions, then you'll at least feel foolish (assuming the doctors are allowing you to feel anything at all).

Creative withdrawal: a tale

When you disagree with most of your group, over the acute-or-chronic nature of a given problem for instance (though there are plenty of other conflicts to be had), you might need to withdraw a bit, physically or emotionally, in order to let you get yourself together, or let them work it out without your unappreciated input. Or, you might have to step in and raise some hell, embracing a little isolation rather than seeing it as a risk to your self-image or your position within the group.

One household I belonged to had a habit of paying the bills that had collected on the table, then going on spending sprees for restaurants and toys and goodies with what was left in the checking account, only to fall into crisis mode when a forgotten bill arrived a few days later, or the next payment on another was substantially larger than anticipated. In one year, this account paid out more than $1,000 in the bank's overdraft fees. This irritated the hell out of me, as I appeared to be the only one who saw the rather obvious chronic nature of the constant "acute" problems. The waste of money to the fees, the red-edged envelopes they came in, the childish glee with which every spare dollar had to be spent rather than saved for big-ticket items, the manic-depressive swings of emotion in the house all were making me very cranky.

I withdrew, pleading a short-term cash crisis of my own to bargain for paying my share of the rent ten days late. This earned me an assortment of teasing and scowls. All was forgiven when I elected to stay home with a book rather than join them on their traditional capitalistic binge; the ones who felt that I needed to be dunned for my slovenly economics accepted this as adequate penance. (Actually, it was a good book and a lovely autumn evening, so I didn't feel particularly deprived.)

Three days later, the telephone bill arrived. One of my housemates had been assigned to pay the previous bill herself, as it contained more than $250 of her long-distance calls. She had, of course, forgotten, and was now as broke as everyone else, including the household's checking account. We were a few days from having our phone service cut off, and nobody was getting paid for another week. Squawk, squawk, squawk, predictably

I held up my checkbook and, in a calm and matter-of-fact tone, offered to pay not just the rent I owed but the next month's amount as well – if I was given complete control of the household account. I also hinted broadly that I was willing to move out even before the telephone stopped working if the situation wasn't improved.

This should have led to argument, tears, threats, and all that sort of thing, for which I was prepared. To my surprise, my "offer" (let's face it: it was a well-timed ultimatum) was met with stunned silence. I felt as if I'd put down an ace-high straight flush when none of the other players could make a pair.

Balancing a checkbook is no big thing, and throwing together a basic budget isn't much more difficult. The job took maybe an hour a week. I made up a short list of fiduciary requirements that would've brought tears of joy from the most hardened banker. For instance, I sugar-coated possible penalties for late payment with positive suggestions, such as recommending that people pay rent every four weeks (two paycheck periods) rather than monthly, thus accumulating a two-week "rent holiday" every six months. (This went over so well that I quietly scrapped my idea to offer discounts for advance payment of rent and phone share.)

Within two months, all household bills were paid to zero, the bank manager was proud of the account's about-face, and our kitchen was so well-stocked that we could probably have eaten well for a week without further purchases. I was established as a tightwad and killjoy, but the grumbling was minor and infrequent. Though spending less overall – there was actually a base amount accumulating in the checking account! – the household *felt* prosperous to everyone including guests. In that sense, we were all quite rich.

And all because I took a chance at losing, and dared to be an individual. My own need for sanity and personal responsibility infected others.

Be your self

Even when things are going quite well, you *must* put occasional effort into ensuring that you are at the top of your form as an individual. Taking care of yourself means you'll be completely in the moment should the crap hit the fan, but beneficial effects are hardly something reserved only for problems. The strength of a group is largely a product of the strengths of its members; if everyone is focused on becoming as similar as possible, as unified, you give away adaptability.

This means refreshing your individuality from time to time, holding onto your curiosities and idiosyncrasies, because these are the very things that make you a vital member, rather than just an interchangeable cog in a social machine. As with so much else, it is a balancing act, a willingness to work on fitting yourself into a community set against the ability to function alone. A picture puzzle made up of identical pieces is either confusing or boring, but a collection of unrelated pieces won't form a unified image. Optimality for everyone involved lies somewhere in the middle.

Make dates with yourself, and don't ever stop. Don't go out of your way to exclude, but don't put effort into togetherness or doing everything as a bunch. Do stuff that is completely free from trying to coordinate schedules and availability.

Find a hobby that has nothing to do with your triad or commune or network. Meet people who have never heard the word "polyamory" and enjoy their company for what it is without proselytizing the lifestyle. Go out to a good restaurant by yourself. Take in a movie that you want to see, without a thought as to what someone else would think of it. Spend an afternoon strolling the park and feeding the ducks. Take in a museum or gallery; go to a play or ballet.

In short: be unique, even as you are a vital part of a community.

69. Time out: sex has limits

Sex demands energy, and it gives energy. I once had a persistent case of bronchitis, and I was amused to notice that I could make love with my partner very strenuously, sometimes for two hours, with absolutely no trouble other than a little minor wheezing. But, like clockwork, I would go into spasmodic coughing shortly after orgasm.

On an emotional level, great sex frightens many people. A woman who considers herself not very sexual (a conclusion reached from lack of exposure to both the affectional and erotic possibilities of sexual interaction) might appear to cool toward her lover after an extraordinary sexual experience. Yes, I've had this happen a few times, and I was startled to discover the cause, as my other lovers would have considered my skills to be above average but hardly a transformative experience. Still, if your lover is used to rather second-rate sex, and you are very attentive and in-the-moment, this might be a bit of a shock to his or her system. The cooling-off reaction is an attempt to step back for the sake of objectivity, and have a long think. When I quizzed one lover, she explained that it had been such a change from how things had been during her married years that she'd been flooded with nagging questions about all that wasted time, and whether her attitudes toward sex hadn't been seriously damaged. She wanted time to think these things over, rather than either attach this upset to me or bury the feelings altogether.

A similar reason is that emotional abuse and sexual molestation of children form a vast problem in our society, largely unrecognized. A person whose erotic pleasure is confined to the pelvic area, or even the genitals, can be overwhelmed when those sensations become more generalized. The newfound ability to experience pleasure is such a primitive, childish (in a positive sense) sensation that it can trigger all sorts of unpleasant memories. I've told people that having sex with me caused two of my lovers to go into therapy, and I am quite proud of facilitating and supporting that possibility for healing and growth. These are barriers and hurdles that I'm pretty sure we can all agree ought to be surmounted. However, not everyone has the mental and emotional reserves to make that leap forward, whether as the one having these experiences, or the one supporting their surfacing.

Sex is important, but it also clouds your judgement. Not just sex per se, but the emotions it raises, the anxieties of pursuit, attendant self-image, and the usual array of odd taboos toted around by you and your partners. When you're juggling so many elements already, the occurrence of some sort of personal growth-point could overload your capacity for complexity. It sometimes makes a great deal of sense that a person on the threshold of a great and possibly life-changing step would want to step back awhile and have some time to think.

There are many good reasons to take a temporary step back from sex. One of the more common is when you've had a messy breakup of a relationship, and don't want to leap right back into possibly making the same errors that led to the explosion. When you're monogamous, this can appear to spell the end of the relationship; there's really no good reason that it has to go that way, but that's how many people handle it – inability to function sexually or procreatively used to be a valid reason to seek divorce or annulment.

For the nonmonogamous, there is the perpetual risk of spreading yourself too thin. With most of my flirtations, my experience has been that it's a given that sex is a possibility... so I don't worry about it. (Why chase after something you're surrounded by?) I've ended up with some treasured sexual experiences that wouldn't have happened if I'd initially been looking for sex. And I've also got some incredible non-sexual friendships.

Multiple intimate relationships can encourage our tendency to grab at every passing opportunity for sex as though there is some sort of expiration date. This feeds into focusing on quantity rather than depth and quality of relating. Taking up frequent opportunity for sex is an excellent way of undermining longevity in other ways.

Someone who fulfills a narrow role in your life becomes interchangeable with someone else, and is easily replaced should a new candidate become more convenient or have slightly more to offer you; should your free time become restricted, you have little incentive to pursue that relationship if the same functions can more easily be filled by someone else to who you have about as little deep attachment.

I think celibacy is an excellent way to heal, and also to improve one's trust in self. The "how long" part is more difficult; "until you're done" is a lame answer, but the best.

The potential trap of celibacy is that it is a kind of inverse hypersexuality, and can become an excuse, a way of hiding from the potential of deep connection with other human beings. If you are truly that damaged, then I can certainly understand a need to cease sexual contact for years or even for the rest of your life – but being in the care of a good therapist would also be part of the solution.

Self-awareness, though, can go a long way toward finding what you need to know about yourself, and in developing the facility to assess others' motivations. Taking some time without sex and all its (admit it) messy trappings can be vital as a way to seed, nurture, or mature that self-awareness, tuning out some of the noise so that you can relax and listen to what your heart or soul or subconscious is trying to tell you.

Once you begin being able to stop viewing sex as a (or *the*) goal, you will be able to fully appreciate its power as part of the process of love and empowerment. Approached consciously, that might mean occasional self-indulgence in seemingly nonstop carnal pleasures, or restricting it to those forms and situations that are best able to provide what you need, or even limiting or ceasing sex altogether with one or more of your sexual partners. It's not as though you are only allowed to make a single decision, with which you will be stuck for the rest of your life – that's more of that ridiculous old-hat thinking; if you aren't going to be monogamous anymore, then cease thinking as if you're monogamous. Experiment, try out the roles, fine-tune an idea until it is what you need, change as you need to change.

As with most things polyamorous, focus on love and respect: learn so that you can trust yourself, and strive to surround yourself with intimates who will support you even when they aren't getting their way.

70. A little more sex education

Before I wind down toward the end of this book, I'd like to briefly introduce the sorts of concepts that you ought to be thinking about if you're going to be happily polyamorous. They're really not much more than a few crib-notes, but they might start a few good conversations between you and your friends.

Orgasm counting (female)

Over a couple of months, while getting some background material for this book, I chanced to find time for heart-to-heart talks with three incredible women. In each case, we were trying to figure out what malign shade possessed us to stop being sexually/romantically involved.

Each told me that, when they were first exploring their sexuality, they were pouted at – even lectured!! – by a sexual partner because they didn't rack off one orgasm after another, with maybe ten minutes' warmup. And (other than with me) this nonsense has resurfaced to this day.

I've practically got a speech where I need to point out that (a) women commonly don't hit sexual maturity until their 20s and I have met a few women who didn't orgasm during intercourse until they'd topped 25, (b) my first lover could vary from two minutes flat to an hour of very meticulous stimulation, and (c) everything depends.

Anyway, though I'm rated highly, it remained (and remains) a problem for each of them, where they "freeze up" if they think they're somehow inconveniencing me!! The three range from 35 to 41, but it's not a generational thing: my previous lover, who is all of 21, tells me that she's gotten the same crap.

Note to guys: sometimes a woman wants to have one orgasm after another for hours, or until her IQ begins to decline permanently, and sometimes she is perfectly contented with an all-over warm-tingly feeling that slides her directly to sleep. Neither extreme is particularly a reflection upon your macho, much less your sexual abilities.

Some women, given a relaxing atmosphere and decent attention, can hit orgasm in about five minutes (sometimes to their surprise); some routinely take an hour. Which extreme is "better"? And even that depends, because sometimes those long-building orgasms are truly incredible… and sometimes the five-minute five-alarm is an historic event…

Orgasm counting (male)

If I've spent all day (or longer) desiring someone, I may not make it to the five-minute mark. Then again, I might continue merrily along for an hour or more. It all depends.

Statistics are misleading. It's true that a healthy human male of 17 can experience a dozen orgasms a day, where alter kackers like myself are only good for two or three. Of course, the average stimulation time for those young bucks is something like five minutes, where I think anything less than an hour is a quickie. So, "great sex" is open to local definition, at best. At the same time, few of the women I've spoken to are favorably impressed with a man whose sexual "prowess" consists almost entirely of pounding away at her for at least an hour; to paraphrase a few of them, "It's nice once in a while, but it gets really old when that's all that happens every time." Relying on one or two such stunts demonstrates a distressing lack of creative imagination.

Time spent at task

All around, the "time" thing tends to be just an extension of the "size queen" tendencies in our society. I've been very lucky in that I've never had reason to worry, though I'm apparently rather average as far as physiognomy. (Digression: who the heck determines what the average penis size is, anyway? Though it could certainly make door-to-door polling for the Census much more interesting: "Now, as to question 37....") My former partner's primary is one of the legendary horse-hung types, about twice (not an exaggeration, or even embellishment) my size in all dimensions; she nevertheless pronounced me incredibly satisfying in all ways.

If I pounce on a lover, and she has an earth-shaking orgasm or three, and the whole show is over in 15 minutes... or if we spend hours and hours going through the entire Kama Sutra and then some... or if one of us doesn't orgasm, maybe neither of us....

It all boils down to the same set of criteria. Did we enjoy it? Did it match our moods? Are we well-and-truly *satisfied*??

If it's positive, then the scorecard's kinda pointless. And it's just as pointless if the results were less than glowing.

It's one of those questions like, "Who's a better lover: someone who comes once a day or someone who can come twice an hour in perpetuity?" The question can't be intelligently answered by the solution set provided.

Everything depends.

Define "sex"

I've always wondered at a particular verbal trap: why does "sex" end when the male partner orgasms? I've noticed this usage even among FMF bi triads.

While, yes, after orgasm I usually do a wonderful impersonation of a stunned ox, if I take a few minutes for my heart to re-start and find the top of my skull, I tend to be immediately interested in kissing and caressing. I've been surprised at how many women are so conditioned that they begin damping down their libido when the male is "done", and actually become wary when I start into the whole "foreplay" thing again, since I tend to have a huge amount of desire for a partner. It worries me that, with the chakras wide-open, we seem to be so afraid – exposed, vulnerable – that we want to change the topic. (The post-coital cigarette makes sense in this light: tobacco closes the heart chakra.) By contrast, I am both so enervated and so **aware** that, despite lethargy, I'm very desirous of passing some of that wonderful feeling back to my beloved.

Related to this, there's one of those goofy artifacts: the only Real Sex is intercourse, everything else is just "playing around." It's always a shock to learn that some of the most fantastic sexual experiences of my life "weren't *really* sex". It's a holdover from Freud and his descent, who tended to lump together things like masturbation and homosexuality as "immature sexuality."

Pay attention to subtleties

My third sexual partner was lovely, but I was disconcerted at how quickly I reached orgasm the first couple of times. Our next evening together, I stepped back a little from lust, and noted that she had a wonderful twist to her hips as she thrust up to meet me, and this produced a very nice, almost dancelike interaction between our bodies. In fact, I guessed, a little *too* nice.

I figured that a small experiment was called for, and unlikely to be seriously distracting. (Little did I know.) All I did was slow down, to maybe half the speed that seemed so natural between us.

To my surprise, she tensed, then closed her eyes, went almost limp, sighed deeply, and for the first time (for us) found orgasm during intercourse.

Diagnosis: we'd been being a tad too aggressive (pronounced "rushed") about our lovemaking. I slowed down (and lasted much longer), and this cued her that "let's get this over with" was *not* on my mind, so she actually allowed herself to get attached to the feelings and *enjoy* the act.

(Odd how an essentially selfish act led to deeper mutual pleasure.)

Poly sex

Does having more than one sexual partner affect your sex drive? Oh, *heck* yes. My lovers have regularly attested that I'm notably more attentive, creative, spontaneous, etc., when I've got more lovers. Moreso when I'm in the NRE phase with someone, when I'm just feeling so darned good that it's contagious.

A couple of suggestions, should you find yourself in such a fortunate situation. Top of the list: **don't neglect your extant partner(s).**

Don't be surprised if your NRE makes your extant partner(s) want (in a positive way) more attention from you – it could easily make you sexier. When I would stop being situationally monogamous, my wife felt freed from the nagging feeling she was *obligated* to have sex with me, in a "last resort" sort of way, and having another lover made her more likely to *want* to have sex with me. (Yes, I've been on all possible sides of *that* situation as well.) This is one of those things that appears "illogical" to non-poly people, but the phenomenon is inarguably real. I'll leave any further theorizing to someone else.

71. Signs that things are going to Hell

Patterns recur. Though we are all unique individuals, most polyamorous people have experienced being brought to adulthood in a particular culture. At an even more subtle level, our brain structures are virtually identical, so we tend largely to see the world in the same manner, and so with our interpretative and problem-solving abilities (the basis of the so-called Jungian unconscious).

I've heard many couples who've said, "We don't need a therapist – we have so much *love*." They rarely last a year without outside help; it's a classic denial symptom. Polyfolk fall into similar patterns of thinking. I wouldn't be surprised to some day find out that most people with a drive toward polyamory have some sort of brain architecture or biochemistry in common.

When it hits the fan

Sooner or later, things polyamorous will go well and truly to Hell for you. And, let me assure you, once you have weathered this crisis, learned from your mistakes, put all the pieces back where they ought to be and moved along, it will happen again. Better still, once you have withstood a certain force of crisis, you will therefore be strengthened for when the Fates throw an even nastier surprise your way.

To top it all off, when you are pretty much ready for anything that can ever possibly happen in your life and relationships, you'll be so busy waiting to take on the next thundering herd of crazed elephants that you won't notice the termites until it's too late.

Call me a fatalist if you wish, but I'm trying to make clear that, if your idea of a good life is one with no crises, no angry shouting, no ghastly surprises, then the passage of time is the only variable until you meet up with abject failure. Artistically satisfying disasters loom everywhere; while they can be very scary-looking, conscientious preparation sucks most of the air out of them and leaves them vulnerable. However, loudly declaring them to be impossible freezes you a few steps short, and each step gives a disaster more power over you.

As I don't want to crib the words of a great man too directly, I will paraphrase Dr. Martin Luther King, Jr. He said that it is easy to believe in a just and kind God as long as things are going your way. Real faith, real conviction, rests on a belief that remains firm when things are going poorly.

You are eventually going to encounter a crisis of faith in polyamory and your immersion in it. Then again, one of your partners might beat you to it. Sheer stubborn determination might be the only thing that gets you through the darkest moments. A short-term dollop of blind trust – in each other, in your goals, in your vision of a better world – could keep you from throwing away what goodness you have found.

Serial sagas

The Internet has its advantages, I suppose. With various polyamory-oriented sites out there, and the proliferation of discussion sites and weblogs, people feel encouraged both to brag about the successes in their relationships and to gripe, whether in search of advice or to vent some spleen at the injustices that are done to them. Once in a while, this forms the sort of self-constructed case study that psychoanalysts everywhere would at one time have been overjoyed to obtain.

Be forewarned: if you choose a site well, you will be facing polyfolk of every possible degree of experience, age, honesty, and therapeutic background. Some of them, though you've never met and possibly never will, will be honestly and deeply concerned about your foibles. The result might be exactly the sort of intervention you need to keep you from digging into an even deeper and messier hole – and it's all out there in public.

After a months-long back-and-forth on one such site, from the two halves of a married couple planning to make an ill-considered leap into nonmonogamy, then doing so and expressing confusion and hurt and anger at the fallout, I posted the following, verbatim. If you've always wondered what the heck an "intervention" is, this bit ought to fill that gap. I was, admittedly, a little peeved. Most of the regulars thought I was being merely mean, but a notable few took my side.

> I gather that a few other folks have been attending the saga since the beginning. Is there anyone else who is tempted to plot the rhythm out on a calendar?
> - Things suck.
> - We've talked and everything is wonderful.
> - Spoke too soon, I'm leaving the relationship.
> - I've had some time to think about it, and I'm comfortable with where we're at.
> - If my spouse doesn't do things my way, we're through, and soon.
> - Thanks for your advice, everyone, but we've worked it out at last.
> - My partner is unreasonable and selfish.

> I've seen two sides of the coin for so long that I have difficulty believing that it's the same coin. He says, she says, and sometimes it's hard to remember that these aren't two entirely unrelated relationships, which merely happen to sound similar. And even when they manage to work things out between the two of them for a couple of days, it's soon back to a week or two of trauma, guilt, accusation, recrimination, and general high-handed ultimatums.

> At this point, a simple choice: (1) get therapy… intensive ongoing therapy; (2) separate; (3) admit that you get a charge out of abusing each other, because it gives each of you a scapegoat for your unresolved individual issues, without forcing either of you to make any serious, lasting changes.

> If they both stand by the "we can't afford counseling" line, then the choice is even simpler.

> The saga has been going on since the first post. Sure, things "take time"… but seven months to get from zero to zero?? I'd gladly hear from both as to the exact points that have improved in that time.

> Firstly, longevity is not a sign of a successful relationship, much less one that is growing, or even healthy; on the flip side, a relationship that has reached a logical end is not necessarily a failure, since relationships are (or should be) living things, all of which must eventually pass.

> They started out wrangling over the possibility of her getting sexually involved with his friend; they progressed to wrangling over the actuality of her being involved with his friend. Perhaps we have disparate definitions of "progress" and "successful" and "healthy" and "loving"; if so, I'm certainly willing to let it go at that.

> As for ending a complaint with "just needed to vent", that's as dishonest as putting someone down in a highly personal manner, then saying, "just kidding!!" If you need to say what's on your mind, then own up to it.

> This is indeed a support group, but not the tea-and-sympathy sort – not a whole lot of "I feel your pain" stuff. The people here have been of great help to me on occasion, and not by sharing in my self-pity – I've been brought up short once or twice, and deservedly so. Unlike most other sites, people here tend to give a damn (goofballs though we all can be), and will at least offer opinions with great sincerity.

> What *are* you looking for, here? Empty sympathy? Validation of your preconceptions? Platitudes? Serious advice?

Not that the couple in question is alone. I've followed a dozen weblogs where the world gets one side of the story, and one day the reader begins falling into a state somewhere between sleepwalking and *deja vu*. Unless that reader is merely a superficial stranger, or truly enjoys watching other peoples' lives as if they were living out a particularly tattered soap opera, there are only two choices: pull the plug (find a more emotionally mature form of pornography), or raise hell. I've seen "people in trouble" cut off by the members of Internet sites after constantly alternating statements of "It's my life and I'll do whatever the hell I want with it, so screw all of you and your stupid advice" with "Please, I need help, maybe I ought to kill myself." The cumulative response can be summarized as, "Look here, you demanded advice, we gave you some excellent advice. Get professional help, then tell us how it works out for you."

The cycle gets old very rapidly for those of us, apparently rare, who are somehow managing to work out the bugs in their own lives. As I once posted:

> I have a dear friend, who I try to support emotionally... but every once in a while I have to leave the room or end the call, because it's about to become a lapel-hoisting event. Her recurring problem is that she's looking for a serious/permanent primary, and for some reason thinks that the best places to do this are campout-type events and science fiction conventions.
>
> Nothing wrong with an "annual relationship" where you see the person every year at the same event or three... but I'm trying to get her to see that these don't automatically translate into great (or even particularly good) day-to-day relationships. It's the ephemerality, the transitoriness that make 'em what they are, after all. The result, for her, is that she spends so much time mooning over the guy-of-the-moment that she probably never sees the ones near-at-hand that could actually be lifetime partners. By the time she figures out that the White Knight is a sot, there's another event... and here we go again.

Mistakes should not merely be tolerated but *accepted*, as learning experiences – once each. One partner who makes an honest mistake should learn from that mistake, as should everyone around them. An unlearned lesson is just a waste for everyone, and pointless repetition wears at the soul. You'll be much happier if you hold the people around you to a high standard – and make the one for yourself a bit higher.

72. The Ref

You're going to find many situations where having someone around who can take no sides and all simultaneously is not only invaluable, but vital. You need a *referee*, someone who is skilled at taking neither side, and both. The referee whacks down any bullying, supports us to defeat self-doubt so that we can attempt to state our case, and prods everyone toward constructive ends.

If you're out in the middle of some cultural wasteland, just the three of you living secretly as a triad, and a hundred miles from a city of at least 50,000 people, you're pretty much screwed. Unless, that is, at least one of you has a suitable combination of skill and experience. (Access to the Internet can help, but it's not at all as good.) The rest of you have it much easier, though this is no guarantee that you can't create a total botch of it if you try really hard, however good the referee.

Really, everyone on the face of the planet ought to learn to be a referee with all the skills of a life-long marriage counselor. Barring that, there are a few things to keep in mind. A nonmonogamous group (whether a triad or a network or anything in between) that has a single talented referee will find that this ability is infectious, and, the more that it is applied, the better the average talent for lovingly interpersonal problem-solving will become.

While no book could possibly teach you techniques to handle all the basic problems you might encounter, much less complex combinations, we'll look at a couple of scenarios. In any case, nothing will be as useful to you as practical experience.

Making your own way

With enough experience, and a little courage, you will be able to not only help others solve their problems, but to deal with your own.

Jason and Barb had been busy for weeks, and finally managed to find a weekend where they could be together, making plans to go to the Renaissance Faire in the morning. Jason's occasional lover, Karen, was working the entrance gate until 10:30, and she was happy to smuggle friends in for free, rather than pay the steep (Jason felt) entrance fees.

A large part of Barb's time had been going to helping out her own occasional lover, Yolanda, who had recently given birth to her second child and was having marital difficulties with her husband, who also happened to work at the Faire. Jason had expressed his concern to Barb that she was cutting deeply into their time together in order to keep the other couple from being forced to confront their problems, even cleaning their house and washing dishes, but he was momentarily mollified that they'd had a nice evening together, a good night's sleep, and were now set for a fun afternoon.

At 9:00, they decided to pull themselves out of bed and get ready to leave. As Jason was stretching, Barb said, "I wonder if Yolanda would like to go."

Since Yolanda had been seeing Barb much more than he had, this bothered Jason, but he set his personal feelings aside. "It's a half-hour drive to the Faire. If we're going to shower and get something for breakfast, we really don't have time. How about if you make plans to go with her next weekend? That way, she can get everything organized that she'll need for the kids without so much rushing around."

"Yeah, I suppose," Barb said. "Do they still sell discount tickets at that gas station around the corner?"

Jason knew the place. "They did last year. But if you go out early enough, I'm sure Karen will walk you all through."

"I'll see if she's up yet." Barb reached for the telephone. Jason went into the bathroom to brush out his hair.

When he returned, Barb was hanging up. "No answer, so I left a message. She's been really tired lately, what with all the problems."

"I'm sure you'll see her sometime this week, and the two of you can make some plans."

"Once she gets the kids up," Barb continued, "it'll take her a while to get them ready to go. We should be able to be out there not too much after noon."

"You'll work it out. Where should we go for breakfast?"

"I wonder how long it will take her to call back?"

Jason began to get the impression that their plans were being changed before his eyes. He'd promised some friends that he would stop by to see them at the Faire. Biting back other comments, he asked, "How long are you planning to wait?"

Barb shrugged. "She'll probably be up by eleven or so. I'm not sure she'll check her voicemail right away. Maybe I should keep calling. But I don't want to wake her before she needs to get up on her own."

"Look," Jason said, "I'm sure it'll all work out, and you will probably see her sometime this week. You can talk about it then." He turned toward the bathroom to shower.

"I suppose so," Barb said, looking thoughtful. "Do you think they'll still have discount tickets after noon?"

Jason stopped. Without looking back, he replied, "I suppose so, but you'll have plenty of time to buy them for next weekend."

"Today, I mean."

"We don't need tickets. Karen is getting us in for free."

"No, I mean for Yolanda and the kids."

At that point, Jason could no longer ignore that he was fighting a losing battle. "I would assume so," he answered tightly, walking out of the room. "You could probably give them a call."

As he showered, Jason seethed. He'd been planning on a little more precious time with Barb, and he was looking forward to getting to the Faire early enough to park close to the gate, avoid the bulk of the crowd for a few hours, and enjoy a little of the morning coolness before the sun was directly overhead. He was especially angry that Barb didn't seem to be hearing him, or even recall that this was supposed to be a day for the two of them.

He looked at it analytically. He had two goals in mind: enjoy the Renaissance Faire, and spend the day with Barb. The latter was clearly in jeopardy, and he felt that any objections he would raise would only start an argument that, at best, would put a dark cloud over the whole thing. Rather than risk such a pointless fight, he considered aborting the entire plan, taking Barb off to a long brunch where they could sort this out. However, she had been becoming very defensive of the increasing time she was devoting to Yolanda, and he knew this discussion would likely lead to disaster as well.

Jason came out of the bathroom toweling his hair, smiling. Barb was still lying in bed, reading a book. She smiled at him, then returned to reading.

After he'd dressed, Jason walked over and kissed Barb on the forehead. "I'm off to the Faire. I'll call you tonight to see if you want to get dinner."

As he turned toward the door, Barb said, puzzled, "I thought we were going together?"

Jason nodded. "So did I. But I've been looking forward to this all week, and you're waiting for Yolanda to call." He grinned. "Maybe next week. I'd really like to see the sights with you."

He waved happily to her, and left the apartment.

A few minutes after entering the grounds of the Faire, Jason stopped to chat briefly with Yolanda, her husband, and the kids. When he mentioned that Barb was waiting for her call, Yolanda rolled her eyes. "I *told* her we were going to be out here all weekend," she said, sighing.

Give that story a little thought. Let's say that Jason had come out of the shower, dressed in angry silence, and stormed out of the apartment. How would you have examined and moderated if Barb had come to you with her side of the tale? Would you have handled it differently if Jason sought you out? Does Jason's logical way of avoiding a (likely nonproductive) blowup affect how you would look at it?

The referee in crisis

I'll finish off this chapter with a composite story that demonstrates the sort of role played by a referee. The tale is taken from real life, including much of the dialogue, though the reality is (as usual) much more complex.

Felicia was back home. Technically, she lived with Brian, but her camera skills had begun to pay off in a big way, and she had been gone for most of a year, working on a documentary project for a small company.

Brian had been involved with Clara for almost two years. The relationship had taken off in Felicia's absence, and the NRE had by this point settled down. Clara owned her own house and had no interest in living elsewhere. Likewise, Felicia and Brian had a comfortable bungalow with a big garden.

Felicia had a month before she needed to recross the country, to spend a few more months assisting in editing the film down to its final release. She'd been talking on the telephone to Brian almost every day, when he was available, which meant three or four times a week they could at least say an affectionate goodnight before bed. Felicia had also encountered Zach, in a decade-long, polyamorously open marriage to Tisha. Zach had become a good virtual companion, and Felicia spoke with him at length every week or so. Though both Felicia and Zach were yet unsure that there was any chemistry that would lead to a relationship, they were looking forward to meeting.

From the beginning of her one-month hiatus, though, Felicia had the nagging feeling that her relationship with Brian was in trouble. She couldn't call attention to anything in particular, but she found herself feeling strangely jealous. Brian would stay up late with Clara, usually coming home after midnight. The next evening, when he had a date with Felicia, he would be worn out, drifting off over dinner, and he'd beg off from going out dancing or even to a movie. On these nights, Brian would make clear that he needed to get some rest, and he was usually sound asleep by 9 pm, "to be ready for work." Most of the time, the following evening would be with Clara, and the cycle would repeat.

Felicia shrugged it off. She had no reason to doubt that Brian loved or desired her any less.

The second Friday she was there, Brian and Felicia were enjoying a light breakfast before he went to work. "Redline is going to be back in town tonight," she said. "We haven't seen them in so long. I'd like to catch them with you."

"Sounds like fun," Brian said, standing up from the table and stretching. "I'd like to do that, as long as we're not out all night."

Biting back a question about how late she deserved his attention, Felicia smiled and kissed Brian goodbye.

After dressing, Felicia called Zach, and they made a date to meet over dinner Sunday evening, when she knew that Brian had a date with Clara. Then Felicia went out for a day of shopping at the small shops around town she'd been missing on her travels.

As the time rolled around toward 5 pm, Felicia hurried home. It had been a good day, and she'd forgotten to get lunch, but there was plenty of time for dinner after Brian got home, maybe on the way to the club to hear Redline. She put away her purchases, humming to herself, then took a decadently long shower.

By the time Felicia was dressing for the evening, she noticed that 6 pm was approaching. Brian was running late. She called his cell phone, knowing that he was rarely without it, and left a message when he didn't answer. After brushing out her hair, Felicia put five CDs into the stereo, picked up the novel she'd been reading, and settled in to wait, looking forward to the evening with Brian.

Two hours later, with the sun going low, and getting a little dizzy and irritable from not having eaten, Felicia went to rifle through the refrigerator, putting together a few things to tide her over.

Brian walked in just before 9:30. He appeared happy to see her, but his smile slid away as he noticed the look on her face. "What's wrong?"

"You'll have to tell me," Felicia replied. "I thought we were going out tonight."

Brian shook his head, already exasperated. "I *told* you I'd see you after work."

"To some people, 'after work' means 'when I'm done, I'll be right there,' not 'some time in the future after this event.'"

"Well I'm *sorry*," Brian said. "I got done with work a little early."

Felicia paused. Given the hour, this made no sense. Almost involuntarily, she said, "What?"

"I had some extra time. I decided you wouldn't be home, so Clara came up to meet me for a late lunch."

"That must have been some lunch."

Brian looked confused. "It was still early, so we went back to her house for a few hours. I lost track of time, I suppose. What's the big deal?"

"So, Clara just happened to get through the switchboard, out of the blue, and you just happened to have your work wrapped up early for once."

"You have no right to control what I do or who I do it with."

"I don't have a problem with Clara, or with you and Clara. I have a problem with wasting an evening waiting for you."

"I got distracted! What was I supposed to do?"

Wordlessly, Felicia pointed toward Brian's belt. His cell phone, to be exact. "And sunset might have been a clue," she added.

With his hands on his hips, Brian said, "Look. I'm here now. If that's not good enough, I'm sure I can find something else to do."

Felicia resisted agreeing that this was abundantly clear.

On Sunday, she and Zach were enjoying dinner, finding many common threads. The incident with Brian had been on her mind, though, and she laid it out for him.

As she reached the end of the story, Zach put down his coffee and sat back in his chair. He had a faraway, thoughtful look in his eyes, and Felicia let him think.

Finally, he looked at her. "Twenty minutes," he said, reaching for his cup.

"What?" said Felicia, startled by the apparent incongruity.

"You don't fully believe in yourself. You didn't set a clear time for the date, so you took on blame for that. If you'd been certain of a specific time, you should have waited twenty minutes, then assumed the date had been yanked away from you, and found something else for fun."

He thought for a moment. "When's your next scheduled evening with Brian?"

"Tuesday."

"What are you planning on doing?"

"The little theater downtown is having a Humphrey Bogart double-feature, one night only, and we thought it'd be nice to see it on the big screen."

Zach nodded. "What time is your date?"

"The first show starts–"

"Nope," Zach interrupted. "Wrong, wrong, wrong. You don't know when Brian is going to get home. You've already set yourself up again."

Felicia flushed, and started to protest.

Brian put up his hands. "Now, just hear me out. You don't know me from Adam – or Eve, for that matter. I know this script, and I must have seen something like it a dozen times. I'm not impugning either you or Brian, but I think you're courting trouble."

"So," he said, leaning forward, "here's what I propose. Tish has class that evening. I was planning on a quiet night at home, but I wouldn't mind seeing Bogie with a friend.

"Tonight, I go home and tell Tisha that I might be going to the movies with you. When does the first show start?"

"Seven."

"Okay. You go home and tell Brian that you will be ready to go at six, so that you won't have to rush. That's me talking – I like to have plenty of time to find parking, get the tickets, and choose a good seat, then I'm relaxed and ready for the show.

"At six-twenty, you call me, and we can enjoy the show together."

"What about Brian?"

"He said he could always make other plans, remember. That was his way of telling you that he has every right to jerk you around if it suits his mood. If you two aren't going to wait for your relationship to blow up from continued inflation with this sort of bullshit, then he has to be willing to recognize it consciously, and to do something to change it. He doesn't have the natural courtesy to even call you to admit he's left you waiting – he should be grateful if you leave him a note when he breaks your date."

Tuesday evening rolled around, and went much as Zach had described. As Felicia was picking up the phone, Brian walked in the door. She set the handset down and Brian grinned. "Was that the new boyfriend?"

"We were going to leave at six," Felicia said evenly.

Brian shrugged. "So I got a little delayed on the way home."

"Did that delay have anything to do with forgetting your briefcase at Clara's house again?"

His eyes went down to his hand, then he spun half-around and scanned the entry.

"The battery on your phone must be dead – I tried to call." She picked up the phone again, and pressed the speed-dial button she'd already programmed for Zach and Tisha,

Zach answered. "Damn," he said, "I thought we ducked the bullet."

"Oh, no," Felicia said brightly, "I was just on my way out."

"Uh-huh. Standing right there, is he?"

"Yeah, I'm really looking forward to it. I'll be there in about ten minutes."

"Great. Let's go grab a banana split after and talk."

"That sounds decadent, but fun – as long as you don't tire me out *too* much." She hung up to Zach's raucous laughter.

Brian looked stunned. "I thought we had the night together!"

Felicia took Brian's hands and smiled at him. "You were right – that's *not* good enough, and I'm sure you *can* find something else to do." She kissed him lightly, adding, "I know I did." She turned toward her bedroom, to check her makeup.

A few minutes later, she called Zach. "I have to make another change," she said. "Brian wants to talk."

"Good!" said Zach.

"He seems a little worried," Felicia added.

"Also good! Give him fifteen minutes, not a second more."

"*What?*"

"You have to make it clear that he's already called off the evening for the two of you, and that he can't simply gloss over it and reclaim control by coming up with a grudging apology. If you stay, you'd be yelling within an hour, because he's still trying to avoid responsibility for his actions. Brian ducked the date, so now it's done and you've made other plans for the remainder. It's your evening now. When's your next planned outing with him?"

"Friday."

"Great. Tell him that the two of you can have the long talk Thursday evening, as soon as he's done with work. Make it clear that you're not going to wait all night. You should have something in mind if you haven't heard from him within thirty minutes."

"But he's already got plans with Clara!"

"Perfect! Then he's got some consequences for being a boob in the first place. For whatever reason, which you'll likely find out Thursday, he has been finding ways to get away with putting you down and blaming it all on you. Right now, he's beginning to realize that he doesn't have you all to himself, because you can call me and I'll be happy to see you. Besides, if you put it off until Friday, you'll be that much more depressed and angry, and he'll use your mood as an excuse to find another delay."

Felicia was beginning to see where this was not a wholly inaccurate assessment of what had been happening. "All right," she said grudgingly, "I'll try it. But you'd better be right."

Zach sighed. "I really wish I weren't – but I know I am. I'm pretty confident that things will look a lot better by Saturday. I'll see you in half an hour."

You're probably horrified – fine. If you've ever been in the position of Felicia, Brian, or Zach (or maybe Clara), though, you know that I'm not exaggerating in the least. Otherwise... well, welcome to polyamory, and I'll break it down a little for you.

It took Zach, an experienced and relatively impartial observer, to spot the behavior cycle that Felicia and Brian were falling into. Rather than let the relationship sink into utter futility, or become an endless cycle of near-abusive interaction, Zach made suggestions that would shatter the cycle. None of his ideas were specifically controlling or manipulating: it was all based in the concept of logical consequences.

There's an aphorism from aikido: "Your opponent does not want you, he wants the space you are occupying. You defeat him by helping him to achieve this goal." So, when someone lunges at me, I step aside, then assist the downward movement of his lunge. Consciously, my attacker wanted to do me harm, but he told his body to crowd me out of that space, which I helped.

That was pretty much Zach's approach to the situation. He quickly saw that Brian was unconsciously demanding freedom from obligations to Felicia, accepting dates with her but turning up "accidentally" late. The gambits he employed put Felicia into a neat (and almost unavoidable) double bind, where no complaints would only lead to more outrageous incursions, yet dissent of any degree would make Felicia the "bad guy" and justify Brian in his actions. Either way, Brian could avoid admitting that he was behaving poorly.

This sort of intervention might indeed *appear* passive-aggressive, or underhanded and backstabbing, or just plain mean, letting Brian walk into a trap that had been set up just for him, and even loaded with appropriate bait. Nothing could be farther from the truth. He established some simple mutual obligations, and backed out on them. After his attention was called to this, his behavior didn't change much.

Any number of underlying reasons could have been behind Brian's annoying new habit. It could have been an expression of fear of losing Felicia entirely, whether to her career or to someone she met on her travels. He might simply have resented her freedom, and been leading up to an ultimatum that she stay with shorter assignments or projects closer to home, else they were through. Maybe he had fallen into a rhythm with Clara, and unconsciously resented Felicia's return.

Brian's concerns, in any case, could have been valid, but the manner in which he was approaching the situation was highly inappropriate, and anti-communication. Where he might have denied any need for relationship counseling, the problem has been called to his attention in an inarguable manner. Zach's intervention forced a sudden return to balance, giving Felicia and Brian common ground to examine a potentially relationship-killing conflict.

73. Falling back in love

One of the common misunderstandings about falling in love is captured in the term NRE, "new relationship energy." This has the unfortunate subconscious effect of telling us that *old* relationships don't have energy! It also implies that, if we want to get back that thrill, that sense of wonder, that we have to go out and find someone new.

Well, nonsense. Falling in love is falling in love. Nowhere does anyone state that falling in love with a particular individual is something you get one pass at and then it's gone, kaput, forever. Sure, that impression lingers, but there is no basis for it.

Before any of you goes off on some strange romantic tangent: no, there is absolutely no need for an Earth-shaking crisis to bring you closer together. While stories abound of people who grow due to adversity, you can't bring growth about by courting disaster. Some people grow, true enough, and most suffer, and some never recover from their tribulations. Relationships are unique objects, not mass-produced items. With the latter, you can choose a random sample, test these to destruction, then infer typical durability. An interpersonal relationship is a work of craft, possibly of art – you make one, then you see whether it works, and (if so) how well, and in any case you note its bad and good qualities for application upon future creations. Sometimes those observations provide insights that allow you to overhaul the inspiring object itself.

Polyamory has one little-acknowledged strength that rarely appears at all in monogamy: the ability to rewrite the rules and proceed from that point – to "start over" with the same person. Really, this is not even a *capability*, but an absolute *necessity* for longevity.

At the same time, though, the odds aren't as high as they probably ought to be. In a nice simple dyad made up from two people very aware of their own unconscious processes and highly capable of reading other people, a stressful time can have a negative impact on the relationship, and vice versa, with the result either way that one or both of the people retreats behind a wall of denial, or pulls away from the relationship. Things are further damaged, communication is impaired and the whole thing spirals rapidly into disintegration and permanent enmity.

Many couples never make it to those heights in the first place. Take that same theoretical couple. Such people are exceedingly rare, and the chances that two of them will not only meet but form a partnership are infinitesimal. Much of our programming drives us to seek out either people that "need to be helped," or the pseudo-alphas that we can look up to and admire. Neither of these has much promise of turning into a dyad of peers. When you try to extend this beyond such a simple two-person unit, the complexity takes off rapidly, and adding multiple relationships of differing intimacy and interaction levels only makes matters messier.

Not that I think the prospects are hopeless – far from it. If you've slogged through most of this book, successfully avoiding temptation to toss it onto a cheery oak blaze in the fireplace, then your odds are improved because you've started to think about some of the things necessary for improvement to take place. As well, if you're going out into the world and practicing polyamory, accepting the mistakes and imperfections and taking your lumps with some slight equanimity, you're better able to roll with the sudden swerving of life without readily losing your balance. "Chance favors the prepared mind," as the saying has it, and I find this hopeful thought very heartening.

Loving relationships, and how we achieve them, ought to be treated for the craft that it is, rather than as some sort of scientific (practically industrial) situation. An apprentice's first efforts are primarily doing the work that the master feels personally demeaning. It is the apprentices of the world who make the coffee, scrub the floors, scour the area for trash, do the broad painting, assemble myriad subassemblies, and so on. Scut-work, in short.

When the apprentice is allowed to actually attempt a project, the results are usually hideous, abominations that seem to parody that particular craft. With time, though, and the development of the skills and dexterity and creativity, an apprentice becomes competent in the craft, and is declared a journeyman – a word that rather bluntly spells out a need for travel. This travel, whether to another region or to another master, or both, seeds those budding nascent skills with a variety of viewpoint, exposing the journeyman to variant ways that similar ends can be accomplished.

Given the effects of time and variety (each of which has elements of both leavening and seasoning, though that would be another analogy entirely), the journeyman is finally recognized as a master at the craft: a competent and trustworthy professional at a standardized trade, yet with a vein of originality.

The constant litany of Forever in our relationships serves to almost entirely bury this sort of evolution as necessary in that part of our lives as well, even those interactions that might involve orgasm. Perhaps it's a model we would do well to copy far more closely. Monogamy can't do that; nonmonogamy, freed from the self-imposed blindness imposed by tradition and societal expectation, can.

A half-competent sub-apprentice won't forever be kept sweeping the floors unless he's repeatedly proven incapable of the most rudimentary portions of the craft, yet we encourage people to latch onto one relationship (which we strongly imply is their only serious try and must be grimly permanent) at an age that for just about everything else we'd call them "not much more than kids" and "irresponsibly young" – but we push them to marry or have children or both, and to repeat that forever. Kids can marry before they can buy cigarettes, which ought to say volumes about our culture. We give them a hundred cues a day that having children is a cure-all for their self-doubts, and then wonder that children too young to drive a car or work after sunset are purposely having babies.

As with an apprenticeship system, mistakes should be allowed for, even encouraged, with the intent of calling up flawed understanding and abilities so that these errors can be entirely corrected. That means, though, a quashing of romantic notions as well as authoritarianism, neither of which is likely to happen without a messy struggle against the culture itself as well as its various institutional and individual stakeholders.

The evolution does sometimes suck. The winners are the ones who do not duck or dodge or run away.

So, too, it is with a loving relationship. When you and another person are in love, you're not both "in love" all the time except maybe at the beginning, when everything is so extreme that it doesn't make much difference whether one of you is somewhat closer to infinity than the other. Often, as the relationship matures, you're not even on the same page, with one in a calm plateau of giving and receiving affection while the other is withdrawn a little and distracted by worldly events and situations. Crises pass, things change, new outlooks are discovered, and two slightly evolved individuals look each other in the eye and realize that there's something different about the spirit, which means that the relationship between them cannot possibly be what it had been previously.

There were many times where, even after years of marriage and steady relationships with another lover or three, I actively lusted after my wife. Even after we were married, I fell in love with Marie at least five times. I'm talking the head-over-heels, calling from work, bringing flowers, breakfast in bed kind of love. This baffled some of my lovers, and clearly delighted and reassured others – I obviously wasn't someone who was going to lose interest easily, and was therefore a better risk for a deeply involved relationship. When you remove this from the context of a dyad, I think you'll see where there's vast possibility for everyone in an intimate group to be regularly falling back in love with one or more of their partners.

It can happen to you, unless you already believe that it's impossible, since then it's a simple matter to ignore or even sabotage it. You can force love away, but you can't force it closer.

Therein lies another of the faults of a romance-sodden monogamy, when people insist on calling matters of duty and obligation "love" rather than labeling them the blackmail they are. If you need to force yourself (or the other person) into being in love, then I'd argue that it ain't love into which you're falling, and likely something quite different into which you're about to step. Watch yourself for thought patterns indicated by "force" words: "How can I make her love me?" or "What can I do to make him respect me?" Such goals cannot be achieved by pressure or sales ability; if methods like that succeed, then the reward is fleeting, and could easily be supplanted by someone else with a better line. The illogical component of love, real deep-seated caring for another human being, is what keeps it from being reduced to the product of a litany of tried-and-true procedures.

74. Toward a culture of polyamory

Is polyamory a "movement"? Oh, gods, I hope not. The *last* thing I want is for polyamory to become mainstream, popular, a fad. The term "bi-curious" still gives me the creeps, even after all these years; I certainly don't want to start hearing "poly curious" used the same way. Call me a snob, but I've worried enough in the past decade about any dilettante and parasite being able to claim to being "poly" without other people willing to check their credentials – serious willingness to risk oneself is the price of admission.

The irony here appears to be that the newbies who could really benefit aren't able to access the info; those who might be ideally suited for polyamory (and would benefit immensely from considering the lifestyle) but don't know about the concept wouldn't know about the information; and the "insiders" who supposedly know all this stuff already are the audience. But at least it'd still be a semi-exclusive club, if only from its obscurity.

There's all shades and flavors of "activism" in the world. In our cultural climate, simply being "out" as poly and willing to discuss it is pretty radical. I'm poly and Wiccan and not the straightest boy on the block; I outed myself in these things back when they were guaranteed to get you into all sorts of trouble with various authorities, just because. Lying has never been my long suit. I certainly cannot recommend this degree of honesty as a general practice – but I certainly sleep better.

When each of these trickled down toward mass culture, I saw my little "community" beset by frauds and fakes, who we initially embraced as kin – fellow deviants. If you've been around the block, you probably know what I mean: people who are "Wicca" because they saw it on a book once; guys who are "bi" because it gets more women (and women who are "bi" because the boyfriend wants another playmate); people who are "into BDSM" and mostly would be swingers but don't have the guts, though they can cause an impressive amount of social and physical damage in the wrong situations; and, of course, "poly" people who want an approved form of promiscuity. Makes me a tad cynical about popularizing the trend.

When setting up the first real convention of committed polyamorous people, *alt.polycon 1*, one of the organizers mentioned that many of the people who contacted her were "looking for the hot bi babes" (her words). This hasn't really changed so much: fully half the members on my favorite polyamory site, PMM, are "Male Seeking Female" or "Couple Seeking Female". Some, I know, are experienced and committed polyamorous people, hoping that lightning will strike; most are fantasizing, and a few just want to get laid with "no strings."

It's very cool to attend conferences relating to polyamory, though I'd say that's more "training" than "activism." Speaking out at, say, a bisexuality conference would be a little outside the box; doing so at a science fiction convention (as I have) would be even more so. And roundtable discussions are much more activist than panel presentations, because they allow more-equal interaction with less of a wall than between audience and lecturers.

In any of the deviant subcultures, there are always a few who think that putting on a nametag makes them *members*. In, say, a poly social, I'm more likely to talk to the ones who say, "How do you arrange household expenses?" than "What are your sleeping arrangements?" but I like those better than "Hi!! I'm poly too! What's your phone number? Let's get together and talk!"

We need to avoid wasting time and energy in constantly re-inventing the wheel. I stopped attending one poly discussion group because literally every third meeting was dominated by "Jealousy: What It Is and How to Deal With It." I know, I know: newbies need help with this, as do people who previously thought they'd ducked the bullet. But those of us who had a handle on it kinda withdrew.

We reinvent the wheel all the time. Someone discovers a polyamory discussion site, doesn't know how to deal with their feelings/situation, and hasn't read the FAQs. We recommend the latter, but give advice anyway, usually variants on the same old stuff. Then the advisee goes away, and we usually don't find out if our advice was even correct.

After you've seen enough "poly" people put the rubric to selfish uses – and possibly take advantage of your friends or loved ones, or actively try to break up you and a lover – you'll be just as cynical as me about poly merging into popular culture.

There's a phrase I saw pop up in the gay community in the 1980s, and cheered when it was stomped down. In a culture of diversity, one group is likely *not* "just like everyone else." To deny that we have different needs, concerns, thought processes, worldview, is to refuse to look at the reason we are supposedly an identifiable community. Having watched the assimilationist effects on my various subcultures for 20 years, I can't agree that striving for the anonymity of the average is a good thing. For instance, if we're "just like everyone else," why can't we overlook the housing codes in many cities that make habitation by more than three unrelated adults a violation that could get the building condemned? After all, it doesn't bother monogamous families – and aren't we just like them?

I'd not be totally happy with having polyamory lumped together with queer and leather communities, for much the same reasons – it'd run very close to saying, "it's all the same," when that's hardly the truth. A friend of mine, a wonderful dyke, says that polyamory in her city will instantly get a gay woman labeled as a dilettante pseudo-lesbian, or merely promiscuous. While clearing this up for the future would be nice, we have the meantime choice as to whether to increase the confusion.

Personally, I do not think that polyamory will ever become a community – and, given the opportunity, it likely shouldn't. There is simply too much diversity among responsibly nonmonogamous people, and it would be a shame to see this become homogenized, structured, or codified. Polyamory is magnificently chaotic, and as such allows all sorts of cross-pollination, evolution, even mutation, rather than winding down toward some sort of boring gray orthodoxy, where the only freedom is to choose from a list of approved possibilities. Polyamorous people, at least at this point in history, are exactly the sort of people who want to stray beyond the fence, which of course does not mark the end of the known world so much as the beginning of the fascinating unknown, risky and potentially dangerous though it may be. It is So Very Cool to find people who are at all like-minded that we sometimes lose track of the vital differences that make us such fascinating individuals. If we want to be more boring, to fall back on the known and the predictable and the (supposedly) safe, then we can always recross the fence line, renounce our wandering ways, and rejoin the herd, with no rancor from either side of the fence.

I belong to a variety of marginal lifestyles. In each and every one, the majority of self-identified members are playing roles – and very few are willing to stand up on their hind legs, to take serious risks with their public image, reputation, psyche, comfort, happiness, soul… call it what you will, they're reluctant to take responsibility for their roles, and therefore the control of them is lost. Roles are powerful transformative tools if they represent ideals into which you are actively and sincerely attempting to grow. A significant part of their power stems from acknowledgement that a role has been assumed. When this isn't done, a fantastic opportunity is lost, and everyone pays just a little.

In my more cynical moments, I suggest that, in polyamory, the vast majority who gravitate to the label (though perhaps not to the defining concept) are either lone males saying "pleeeeeeze let me join!!" or couples saying "move into our house and follow our rules" (almost always looking for bisexual females). When more lucid, I can't entirely shake that impression. If this was a lifestyle to which we were dedicated, a lifestyle which we see as potentially transforming the sense of "community" as we know it – if not the entire culture! – wouldn't *someone* occasionally say, "Come. Let us reason together. Let us put each of us where we can do the most good, and thus come to full fruition as individuals"? I'd be overjoyed to hear of two married couples who, a couple of years into a poly foursome, sell *all* their "coupled" property and find something that suits them as a community, as a tribe, as a family.

It's a risk, but as products of our culture we are so entranced by our own (well-founded!) cynicism that we can't take emotional risks even slightly analogous to the physical hardships endured by our ancestors just a few generations ago. Most people would rather cling to the known-and-failed than take a chance; it worries me that I cannot say whether they're more afraid of potential failure, or of potential success. Though thus far disappointed, I remain optimistic for the future.

Until more people make it to that jumping-off point, what I *want* to see is people **talking** – about the ups-and-downs, the nuts-and-bolts. About how poly relationships can suddenly disintegrate, just like they can suddenly spring from out of the blue. About doubts and fears, about the existential realizations that only multiple lovers can inspire, about the magnificent lows and highs we exist in the thick of. I want to hear stories about what it's like to live day-to-day with two-plus lovers, to juggle schedules, to form a community – warts and all, as they say. I'm hoping that, by bringing it out in the open, people can (a) realize they have doubts, (b) compare those doubts, and (c) get done with the bad parts that vanish when exposed to sunlight – and *then* the odds of finding family or community or village or household or simple happiness increase greatly.

I am primarily a storyteller, an historian. This is far more vital than our culture remembers; we have largely lost the role of the bard, the keeper of the fables that contain great truth. When we don't tell the stories, the history dies. Without a living history, we are doomed to repeat ourselves, over and over – we must repeat our learning experiences, we must grow talents again and again, we must suffer through honest error and egregious hubris alike. Largely, this is done from a partially hidden belief that newness and novelty are superior to experience and stability, yet another of our ingrained social myths.

But maybe, just maybe, we can make it better if we keep the stories alive.

75. About this book

Yeah; heck of a place to put this chapter. But if I have done the job that I set out aiming for, you've absorbed some very serious lessons that ought to give you a serious shot at happiness.

Becoming polyamorous is not like flipping a switch. The change is *not* a matter of waking up one bright morning and saying, "Hey – I'm polyamorous!" whence the scales fall away from your eyes, and everything is forever after absolutely peachy. Nothing in life works like that, yet many people behave in exactly that manner when it comes to polyamory.

If you set out to have multiple sexual partners and nothing more, then you have merely traded the narrow depth attributed (however erroneously) to monogamy for a life of shallow breadth.

That isn't polyamory. What I advocate, what I have experienced, and what I hope for you is both breadth and depth, simultaneous. That takes self-awareness. That takes honesty. That takes resilience. That takes an amazing level of emotional risk-taking. That takes an almost superhuman ability to understand the damage that each of us carries. That requires an extraordinarily high degree of problem-solving and communication skills.

The thing is, all these abilities are within your grasp. Though you've been raised from birth to believe that none of these is likely possible for you, I disagree and I disagree heartily. You've slogged your way through a mammoth book, and you've comprehended most of the big words. Many of the concepts I have raised are new to you, and though you might think that most do not apply to your situation, and may never, you've nevertheless read and digested them. That shows a dedication, a willingness to learn that I believe still flickers in the hearts of most human beings. By making it this far, you've shown a degree of comprehension that can fan those few banked embers.

You need to plan far in advance, a strategy that is totally at odds with our culture of instant gratification. You need to prepare for crises that may never occur. You need to develop skills that you might use once, or not at all. That, ultimately, is the lesson I have hoped to impart. Anything less will not allow you to be polyamorous – you'll merely be burning repetitiously through shallow relationships at a faster rate than monogamy would allow. I believe that you are capable of far better.

Six months from now, or maybe a year, come back and read this book again. In the meantime, if a question pops up, look it up, or reach out to other flawed, hopeful people like yourself, then apply your inherent reasoning abilities. Do some reading, find some time to ponder, make some notes.

It's time that you write your own stories. I'm expecting them to be good.

Epilogue: Real Community; or, Why I Sound Like an Activist

First they ignore you, then they ridicule you, then they fight you, then you win.

Gandhi

There is an analogy I haven't been able to get out of my head. Call it a dream-image.

I'm living in some run-down place, scrabbling for existence, but I'm a survivor, so I have enough food to get by. People like me; I'm always ready with a funny story, so when I stop by to chat, they're usually happy to give me what they don't want. I soon establish a routine where I regularly have plenty of wilted vegetables and even shankbones. I can make a heck of a soup, not a cure-all, but enough to make you feel right and keep you going for an entire day.

I'm lucky, or I'm talented, take your pick, but it comes out either way that I'm more fortunate than most of the people near me. Every day, I can make a pot of soup big enough to feed a dozen people, including me. I find people nearby, or they find me, and we sit down together to eat.

I notice that usually my guests are in better shape than most people out on the streets. I'm pretty sure that they live this way, going from handout to handout, making their rounds. The difference between them and me is that they stuff themselves as often as possible, filling their pockets with what they can carry, most of which is wasted because they have plenty even though they tell themselves they need more, more, more, and the more they have the more security and safety they have. They live in the moment, and most of what they take away goes to waste because they have more than enough for the moment. They don't seek out others to give it to, they don't share, because the food they waste represents their security.

But out of my guests, one is regularly thankful, even arriving early to help me in the preparation, and staying behind to put things in order. The rest of my guests unerringly show up as the soup is being ladled out, pour it down their throats, and are gone as soon as the pot's empty.

The way we're taught, all of us, me and you and you, is to think that I'm a sap. There I am, day in and day out, wandering around town half the day to collect rubbery carrots and get the bones and scraps before they go to the dogs, feeding ten greedy scavengers and one good person. I hear all the time, "Ten to one! What are you, stupid? You're just feeding these parasites, when we ought to be letting them all starve. Take care of yourself, and let it stand at that." One to ten – what a fool!

But I can only look at it the other way around. I feed ten people a day who are less appreciative than the dogs whose dinner-bones I've appropriated. And for this effort, I have meaningful labor, my own belly is full, I get my evening news of the neighborhood... and I've met one good person, the greatest reward of all. One to ten – what an accomplishment!

So, I say to this person, "Join me. Let me show you how I do what I do, and the work for us both will be less, even if we cannot feed more." We still have a dozen at dinner, but now, on average, I feed five guests, he feeds five.

I tell him, "Watch for others like us."

And they trickle in.

As you may have noted, hoarding doesn't work with me. If I have something of value, I want to find someone to share it with. I see things that would otherwise go to waste, and I can't help but wonder what use I could put them to. Most importantly, I'm looking for those few people who are worth it, who can share with me, not just take, and take, and take.

The funny thing is, as the weeks and months run by, one of the most greedy and grasping of our guests begins to show up before the meals, and quietly clears the table and puts out the bowls as I chatter with my erstwhile partner over the preparations. After a while, this stranger also begins quietly clearing up after the meal, and is gone before we notice. He's learning how to be part of a community (albeit small) by giving back to it. Eventually, he is part of our conversations, shows up earlier and earlier, stays ever later. One day, he shows up with a couple of discarded turnips, slices off and discards the mushy parts, adds them to the pot, and we know he's joined us.

This little story comes up here because I'm usually seen as the cynical one when it comes to community-building. The problem is not in attracting good people, but in making sure there's a place for them at the table. The door is crowded with bullies and parasitical sorts who would almost force their way in, grab the pot, and walk calmly out the door as if it is their right. I face myself constantly with questions like: how do we give people a chance, yet determine when that chance is used up and someone else should be given their seat at the table?

I want to put together a community, and say, "Come to meet us. See what we have, what we do, and imagine yourself as part of this. Bring your family, and join it with ours."

We all come from a culture of fear, of shame, of the "starvation mentality." (Don't bother to deny its effect on you: I'm exceptional, in upbringing and experience and intelligence, and it still lurks.) I can tell you what this would result in for a community with open borders. Women would arrive, believing that they could trade their sexual desirability for leisure, likely not even being civil to the people around them. Men would arrive, convinced that they would be able to gratify their infantile sexual fantasies, quickly rounding up a personal harem to indulge their silly whims between televised football games. Couples would arrive, intent on having sex with as many women as possible without giving up the protective shell of their couplehood, and of soon finding The One and pulling her into that shell, property of conquest and not to be "shared" with others. Individuals of all stripes would harbor thoughts of finding someone to take care of them, allowing them to live a life of brainless Lethe. Most, of whatever shading or motive, would demand "their space" as if the could own the air or the soil.

Few would say, "Hi. I'm new here. What needs to be done first?" Few would stack their bags in a closet and dive headlong, smiling, into a day that regularly consisted of five hours of work for the community, five hours of work for others, and five hours of work on their own projects. I can hear it now: "Hell, if I wanted to be working all the time, I coulda stayed with IBM!!"

And, because I'm a crabby old bastard, I might go and start packing for them. To even think that way suggests they haven't gotten – and aren't getting – the point.

So, we need a way to filter out the bullies, the parasites, the obsessively arrogant. We need a way to push the couch potatoes gently toward the airlock, yet to allow for the good people to have their quiet time, their sad moments, their periods of recuperation.

The starvation mentality each of us carries is pernicious. It's a time-bomb, a virus, our society's way of killing off deviant subcultures. We talk about "long-term" this and "lifetime" that, and it's all made empty because we scrabble madly for both false security and cheap thrills, telling ourselves with each shallow sexual encounter, "This could be the one I spend the rest of my life with," as if to justify a waste of time as relationship-seeking – we even can't properly accept the joy of the moment, then, because we're trying to cast it as Something Serious.

A few years ago, I had a lover who broke off our relationship, but Amy was articulate enough to understand her motivations and their irrational root. "Real life isn't like this," she told me. "I love you, and I love Jon, and you're both okay with it, and you even talk to me about each other and try to help when there are problems. And it's so cool, but this isn't how the world is."

(What could I do? I agreed with her, "but I refuse to believe that the world *has* to be that way.")

Much like Amy, good people are likely to show up, become easily integrated in the community... then that virus activates as programmed. The doubts, the fears, resentment, anger that had never had a use or even a safe place in which to be expressed, all come bubbling up. Anyone who's dealt with abused codependent partners has eventually noticed that, taken out of abusive situations and surrounded by support and tolerance and love, abused people become abusive. They are trying to recreate the world they've internalized: I deserve to be abused, and if I push you far enough, you'll abuse me, which will show me that I'm needed, and justify this pattern of thinking. Good people, given Utopia, will try to sabotage it, because they're programmed to believe that it's all a trick, an illusion, and they want to believe in it with every fiber of their being, and every time they've done that they've lost. Easier to set a torch to it. It's easier to believe in someone who's a transparent liar than someone who might be handing out tickets to Eldorado.

I am probably talking about you. Make no mistake about that. Our society has poisoned us all... though we're not dead yet. As the walking wounded, we need to recognize each other, and learn to spot who needs a little assistance. We need to be brave and calm in the face of screaming and crying and verbal abuse – especially our own. By that I mean, when this garbage comes bubbling up, I've seen good people who were finally allowing this to escape and stop poisoning their world, then proceed to beat themselves up for being so terrible and saying all those things, and they withdraw from the people they'd attacked, with the result that no good ever comes from what could've been incredibly healing all around.

If I were to put forward a Rule 1, it'd look something like this: Express yourself fully and honestly, but *own* your mistakes, don't shrink from an honestly unpolished outburst, and give yourself the same trust you want to give others.

My experience is that these are the people who will receive the most criticism, rather than those who are simply there to leech off the community ecosystem. A sane parasite doesn't kill its host, or even make it very sick. The leeches in the community would do basic work, control the meetings through bullying and disdain and sarcasm, and try to squeeze out the ones who really need help and who could greatly benefit from a little assistance. The bullies will control whatever governing committee exists, yet not actually serve on it, because that would require some degree of commitment, even work. I don't hate them, but I don't feel like they deserve my time.

As for the rest of you, few that you are: let's converse, and see where it all leads when we're paying attention. In the meantime, welcome to my table, and I thank you for your company.

Resources:
Real people in virtual bunches

I'm a bit of a Luddite, so I've been using the power of the Internet since just 1999. If you want to look into polyamory, then, in my highly biased opinion, there are only two possible Internet points to begin. (Until I get my own website started, of course.) While people associated with both groups do occasionally descend into whirls of cliquish silliness, self-congratulation, groupthink and gatekeeping, they are for the most part warm and welcoming to people at any level of interest and experience – as long as you're forthright and sincere. If you poke around a bit, or join up and ask the members, they can likely help you to find nearby social groups, as well as regional and national organizations.

Loving More

Though by 1985 I had already been living a life of responsible nonmonogamy for a few years, I was very glad to find Polyfidelitous Educational Products (PEP), a sideline business run by a closed MFM triad in Eugene, Oregon, the F being Ryam Nearing. I wrote an occasional article for their quarterly newsletter, *Loving More*. Mostly, I rankled some of the other members for suggesting that open relating was just as "moral" and just as feasible as closed egalitarian relationships.

Well, PEP went through its changes, including moving to Hawaii, then becoming (with no fanfare) an open relationship, then Nearing moving to Colorado with her newest partner, Brett Hill. Somewhere along the line, *Loving More* became an actual slick-paper quarterly magazine. In the 1990s, the enterprise spawned an Internet presence, *www.lovemore.com*.

One of the best things about this site is that you can browse around all you want, and only have to sign up as a member (it's free) if you want to add your two cents to the discussion postings. Their archives of these member-driven discussions are pretty impressive, dating back to the mid-1990s.

PMM

More recently, Poly MatchMaker, commonly known as PMM, appeared on the Internet as *www.polymatchmaker.com*. The couple that started this enterprise was very new to the concept, but they hit the ground running in 2000, and the virtual community has since led to many real-world relationships, and a handful of networks and households. At any given moment, the member count hovers around 5,000.

Basic-level membership is free, and (like the Loving More site) you don't have to worry about your information ending up in the hands of spammers. In order to get past the opening screens, though, you will need to register with the administrator, and wait a few minutes to receive your password.

For me, the PMM discussion areas are the big draw, but each member is strongly encouraged to post a profile, a verbose biography and photograph, with many check-boxes that outline your current relational status and what you are hoping to find in the unfolding future. The site's software is excellent, and Cyberfunk (the co-founder) has created some impressive capabilities; I searched the word "editor" in the profiles, and in about 15 seconds had a list of all PMM members that used that word. There is also an internal "e-mail" system that allows members to drop notes to each other, which might be reassuring to those of you who are concerned about being exposed to the hard light of day. As some of the "members" of PMM are couples or groups, the number of people with access to the site is likely significantly higher.

People on this site are scattered around the world, but the two centers appear to be southern California and the Portland (Oregon) area. Thanks to the Cyberfunk search engine, I have also managed to get top-quality advice on audio recording, options investing, and Java design from PMM members, rather than dig through the Web, so there are benefits beyond your interest in polyamory.

More points of potential interest

The following list is hardly exhaustive, but each will point you to other resources, including some of the more ephemeral ones in such areas as Yahoo! groups as well as various on-line diaries and weblogs.

The Sacred Space Institute: www.lovewithoutlimits.com

Southwest Polyamory Connection: www.twomoons.com/polyamory/swpc

The Polyamory Society: www.polyamorysociety.org

An Unconditional Love: ropi.net/aul

Polyamory.com: www.polyamory.com

alt.polyamory: www.polyamory.org

Further reading

Most people who cite the book *Open Marriage* as if it were divine revelation have never read it. If they had, they wouldn't mention it so freely. In that regard, it's hardly unique.

When you glance over the shelves at the bookstore or your library, you'll quickly locate many hundreds of books on topics that directly affect your interpersonal relationships. The bad news is, almost all of them are crap. You have a choice between the high-minded crap, the scholarly crap, the big-name crap, the condescending crap, and the simplistic crap. (Perhaps you've noted the pattern here.) You choose your fad, lay down your cash, and then you're on your own, unless you know people who subscribe to the method.

I've been quite blessed over the years, accumulating contacts with librarians, booksellers, authors, publishers, and various organizations that cater to the respective needs of these people. The following list is primarily of books you've never so much as heard of. If you know a bunch of people who are interested in polyamory, you ought to consider pooling your cash, becoming a regular customer on Amazon.com (or similar), and building a small library of these, starting at the top. Better still, maybe you could help found an information exchange network via the Internet, even if it's nothing more glamorous than mailing books to each other. My own collection has been 20 years in the making, and largely comes from many hours spent in wonderfully obscure used-book stores near major universities.

Many of these titles may have no first-glance relation to polyamory. After you read them, I think you'll find yourself putting to use what you encounter. Most especially, I've recommended some business-related books: our culture does not really recognize multilinear relating as a paradigm, but does provide some wonderful advice to businesses, partnerships, and corporations that has direct bearing upon nonmonogamy.

I have to say that about a dozen of these books had no influence on my own writing, as I stumbled across them in the final stages of this volume. This serendipity was quite heartening while I slogged through correcting my occasionally ghastly misspellings. In future, I may have opportunity to create a new edition, when I will tie my musings to theirs. Until then, rest assured that, unless noted, the thoughts in the foregoing are entirely my own and I am culpable. Look through this list if you'd like to see proper expansion on concepts and themes that I have raised.

Absolutely necessary

Leonard, Thomas J., *The Portable Coach*. It's no stretch of your credulity that I put this book at the top. You'd be unlikely to a find a better book for self-motivation.

Hendricks, Gay & Kate Ludeman, *The Corporate Mystic: A Guidebook for Visionaries with Their Feet on the Ground*. An impressive little book drawn from the authors' years of corporate consulting. Their comments on integrity, communication, and growth are invaluable. This is a must-read, and not difficult to locate.

Dreikurs, Rudolf, *The New Approach to Discipline: Logical Consequences*. I first ran into the "logical consequences" concept years ago, just before my daughter was born. It is a powerful way of providing reliable and well-defined boundaries for kids – and adults, too. This can give you the calm stability you need to turn any disagreement into an opportunity for growth.

Poole, Liz & Amanda McKenzie, *The Share-House Survival Guide*. An Australian book with advice for those who think they want to share living space. The authors have peppered it with hilarious real-life horror stories told to them, which ought to go a long way toward convincing you of the benefits of planning.

Klein, Fred, *The Bisexual Option: A Concept of One Hundred Percent Intimacy*. Probably the first book to point out how different bisexuality is from homosexuality – hey, that was a radical thought not too long ago. Klein's writing is thorough without descending to either rah-rah polemic or academic stuffiness.

Kiyosaki, Robert T., *Rich Dad, Poor Dad*. Actually, there is a great deal of value in all of the books that have been spun off from Kiyosaki's core writing, but this is the place to start. If it doesn't grab you, then further books in the series probably won't either; if something in you resonates, then at least read the other Kiyosaki-authored titles. These books provide an outlook that is entirely too rare in the "self help" category, with direct bearing on multilateral intimacy.

Seabury, David, *The Art of Selfishness*. I have yet to find a bad edition of this book, so glom onto whatever you can turn up. Read it thoroughly. A month or two later, read it again and take notes on your thoughts, even if you happen to disagree with the author. Read it once or twice a year. Force all of your partners and friends to read it. The author's core thesis is that too many people destroy their lives and the lives of people around them for fear of appearing selfish, and that we likely ought to spend a little *more* time taking care of our individual needs and choosing our crusades wisely, so that more people can end up happier. What a radical. First published in 1937, and its empathetically in-your-face style remains as fresh as ever.

Weitzman, Lenore J., *The Marriage Contract: A Guide to Living With Lovers and Spouses*. Perhaps the ultimate written history of institutionalized monogamy. Until I read this, I had no idea what a weird legalistic snakepit marriage was, well into the 1970s. The prime guide to things that should never become features of polyamory.

Bach, George R. & Peter Wyden, *The Intimate Enemy: How to Fight Fair in Love and Marriage*. You need this book, so that you can learn how to defuse the negative games that you play; after that, you can maybe work on your loved ones. I was already exceptional at "reading" other people, and this book made me feel like a novice, so I read it through twice the first time I encountered it.

Hendrix, Harville, *Keeping the Love You Find: A Personal Guide*. I approve of anything from Hendrix, but this is the book that applies directly to maintaining the strength of a dyad in such a way that nonmonogamy has a decent chance of lasting long enough to function. Reminds me strongly of Eric Berne's work – not as deep, but much more approachable. The exercises are quite practical. If you fill out the "Self-Knowledge Inventory" and compare notes with your partner, you may be surprised to discover how little you know about communication.

Faludi, Susan, *Stiffed: The Betrayal of the American Man*. While Faludi's previous book, *Backlash*, was a remarkable and thorough examination of the forces that continue to keep women down, most of us knew that already. In this book, she shows that men really don't come out much better merely because they're on the other side of the divide. The interviews with Sylvester Stallone are worth the price.

Quinn, Daniel, *Beyond Civilization: Humanity's Next Great Adventure*. Advanced nonfiction, which pulls together many of the underlying ideas in Quinn's fiction. A must-read for anyone who sees themselves in some sort of community-builder role.

Quinn, Daniel, *My Ishmael: A Sequel*. As much as I enjoyed *Ishmael*, the sequel stands up very well on its own. You'll plow through the story, and only afterwards realize that it has deviously planted some very disturbing and fascinating ideas in your head.

Slater, Philip, *The Pursuit of Loneliness: American Culture at the Breaking Point.* I have the second edition (1976) of this book, and it remains a startlingly apt analysis of the culture from which polyamory is developing. The central thesis is basically that the drive in the United States toward individualistic autonomy has all but eliminated our capability for interdependence, cooperation and emotional risk-taking. His analysis of romantic love as a mechanism for maintaining a sense of scarcity of love and sex is amazing.

Machiavelli, Niccolo, *The Prince.* This guy has gotten such a bad rap over the years. You probably have no idea of how much Machiavelli laments the failure of humans to work constructively for the greater good, and this is more a treatise on how to curb greed, shortsightedness, and obsession in order to keep a community functioning in the long term, rather than the guide to oppressing the peasants you likely think it.

Corcodilos, Nick A., *Ask the Headhunter: Reinventing the Interview to Do the Job.* One of the best places to learn how to examine your own motives, and to present yourself in such a way as to point up your strengths. Especially useful if you have poor self-image, or you're one of those people who gets panicky in any sort of presentation before others, even one-on-one interviews. If you want others to see you in the best possible honest light, then study this book.

Burke, Dan & Alan Morrison, *Business @ the Speed of Stupid.* A great book about how to manage technology within businesses to avoid being sucked down by "the acceleration of stupidity." Actually, it's an excellent analysis of how to work with people in such a way as to avoid their weaknesses, maximize their strengths, and move the whole group forward. Their comments on the Industrial Revolution and systems thinking are startlingly similar to some of my own thoughts.

Huff, Darrell, *How to Lie With Statistics.* A pocket-size graduate seminar in critical thinking, with many hilarious real-life examples of how numbers and graphs are used to override your thinking processes. Since it was first published in 1954, the examples are a bit dusty, but you should be able to grasp the point easily. You'll never again look at media as a passive, naïve consumer.

Out-of-print but very worth the search

Constantine, Larry L. & Joan M., *Group Marriage: A Study of Contemporary Multilateral Marriage.* The book I wanted to redo twelve years ago. The authors spent years tracking down a handful of functioning group marriages, and draw many invaluable facts from their research. Though a little long in the tooth, the book holds up very well after three decades.

Sintetos, Lorre H., *Housemates: How to Find Them, Screen Them, and Live With Them.* A very nice book, divided about half-and-half between advice for the "househunter" and "householder." Starts with probing questions to help determine what you're really looking for, progresses through how to write (and read) ads, how to handle interview and selection processes, and the final two chapters are on living well with others and solving the inevitable problems. *The Share-House Survival Guide* (mentioned previously) is the wacky younger cousin of this book, and together they offer a solid basis for learning how to live with other people.

Raimy, Eric, *Shared Houses, Shared Lives: The New Extended Families and How They Work*. Much more serious than *The Share-House Survival Guide*, and even *Housemates*. Raimy begins from the assumption that you're going to go ahead and do it, so he might as well focus on problem-solving. Not that it's stuffy or gloomy: he takes an entire appendix outlining how to rent or buy a house as a group, and another on how to draft a formal co-ownership agreement. My introduction to the concept of co-housing (though I don't think he actually uses the term). Raimy also doesn't shrink from the topic of nonmonogamy, devoting most of chapter 3 ("Community and Privacy") to the topic. A very positive but no-nonsense book that will start you thinking about the incredible range of choices embodied in the words "living together."

Goldstein, Lee, *Communes, Law & Commonsense*. Very outdated due to changes in laws over the past 30 years, yet can provide an excellent starting point for putting together your own list of potential legal problems and possible solutions.

Young-Eisendrath, Polly, *You're Not What I Expected*. The author is a post-Jungian marriage therapist, and here examines her observation that people often fall in love not with a real person, but with someone on whom they can project their fantasies, and that marital problems stem from the point at which the real person inconveniently shows through.

Ramey, James, *Intimate Friendships*. If this title were in print, I would have placed it at the top of the bibliography. Ramey had been a decade into studying alternatives to monogamy, marriage, and the restricted concept of family. The stories alone are worth the search, and there is much more to be found here.

Curran, Dolores, *Traits of a Healthy Family*. An expansion of a brief study that focused on functional families, and does a good job of showing what they're doing right, a very useful reversal of the preponderance that would rather dissect "troubled" families.

Van Deusen, Edmund L., *Contract Cohabitation: An Alternative to Marriage*. The author – an engineer, writer, sculptor, and political strategist among other things – lays out the details of his foray into hiring a woman to live with him. Though published in 1974, Van Deusen's almost painful honesty is a pleasant shock. The book also contains the most skillful criticism of *Open Marriage* that I have yet seen. Overall, an amazing tale of an individual's decision to understand and meet his own needs without restricting anyone's individuality. The final chapters, "A Cohabitation Handbook," ought to be a pamphlet, forming the outline of a mutually beneficial living-together contract.

Kantor, David & William Lehr, *Inside the Family: Toward a Theory of Family Process*. A well-illustrated scholarly study of intrafamilial dynamics. Valuable both as an examination of where we're coming from and of where intelligently approached communitarian impulses could take us and our society.

SIECUS (eds.), *Sexuality and Man*. An edited compilation from 1970 of a dozen study guides put out by the – imagine how radical this must have sounded in the late 1960s! – Sex Information and Education Council of the United States. (They certainly carved out a Herculean task for themselves, for which wonderful hubris I applaud them.) A blunt summary of the problems caused by our culture's sexual attitudes. For instance, the authors state that, in order to "prevent homosexuality," we would first have to answer some questions, the examination of which would be much more uncomfortable than letting homosexuality continue unimpeded.

Libby, Roger W. & Robert N. Whitehurst (eds.), *Renovating Marriage*. As you'll note shortly, I have a penchant for collections of good papers on alternatives to monogamy (and am damned irritated that these were regularly published in a brief flurry thirty-some years ago, then almost entirely ceased as a phenomenon). This contains 22 articles from a variety of disciplines, examining the flaws and strengths of marriage as practiced. Authors include the Constantines, the Roys, Mazur, Schwartz, the Francoeurs, Rimmer, Clanton, and Bernard. The best articles are Varni's comments on swingers, Miller's paper on the Apollonian/Dionysian dichotomy, and Ford's contention that nonmonogamous sex of any form tends to force new patterns of thinking. Not the best of the anthologies, but certainly worth taking home if you find a copy.

Gordon, Sol & Roger W. Libby (eds.), *Sexuality Today and Tomorrow*. A thoroughgoing collection, 40 articles plus eight shorter pieces. Looks at sex, gender, and sexuality, then at how these affect and are affected by society, religion, politics, and the medical establishment, with considerations of STDs, personal growth, and ethics.

Libby, Roger W. & Robert N. Whitehurst (eds.), *Marriage and Alternatives: Exploring Intimate Relationships*. I think of this as the final volume of the "Libby trilogy." The two mentioned previously look at marriage and at sex, respectively. This 1977 collection begins from three papers examining the state of monogamous marriage, moves through various facets of change (chosen singlehood, unmarried cohabitation, adultery, sexually open marriage, swinging, group marriage), stirs other then-neglected topics into the conversation (the sexual double-standard, bisexuality, effects on offspring), and is rounded out with considerations of possible long-term positive outcomes on both the individual and cultural levels. Possibly the collection most relevant to general modern nonmonogamy.

Delora, Joann S. & Jack R. (eds.), *Intimate Life Styles: Marriage and Its Alternatives*. Though I have very high respect for Roger Libby, this is the collection to which I have turned most frequently. Published in 1972, it is invaluable for anyone trying to understand polyamory, especially those in complex living situations with their various partners. Manages to contain 51 articles divided into seven sections: factors and methods of mate selection, sex from a sociological standpoint, sex from an individual standpoint, problems of marriage and family, demands for change of sexual and gender roles, emergent alternatives and their problems, and potential paths for overhauling or transforming extant practices.

Wells, J. Gipson (ed.), *Current Issues in Marriage and the Family*. A happenstance companion on my shelf to *Intimate Life Styles*, with 26 articles in nine sections: marriage vs. singlehood (the latter was once a very radical choice, more usually something forced upon you rather than sought); marriage vs. cohabitation; the shifting ground rules in the social concept of marriage; the socioeconomics of childbearing; reform of abortion; reform of divorce; questions of adultery (including Albert Ellis' pointed "Healthy and Disturbed Reasons for Having Extramarital Relations"); and speculation on the future of marriage and family. Whether you begin here or use it to round out your reading, it's worth getting.

Obscure but useful

Hoffer, Eric, *The True Believer*. Written by an amateur scholar, who traveled the world for years as a seaman and decided to categorize and examine his observations. Though certainly flawed, and more a philosophical essay than a scientific paper, this is still one of the best studies of the "true believer" in various cultures.

Carden, Maren Lockwood, *Oneida: Utopian Community to Modern Corporation*. A good history of what for some years was an extremely successful nonmonogamous community. The author shows Oneida's strengths and flaws in the same light.

Burns, Scott, *The Household Economy: Its Shape, Origins, & Future*. Beginning from the premise that the household is the material basis of family, this book examines many benefits that could be realized if households are treated and run in a business-like manner. Previously published as *Home, Inc.* (which I think is a much cooler title).

Kotler, Milton, *Neighborhood Government: The Local Foundations of Political Life*. Posits that cities would be easier to run and residents would be happier if economics, services, taxes, and politics were based more around the unique strengths and characteristics of each area, rather than trying to homogenize everything across a bewildering range of needs.

Reich, Wilhelm, *The Sexual Revolution: Toward a Self-Governing Character Structure*. Examines society as an ecological system, where defining sexuality as a commodity creates a culture that perpetuates erotic suppression in order to maintain itself, even though this downward spiral leads inexorably toward such "pinnacles" as Nazism. Particularly poignant since the original edition was published in Germany in 1930 (and led eventually to 1946's *The Mass Psychology of Fascism*). The second part of the book takes the Soviet Union as a contemporary example of the unavoidable tendency of restrictive cultures to be self-defeating and ultimately self-destructive. Variant and expressed sexuality is chaotic, and Reich is a reminder that the opposite of chaos is the decline and death known as entropy – and that such an end does not take centuries, but only a few brief, ugly years.

Lindsey, Ben B. & Wainwright Evans, *The Companionate Marriage*. An extremely controversial book for its time. Lindsey was a judge who regularly had to deal with the societal fallout from dysfunctional families, and proposed that perhaps people should marry primarily on the basis of long-term partnership, with sexual exclusivity falling by the wayside as a factor that distracted from solid, sane families. The book was widely burned, and ended Lindsey's career as a jurist.

Neubeck, Gerhard (ed.), *Extramarital Relations*. This collection (13 pieces from 1969) deals fairly with adultery, and asks whether such "illegitimate" intimacy doesn't indeed have healthy purpose. Neubeck was a professor of marriage counseling at my alma mater, and headed the quietly subversive Family Study Center (I happily bought up a few dozen of their "outdated" books when they cleaned their shelves). Includes papers from Whitehurst, Ellis, and Cuber.

Otto, Herbert A. (ed.), *The Family in Search of a Future*. This is possibly the best of the brief topical collections, as the authors aren't wild-eyed radicals, but thoughtful scholars proposing an atmosphere of free social experimentation to address the undeniable problems of the world. Fifteen articles, collected 1970, including contributions from heavy hitters like Herbert Otto, Margaret Mead, and Albert Ellis.

Packard, Vance, *The Sexual Wilderness: The Contemporary Upheaval in Male-Female Relationships*. I'm a fan of Packard's mammoth (and surprisingly popular) tomes. This one does a credible job of examining the cognitive dissonance between our societal self-image concerning sex and what is actually going on out in reality, then lays out various proposals for bridging the gap. The focus, of course, is still on monogamous marriage-for-life (it was published in 1968, after all), but more than a few of the suggestions would appear radical if presented today. Moves very nicely from history to future.

Blumstein, Philip & Pepper Schwartz, *American Couples*. A massive book packed with quotations from interviews. The authors aimed for a thorough study of couplehood, and so included unmarried couples who were straight, gay, and lesbian; the latter half of the book consists of in-depth examinations of twenty couples, five from each grouping. Not only is there a thorough chapter on nonmonogamy, but the book itself ends with an epilogue about the couples that separated during the study and examines their reasons for doing so.

Ford, Clellan S. & Frank A. Beach, *Patterns of Sexual Behavior*. Probably the primary anthropological examination of sexual expression throughout the animal kingdom. A great place to begin your study if you retain squeamishness about (literally) natural impulses.

Karlen, Arno, *Threesomes: Studies in Sex, Power, and Intimacy*. This is likely the only reasonably thorough examination of the triad. Karlen looks at swingers and committed triads alike, devotes a whole chapter to the fantasy element ("Orgy, Ecstasy, and Reality"), and gives two to effects of same-gender interaction. Not unsympathetic, but not cheery propaganda.

Wells, John Warren, *3 is Not a Crowd*. A bit of a potboiler, but the slightly sensational tone doesn't obscure the impact of very candid interviews with the members of various threesomes. I picked this up for a laugh, and ended up touched by the depth and variety of motivations presented by the interviewees.

Lipton, Lawrence, *The Erotic Revolution*. A very good overview on why our culture is both fascinated and repelled by sex. The down side is that the author holds out hope for success of a "sexual revolution" that has in actuality not yet gotten off the ground.

Dowling, Colette, *The Cinderella Complex: Women's Hidden Fear of Independence*. This book began from a very poignant place, as the author questioned the bases for her own self-sabotage. Dowling has evolved a very solid paradigm, and this book ought to be studied by anyone who is or loves a female raised in modern Western culture. As the "complex" now directly affects more than a few men, it probably ought to be much more widely read.

Schwartz, Pepper, *Peer Marriage: How Love Between Equals Really Works*. Not as out of place as may appear at first blush. As with Harville Hendrix's books, you will probably find *Peer Marriage* very useful in maintaining your core dyads within complex relational structures.

Rimmer, Robert H., *Proposition 31*. Everyone knows about Robert Heinlein's novels that feature nonmonogamy (*The Moon is a Harsh Mistress*, *Stranger in a Strange Land*, *Friday*, etc.), but few are aware that Heinlein and Rimmer cribbed from each other. In this novel, the main characters form a group marriage after reading *Stranger in a Strange Land*, then set out to change California laws to recognize and benefit expanded family models. Their first step is organizing as a Subchapter S corporation, a concept subsequently borrowed by Heinlein for the "S-group" that Friday joins. A little outdated (especially insofar as tax law post-1986), but a believable tale of the trials, risks, and rewards of group marriage.

Rimmer, Robert H., *The Rebellion of Yale Marratt*. I consider this Rimmer's most extraordinary novel. The protagonist, through nobody's fault, finds himself married to two women, which causes a little consternation, not the least for his girlfriend. Not comedy, not pathos, not melodrama, just a surprisingly believable Everyman tale. Marratt is the (sane) Howard Roark of nonmonogamy.

Rimmer, Robert H., *The Harrad Experiment*. Specifically, I am recommending the 25th anniversary edition published in 1990—yes, the original has really been around that long, and it's a true shame that Rimmer's ideas are no less radical now than they were in 1966; the world has yet to catch up to him. This version contains the entire novel, plus Rimmer's autobiography, where he describes the events in his life that led him to propose the viability and even necessity of social experiments and changes that stand out so starkly from societal norms.

Berne, Eric, *Sex in Human Loving*. A witty, entertaining little book that examines sex in various concepts of human interaction, and how it is exploited as both means and end, used by individuals to manipulate other individuals and society (and to hide my lies from my own sight even though others may be blinded by the glare), and by society to manipulate the individual. Assembled from a set of lecture notes shortly after Berne's death, but shows the good doctor at peak form. This is an enjoyable sidelight to transactional analysis in general. Much applies directly to polyamory and its cousins, such as his five categories of "Intermediate Sex Education" in our society: Sex is a Giant Squid; Sex is a Gift of the Angels; Sex is a Triumph of Mechanical Engineering; Sex is Naughty; Sex is Fun. How do *you* view sex?

Berne, Eric, *What Do You Say After You Say Hello?: The Psychology of Human Destiny*. If you are acquainted with *Games People Play* (or *I'm O.K.–You're O.K.*, which stems largely from a further simplification of Berne), then you might want to add this to your reading list. I didn't like Berne's popular work because it felt incomplete and superficial; this book validated that feeling. As my subsequent study largely led me to the symbolic interactionist faction, I've found Berne's paradigms of "games" and "scripts" to be very powerful in analyzing human action and interaction. Not half as stuffy as that makes it sound, and actually a very entertaining read.

Glasser, William, *Reality Therapy: A New Approach to Psychiatry*. Glasser, a widely experienced clinician, begins from the well-grounded belief that (barring brain damage) every individual possesses a moral sense and can tell right from wrong, and therefore can learn to act in a manner consonant with this inherent understanding. The equating of "teacher" and "therapist" never fails to inspire me.

Peter, Laurence J. & Raymond Hull, *The Peter Principle: Why Things Always Go Wrong*. A deserved classic in business literature, with wide application to daily life, especially when dealing with other people.

Roy, Rustum & Della, *Honest Sex: A Revolutionary Sex Ethic By and For Concerned Christians*. Though only a beginning, I cannot heap enough praise on the authors of this book, representative of brave Christians who dared look so honestly at the flaws in modern monogamistic thinking and practice. Really, this ought to have been the first volume in a series.

Ellul, Jacques, *Propaganda: The Formation of Men's Attitudes*. The only book I have found to adequately deal in a readily understandable way with what social psychologists call "attitudes and persuasion." Among other things, you can discover how easily the educational process can be abused, even unconsciously.

Brooks, David, *BOBOS in Paradise: The New Upper Class and How They Got There*. We are living in a rapidly changing world, and this is an excellent, funny, and thought-provoking overview of the paradoxes with which we increasingly surround ourselves.

Mathews, Ryan & Watts Wacker, *The Deviant's Advantage: How Fringe Ideas Create Mass Markets*. While on the surface this is a business-oriented book, the authors examine how ideas make the trip from wild weirdness to mainstream acceptance, and occasionally to old-hat obscurity. There are many lessons to be drawn for those with even an academic curiosity about polyamory, group marriage, communes, or the misnamed Sexual Revolution.

Bartell, Gilbert D., *Group Sex: An Eyewitness Report on the American Way of Swinging*. There are no thrills to speak of here, as the author spends a few years traveling around the country as a non-participating swinger. Bartell shows what a wide variety of lifestyles are encompassed in "swinging," and draws many interesting conclusions about Western sexual expression.

Hatfield, Tom, *Sandstone Experience*. A history of what is perhaps the most successful swing club of all time, told by one of the insiders. The book follows the organization from start to finish, and you get a strong feeling for the various motivations of its members, as well as what succeeded and how the whole thing ultimately collapsed. A very good overview of a "sex positive" group.

Crowther, C. Edward & Gayle Stone, *Intimacy: Strategies for Successful Relationships*. A very good little book, and easily "translatable" out of its generally monogamist focus. Contains some very good ideas (and, not unimportantly, cheerleading) on how to recognize, nurture, rebuild, and expand interpersonal intimacy with a partner. Doesn't go very far in helping people to recognize and withdraw from an emotionally toxic situation, but otherwise worthy of reading, and contains some very good "self tests" that could open or maintain dialogue in your own relationships.

Casler, Lawrence, *Is Marriage Necessary?* Neither a defense of nor an attack upon marriage, but a very close analysis of underlying motivations for marriage, on an individual and a societal level. The author is not afraid to consider how else the same needs could be met – perhaps met better.

Unread but probably worth finding

I normally do not recommend books that I haven't even held in my hands, but I receive suggestions from others, and I have the very firm belief that a healthy flow of information is best for everyone. Therefore, so that I don't leave out too many books that might be of high value to you personally, I include the following suggestions.

Anapol, Deborah, *Polyamory: The New Love Without Limits*.

Hutchins, Loraine & Lani Kaahumanu (eds.), *Bi Any Other Name*.

Nearing, Ryam & Brett Hill (eds.), *The Best of* Loving More.

Easton, Dossie & Catherine A. Liszt, *The Ethical Slut*.

West, Celeste, *Lesbian Polyfidelity*.

McGarey, Robert, *Poly Communication Survival Kit*.